Windows 10 At Work

FOR DUMMIES®
A Wiley Brand

by Ciprian Adrian Rusen

Windows 10 At Work For Dummies®

Published by:
John Wiley & Sons, Inc.,
111 River Street,
Hoboken, NJ 07030-5774,
www.wiley.com

For general information on our other products and services, please contact our Customer Care Department within the U.S. at 877-762-2974, outside the U.S. at 317-572-3993, or fax 317-572-4002. For technical support, please visit www.wiley.com/techsupport.

Wiley publishes in a variety of print and electronic formats and by print-on-demand. Some material included with standard print versions of this book may not be included in e-books or in print-on-demand. If this book refers to media such as a CD or DVD that is not included in the version you purchased, you may download this material at http://booksupport.wiley.com. For more information about Wiley products, visit www.wiley.com.

Library of Congress Control Number: 2015947376

ISBN 978-1-119-05185-5 (pbk); ISBN 978-1-119-08476-1 (epub); 978-1-119-08475-4 (epdf)

Manufactured in the United States of America

10 9 8 7 6 5 4 3 2 1

CONTENTS AT A GLANCE

TABLE OF CONTENTS

INTRODUCTION

Microsoft's latest operating system is Windows 10, and rolled into it are the things that work in Windows 8.1, some of our favorites in Windows 7, and some great features in Windows Phone. I consider Windows 10 a more-than-worthy upgrade for all Windows 7 and Windows 8 users. However, *Windows 10 At Work For Dummies* is for professionals who daily log on to a Windows computer, wherever they work.

I designed this book for time-pressed Windows users who simply want to figure out the task at hand without spending a lot of time looking for answers. This full-color book presents the most common Windows tasks in illustrated, step-by-step instructions and organizes them so that they're easy to find, read, and apply. It covers classic Windows tasks such as setting up accounts, customizing the interface, and managing applications, along with the newest features of Windows 10.

About This Book

This book is organized into chapters, each split into a series of common tasks. It begins by familiarizing you with Windows 10 and showing you how to perform basic tasks such as signing in to Windows. Each chapter covers important features, apps, and tools that you're likely to encounter while working on your Windows 10 computer or device. You see how to use the new Start Menu, and then you go into using apps such as Internet Explorer, File Explorer, Mail, Calendar, and Skype. As you advance through the book, the content becomes more specialized. By the end of the book, you read about powerful user skills such as sharing content on a network, improving your privacy and security, and preventing problems with Windows 10.

You can read the chapters in any order, at any time. Although each task is explained step by step, if you have trouble with a particular task, I recommend reading the entire chapter for that task — it's just possible that you'll find a different, better approach to accomplishing the task.

Windows 10 Editions

Just like any other version of Windows, Windows 10 is available in several editions:

- **Windows 10 Home:** This edition is the consumer-focused desktop edition. You can use it on PCs, tablets, and 2-in-1s. It doesn't include business-oriented features such as BitLocker encryption, and you can't control how Windows updates itself.

- **Windows 10 Mobile:** This edition is aimed at smartphones and small tablets. With the help of the Continuum feature, Windows 10 Mobile users may be able to turn their smartphones into fully featured PCs by connecting them to a display, keyboard, and mouse.
- **Windows 10 Pro:** This edition is aimed at small businesses and technical users who want the entire feature set of Windows 10, including tools such as BitLocker encryption. This edition is also a good choice if you want to control how Windows updates itself.
- **Windows 10 Enterprise:** This edition builds on Windows 10 Pro, adding advanced features designed to meet the demands of medium- and large-size organizations. Windows 10 Enterprise is available only to Volume Licensing customers, which generally are large institutions such as international corporations.
- **Windows 10 Mobile Enterprise:** This edition is designed to deliver the best customer experience to business customers on smartphones and small tablets. It's only available to Volume Licensing customers.
- **Windows 10 Education:** This edition builds on Windows 10 Enterprise and is designed to meet the needs of schools — staff, administrators, teachers, and students. This edition is available through academic Volume Licensing and offers paths for schools and students using Windows 10 Home and Windows 10 Pro devices to upgrade to Windows 10 Education.

If you're using Windows 10 at work, you're probably using either Windows 10 Pro or Windows 10 Enterprise. With that in mind, I wrote this book to illustrate important Windows 10 Enterprise featuresthat you may use at work.

Foolish Assumptions

First, I assume that you're familiar with computer basics, such as using a mouse and keyboard; opening, viewing, and saving files; switching between windows and finding content; and so forth. Second, if you're reading this book, I assume that you're a time-pressed professional, that you've been using a version of Windows earlier than Windows 10 on your company's computers and devices, that your company has upgraded to Windows 10, and that you must quickly learn how to use new Windows 10 devices and apps in order to be productive in your daily work.

Icons Used in This Book

The following icons highlight important or useful information in this book.

Tips can save you time or make it easier to do something.

This icon emphasizes useful information to keep in mind when using Windows 10.

Watch out! This icon alerts you about something that can hurt or wipe out important data. Read this information before making a mistake that you may not be able to recover from.

This icon targets interesting information that you don't really need while you work but that may answer some questions about why Windows 10 works a certain way.

Beyond the Book

`www.dummies.com` has a heaping handful of additional Windows 10 information:

- You can find a cheat sheet with shortcuts for working in Windows 10 at `www.dummies.com/cheatsheet/windows10atwork`.
- Visit `www.dummies.com/go/dummiesvideo` to access the *Windows 10 For Dummies* online video course, featuring 150 how-to videos on Windows 10.

To gain access to the online video, all you have to do is register. Just follow these simple steps:

1. **Find your PIN code.**
   - **Print book:** If you purchased a hard copy of this book, turn to the inside back cover of this book to find your PIN.
   - **E-book:** If you purchased this book as an e-book, you can get your PIN by registering your e-book. Go to `www.dummies.com/go/dummiesvideo`, click the link to register to get a PIN, and follow the instructions. You'll be asked to fill in some registration information and answer a security question to verify your purchase. Once you handle those steps, you'll receive an e-mail with your PIN.
2. **Go to `www.dummies.com/go/dummiesvideo`.**

3. **Click the link to go to the video resource site and follow the on-screen instructions to create an account, enter your PIN, and establish your own login information.**

Now you're ready to start watching your videos! Your PIN gives you access to watch as often as you want for 12 months after you register. Once you create your registration, simply return to the video site and log on with the username and password you created. No need to enter your PIN a second time.

If you have trouble with your PIN or can't find it, contact Wiley Product Technical Support at 877-762-2974 or go to `http://support.wiley.com`.

Where to Go from Here

You can work through this book from beginning to end or simply look at the table of contents and find the information you need to solve a problem or learn a new skill. The steps in each task quickly get you where you want to go.

If you're new to Windows 10, I recommend that you start by reading Chapter 1, which introduces new Windows 10 concepts you may not be familiar with. If you're using a Windows 10 tablet or hybrid device, be sure to read Chapter 3, too. With the information in these chapters, you can easily work through all the chapters.

CHAPTERONE

Getting Started with Windows 10

Windows 10 is another revolution in the world of Microsoft operating systems. It's the first operating system to work on a huge number of devices, such as smartphones, tablets, traditional desktop PCs, consoles, and industrial devices. That also means it's designed to minimize hardware requirements. A Windows this slim and fast hasn't been built in a long time.

To make Windows 10 work on a variety of devices, with very different form factors, Microsoft developed a new user interface that's different from what you may have used with Windows 7 or Windows XP. Getting the first steps right when using Windows 10, goes a long way in having a pleasant user experience with this operating system. This chapter is your introduction to doing so.

Windows 10 uses concepts that may be new to you, such as the Lock Screen (introduced in Windows 8); a completely new Start Menu; the WinX menu (introduced in Windows 8); a new Settings panel that replaces the old Control Panel; the new Task View; and a new Action Center. Some items in this chapter are very simple, but you need to get them right in order to use Windows 10 productively. So, roll up your sleeves and arm yourself with a bit of patience. It's time to go to work!

In This Chapter

- Getting past the Lock Screen and signing in to Windows
- Using the new Start Menu to start your apps
- Using the hidden WinX menu
- Accessing the Desktop
- Accessing Settings and Control Panel
- Performing simple searches
- Using notifications
- Working with multiple apps and Desktops at once
- Closing apps and desktops
- Signing out and locking your Windows 10 device
- Shutting down and restarting Windows

Use the Lock Screen

The first screen you see after Windows 10 loads on your computer or device is the Lock Screen. This concept was introduced in Windows 8 and continues in Windows 10. The Lock Screen is basically a full-screen wallpaper. By default, it shows you the time and the date and whether you're connected to a network (see Figure 1-1). You can customize it to also show the detailed status of an app as well as small icons of your favorite apps so that you can see the status of those apps without leaving the Lock Screen. Along with all that, you can customize the Lock Screen's image.

Figure 1-1: The Lock Screen in Windows 10.

How you unlock the Lock Screen depends on the type of computer you're using:

- **A Windows 10 desktop computer without touch:**
  - Press any key on the keyboard.
  - Click the mouse anywhere on the screen.
  - Drag upward from the bottom of the screen.
- **A Windows 10 laptop with a touchpad:**
  - Press any key on the keyboard.
  - Click the mouse or the left-click trackpad button anywhere on the screen.
  - Hold down the left trackpad button and drag your cursor upward.

- **Any Windows 10 device with a touchscreen (such as a tablet or a 2-in-1 device):**
    - Place your finger anywhere near the middle or bottom of the screen and flick upward.

Chapter 8 shows how to customize the Lock Screen.

Sign In to Windows 10

Once you get past the Lock Screen, you can sign in to Windows 10. You're asked to enter the password and click or tap the Sign In button for your user account (or the last account that was used on your device). The Sign In button is a right-pointing arrow (see Figure 1-2).

If there are other user accounts on this computer, they're listed on the bottom-left side of the Sign In screen. To sign in with one of these other user accounts, click the account that you want, enter the password, and click or tap the Sign In button.

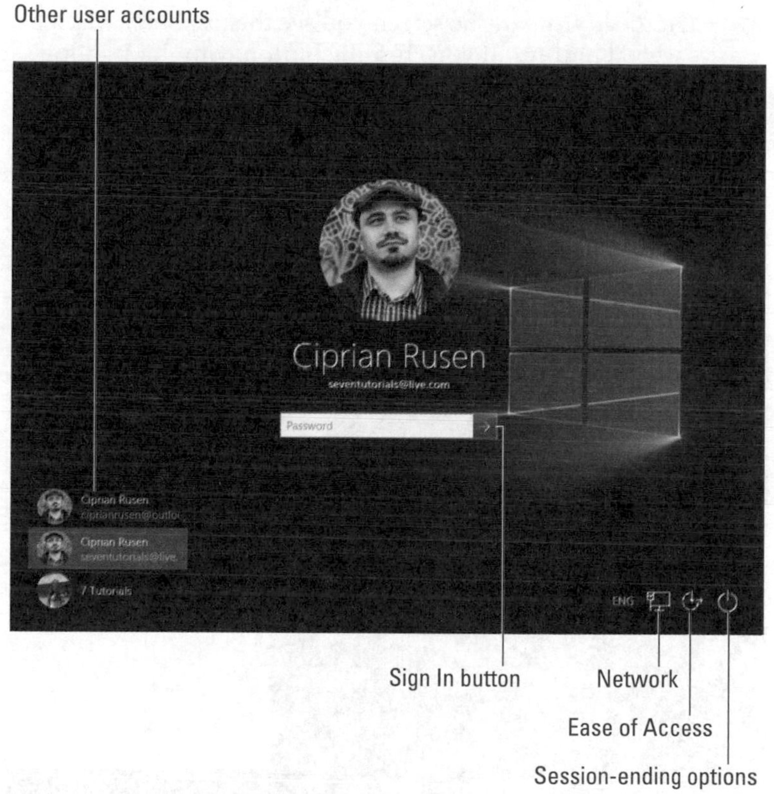

Figure 1-2: The Sign In screen in Windows 10.

On the bottom right of the sign in screen, you see three accessible buttons:

- Network Connections
- Ease of Access options for starting such tools as the Narrator, Magnifier, and On-Screen keyboard
- Session-ending options (such as Sleep, Shut down, and Restart)

Chapter 21 covers the ins and outs of user accounts, passwords, and different ways of signing into Windows 10.

Use the Start Menu

After you sign in to Windows 10, the user interface of the operating system loads:

- On a classic PC, the Desktop loads.
- On a touch-enabled device that's set to work in Tablet mode, the Start Menu loads.

At the bottom of the screen you see the taskbar, a black bar with several buttons. If you click the button with the Windows logo (which is called the Start button), the Start Menu opens.

On classic PCs, the Start Menu covers only part of the screen and looks similar to what is shown in Figure 1-3.

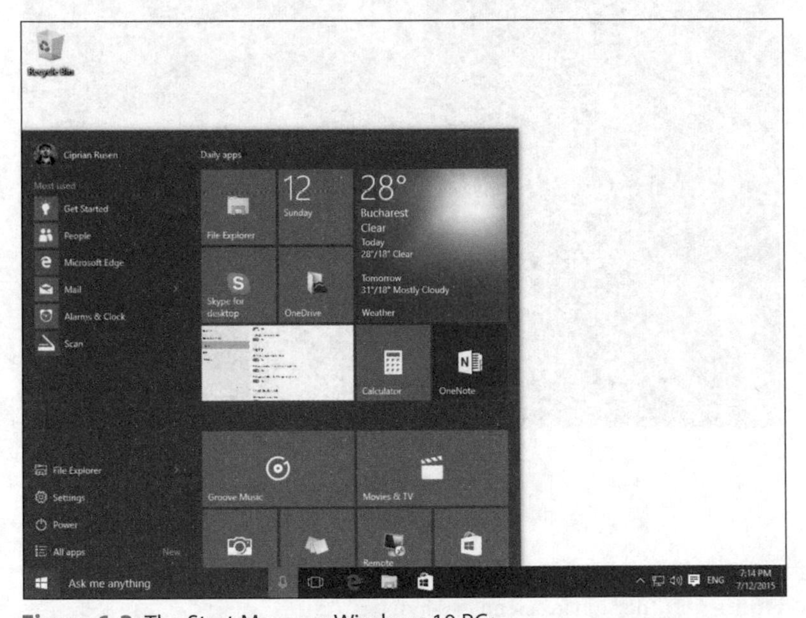

Figure 1-3: The Start Menu on Windows 10 PCs.

On the right side of the Start Menu, you see several tiles of different sizes. Tiles are like shortcuts, and clicking them opens the app that they represent. However, some tiles can also display up-to-date information for the app they represent. These are interactive *live tiles*. You don't need to open the app to view the basic data a live tile offers. For example, after you configure the Weather app, it can show up-to-date weather information for a city, and the Photos app can show your pictures. This data appears on the Start Menu so that you have access to it without opening the app itself. The information is dynamic and changes as the information it represents does.

If you need to see more than a preview of the information, click the tile. The app opens in a window from which you can access all its features.

On the left side of the Start Menu, you see a column that contains your user account name, a list with your most used apps, a Power button and an All Apps button. Clicking an app's name opens that app.

If you're on a device that's working in Tablet mode, the Start Menu consumes the whole screen, so you don't see the Desktop (see Figure 1-4).

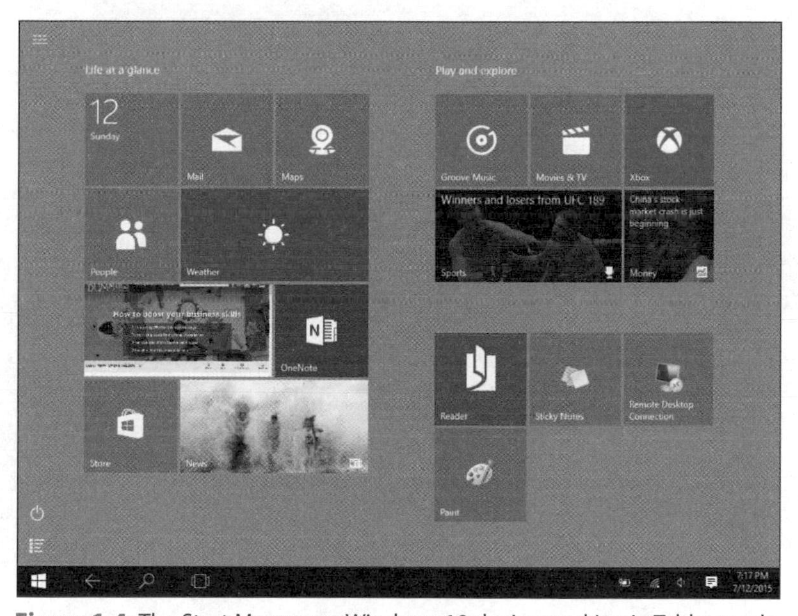

Figure 1-4: The Start Menu on a Windows 10 device working in Tablet mode.

The Start Menu displays a list with all your tiles, including the live tiles of apps that are pinned to the Start Menu. To access the column on the left with your user account name, the list of your Most Used apps, the Power button, and the All Apps button, you tap what's called a hamburger button (or just *burger button)* located at the top-left corner of the screen (the button is called a burger button because its three parallel lines look like a burger on a bun), which is found on the top-left corner of the screen. Tapping the burger button shows or hides this column, depending on its status.

Wherever you see the burger button, clicking or tapping it opens a menu.

From here on, navigating the Start Menu works just like it does on desktop PCs. The only difference is that instead of clicking, you tap with your finger or stylus.

Chapter 3 covers using Tablet mode and touch in Windows 10.

Use the All Apps List to Start Your Apps

All Apps is a list with all the apps that are installed on your Windows 10 device. Here's how to access it and start any app you want:

1. **Sign in to Windows 10.**

   The Desktop appears.

2. **Click the Windows logo.**

   The Start Menu appears.

3. **In the Start Menu, click the All Apps button.**

   A list with all your apps appears.

4. **Scroll down the list of apps until you find the one that you want to start (see Figure 1-5).**

5. **Click the app that you want to start.**

On touch-enabled devices that work in Tablet mode, after Step 2, tap the burger button and then follow the instructions from Step 3 onward. Also, don't forget to replace the click with a tap.

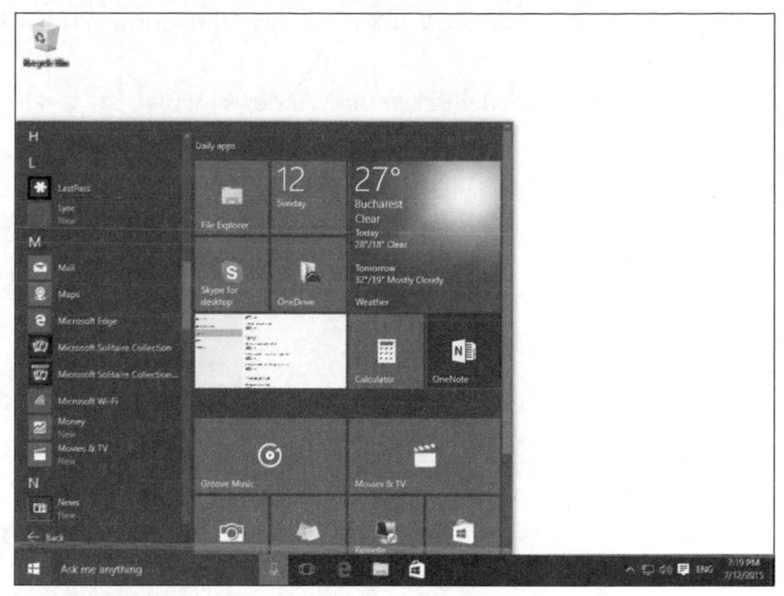

Figure 1-5: The All Apps list in Windows 10.

Use the WinX Menu

In Windows 10, a hidden menu, the WinX menu, produces shortcuts to such useful tools and apps as Computer Management, the Control Panel, the Command Prompt, and the Task Manager. The menu's name comes from the keyboard shortcut that you press to open the menu: Windows+X (see Figure 1-6).

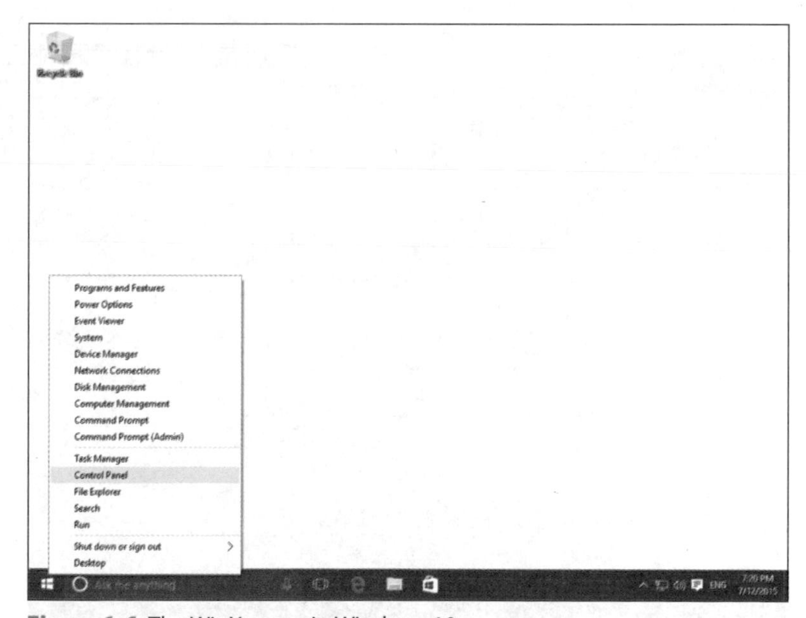

Figure 1-6: The WinX menu in Windows 10.

You can also open the WinX menu with the mouse or by using touch:

- With a mouse, right-click the Windows logo on the taskbar.
- With a touch-sensitive screen, press and hold the Windows logo until the WinX menu appears.

To start any of the tools available in the WinX menu, simply click or tap them.

Access the Desktop

On a computer or device that isn't set to work in Tablet mode, you can access the Desktop and its contents. If several apps are open and they completely cover the Desktop, just press Windows+D on the keyboard. All apps are minimized, and you can see the Desktop. Another solution is to minimize or close all apps, one by one.

Access Settings

In Windows 10, the old Control Panel is somewhat hidden, but it's there and you can use it. It's hidden because Microsoft developed an alternative "control panel" that works well on both classic desktop PCs with a mouse and keyboard and touch-enabled devices. This new "control panel" is named Settings, and it includes most of the settings that you adjust while using Windows 10 (see Figure 1-7).

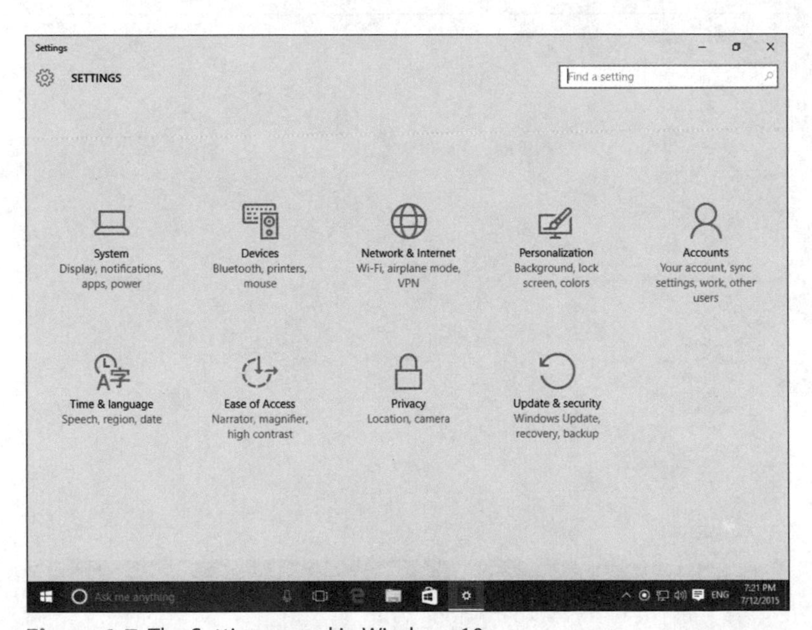

Figure 1-7: The Settings panel in Windows 10.

To access the Settings panel, follow these steps:

1. **Open the Start Menu.**

   If you're using a touch-enabled device in Tablet mode, tap the burger button now.

2. **Click Settings.**

   The Settings window appears.

3. **Click any of the sections to access the available settings.**

   On touch-enabled devices that work in Tablet mode, replace the click with a tap.

Access the Control Panel

The Control Panel still exists in Windows 10, and it works the same as in previous versions of Windows. The easiest way to access the Control Panel is to start it from the WinX menu, like this:

1. **Right-click the Windows logo (Start button) on the taskbar.**

   The WinX menu appears.

2. **In the WinX menu, click Control Panel.**

3. **Navigate Control Panel to find what you're looking for (see Figure 1-8).**

   As you can see, the Control Panel is just like Windows 7 or Windows 8.1.

4. **When you're done, close the Control Panel.**

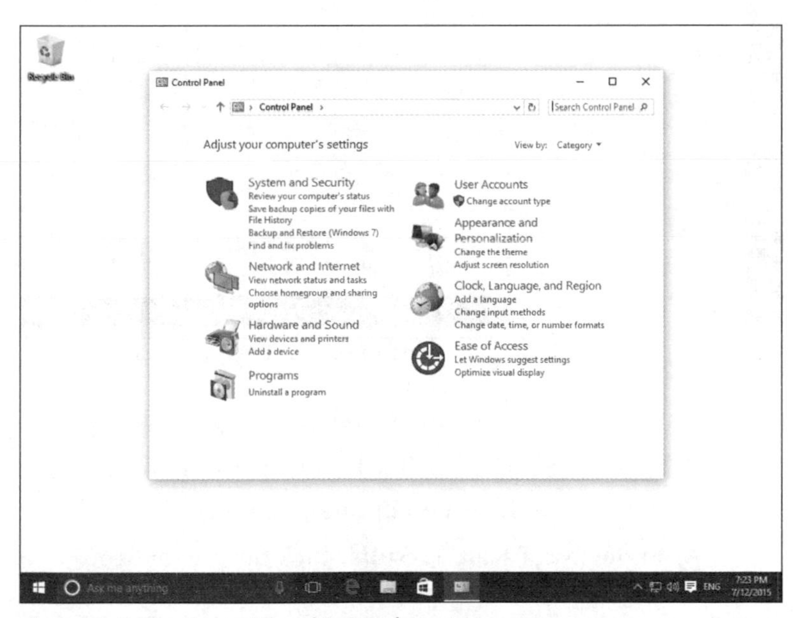

Figure 1-8: The Control Panel in Windows 10.

Perform Simple Searches

On the right side of the Start button, you see the Ask Me Anything search box. That's Cortana: an intelligent personal assistant that's built into Windows 10. With Cortana, you can do basic searches for apps and files on your computer, or you can interact by using voice and text and get all kinds of information.

While Chapter 14 explains how to use Cortana in detail, it's good to know how to perform a basic search using this intelligent search box. Here's an example of finding an app and a file:

1. **Click inside the search bar on the taskbar.**
2. **Type the name of the app that you want to use (for example, Camera).**

   A list of search results appears.
3. **In the list of search results, click the app that you want to use (see Figure 1-9).**

   The app starts.

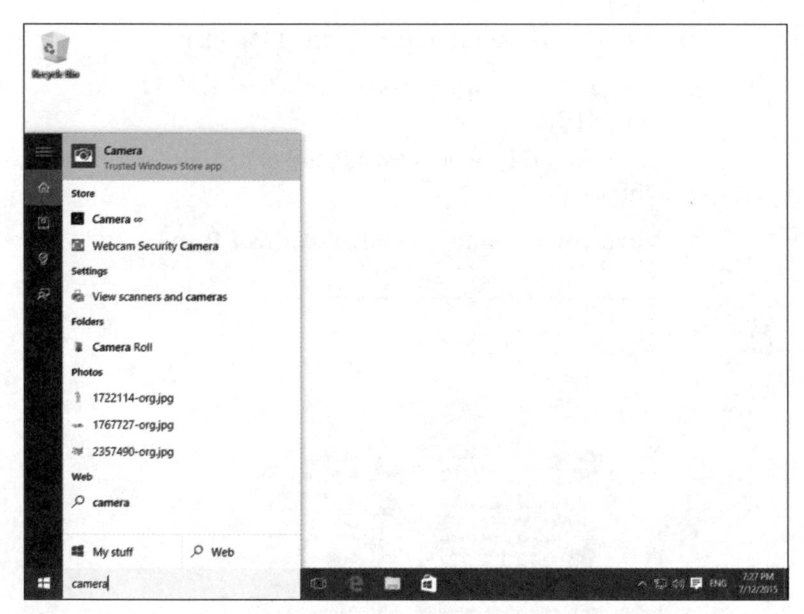

Figure 1-9: Searching for apps by using the search bar on the taskbar.

4. **Click again inside the search bar on the taskbar.**
5. **Type the name of the file that you want to find.**

   A list of search results appears.
6. **In the list of search results, click the file that you want to find, and it opens.**

Use the Action Center

When you use Windows 10, you get all kinds of notifications. They can be notifications from apps, such as a new email message was a received, or notifications from Windows saying that it detected a removable disk that you just plugged into your computer. All these notifications are centralized in the Action Center, which you can access at any time (see Figure 1-10).

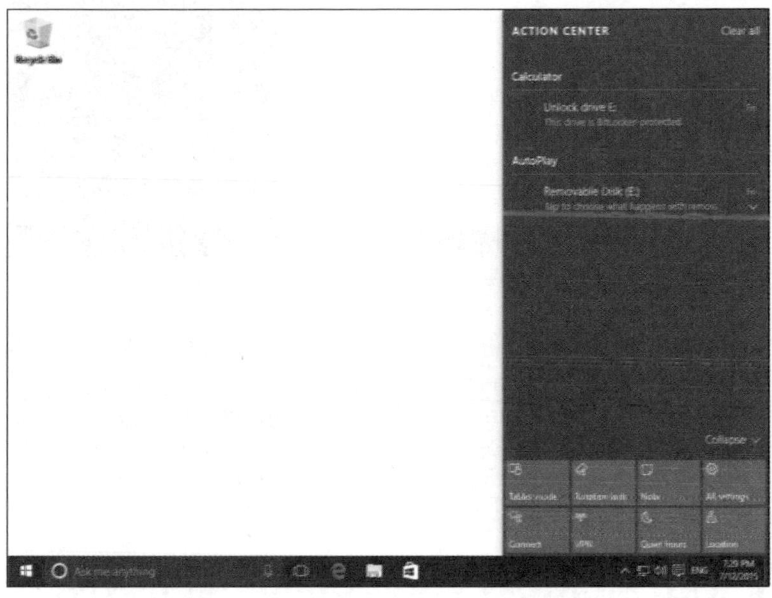

Figure 1-10: The Action Center in Windows 10.

All your notifications are grouped according to the app that generated them:

- For more details about a notification, click it, and the app that generated it opens and shows you more details.

  After you open a notification, it disappears from the Action Center.

- To remove a notification without opening it, move the mouse cursor to its top-right corner and click the X button shown in Figure 1-11.

- To remove all notifications without opening them, click Clear All at the top-right side of the Action Center (see Figure 1-11).

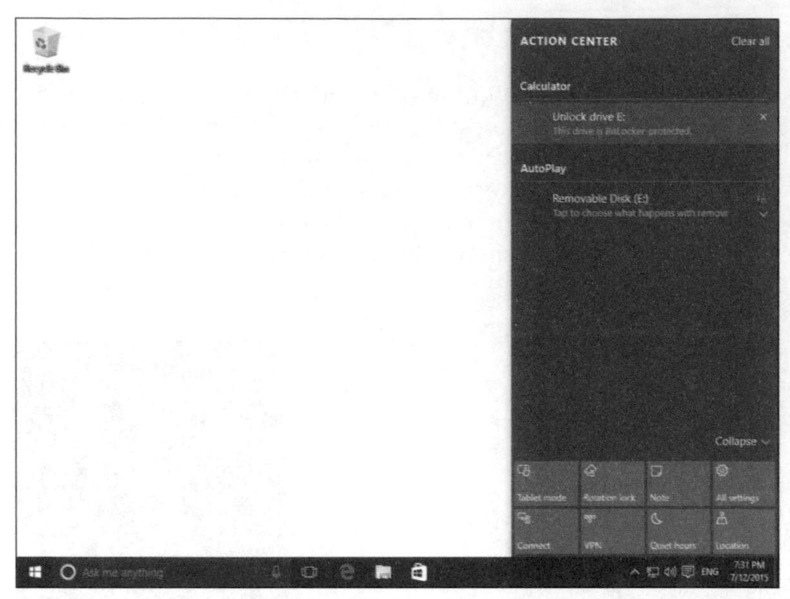

Figure 1-11: How to remove a notification from the Action Center.

At the bottom of the Action Center shown in Figure 1-11, you see such shortcuts as Tablet Mode, VPN, Connect, All Settings, Rotation Lock, and Location. The number of shortcuts displayed varies from device to device, depending on its capabilities. Click or tap on these shortcuts to start the tools that they represent and see what they do.

Work with Multiple Apps Simultaneously

Clicking a shortcut or a tile from the Start Menu starts the app that the shortcut represents.

On a desktop computer, these apps are opened one by one, and their icons appear on the taskbar. To switch to another app that's open, click its icon in the taskbar. Figure 1-12 shows an example of multiple opened apps and their icons on the taskbar.

On a device that's running in Tablet mode, you switch between apps using the Task View. The following section shows how.

To switch between apps very quickly, you can also press Alt+Tab on your keyboard. This accesses a list with all opened apps. Keep the Alt key pressed and then press Tab to navigate between apps. When you reach the app you want to switch to, release both keys.

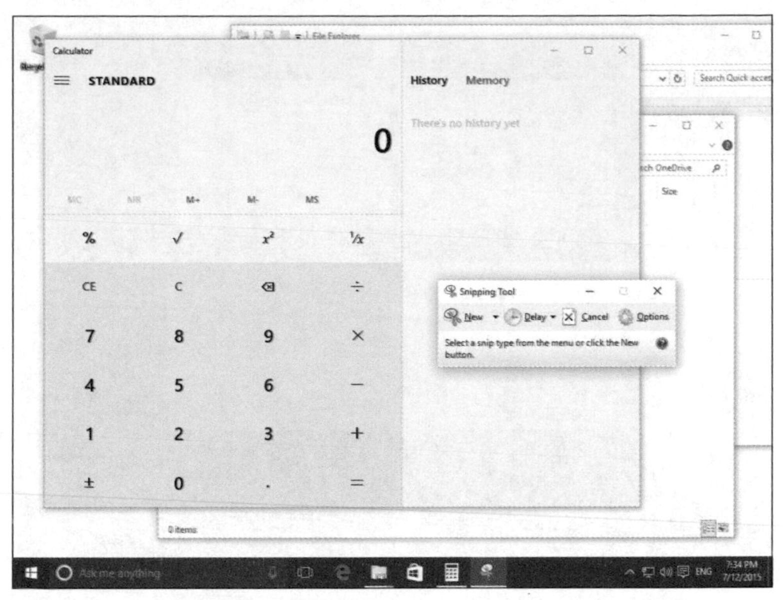

Figure 1-12: Multiple apps opened at the same time in Windows 10.

Switch Between Apps with the Task View

The Task View is like a more advanced Alt+Tab list that shows you the Desktops that are open and the apps that are open in each Desktop. (See the "Switch Between Multiple Desktops" section, later this chapter, to find out how to use more than one Desktop in Windows 10.) Here's how to use the Task View to switch between apps:

1. **On the taskbar, click the Task View button near the Search bar.**

   The Task View button looks like two rectangles stacked on each other (see Figure 1-13).

2. **In the list of apps that appears, click the app that you want to switch to.**

On a touch-enabled device, you can access the Task View by flicking from the left side of the screen to the right.

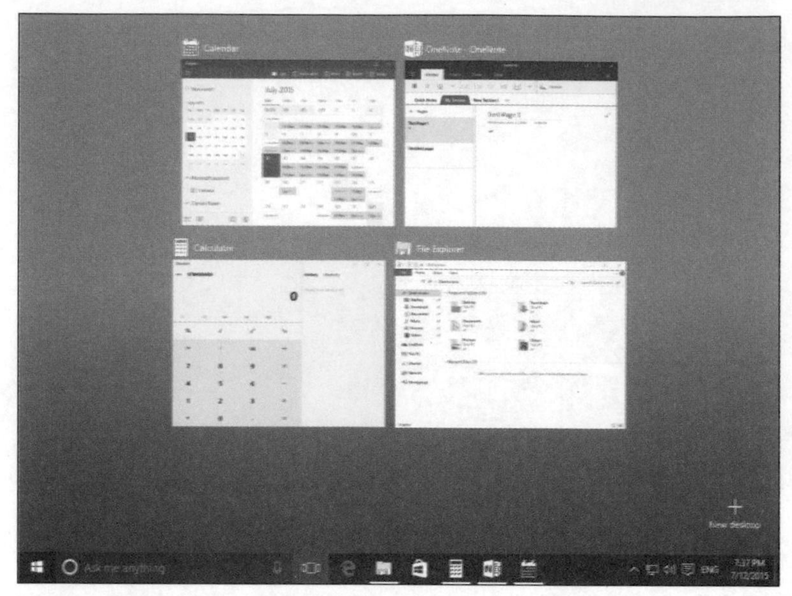

Figure 1-13: How to use the Task View in Windows 10.

Close an App

You close apps in Windows 10 like you did in older versions of Windows. When you open an app on the Desktop, you can close it by pressing Alt+F4 on your keyboard or by clicking the X (the exit button) located at the top-right corner of its window (see Figure 1-14).

Figure 1-14: The X (or exit) button for closing an app in Windows 10.

If you're using Tablet mode on a touch-enabled device, apps consume the whole screen, and exit button isn't shown. To close an app, use your finger to drag an app down from the top.

Create a New Desktop

Although Windows has long supported virtual Desktops (with the help of third-party tools), Microsoft declined to make this feature available to users until Windows 10. Now you can easily create and manage multiple Desktops, which you can use to separate related tasks into their own workspaces. This is useful in business environments where you can keep your personal apps and files in one Desktop and your work-related apps and files in another.

To create a new Desktop in Windows 10, follow these steps:

1. **Click the Task View button.**

   The Task View appears.

2. **Click New Desktop (see Figure 1-15).**

   A new Desktop is created.

Figure 1-15: The New desktop button in the Task View.

3. **Click the Desktop that you want to use.**

You can also use the keyboard shortcut Windows+Ctrl+D.

Switch Between Multiple Desktops

Switching between Desktops is as easy as switching between apps. Just use the Task View, like this:

1. **Click the Task View button.**

   The Task View appears.

2. **Click the Desktop that you want to use.**

You can also use these keyboard shortcuts: Windows+Ctrl+left arrow for the previous Desktop and Windows+Ctrl+right arrow for the next Desktop.

Send an App to Another Desktop

As you start populating each Desktop with open apps, you may want to move an app from one Desktop to another. Here's how to move an app:

1. **Click the Task View button.**

   The Task View appears.

2. **Right-click the app that you want to move to another Desktop.**

   The right-click menu appears.

3. **Click Move To.**

4. **Click the Desktop that you want to move the app to (see Figure 1-16).**

5. **Click the Desktop that you want to use.**

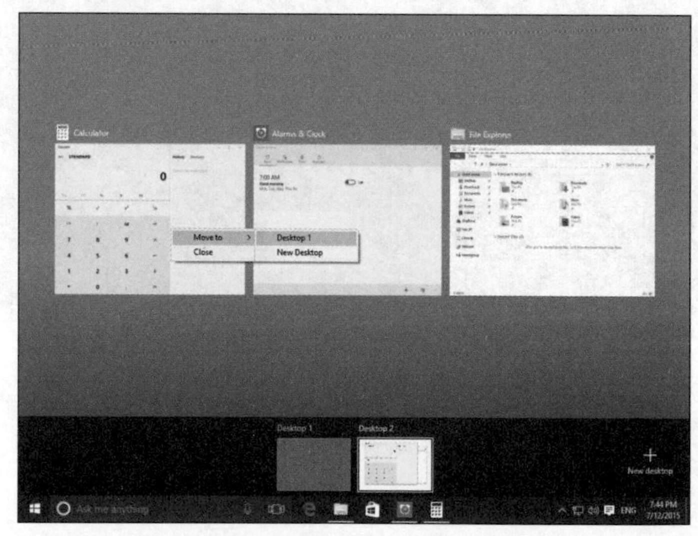

Figure 1-16: How to move an app to another Desktop.

Close a Desktop

You can close any Desktop that you've opened, at any time. When you close a Desktop, the apps that were open on it are moved to the remaining Desktops. To close a Desktop, follow these steps:

1. **Click the Task View button.**

   The Task View appears.

2. **Move the mouse to the top-right corner of the thumbnail of the Desktop that you want to close.**

3. **Click the X (exit) button at its top-right corner (see Figure 1-17).**

4. **Click the Desktop that you want to use.**

Figure 1-17: How to close a Desktop in Windows 10.

Sign Out or Lock Your Windows 10 Device

When you leave your desk, you need to secure your computer so that others can't access it. The easiest way to do so is by locking it. After you lock your computer, you must enter your user account password when you're ready to use your computer again. When you enter your password, the computer is just as you left it, with the same apps and files open. Lock your computer anytime you leave it unattended.

You can also sign out of your computer. When you sign out, you're prompted to save any open files, and you might be prompted to close open apps. With that done, Windows closes your computing session as if you were turning off the computer, but it doesn't turn the computer off. You're signed out of your user account, and you can let others use your computer, if they want to sign in with their user account. You can also log on again to start a new computing session.

To lock your Windows 10 computer or to sign out, follow these steps:

1. **Click the Windows logo (Start button.)**

   The Start Menu appears.

2. **If you're in Tablet mode, tap the burger button.**
3. **Click your username.**

   A menu appears beneath your username.

4. **Click Lock or Sign Out, depending on what you want to do (see Figure 1-18).**

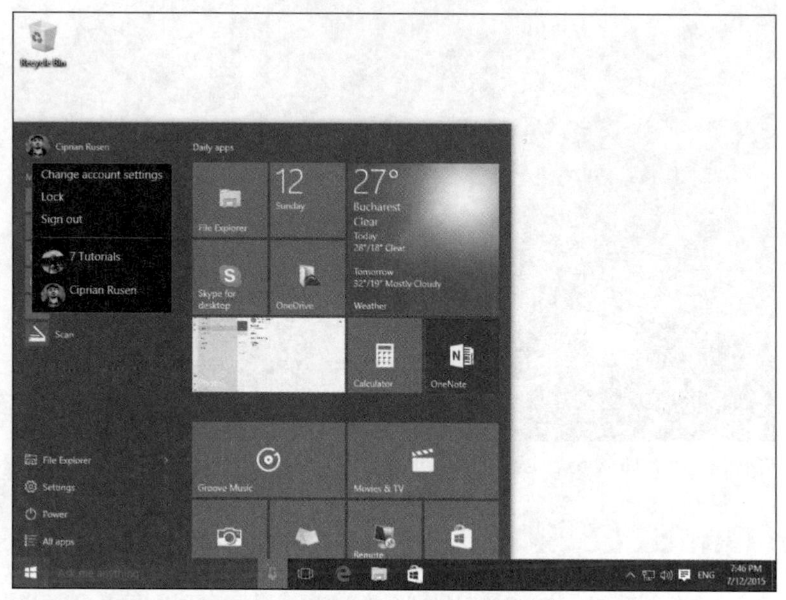

Figure 1-18: How to lock or sign out from Windows 10.

You can quickly lock your computer by pressing Windows+L on your keyboard.

Shut Down or Restart Windows 10

If you need to shut down or restart your Windows 10 computer or device, close all your open files and apps and follow these steps:

1. **Click the Windows logo (Start button.)**

   The Start Menu appears.

2. **Click the Power button (the icon is a power symbol; see Figure 1-19).**

   A menu appears with power-related options.

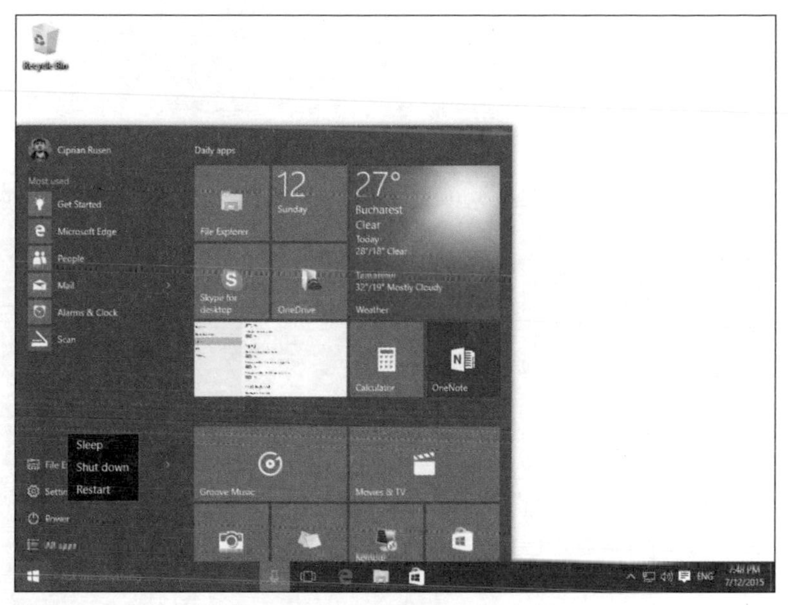

Figure 1-19: How to shut down or restart Windows 10.

3. **Click Shut Down or Restart, depending on what you want.**

The Power button is available also on the Sign In screen, and this button offers you the same options as when you access it from the Start Menu.

CHAPTERTWO

Using the New Start Menu

In This Chapter

- Accessing a list with all your apps
- Expanding and minimizing the Start Menu
- Pinning apps and files
- Moving tiles and shortcuts
- Resizing tiles and shortcuts
- Naming groups of tiles and shortcuts
- Unpinning items from the Start Menu

One of the most important changes in Windows 8 was replacing the Start Menu with the Start screen. Most people didn't like this change and were very vocal in saying so. As a result, Windows 10 brings the old Start Menu back but in a modified form that mixes the best of Windows 7 and Windows 8. So, if you're a Windows 7 user, you'll feel right at home and have no trouble getting up to speed with the new Start Menu. If you use Windows 8 and love the Start screen, the good news is that you can easily set the Start Menu to utilize the whole screen and to behave like the former Start screen.

This chapter shows you how to use the new Start Menu, how to customize it, and how to improve the privacy of the data shown by the tiles you pin to it.

Access the All Apps List in the Start Menu

For a list of all the apps that you can access from the Start Menu, follow these steps:

1. **Click Start to open the Start Menu.**

   The Start button is in the left corner on the taskbar. It has the Windows logo.

2. **Click All Apps (see Figure 2-1).**

   A list of apps appears.

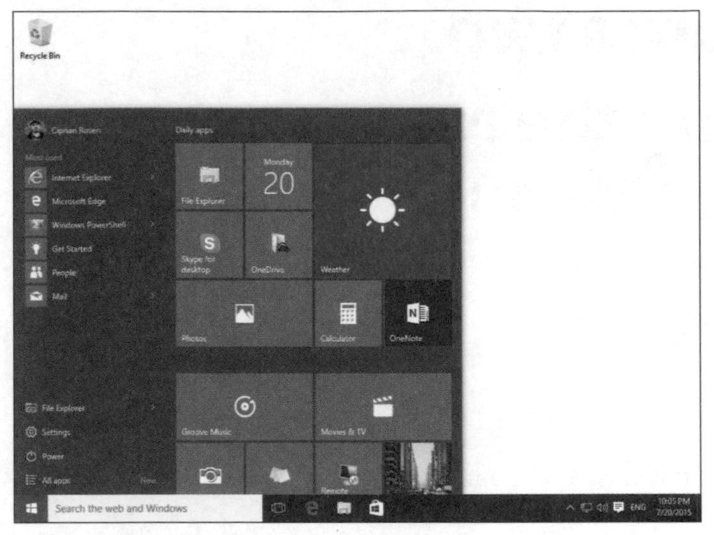

Figure 2-1: The Start Menu in Windows 10.

3. **Navigate through the list to find the app you want.**
4. **Select the app that you want to start.**

Expand the Start Menu in Windows 10

You can expand the new Start Menu so it fills the entire screen and shows more shortcuts, tiles, live tiles, and data for these tiles. (Chapter 1 explains live tiles.)

To expand the Start Menu, follow these steps:

1. **Click Start to open the Start Menu.**
2. **Move the mouse cursor to the right-margin of the Start Menu.**

   You should see a double-arrow icon, pointing both left and right (see Figure 2-2).
3. **Click the double-arrow icon and drag the Start Menu to the right side of the screen to expand it (see Figure 2-2).**

   The Start Menu fills more of the screen and shows more data.
4. **Click anywhere outside the Start Menu to close it.**

The Start Menu remembers your last setting. If you expand the Start Menu, it always opens in an expanded form until you manually restore it to its default size.

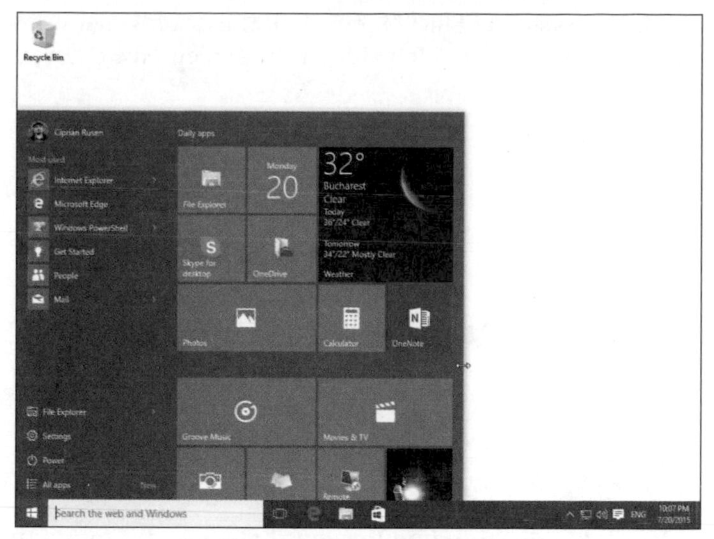

Figure 2-2: The double-arrow icon for expanding the Start Menu.

Restore the Start Menu in Windows 10

If you no longer want to use the Start Menu in expanded form, here's how to restore it to its default size:

1. **Click the Start button to open the Start Menu.**
2. **Move the mouse cursor to the right-margin of the Start Menu.**

   You should see a double-arrow icon, pointing both left and right (see Figure 2-3).

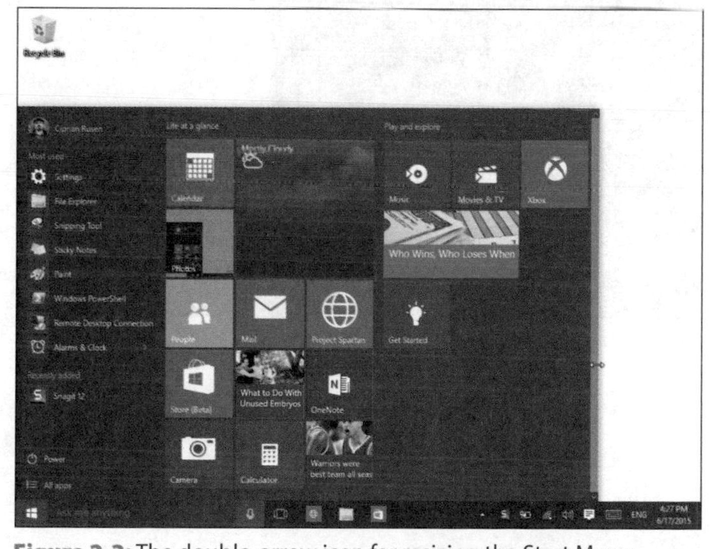

Figure 2-3: The double-arrow icon for resizing the Start Menu.

3. **To resize the Start Menu, click the double-arrow and drag the menu to the left side of the screen (see Figure 2-3).**

   The Start Menu is resized.

4. **Click Start to close it.**

The Start Menu remembers your last setting. If you restore the Start Menu, it always opens with its default size until you expand it.

Pin Apps to the Start Menu

You can easily pin any app to the Start Menu. Follow these steps:

1. **Click Start to open the Start Menu.**
2. **Click All Apps.**
3. **Scroll down to find the app that you want to pin to the Start Menu, then right-click the app.**
4. **In the list, click Pin to start (see Figure 2-4).**

   The app is now pinned to the right side of the Start Menu.

5. **Click Start to close the Start Menu.**

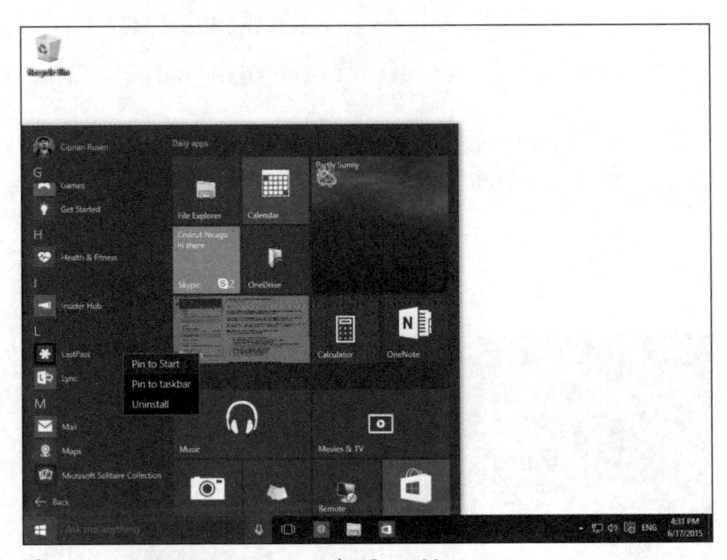

Figure 2-4: Pinning an app to the Start Menu.

Pin Executable Files to the Start Menu

Pinning files to the Start Menu is just as easy as pinning apps.

The only rule is that you can pin only executable files with the file extension `.exe`.

To pin an executable file to the Start Menu, follow these steps:

1. **Click the File Explorer icon on the taskbar to start this application.**
2. **Navigate to the location of the executable file that you want to pin and right-click it.**
3. **In the list that appears, click Pin to Start (see Figure 2-5).**
4. **Close File Explorer and then click Start.**

   The file is pinned to the bottom of the Start Menu.

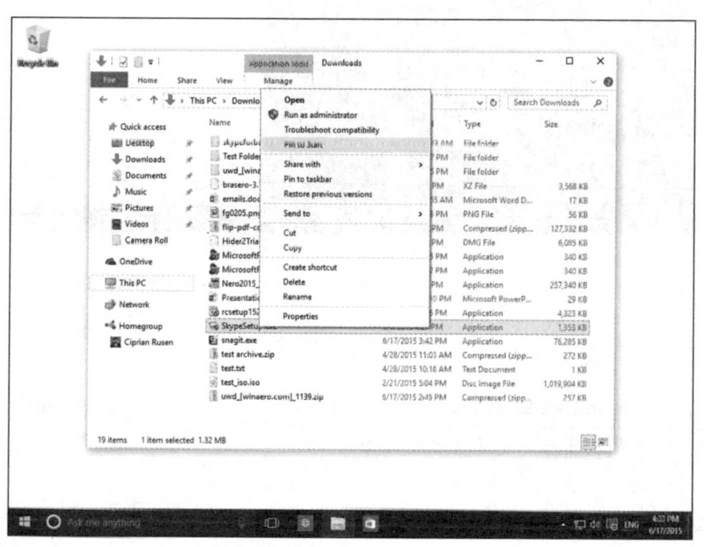

Figure 2-5: Pinning a file to the Start Menu.

Move Tiles and Shortcuts Across the Start Menu

You can reorganize and change the position of apps, files, and websites that are pinned to the Start Menu. To move a tile or shortcut to another place on the Start Menu, follow these steps:

1. **Click Start to open the Start Menu.**
2. **Click and hold the left mouse button on the tile or shortcut that you want to move.**

The item you select is highlighted, and the others are grayed out, which means they're disabled.

3. **Still pressing the left mouse button, move the selected item to the desired location (see Figure 2-6).**

   Other elements automatically change their positions to make room for your item.

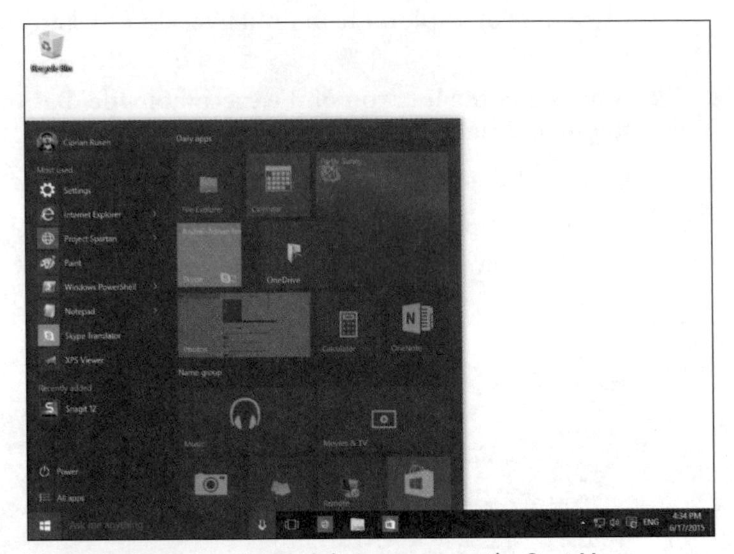

Figure 2-6: Moving tiles and shortcuts across the Start Menu.

4. **Release the left mouse button when the item is where you want it.**

You can use these steps to arrange all the items on the Start Menu just as you want them to be.

Resize Tiles and Shortcuts

You can change the size of all the items on the Start Menu. The choices are small, medium, wide, and large.

To change the size of a tile or shortcut on the Start Menu, follow these steps:

1. **Click Start to open the Start Menu.**
2. **Right-click the item that you want to resize.**
3. **In the list that appears, click Resize (see Figure 2-7).**

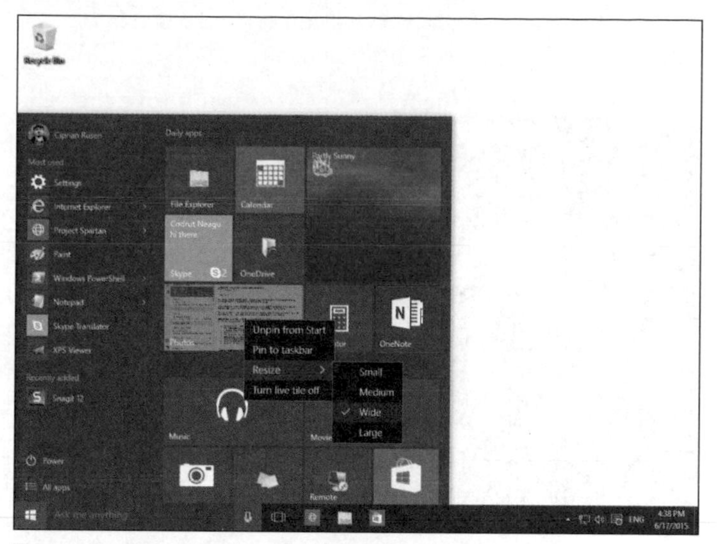

Figure 2-7: Resizing tiles and shortcuts on the Start Menu.

4. **In the list of available sizes, click the size you want for the item (see Figure 2-7).**

   The selected item is now resized.

The maximum size that you can set for a tile or shortcut varies from app to app. For example, only a few apps have tiles that can be set as Large. Shortcuts to desktop apps can be set only to small and medium.

Name Groups of Tiles and Shortcuts

One of the not-so-obvious features of the Start Menu is the capability to name groups of shortcuts and tiles, which enables you to organize them more efficiently. To name a group, follow these steps:

1. **Click Start.**
2. **Move the mouse to the top-right corner of the group of tiles and shortcuts that you want to name.**

   A symbol resembling the equal (=) sign appears at the top-right corner of the group.
3. **Click on the empty space at the left of the equal sign.**

   An empty text box appears.
4. **Type the name that you want for that group (see Figure 2-8).**
5. **After you name the group, click somewhere else in the empty space available on the Start Menu or the Desktop.**

   The group now uses the name you chose.

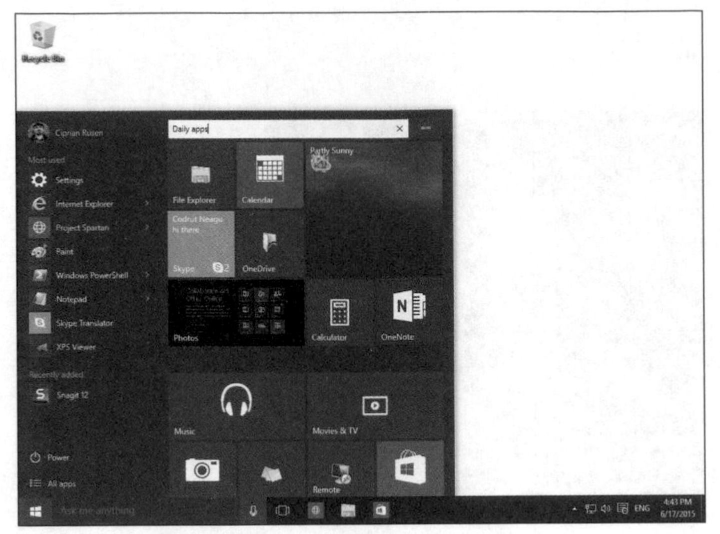

Figure 2-8: Naming a group of shortcuts and tiles.

If you no longer want to use a name for a group of shortcuts and tiles, follow the same procedure and delete the existing name you typed in Step 4.

Store and Display Recently Opened Programs

By default, Windows 10 stores and displays recently opened programs and items in the Start Menu and on the taskbar. However, on computers that are managed by a network administrator, this feature might be disabled. Here's what you need to do to enable this feature:

1. **Open Settings.**
2. **Click Personalization.**

   A list with personalization options and settings appears, split into several categories.
3. **Click Start.**
4. **In the Customize list section, find the switch that says "Store and display recently opened programs in Start".**
5. **Set this switch to On, if you want it to display recently opened programs (see Figure 2-9).**

   Set the switch to Off, if you don't want it to display recently opened programs.
6. **Close Settings.**

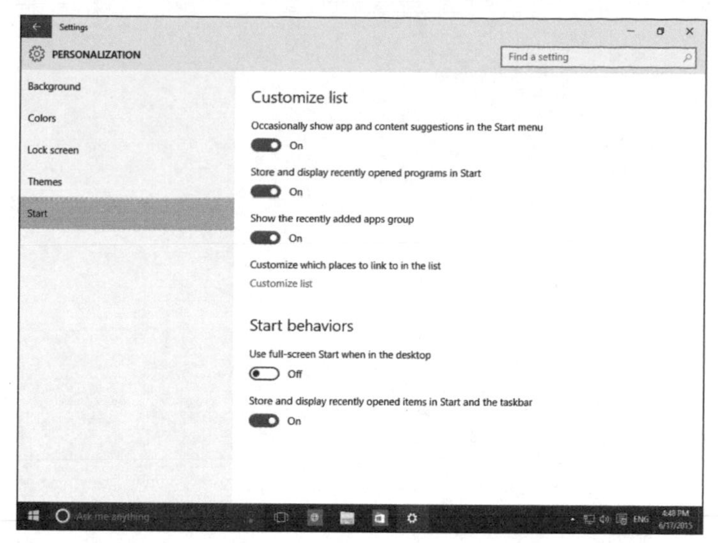

Figure 2-9: Customizing the programs shown on the Start Menu.

Unpin Items from the Start Menu

To remove a tile or shortcut from the Start Menu, follow these steps:

1. **Click Start.**
2. **Right-click the tile or shortcut that you want to unpin.**
3. **In the list that appears, click Unpin from Start (see Figure 2-10).**
4. **Click Start to close the Start Menu.**

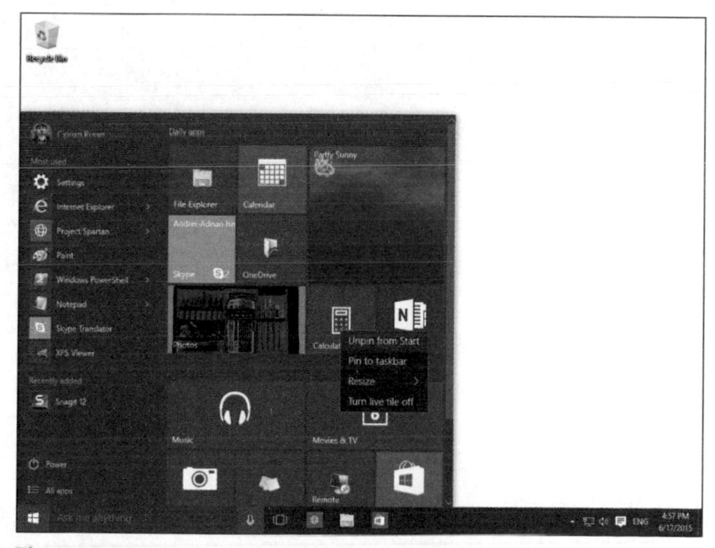

Figure 2-10: Unpinning an item from the Start Menu.

CHAPTER THREE

Using Touch and Touchpads

Since Windows 8 was launched, many new devices have made their way to the marketplace. Now, along with Windows desktops and laptops, you can find tablets and hybrid devices (also referred to as 2-in-1s) such as the Microsoft Surface, ASUS Transformer T100, and Lenovo Yoga. This trend continues with Windows 10, and many devices that ship with this operating system have touchscreens, precision touchpads, or pens.

This chapter shows you how to use touch gestures for touchscreens and precision touchpads. You find out how to use Windows 10 in Tablet Mode and customize the touch keyboard, pen, touchpad, and mouse. Also, you see how to configure the typing and spelling features in Windows 10.

In This Chapter

- Using touch gestures for touchscreens and precision touchpads
- Using the Tablet mode
- Configuring the Tablet Mode
- Using the touch keyboard
- Configuring the touch keyboard
- Configuring typing and spelling
- Configuring the pen, touchpad, and mouse

Use Touch Gestures for Touchscreens

If you have a tablet with Windows 10, a 2-in-1 device such as Microsoft Surface, or simply a laptop with touch, you can use all kinds of touch gestures to interact with the operating system and the apps that you're using. Here is a list of the touch gestures available in Windows 10, how to use them, and what they do. Figure 3-1 shows these gestures:

- **Tap:** Tap once on an item to open, select, or activate it.

  This gesture is similar to a left-click with a mouse.

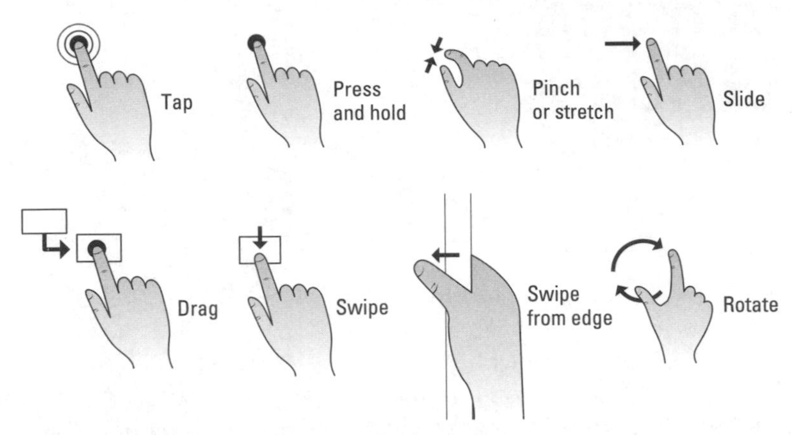

Figure 3-1: The touch gestures in Windows 10.

- **Press and hold:** When you press and hold your finger on an item, Windows shows information about the item or opens a menu that is specific to what you're doing.

  For example, if you press and hold on a tile on the Start menu, options to rearrange and resize it appear. In File Explorer, if you press and hold on a file, the right-click menu pops up.

- **Pinch or stretch:** Touch the screen or an item with two or more fingers, then either move the fingers toward each other (pinch) to zoom in or away from each other (stretch) to zoom out

  This is especially useful when you work with pictures in the Photos app or in similar apps.

- **Slide:** Drag your finger on the screen to the left, right, top, and bottom to scroll and move through what is on the screen.

  The slide gesture is similar to scrolling with the mouse. It's especially useful when working with documents in such apps as Reader, Excel, and Word.

- **Drag:** To move an item, press and briefly drag it opposite the way the page scrolls and then move it wherever you want (this is similar to the way you drag with the mouse).

  For example, if the page scrolls left or right, drag the item up or down. After you move the item to the new location, release it.

- **Swipe:** When you swipe an item with a short, quick movement opposite the direction the page scrolls, you select that item. Depending on the app you're using, the app's commands appear.

  For example, if the page scrolls left or right, swipe the item up or down to select it. If the page scrolls up or down, swipe the item left or right to select it.
- **Swipe from edge:** When you swipe your finger quickly, without lifting it, from the right side of the screen to the left, the Action Center appears. If you swipe your finger quickly, without lifting it, from the left side of the screen to the right, a list of all the open apps appears. You can then switch between apps by tapping the app that you want. This action is somewhat like pressing Alt+Tab on your keyboard.
- **Rotate:** When you put two or more fingers on an item and turn your hand, you rotate the item in the direction that your hand turns.

  This gesture works only in a few apps, and mostly with images.

Use Touch Gestures for Precision Touchpads

In Windows 10, Microsoft introduces new gestures for controlling the operating system with the help of precision touchpads. These touchpads are included on many modern laptops and Ultrabooks, and they're especially useful when you don't have a mouse at hand.

Figure 3-2 shows a summary of the gestures you can perform on a precision touchpad (the number of dots represents the number of fingers that you use for each gesture):

- **Left-click an item:** Tap one finger.
- **Double-click an item:** Double-tap one finger.
- **Move the cursor on the screen:** Place one finger on the touchpad and move it across the touchpad.
- **Tap and slide to the left/right:** Moves through what's on the screen. Similar to scrolling horizontally with a mouse.
- **Right-click an item:** Tap two fingers on the touchpad after moving the cursor on top of that item.
- **Scroll and move any direction on the screen:** Drag two fingers on the touchpad to the direction you want to scroll.
- **Scroll or pan:** Place two fingers on the touchpad and move them in the direction that you want.

- **Zoom in:** Touch the touchpad with two or more fingers, then move the fingers toward each other (pinch).
- **Zoom out:** Touch the touchpad with two or more fingers, then move the fingers apart (stretch).
- **Wake up Cortana:** Tap three fingers on the touchpad.
- **Open the Action Center:** Tap four fingers on the touchpad.

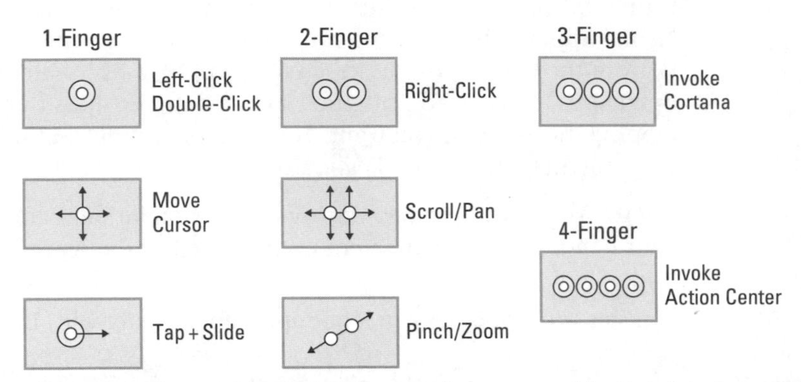

Figure 3-2: The gestures that you can perform on precision touchpads.

You can also put three fingers on the touchpad for *multitasking gestures,* which are useful when working with different apps at once. Figure 3-3 shows several examples of how to use these gestures to multitask:

- **Open the Task View:** Move three fingers from the bottom margin to the top of the touchpad.
- **Hide the Task View:** Move three fingers from the top margin to the bottom of the touchpad; you see what was previously opened.
- **Switch to the next open app:** Move three fingers from left to the right of the touchpad.
- **Switch to the previous open app:** Move three fingers from the right to the left of the touchpad.
- **Select any open app:**
  1. *Press three fingers on the touchpad and move them to the left or right (keep holding them down).*

     The Alt+Tab window lists all opened apps.
  2. *With those three fingers still down, move to the left or right to select the app that you want to open.*
  3. *When the app is selected, release your fingers from the touchpad.*

- **Minimize all open apps (show the Desktop):** Move three fingers from the top to the bottom of the touchpad.

  Show all minimized apps: Move three fingers from the bottom to the top of the touchpad.

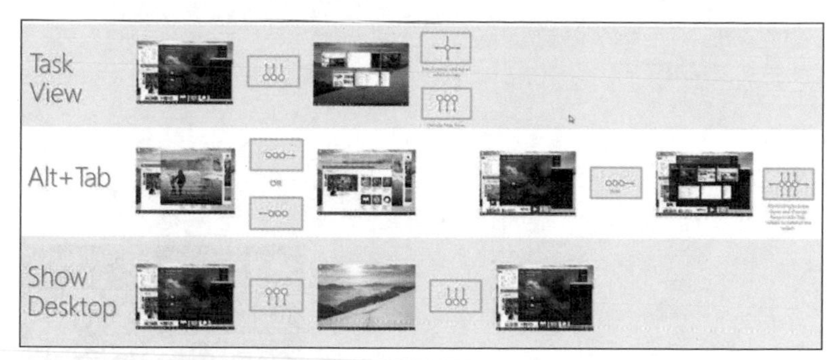

Figure 3-3: Multitasking gestures that you can perform on precision touchpads.

Precision touchpads were first introduced in October 2013 on devices with Windows 8.1. If your laptop or Ultrabook was made before that time, it probably doesn't have a precision touchpad. Also, basic devices with Windows 10 may not have a precision touchpad; instead, they may have a standard touchpad that doesn't support gestures. To find out whether this feature of Windows 10 works on your device, check your owner's manual or the manufacturer's website for more information.

Enter the Tablet mode

Tablet mode is a new feature of Windows 10 that allows hybrid devices to run in full-screen continuum mode, which removes windowed apps and turns the Start menu into a Start screen. The Desktop is hidden and all apps (including desktop apps) take the whole screen. When working in this mode, you can only minimize apps; you can't resize them. Everything either occupies the whole screen or is minimized in the background.

If you have a hybrid device such as Microsoft Surface and you remove the keyboard, Windows 10 automatically asks whether you want to enter Tablet mode (see Figure 3-4). Tap Yes, and Tablet mode is enabled immediately.

However, you can enter Tablet mode at any time, even if you haven't removed your device's keyboard. Just follow these steps:

1. **Go to the Notification area on the taskbar and click the Notifications icon.**

   The Action Center appears.

Figure 3-4: The prompt for entering Tablet mode.

2. **Click the Tablet Mode icon to enable Tablet mode (see Figure 3-5).**

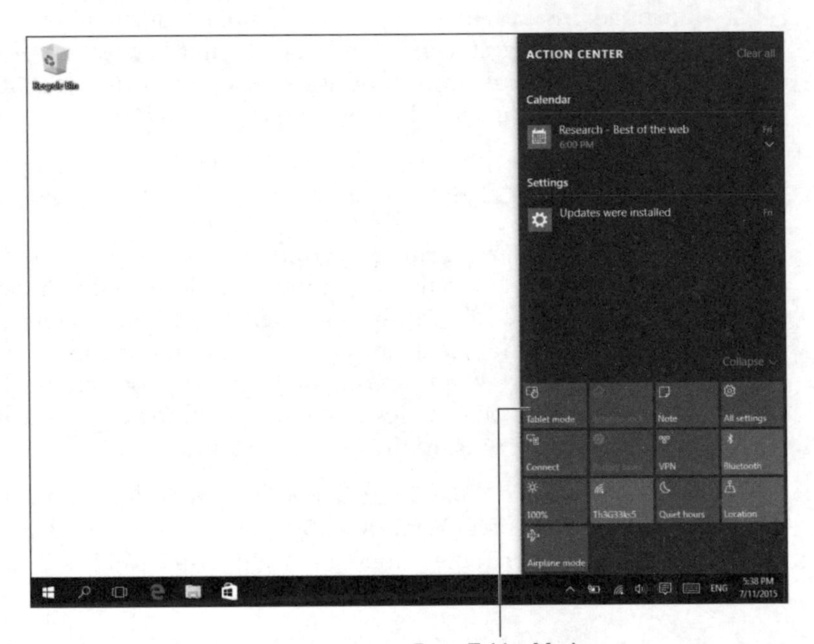

Enter Tablet Mode

Figure 3-5: Enabling the Tablet mode.

3. **Tap somewhere else on the screen to hide the Action Center.**

Exit the Tablet mode

You can exit the Tablet mode at any time, even if a keyboard isn't attached to your hybrid device. Here's how:

1. **Go to the Notification area on the taskbar and tap the icon for the Notifications.**

   The Action Center appears.

2. **Tap the Tablet Mode icon to exit the Tablet mode.**
3. **Click or tap somewhere else on the screen to hide the Action Center.**

When you reattach the keyboard to your hybrid device, Windows 10 asks if you want to exit Tablet Mode. Click or tap Yes if you want to exit it.

Configure the Tablet mode

Windows 10 offers several settings for customizing Tablet mode. First, you can enable or disable this feature, though it's best to disable it only on desktop computers and laptops without touchscreens. You can set how you want Tablet mode to behave in Windows 10 when you sign in. For example, you can set it to keep the mode you were previously in, to immediately enter Tablet mode, or to take you to the Desktop.

Also, you can set when your device can switch modes. You can set it to show a prompt to confirm whether you want to enter or exit Tablet mode, to never prompt you about this change and always stay in your current mode, or to never prompt you but always change modes depending on whether you keep the keyboard attached to your device. Finally, you can set Windows 10 to hide or show app icons on the taskbar when in Tablet mode.

Here's how to access all these settings and change them in Windows 10:

1. **Open Settings.**
2. **Click System.**

   A list of system settings appears.

3. **Click Tablet Mode.**
4. **Set Tablet mode as you want it to work (see Figure 3-6).**
5. **Close the Settings window.**

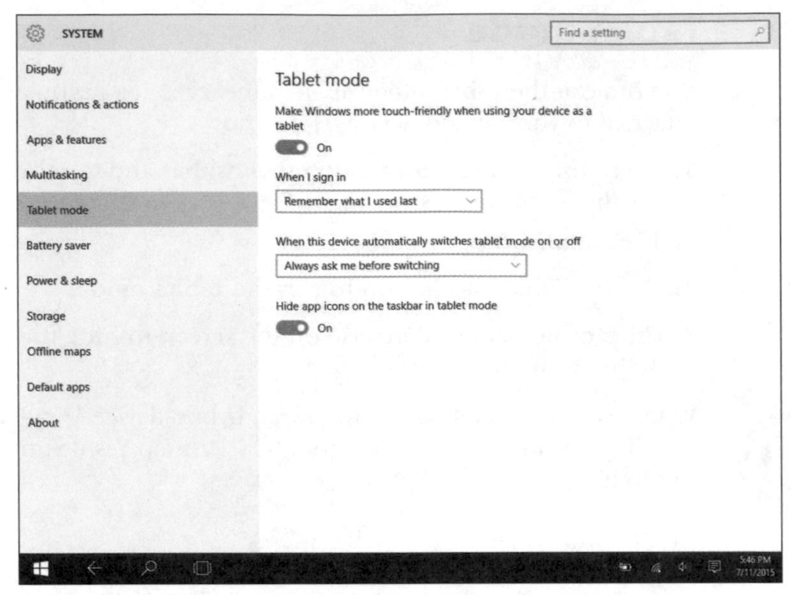

Figure 3-6: Configuring Tablet mode.

Use the Touch Keyboard

Windows 10 features an improved touch keyboard that you can activate when you want to type on a touchscreen. When you're using a Windows 10 device with touch and you tap in a text field, the touch keyboard comes up automatically (see Figure 3-7).

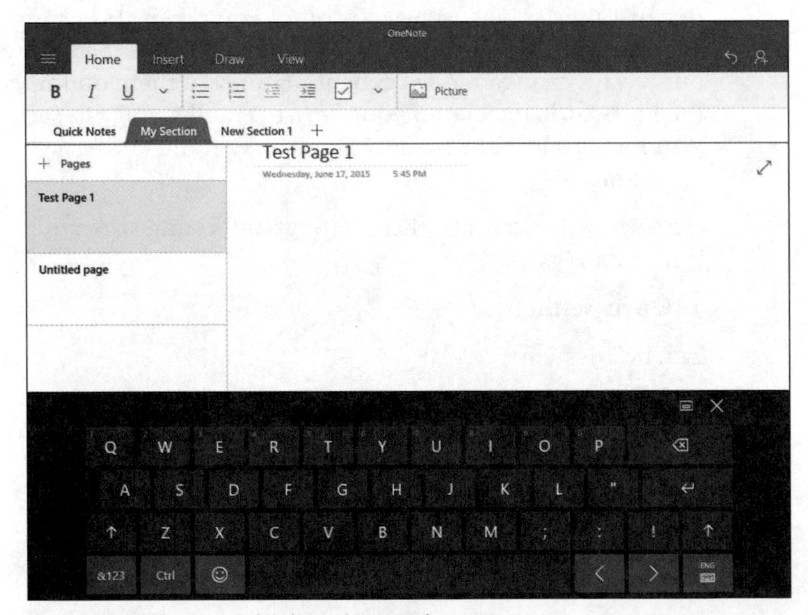

Figure 3-7: The touch keyboard in Windows 10.

You get suggestions as you type, which enables you to type faster and correct typos along the way. When a suggestion appears, tap it to insert it into your text or press the spacebar to get the same result.

Press and hold a key to get other letters, numbers, and symbols. Slide your finger to the character you want and release to enter the character into your text (see Figure 3-8).

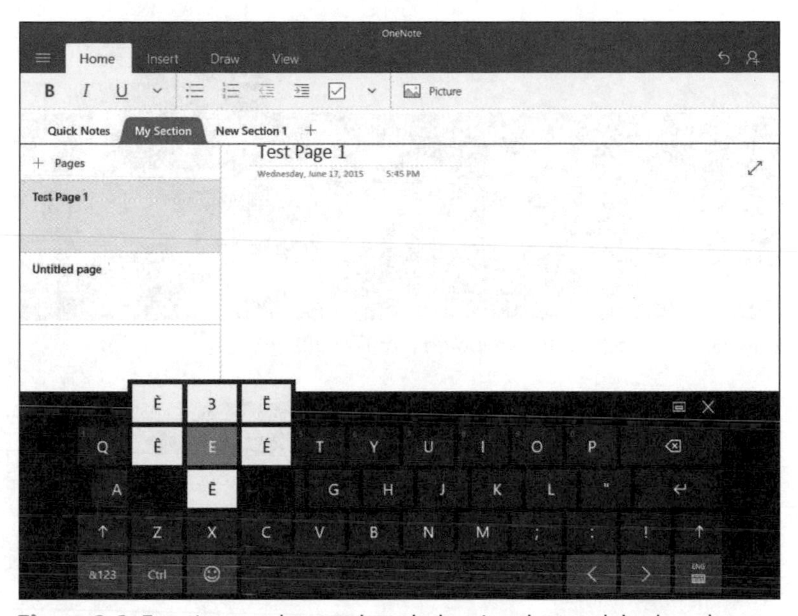

Figure 3-8: Entering numbers and symbols using the touch keyboard.

The characters on the top row of the keyboard have letters and numbers on their top-left corners. To quickly enter a number, swipe up from the character's key. When you finish typing, tap outside the keyboard to hide it.

On tablets and other devices with touch, you can also switch to the thumb keyboard. To do so, tap the keyboard icon and then tap the thumb keyboard.

If you have multiple keyboard input languages installed, you can also switch between languages by tapping the language that you want to use. You can view all these options when you tap the keyboard icon on the bottom-left corner of the keyboard (see Figure 3-9).

When using the thumb keyboard, you can adjust its size by pressing and sliding the three dots that are available. Switch through the available sizes until you get the size that best fits your needs (see Figure 3-10).

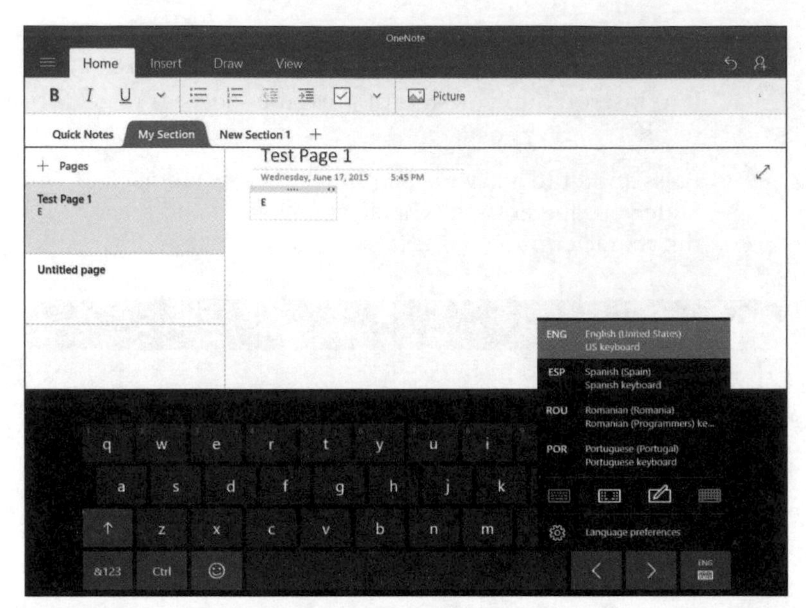

Figure 3-9: Switching the keyboard input language.

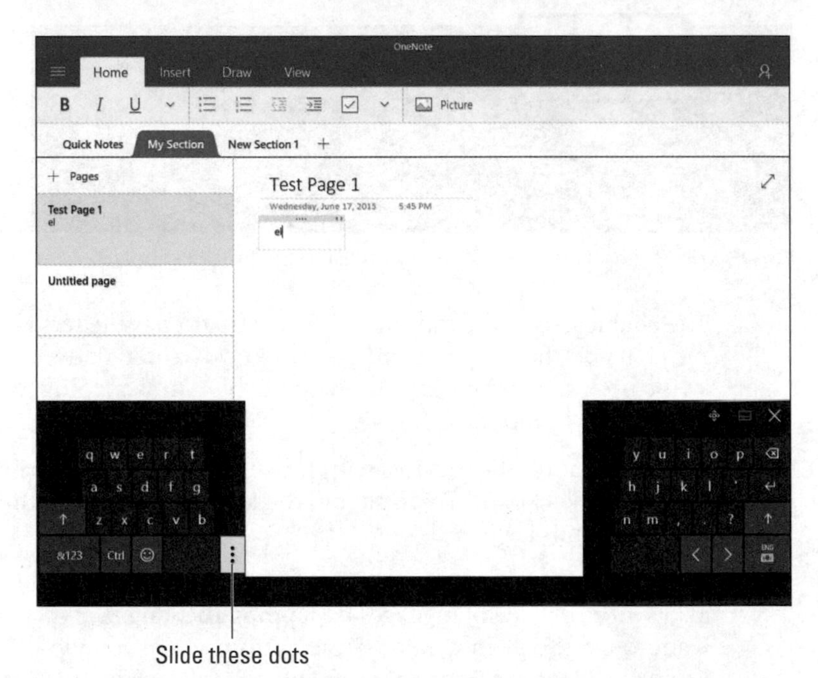

Figure 3-10: The three dots for changing the size of the thumb keyboard.

The touch keyboard activates itself only in Tablet mode. It isn't available in other modes. Also, if you don't have a device with touch, you can't use the touch keyboard without manually turning it on in the Windows settings.

Configure the Touch Keyboard

Windows 10 allows you to configure how a touch keyboard works. You can enable or disable sounds as you type, capitalize the first letter of each sentence, use all uppercase letters when you double-tap Shift, add the standard keyboard layout as a touch keyboard option, and more. You can find all settings related to the touch keyboard by following these steps:

1. **Open Settings.**
2. **Tap Devices.**

   The settings for your devices are shown.
3. **Tap Typing.**

   Your typing and spelling settings are shown.
4. **Scroll down to the Touch Keyboard settings (see Figure 3-11).**

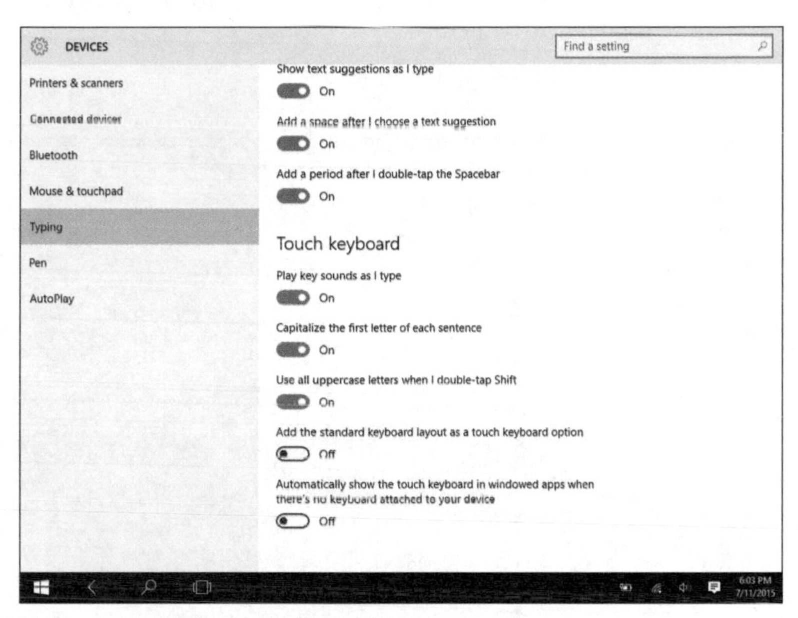

Figure 3-11: The Touch Keyboard settings.

5. **Change the settings that you're interested in by setting the appropriate switches to On or Off.**
6. **Close the Settings window.**

Configure Typing and Spelling

In Windows 10, you can configure the spelling and typing behaviors when you use a touch keyboard. You can set the spelling feature to autocorrect misspelled words or highlight them, and you can set the typing feature to show suggestions as you type, to add a space after you choose a text suggestion, and to add a period after you double-tap the spacebar.

Here's how to set the spelling and typing features in Windows 10:

1. **Open Settings.**
2. **Tap Devices.**

   The settings for your devices are shown.
3. **Tap Typing.**

   Your typing and spelling settings are shown.
4. **In the Spelling group, change the settings that you're interested in by setting the appropriate switches to On or Off (see Figure 3-12).**
5. **In the Typing group, change the settings that you're interested in by setting the appropriate switches to On or Off (see Figure 3-12).**
6. **Close the Settings window.**

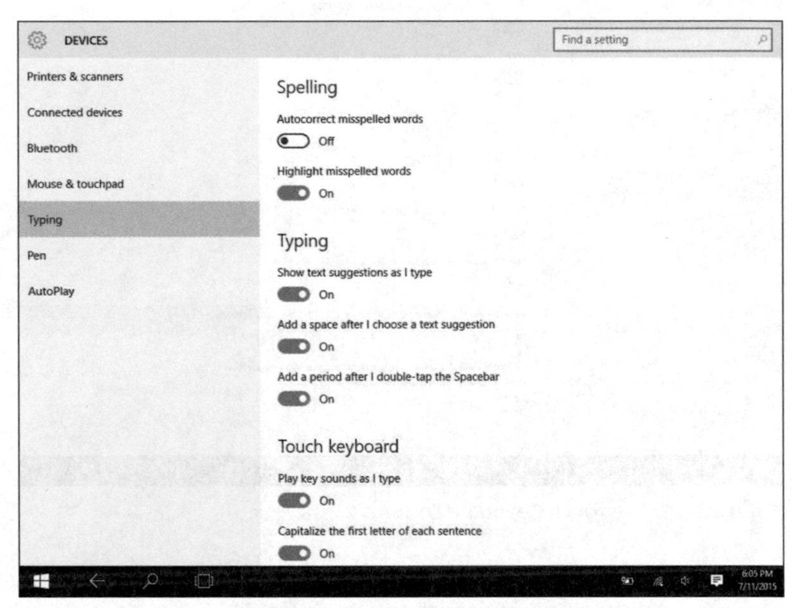

Figure 3-12: The Spelling and Typing settings in Windows 10.

Configure the Pen

If you have a device with a pen, such as the Surface Pro 3, you can use the pen for common tasks, such as taking notes in OneNote and taking screenshots. You can also configure how the pen works and change things like the hand you write with and whether to show the cursor and visual effects while using it. Here's how to configure the pen in Windows 10:

1. **Open Settings.**
2. **Tap Devices.**

   The settings for your devices are shown.
3. **Tap Pen.**

   Your pen settings are shown.
4. **Change the settings that you're interested in (see Figure 3-13).**
5. **Close the Settings window.**

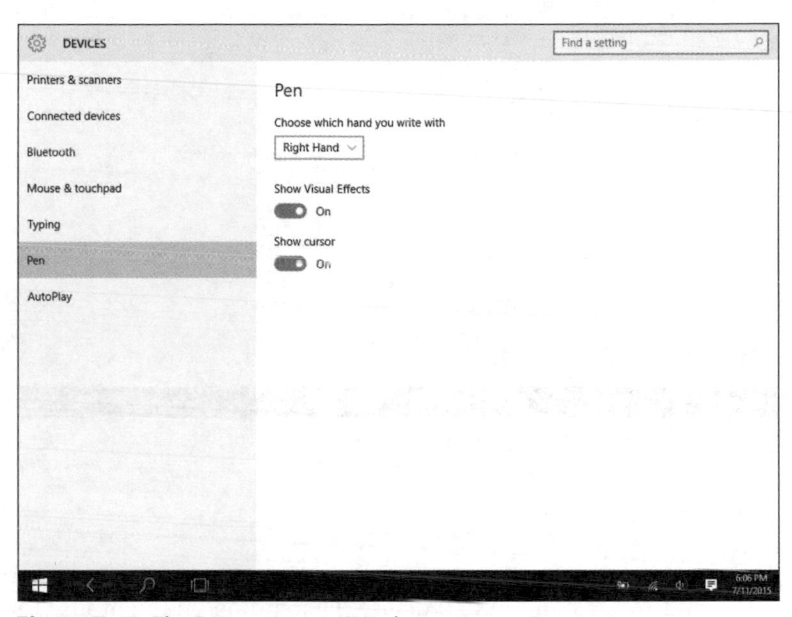

Figure 3-13: The Pen settings in Windows 10.

Configure the Touchpad

If you're working on a Windows 10 device that has a touchpad (for example, Ultrabook or a 2-in-1 device such as Microsoft Surface), you can configure in detail how the touchpad works. The configuration options differ from device to device but should include values such as turning the touchpad on or off, keeping the device turned on when you connect a mouse, and configuring the scrolling direction and cursor speed. Here's how to configure the touchpad in Windows 10:

1. **Open Settings.**
2. **Tap Devices.**

   The settings for your devices are shown.

3. **Click Mouse & Touchpad.**

   Your mouse and touchpad settings are shown.

4. **In the Touchpad group, change the settings that you're interested in (see Figure 3-14).**

5. **Close Settings.**

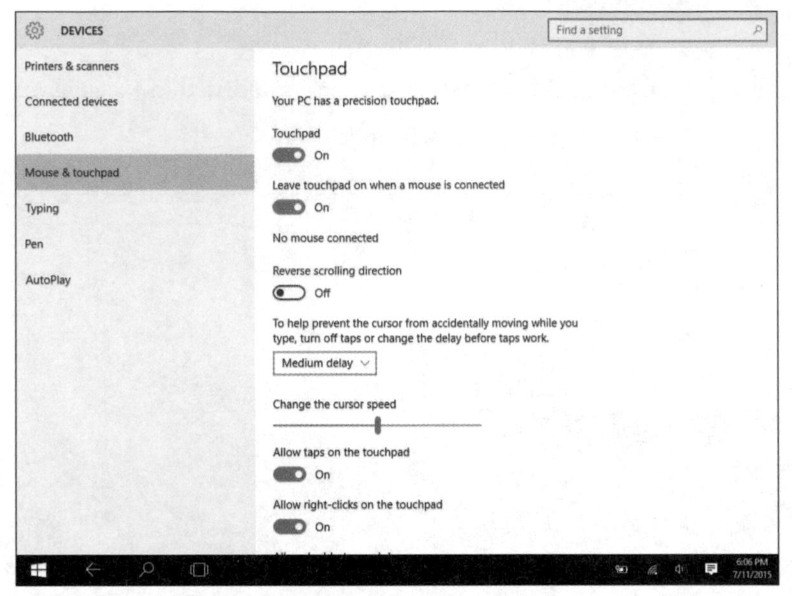

Figure 3-14: The Touchpad settings in Windows 10.

Configure the Mouse

You can also configure how the mouse works when you connect it to your Windows 10 device. Depending on the mouse that you have and its drivers, you can configure more or fewer options. However, in most cases, you can configure options such as your primary button and how many lines you scroll each time you use the scroll wheel. To configure how your mouse works, follow these steps:

1. **Open Settings.**

2. **Tap Devices.**

   The settings for your devices are shown.

3. **Click Mouse & Touchpad.**

   Your mouse and touchpad settings are shown.

4. **In the Mouse group, change the settings that you're interested in (see Figure 3-15).**

5. **Close Settings.**

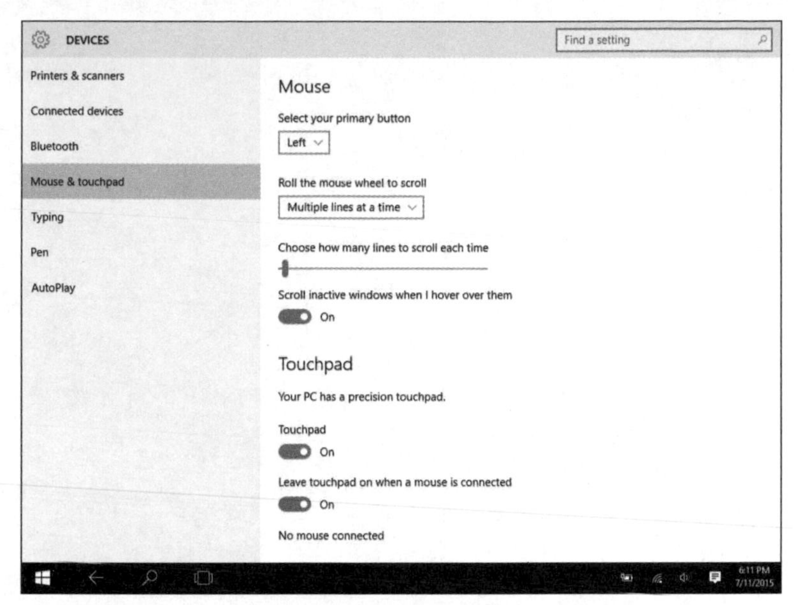

Figure 3-15: The Mouse settings in Windows 10.

CHAPTERFOUR

Connecting to Wi-Fi Networks and the Internet

In order to be productive, you need to connect to your company's network as well as the Internet. If you have a laptop or 2-in-1 device with Windows 10, then you probably need to connect to the company's network through Wi-Fi. That's why in this chapter I first show you how to turn the Wi-Fi on and off in Windows 10 and how to connect to all kinds of wireless networks.

Business workers also travel a lot, and they need to connect to the Internet from all kinds of places like airports, coffee shops, and business and public buildings. One way to connect to the Internet is to use a mobile USB modem that connects to your telecom's network. This chapter shows you how.

When you connect to any new network, Windows 10 asks whether you want to find PCs, devices, and content on that network. Depending on your answer, Windows 10 assigns a specific network profile that determines whether you can share with others on the network, and determines your level of security and firewall protection. This chapter shows what a network profile is, how to assign it correctly, and how to change it if you didn't get it right the first time.

Finally, many companies use proxy servers as intermediaries between their company PCs and devices and the Internet. Proxies bring many benefits ranging from bandwidth savings to privacy and security

In This Chapter

- Turning the Wi-Fi connection on and off
- Connecting to wireless networks
- Connecting to the Internet using a mobile USB modem
- Setting the correct network profile
- Managing your Wi-Fi settings
- Setting up connections through proxies

improvements. This chapter shows you how to set up and disable a proxy server on your Windows 10 work computer or device.

Turn the Wi-Fi On and Off

Before connecting to a wireless network, you need to ensure that your Wi-Fi network card is turned on. Windows 10 offers a quick way to switch your Wi-Fi network card on or off. Here's how:

1. **On the Desktop, either slide from the right side of the screen to the left (on a screen with touch) or click the Notifications icon in the notification area on the taskbar.**

   The Action Center appears on the screen, as shown in Figure 4-1.

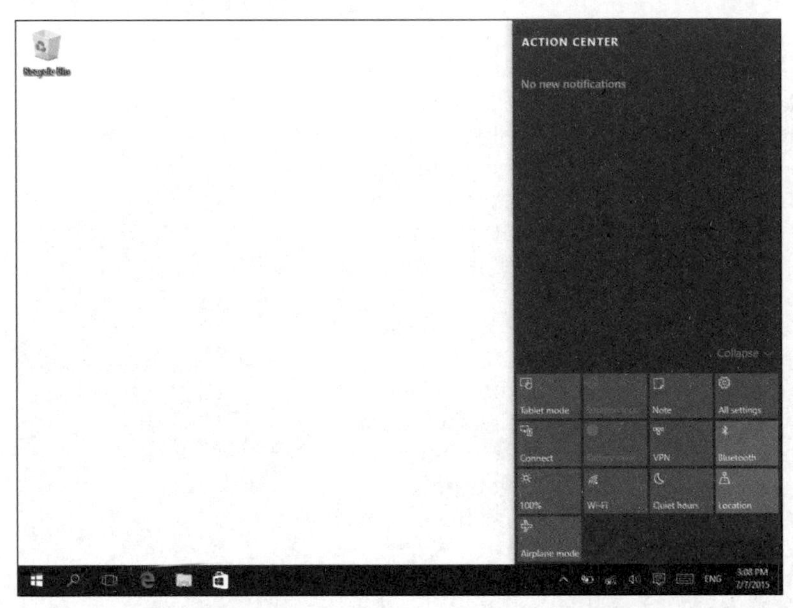

Figure 4-1: The Action Center.

2. **Click or tap the Wi-Fi icon to change the status of the wireless network.**

   If the Wi-Fi is turned on, you just turn it off, and vice versa.

Connect to a Wireless Network

If you need to connect to a wireless network, the procedure is simple. You just need to know the network name and its password. To connect to the wireless network, follow these steps:

1. **Click the wireless network icon on the taskbar.**

   A list appears showing all the wireless networks in the area.

2. **Click the network you want to connect to.**
3. **Leave the box Connect Automatically checked; then click Connect.**

   You're asked to enter the password or the network security key.
4. **Type the password or the network security key in the appropriate field (see Figure 4-2).**
5. **Check whether you want to share the network connection details with your contacts, then click Next.**

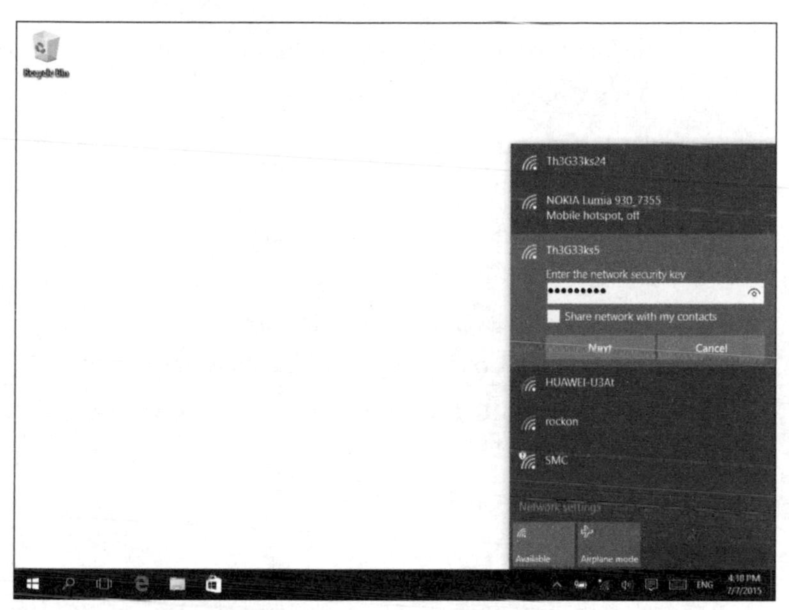

Figure 4-2: Connecting to a wireless network.

   You're asked whether you want to allow your PC to be discoverable by other PCs and devices on this network. If you answer Yes, you can find PCs, devices, and content on the network you connected to.
6. **Click Yes or No, depending on what you prefer.**

You're now connected to the network, and you can start using it. In the future, Windows 10 automatically connects to this network each time the network is detected in your area. You don't have to go through this procedure again.

Setting whether you want to find PCs, devices, and content on the network you connected to affects what you can do on the network and how secure your Windows computer or device is after you connect. In order to better understand how this setting works and its effects, see the "Set the Correct Network Profile" section, later in this chapter.

Connect to a Hidden Wireless Network

Hidden wireless networks broadcast their signal in a geographical area without making their name public. When you look for wireless networks in Windows 10, hidden networks aren't visible in the list with wireless networks. However, some companies use hidden wireless networks in some of their offices. In that case, you need to know the network's name, security type and password before connecting to it. Follow these steps to connect to the hidden network:

1. **Open Control Panel.**
2. **Click Network and Internet.**

   A list with network and internet related settings appears.
3. **Click Network and Sharing Center.**

   A window with the same name opens.
4. **Click Set Up a New Connection or Network.**

   The Set Up a Connection or Network wizard opens.
5. **Select Manually Connect to a Wireless Network, then click Next.**

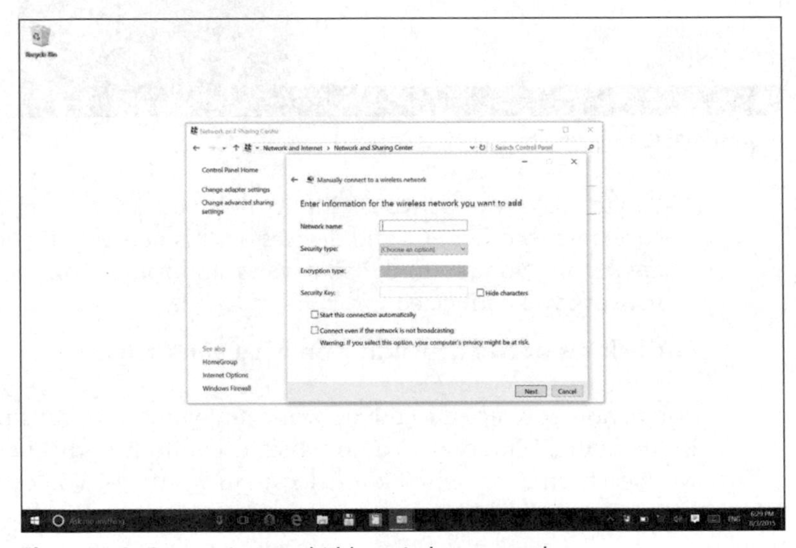

Figure 4-3: Connecting to a hidden wireless network.

   You're asked to enter the name (SSID) for the network and other details, such as the security type, encryption type, and security key.

6. **Type the network name in the appropriate field.**
7. **In the Security Type field, choose the type of security used for the hidden wireless network.**
8. **In the Security Key field, type the network password.**
9. **Check whether you want to start this connection automatically, then click Next.**

   Windows 10 notifies you that it has successfully added the wireless network.
10. **Click Close.**

Connect to the Internet Using a Mobile USB Modem or SIM Card

If you have a laptop or a 2-in-1 device with Windows 10, you can connect to the Internet while on the go, by using a USB mobile modem from your telecom provider. In order to use it, you need to plug the modem into a USB port and wait for Windows 10 to detect and install it.

Once that's done, find the setup of a desktop app that's made available by the telecom provider on your modem. You need to install this app in order to connect to the mobile network of your telecom provider.

The app's name depends on your telecom provider. For example, in the United States, AT&T offers AT&T Communication Manager for its users that have a mobile modem that can connect to their network and the Internet.

After you install the app, you can use it to connect to your telecom's mobile network and the Internet.

Figure 4-4 shows an example of a desktop app that's offered by Vodafone, a major telecom provider in Europe.

These desktop apps vary from provider to provider, and there's no one way of doing things.

Some Windows 10 devices have a slot for inserting a SIM card that you can then use to connect to the network of your telecom provider. If that's the case for you, plug in the SIM card and then go to the Windows Store. There, search for the app offered by your telecom and install it. You can use that app to connect to your telecom's mobile network and the Internet. For example, in the United States, Verizon offers the Verizon Connection Manager app, which you can use to manage your mobile broadband experiences (see Figure 4-5, which shows this app's Windows Store page).

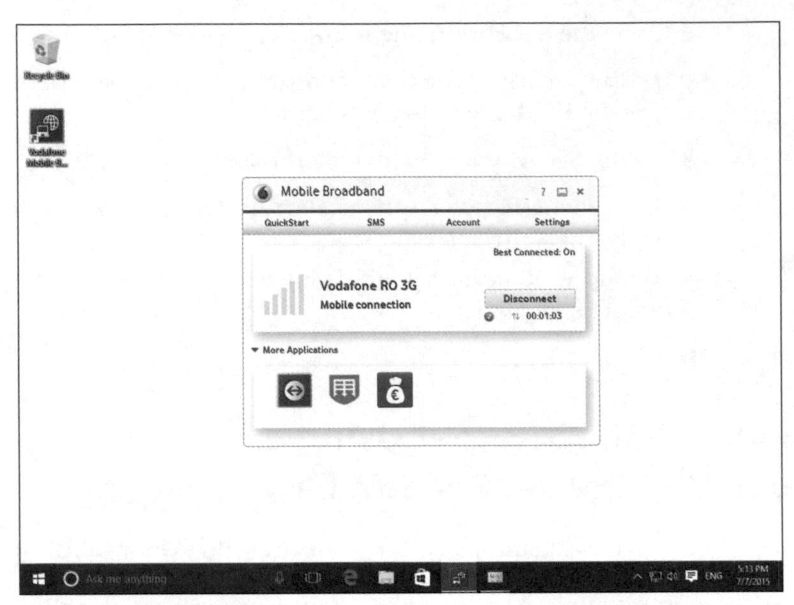

Figure 4-4: The desktop app offered by Vodafone for its mobile USB modems.

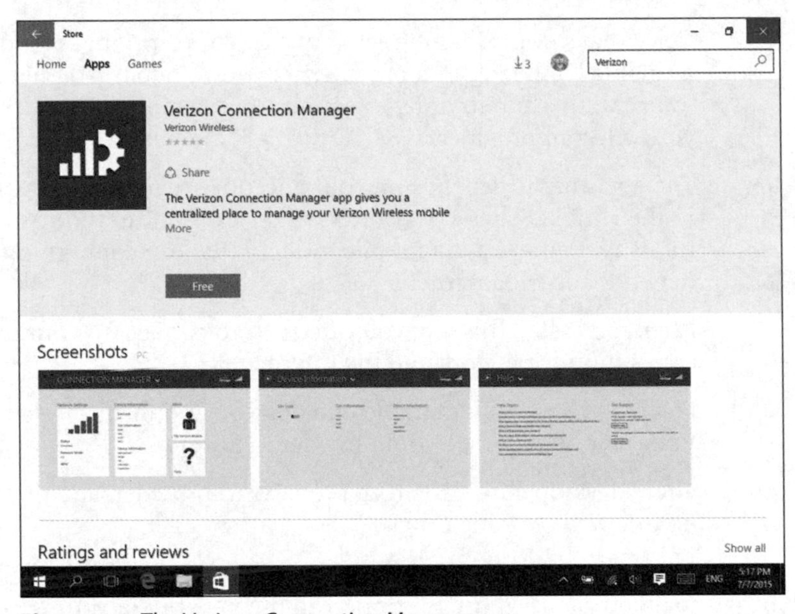

Figure 4-5: The Verizon Connection Manager app.

Set the Correct Network Profile

When you connect for the first time to a new network, through a wireless network, a cable network, or a mobile USB modem, you're asked whether you want to allow your PC to be discoverable by other PCs and devices on that network. If you select Yes, your computer can find PCs, devices, and content on this network and to automatically connect to devices like printers and TVs (see Figure 4-6). When you select Yes, you set the network profile to Private.

Make your home or work network private if it's used by people and devices you trust. By default, network discovery is turned on, and you can see other computers and devices that are part of the network. This allows other computers from the network to access your computer, and you can create or join a HomeGroup.

If you select No, you disable all these preceding features, and you set the network profile to Public. This profile is appropriate when you're in public places such as airports, cafes, and libraries. Network discovery and sharing are turned off. Other computers from the network can't see your computer. This setting is also useful when your computer is directly connected to the Internet (such as via direct cable/modem connection or mobile Internet).

A third network location profile called a domain network is available for enterprise workplaces. Only a network administrator can set it or change it. This profile is applied only when you're connected to the network at your workplace.

Except for a domain network, you can easily change profiles for a network after you connect to it, as you see in the next section.

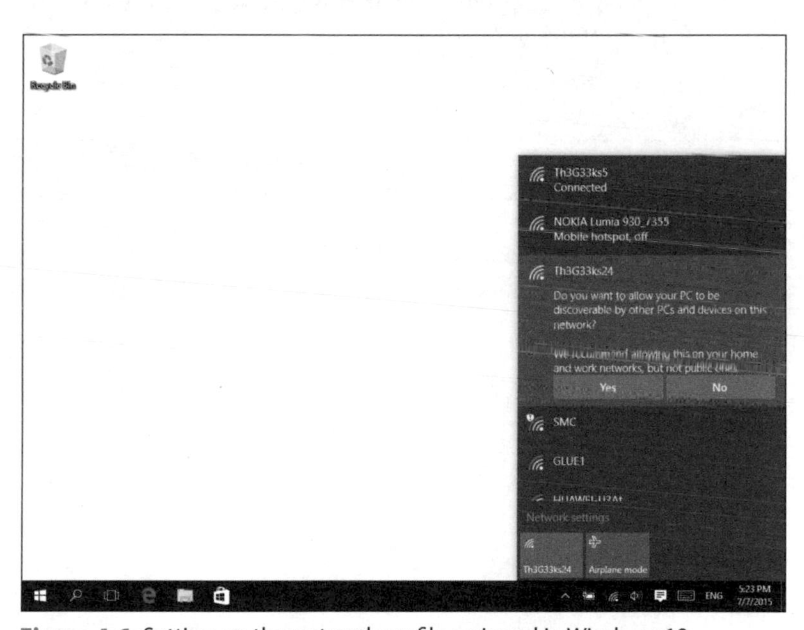

Figure 4-6: Setting up the network profile assigned in Windows 10.

Change the Network Profile

If you set an incorrect profile when you connect to a new network, you can always change the profile. If you agreed to allow

Windows 10 find PCs, devices, and content on your network, then you have set the Private network profile, which makes your Windows 10 device discoverable on the network. If you didn't agree to let Windows 10 find PCs, devices, and content, you set the Public network profile, which doesn't allow network sharing.

To change the network profile in Windows 10, follow these steps:

1. **Open Settings.**
2. **Click Network & Internet.**

   The list of network and Internet related settings appears.
3. **Click Ethernet or Wi-Fi, depending on the type of network you're connected to.**

   Information about the network you're connected to appears.
4. **If you're connected to a wired network, click the name of the network you're connected to. If you're connected to a wireless network, click Advanced Options under the list of available wireless networks.**

   The list of settings available for your network connection is shown.
5. **Set the Find Devices and Content switch to Off or On, depending on whether or not you want to turn on sharing (see Figure 4-7).**
6. **Close Settings.**

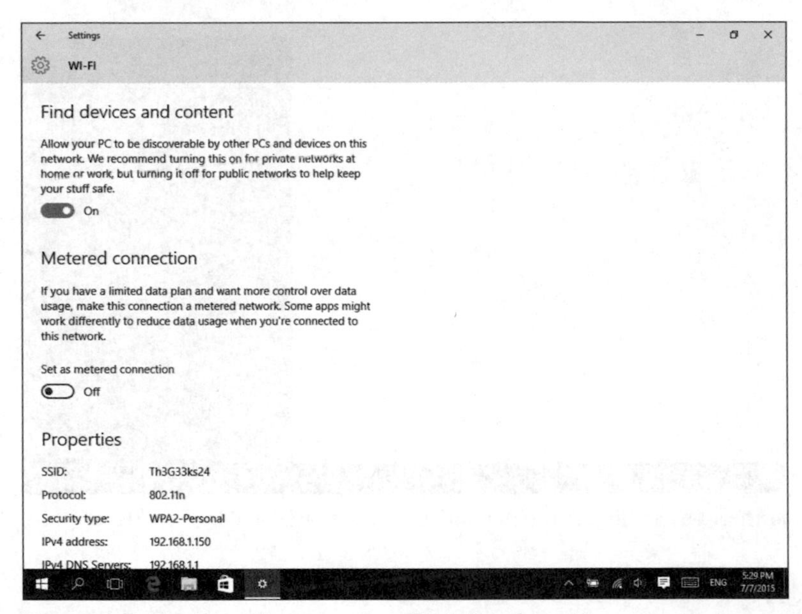

Figure 4-7: Changing the network profile in Windows 10.

To enable network sharing, set the Find Devices and Content switch to On. To disable network sharing, set the switch to Off.

Manage Your Wi-Fi Settings

With the help of the new Wi-Fi feature, Wi-Fi Sense, Windows 10 can connect to Wi-Fi hotspots and networks that your contacts share with you. You can also share your networks and their details with your contacts. When Wi-Fi Sense is enabled, you agree that this feature can use your location in order to work and do what it was designed to do. Obviously, you can easily disable this feature, if you don't want to use it. You can also set whether you want to exchange Wi-Fi network access with your contacts and which group of contacts you want to make this exchange with.

Here's how to customize your Wi-Fi settings:

1. **Click the wireless network icon on the taskbar.**

   The list of available wireless networks appears.

2. **Click Network Settings.**

   Your wireless network settings are shown.

3. **Scroll down to the end of the list of wireless networks.**

4. **Click Manage Wi-Fi Settings.**

   The Manage Wi-Fi Settings window is shown.

5. **Set the Connect To Suggested Open Hotspots switch to Off if you want to disable this feature (see Figure 4-8).**

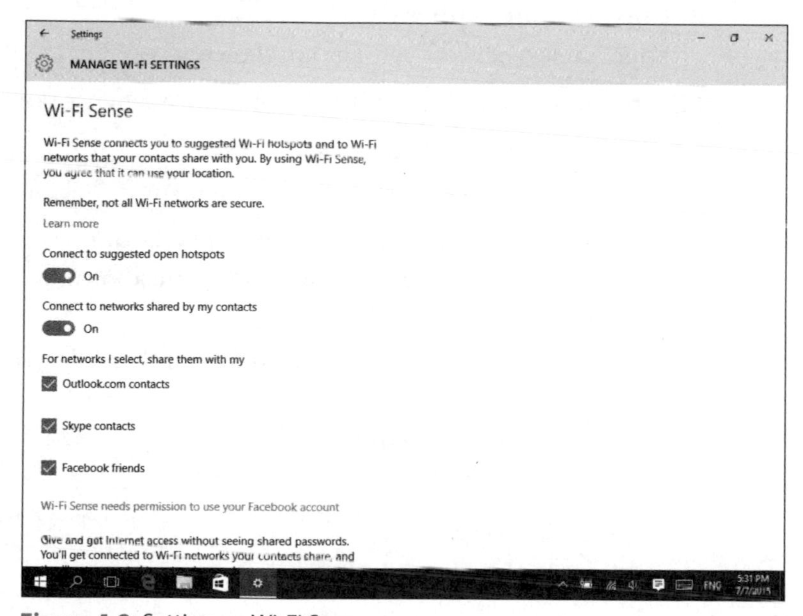

Figure 4-8: Setting up Wi-Fi Sense.

6. **Set Connect To Networks Shared By My Contacts to Off if you want to disable this feature.**
7. **If you want to keep these features turned On but customize which contacts you're sharing with, select the types of contacts you're interested in and deselect those you don't want to share with.**
8. **Close Manage Wi-Fi Settings window.**

Forget a Wireless Network You Connected To

You can easily "forget" a wireless network you connected to in the past. When doing so, Windows 10 deletes all the information it stored about the network and it can't connect to it automatically. If you want to connect to it later, you must go through the whole procedure of connecting to that network, as though you're connecting to it for the first time.

Forgetting a network is very useful when its settings have been changed, such as its security password.

Because Windows 10 stored details about a wireless network that are no longer valid, you may no longer be able to connect to it. Forgetting a wireless network forces Windows 10 to ask you for its latest connection details the next time you try to connect to it. Here's how to forget a wireless network in Windows 10:

1. **Click the wireless network icon on the taskbar.**

   The list of available wireless networks appears.
2. **Click Network Settings.**

   Your wireless network settings are shown.
3. **Scroll down to the end of the list of wireless networks.**
4. **Click Manage Wi-Fi Settings.**

   The Manage Wi-Fi Settings window is shown.
5. **Scroll to the Manage Known Networks section.**

   You can see all the wireless networks that are known by Windows 10.
6. **Click the network that you want to forget; then click Forget (see Figure 4-9).**
7. **Close Manage Wi-Fi Settings window.**

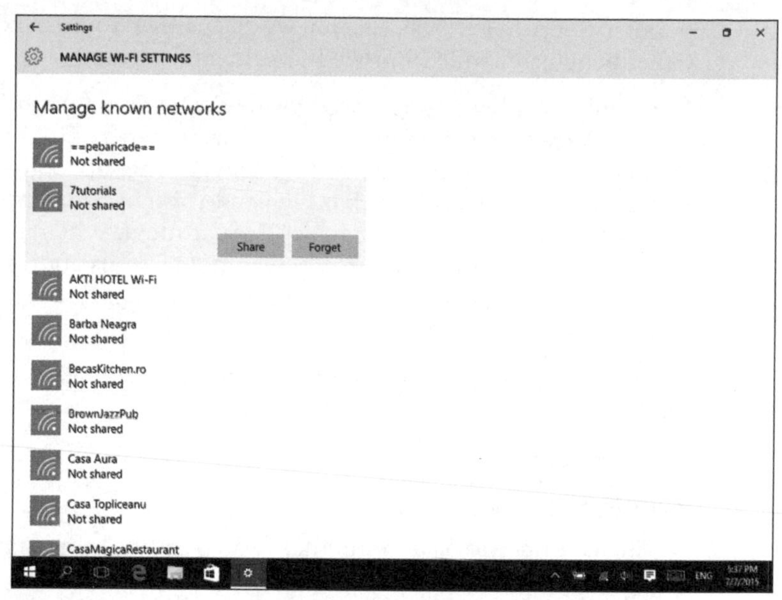

Figure 4-9: Forgetting a wireless network.

If you chose to "forget" a network because you could no longer connect to it and you still can't connect after forgetting it, then talk to your company's network administrator or IT support department. The problem may be that the network is now set up so that it's no longer compatible with the wireless network card on your Windows 10 device.

Set Up a Proxy Using an Automatic Configuration Script

A proxy server is an intermediary between your PC or device and the Internet. This server makes requests to websites, servers, and services on the Internet for you. For example, say that you use a web browser to visit `www.wiley.com` and your browser is set to use a proxy server. After you type **www.wiley.com**, the request is sent to the proxy server. The server then sends the request to the server where the website is hosted. The homepage of the Wiley website is returned to the proxy server which, in turn, returns the homepage to you.

One reason companies use proxy servers is that doing so helps them save precious bandwidth. Proxy servers can compress traffic, cache files and web pages from the Internet, and even strip ads from websites before they reach your computer. This allows companies to save bandwidth, especially when they have hundreds or thousands of employees accessing mostly the same popular websites (such as CNN news or *The New York Times*). Other benefits include improved security and privacy.

By default, Windows 10 is set to automatically detect proxy settings. However, this may not work when you're connected to your company's business network. One way to set up a proxy is to specify a script address that is given to you by the network administrator or by the company's IT department. When using a configuration script for a proxy server, note that its address is similar to a URL (the address of a website), such as `http://my.proxy.server:8000/`.

To set a proxy using an automatic configuration script, follow these steps:

1. **Open Settings.**
2. **Click Network & Internet.**

   The list of network- and Internet-related settings appears.
3. **Click Proxy.**

   The list of available proxy settings appears.
4. **In the Automatic Proxy Setup section, set the Use Setup Script switch to On (see Figure 4-10).**

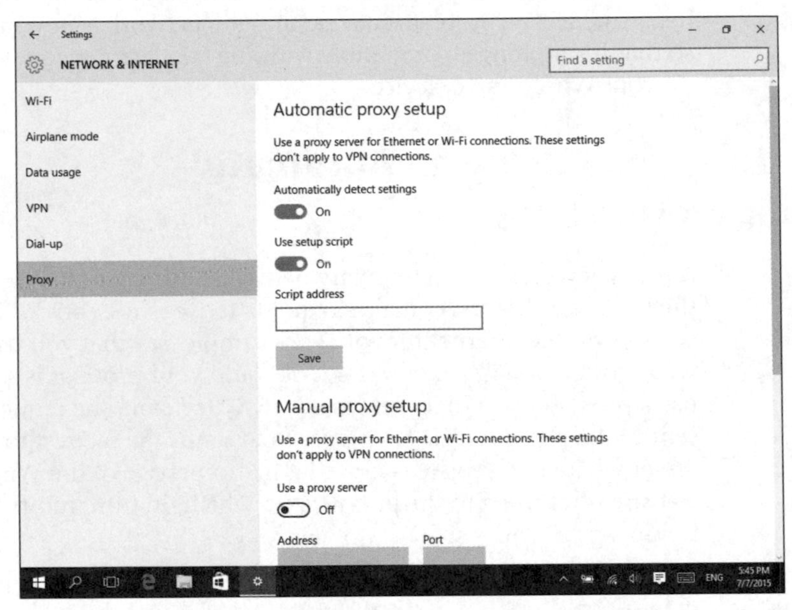

Figure 4-10: Setting up an automatic proxy configuration script.

5. **Enter the script address as it was given to you; then click Save.**
6. **Close Settings.**

To disable the proxy, follow the same steps and, at Step 4, set the Use Setup Script switch to Off.

Set Up a Proxy Manually

Another way to set a proxy is to manually enter its IP address and port number. The address of a proxy server is similar to that of any computer on the network, and it could be something like: 192.168.1.211. The port can be any combination of up to four figures. It can be any combination of digits, including 80 or 8080, depending on how its administrator(s) set it. The IP address and port of your company's proxy server are given to you by the network administrator or by the company's IT department. Here's how to set a proxy manually in Windows 10:

1. **Open Settings.**
2. **Click Network & Internet.**

   The list of network- and Internet-related settings appears.
3. **Click Proxy.**

   The list of available proxy settings appears.
4. **In the Manual Proxy Setup section, set the Use a Proxy Server switch to On (see Figure 4-11).**

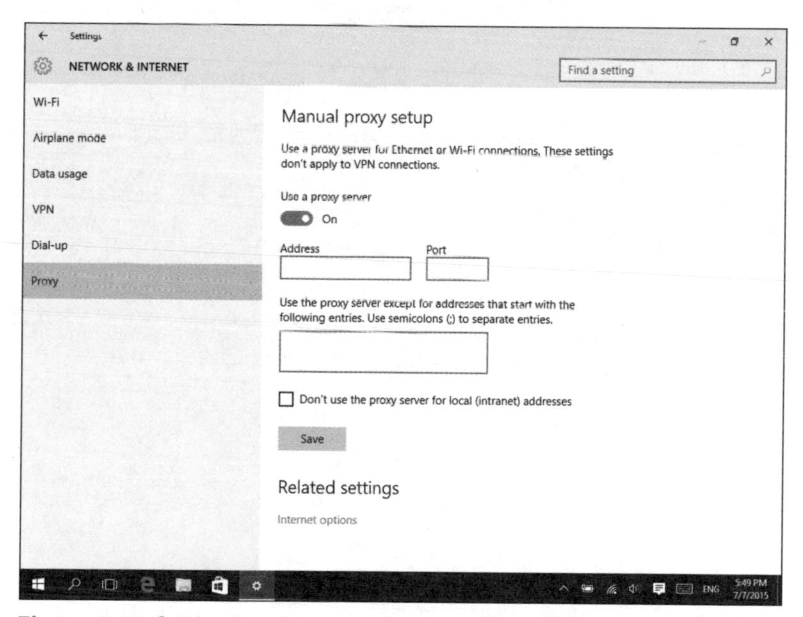

Figure 4-11: Setting up a proxy server manually.

5. **In the Address field, type the IP address.**
6. **In the Port field, type the port.**
7. **Click Save; then close the Settings window.**

To disable the proxy, follow the same steps; at Step 4, set the Use a Proxy Server switch to Off.

CHAPTERFIVE

Using Internet Explorer

In This Chapter

- Browse the web with Internet Explorer
- Download files and manage your downloads
- Work with multiple tabs
- Add web pages as favorites and access them later
- Pin a website to the Apps list in the Start Menu
- Change the homepage
- Set Internet Explorer to start with tabs from the last session
- Add a website to Compatibility View
- Browse the web using InPrivate Browsing
- Delete your browsing history

Windows 10 is the first Microsoft operating system with two web browsers: Internet Explorer and Microsoft Edge. When Windows 10 was released, Microsoft Edge wasn't fully finalized, and its feature set still needs to be expanded. If you also consider that many businesses don't have modern web apps and intranet websites that work with Microsoft Edge, it's obvious that Microsoft couldn't ditch Internet Explorer in Windows 10. At least not in the version for enterprise customers. I don't expect many businesses to provide support for Microsoft Edge for quite some time, so I cover Internet Explorer 11 in this book. It's the browser that you're most likely to use at work to access your company's websites and web services.

In this chapter, I start by showing you the basics on using Internet Explorer: how to visit websites, how to download files, and how to manage downloads and work with multiple tabs simultaneously. Then I move on to more advanced tasks such as adding web pages to your favorites and accessing them, adding websites to the list of apps in the Start Menu, and changing the Internet Explorer homepage.

Finally, I provide some productivity tips such as how to set Internet Explorer to start with tabs from the previous session, how to add sites with rendering issues to the

Compatibility View list, how to browse the web privately, and how to delete your browsing history in Internet Explorer.

Browse the Web in Internet Explorer

The following example shows the basics on using Internet Explorer. To start Internet Explorer, type a website address, navigate that website, and then use the Back and Forward buttons to move to the previous page and the next page, respectively.

1. **Click in the search bar on the taskbar.**
2. **Type the word** internet.

   A list of search results appears.
3. **Click the Internet Explorer search result.**
4. **Click in the address bar located at the upper-left of the Internet Explorer window.**
5. **Type** dummies.com**; then press Enter (see Figure 5-1).**

   The For Dummies website appears.

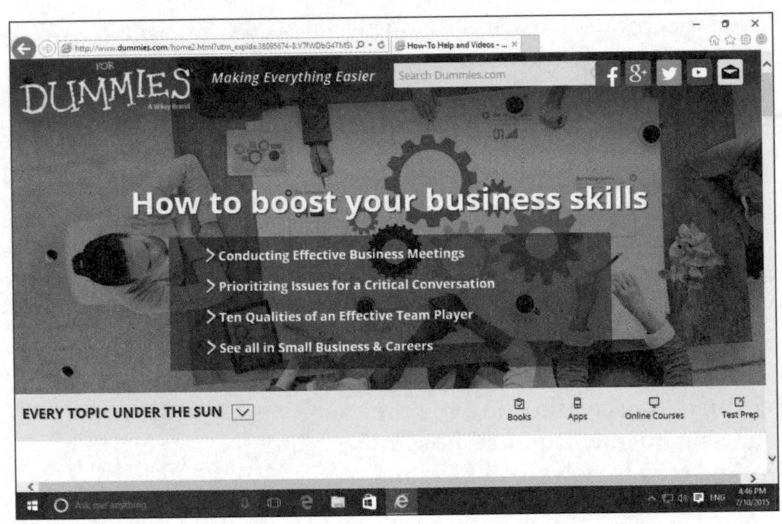

Figure 5-1: How to enter a website's address in the Address bar.

6. **Click the Books link on the For Dummies website.**
7. **After the For Dummies Store page loads, click the Back (left-pointing arrow) button, located at the top-left corner of the Internet Explorer window (see Figure 5-2).**

   You're now back at the For Dummies homepage.

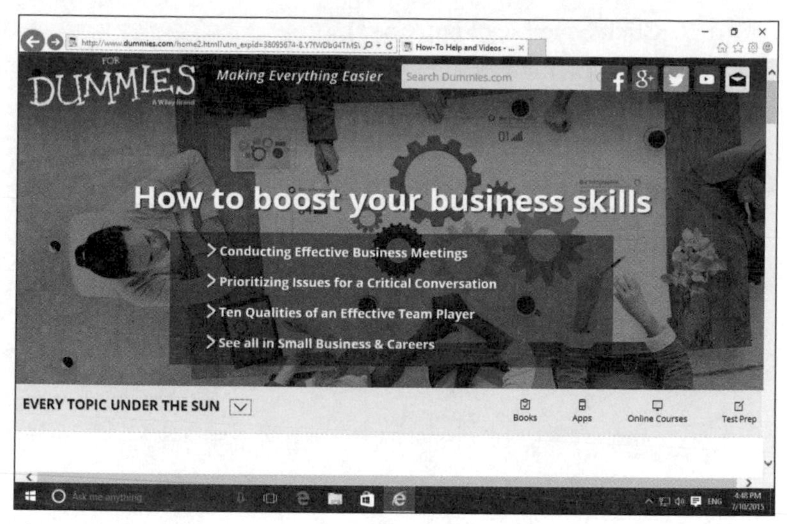

Figure 5-2: Using the Back and Forward buttons.

8. **Click the Forward button (right-pointing arrow), located at the top-left corner of the Internet Explorer window.**

   You're now back at the For Dummies Store page.

9. **Close Internet Explorer.**

Download Files in Internet Explorer

Downloading files in Internet Explorer involves just a few clicks. If you download an executable file, Internet Explorer asks whether you want to run it or save it. When you download other types of files, such as PDF documents or file archives, Internet Explorer asks whether you want to open or save them.

It's better to save a downloaded file and then run or open it. Directly opening or running a file without selecting Save means it's saved to a temporary location on your computer, and when you close a temporary file, it's difficult to find.

Here's an example of downloading a file in Internet Explorer from the Skype website:

1. **Start Internet Explorer.**
2. **In the Address bar, type** skype.com; **then press Enter.**
3. **Once the Skype website loads, click Download Skype.**
4. **Click Get Skype for Windows Desktop.**

   Internet Explorer shows a prompt asking whether you want to run or save the SkypeSetup.exe file.

5. **Click Save (see Figure 5-3).**

   After the file is downloaded and saved on your computer, you receive a message to that effect.

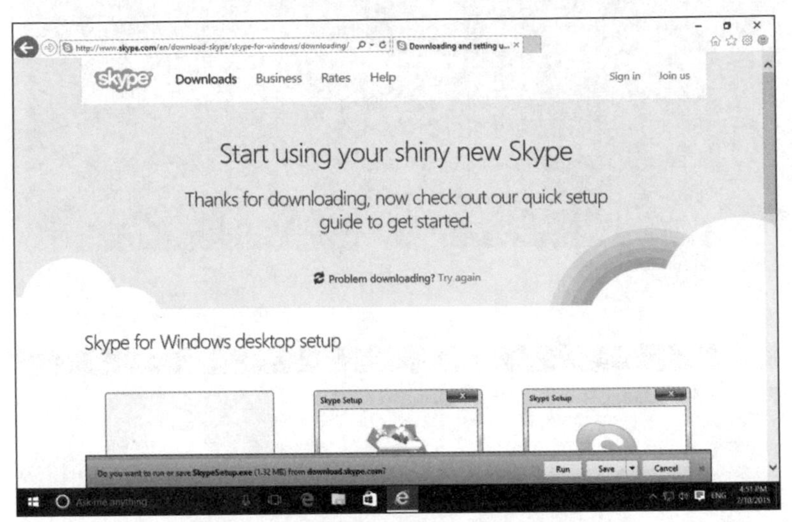

Figure 5-3: How to download Skype in Internet Explorer.

6. **In the window informing you that the download has completed, click Open Folder.**

   A File Explorer window appears showing you where the downloaded file is stored.

7. **Close File Explorer.**
8. **Close Internet Explorer.**

Downloads are saved, by default, in the Downloads folder of your user account.

View and Manage Your Downloads in Internet Explorer

In Internet Explorer, you can download multiple files at the same time, and you can manage them from the View Downloads window. Here, you see a list of the files that were downloaded recently, as well as ongoing downloads. You can pause active downloads or cancel them (see Figure 5-4).

You can also remove a downloaded file from the list by selecting it and then clicking the small x at the top-right corner of its entry, as shown in Figure 5-5.

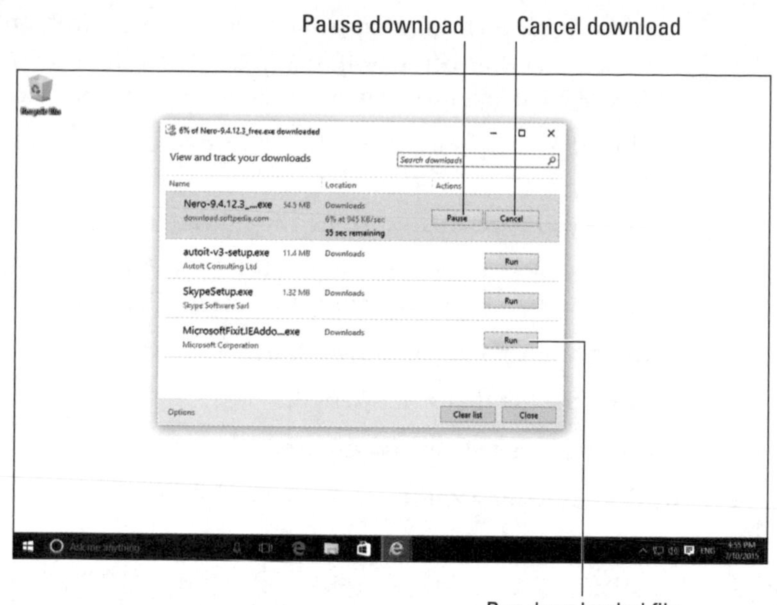

Figure 5-4: Tracking downloads in Internet Explorer.

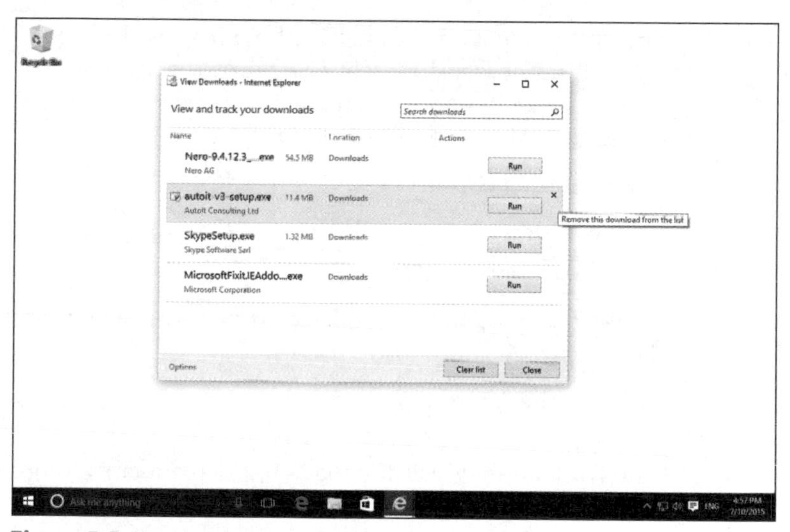

Figure 5-5: How to remove a download from the list.

When you browse the web with Internet Explorer, here's how to access the View Downloads window and use it to manage downloads:

1. **Click the Tools button in Internet Explorer.**

   The Tools button is shaped like a gear wheel.

2. **In the Tools menu that appears, select View Downloads.**

   The View Downloads window shows the files that have been downloaded and files that currently are downloaded (if any).

3. **Click the Pause button for the download that you want to pause.**
4. **When you're ready to resume the download, click Resume.**
5. **To remove a file from the list, select it by clicking it, then click the small x at the top-right corner of its entry.**
6. **To open files that you downloaded, click Open.**
7. **Close the file that you opened.**
8. **Close the View Downloads window.**
9. **Close Internet Explorer.**

The keyboard shortcut Ctrl+J opens the View Downloads window.

Work with Multiple Tabs in Internet Explorer

Tabbed browsing is an Internet Explorer feature that allows you to open multiple websites in a single browser window. You can open web pages in new tabs and switch between the pages by clicking their tabs. Here's how to do so:

1. **Start Internet Explorer.**
2. **In the Address bar, type** skype.com; **then press Enter.**

   The Skype website appears.

3. **Click the New Tab button, located near the Skype tab (see Figure 5-6).**
4. **Click in the Address bar, type** dummies.com, **and press Enter.**

   The For Dummies website loads in a second tab, alongside the Skype website.

5. **Click the Skype tab to return to it.**
6. **Click the small x at the right of the Skype tab to close it (see Figure 5-7).**

   Now only the *For Dummies* website tab remains.

7. **Close Internet Explorer.**

The keyboard shortcut Ctrl+T opens a new tab in Internet Explorer.

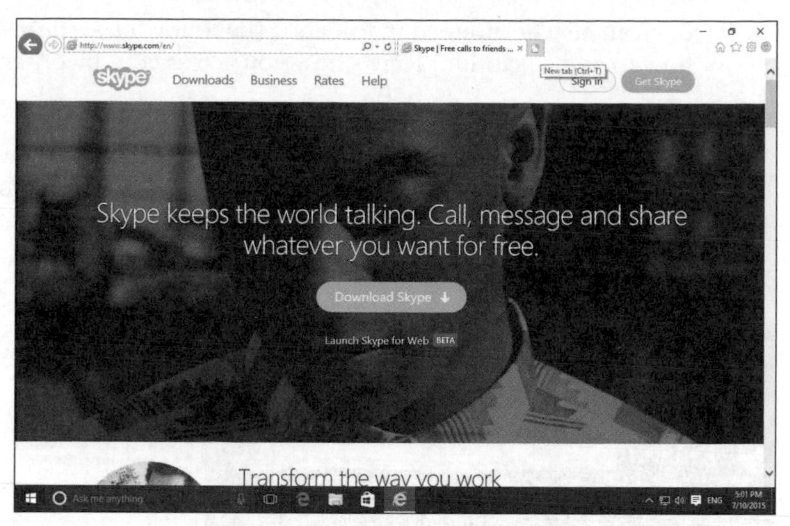

Figure 5-6: How to open a new tab in Internet Explorer.

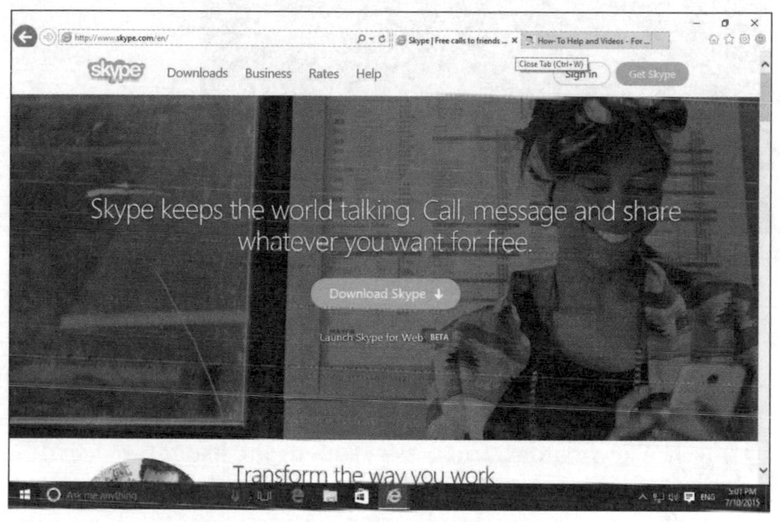

Figure 5-7: How to close a tab in Internet Explorer.

Access Your Favorite Web Pages in Internet Explorer

You can mark a web page as a favorite and then access it very quickly, with just a few clicks, without having to type its address or remember it, which is very useful, especially when you encounter a web page with content that you want to get back to later. Favorites are organized as lists of shortcuts to web pages that can also be grouped in folders. (The following section shows how to add a favorite.) Here's how you access your favorites:

1. **Start Internet Explorer.**
2. **In the top-right corner of the Internet Explorer window, click the button that looks like a star (it's referred to as the View Favorites, Feeds, and History button).**

   A list with your favorites appears.

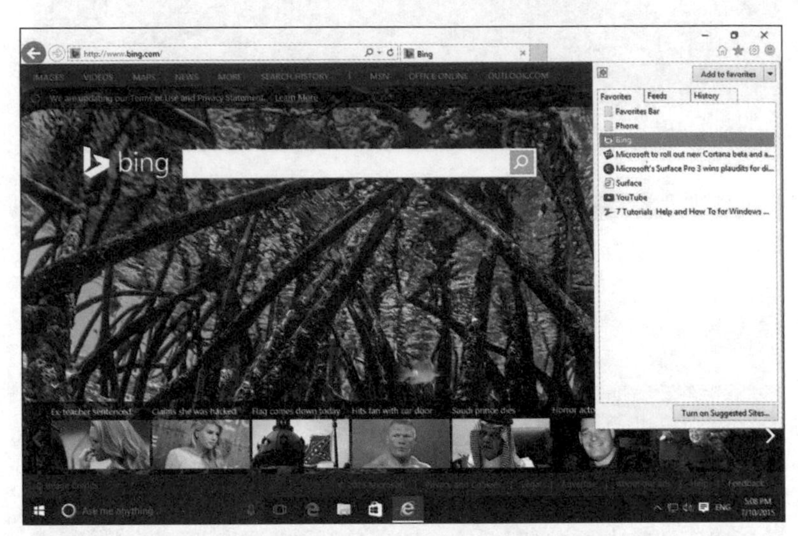

Figure 5-8: Accessing your favorites in Internet Explorer.

3. **Click one of your favorites (see Figure 5-8).**
4. **Close Internet Explorer after the selected favorite webpage loads.**

The keyboard shortcut Alt+C opens the list of favorites.

Add a Web Page to Your Favorites

In order to add a web page to the list of Internet Explorer favorites, follow these steps:

1. **Start Internet Explorer.**
2. **In the Address bar, type the address of the web page that you want to add as a favorite; then press Enter.**
3. **After the web page loads, click the button that looks like a star, at the top-right of the Internet Explorer window (it's referred to as the View Favorites, Feeds, and History button).**
4. **Click Add to Favorites.**

5. **Click inside the Create In drop-down list and choose the folder where you want to save your favorite; then click Add (see Figure 5-9).**

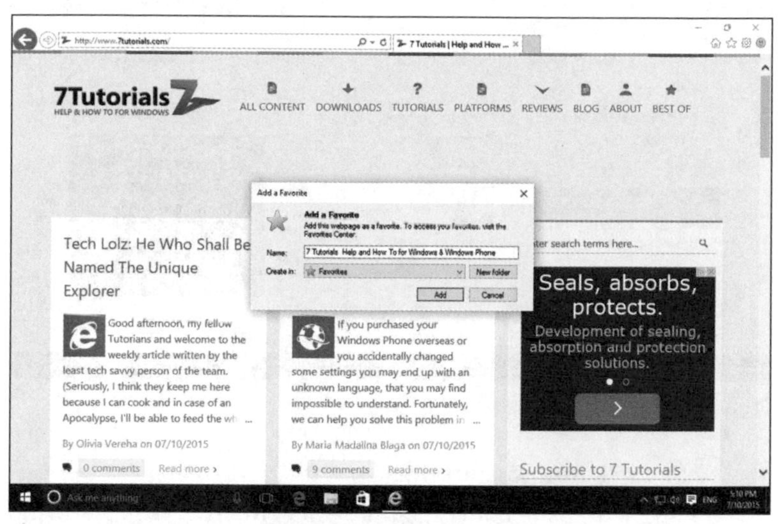

Figure 5-9: How to add a web page as a favorite.

6. **Access the list of favorites again to see the newly added entry in the folder that you selected.**
7. **Close Internet Explorer.**

Pin a Website to the List of Apps in the Start Menu

In Windows 10, you can pin a website to the list of Apps that's shown when you access the Start Menu. Once you pin a website, its shortcut appears in the All Apps list, as though it were an app. If you use a website often (such as a corporate intranet page or a vendor's website), having it in the list of apps will save time.

To pin a website to the list of apps shown in the Start Menu, follow these steps:

1. **Start Internet Explorer.**
2. **In the Address bar, type the address of the web page that you want to pin; then press Enter.**

   The web page is loaded in Internet Explorer.
3. **Click the Tools button (shaped like a gear wheel).**

   The Tools menu appears.
4. **In the Tools menu, click Add Site to Apps (see Figure 5-10).**

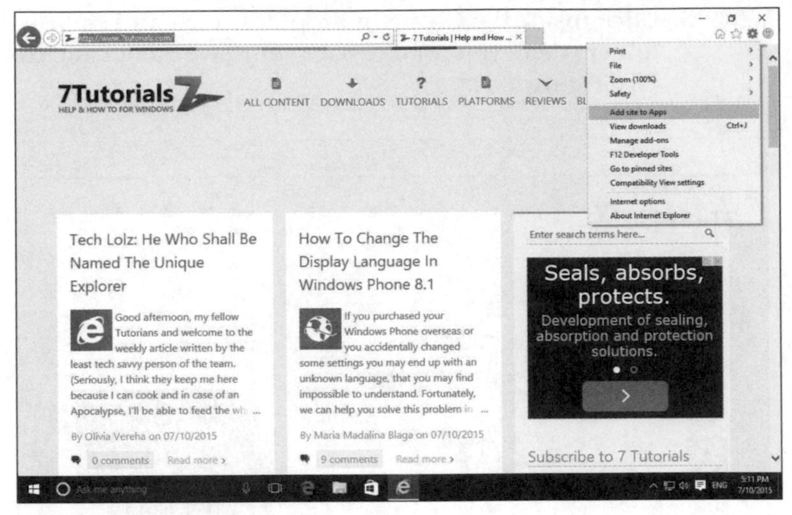

Figure 5-10: How to add a site to Apps.

5. **Click Add to confirm.**

   The website loads again in a new Internet Explorer window which has the website's logo as an icon, in the top-left corner of the window.

6. **Close Internet Explorer.**

If you open the Start Menu and go to All Apps, you see the newly pined website in the list of available apps.

Change the Homepage in Internet Explorer

The homepage in Internet Explorer is the page that loads automatically each time you start this browser. You can easily change the homepage and make it anything you want. It can be any web page on the Internet, or a web page from your company's internal network. It can be the default page provided by Internet Explorer when you install Windows 10, the current page that's loaded in the active tab, or a new, empty tab.

To change the Internet Explorer homepage, follow these steps:

1. **Start Internet Explorer.**
2. **In the Address bar, type the address of the web page that you want to set as the homepage and press Enter.**

   The web page is loaded in Internet Explorer.
3. **Click the Tools button (shaped like a gear wheel).**

   The Tools menu appears.

4. **Click Internet Options.**

   The Internet Options window appears.

5. **In the General tab, find the Home Page section.**
6. **Click the Use Current button (see Figure 5-11).**

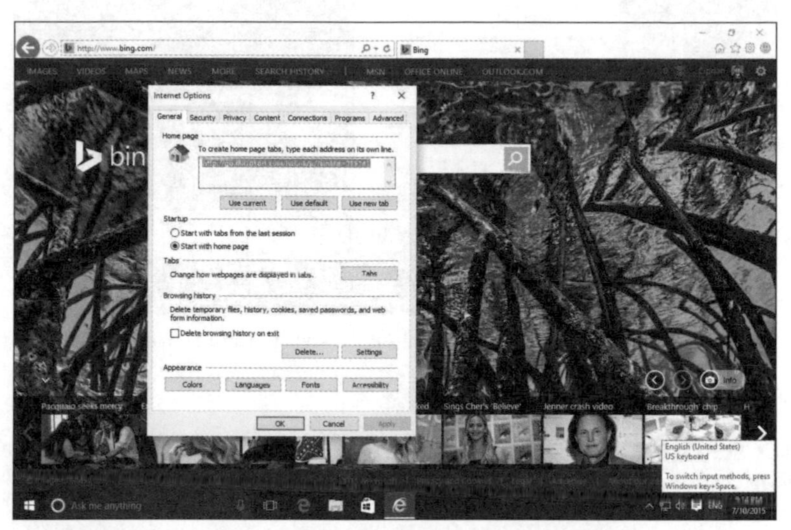

Figure 5-11: How to change the homepage in Internet Explorer.

7. **Click OK (see Figure 5-11).**
8. **Close Internet Explorer.**

Set Internet Explorer to Start with the Tabs from the Last Session

You can set Internet Explorer so that it automatically loads the tabs that were open the last time you closed it. This is handy if you regularly work on several websites or web pages. Here's how to do so:

1. **Start Internet Explorer.**
2. **Click the Tools button (shaped like a gear wheel).**

   The Tools menu appears.

3. **Click Internet Options.**

   The Internet Options window appears.

4. **In the General tab, find the Startup section.**
5. **Select Start with Tabs from the Last Session; then click OK (see Figure 5-12).**
6. **Close Internet Explorer.**

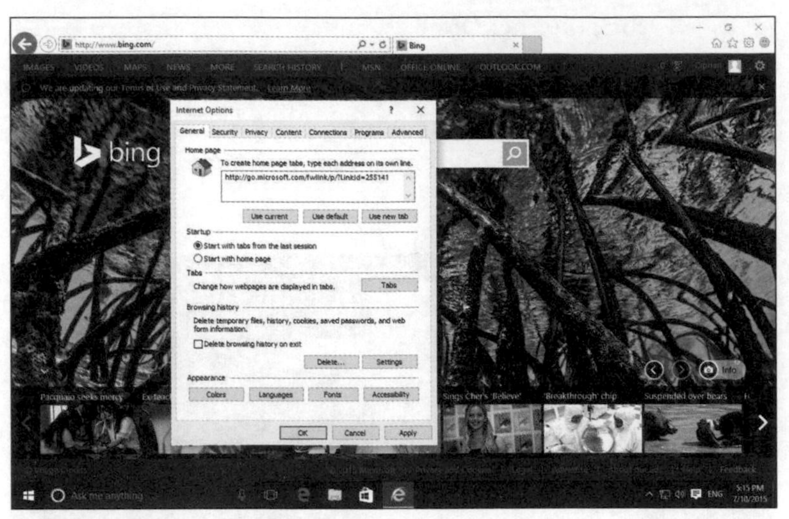

Figure 5-12: How to set Internet Explorer to start with tabs from the last session.

When you set Internet Explorer to start with tabs from the last session, it ignores the homepage that you set.

Add a Website to Compatibility View

Sometimes websites don't look like you expect them to. Images might not appear correctly, menus might be out of place, and text may be jumbled together. Such problems can be caused by incompatibility between Internet Explorer and the website you're on. This situation may be especially the case with intranet websites that companies created many years ago. However, incompatibility can also happen with public websites on the Internet.

If a website doesn't look right in Internet Explorer, you may be able to fix the problem by adding the site to the Compatibility View list. Once you turn on Compatibility View, Internet Explorer automatically shows that site in Compatibility View each time you visit the site. You can turn off the Compatibility View for that site by removing it from your compatibility list.

Here's how to add websites to the Compatibility View list:

1. **Start Internet Explorer.**
2. **In the Address bar, type the address of the website you're having trouble with and press Enter.**

   The website is loaded in Internet Explorer.
3. **Click the Tools button (shaped like a gear wheel).**

   The Tools menu appears.

4. **Click Compatibility View Settings.**

   The Compatibility View Settings window appears (see Figure 5-13).

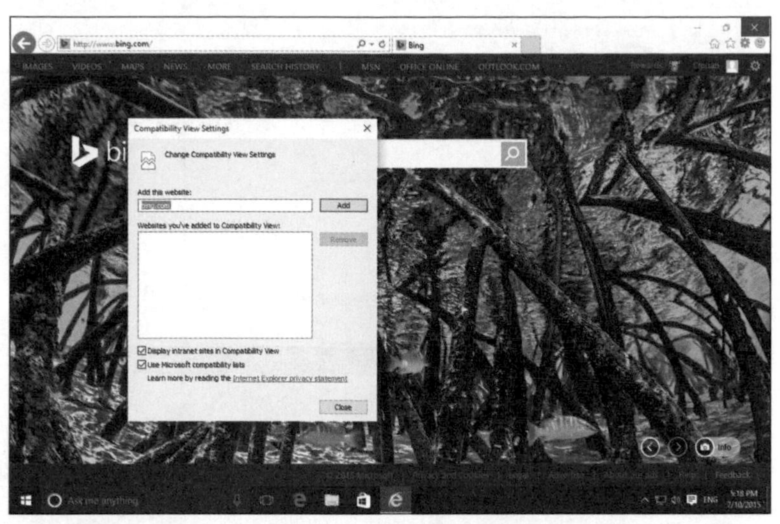

Figure 5-13: How to add a website to the Compatibility View list.

5. **Click Add and then click Close.**

   The site loads again, using Internet Explorer's Compatibility View.

If you add a site to the Compatibility View list and the page looks worse, the problem may not be compatibility. In this case, remove the site from the list.

Browse the Web Using InPrivate Browsing

InPrivate Browsing in Internet Explorer enables you to surf the web without leaving a trail in your browser. This helps prevent others using your computer from seeing what sites you visited and what you looked at on the web.

When you start InPrivate Browsing, Internet Explorer opens a new browser window. The protection that is provided is in effect only during the time that you use that window. You can open as many tabs as you want in that window, and they're all protected. However, if you open another browser window, that window isn't protected by InPrivate Browsing. You can see an InPrivate Browsing window in Figure 5-14.

While you're surfing the web using InPrivate Browsing, Internet Explorer stores some information like cookies and temporary Internet files so that the web pages you visit work correctly.

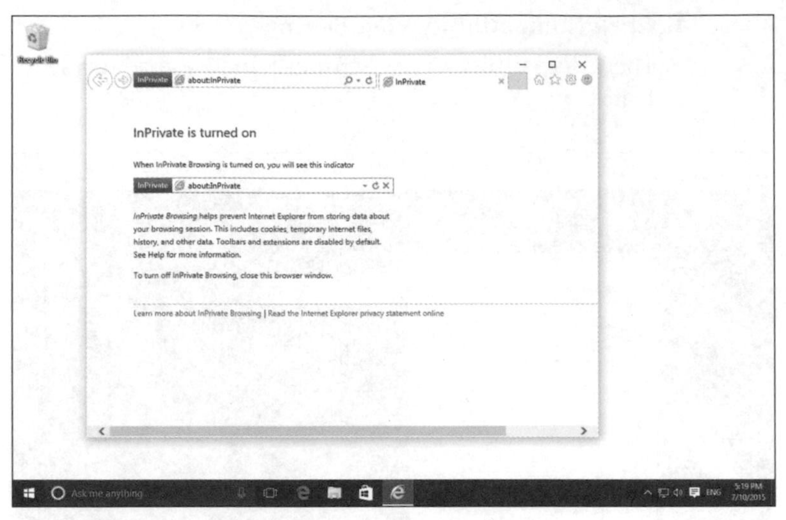

Figure 5-14: InPrivate Browsing in Internet Explorer.

However, at the end of your InPrivate Browsing session, this information is discarded.

Here's how to start InPrivate Browsing in Internet Explorer:

1. **Start Internet Explorer.**

   The window that opens isn't protected by InPrivate Browsing.

2. **Click the Tools button (shaped like a gear wheel).**

   The Tools menu appears.

3. **Click Safety (see Figure 5-15).**

   The Safety menu appears.

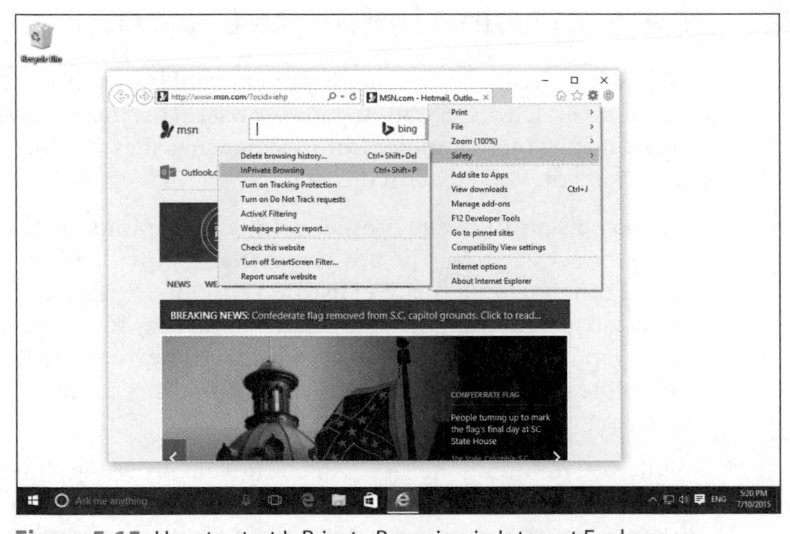

Figure 5-15: How to start InPrivate Browsing in Internet Explorer.

4. **Click InPrivate Browsing (see Figure 5-15).**

   An InPrivate Browsing window opens.

5. **Navigate the web as usual in this window.**
6. **Close the InPrivate window when you finish.**
7. **Close Internet Explorer.**

The keyboard shortcut Ctrl+Shift+P starts an InPrivate Browsing session.

Delete Your Browsing History in Internet Explorer

As you use Internet Explorer, the browser stores temporary files, your browsing history, cookies from the websites that you're visiting, saved passwords, and web form information. All web browsers do this so that they can load web pages faster and quickly provide you with the data you need. However, over time the browser may start to slow down. One way to speed it up is to delete all the stored browsing history.

Deleting your browsing history is useful when you don't want others to see which websites you visited.

To clear all the browsing history stored by Internet Explorer, follow these steps:

1. **Start Internet Explorer.**
2. **Click the Tools button (shaped like a gear wheel).**

   The Tools menu appears.

3. **Click Internet Options.**

   The Internet Options window appears.

4. **In the General tab, find the Browsing History section (at the bottom of the Internet Options window).**
5. **Click the Delete button.**

   The Delete Browsing History window opens.

6. **Select all the types of data that you want removed and click Delete (see Figure 5-16).**

   After Internet Explorer deletes the selected browsing history, a message confirms it.

7. **Click OK in the Internet Options window.**
8. **Close Internet Explorer.**

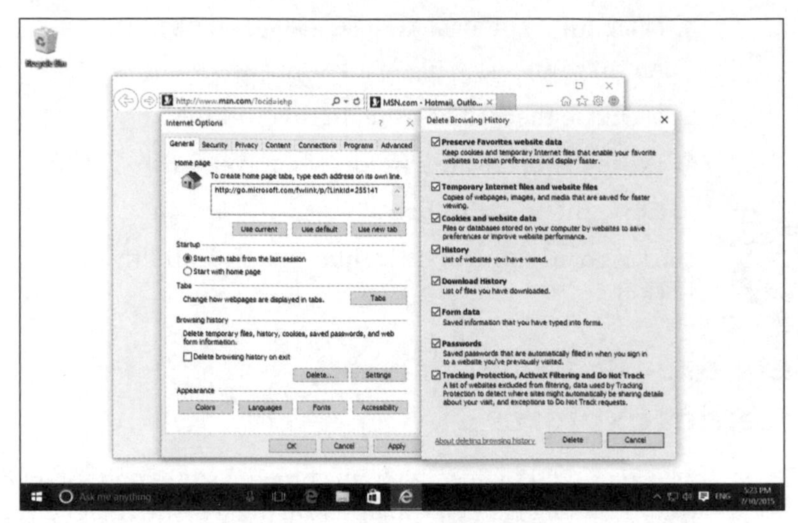

Figure 5-16: How to delete your browsing history in Internet Explorer.

CHAPTER SIX

Managing Files and Folders

When you work on a Windows computer or device, you spend a lot of time browsing and managing files and folders. You may want to look at your pictures, create documents, watch movies, and organize your files. You may also want to burn your files onto a DVD or Blu-Ray disc.

File Explorer is Windows' most important tool for doing all the above, and, once you're familiar with it, you find that you can do a lot with File Explorer, which is what this chapter tells you about.

In This Chapter

- Using File Explorer to browse files and folders
- Using the Ribbon in File Explorer
- Managing files and folders with File Explorer
- Selecting multiple files and folders
- Working with file archives
- Burning files to a disc
- Working with ISO images

Key Terms

Before getting down to the business of working with Windows 10's File Explorer, I'd like to go over a few basic terms. Once you understand them, the rest of the chapter will be much clearer:

- **Files:** A file is any unique, stand-alone piece of data. It can be a document, a presentation, a picture, or a video.

  To help keep track of your files, you save them in folders.
- **Folders:** Folders on your computer are the digital equivalent of the file folders used to hold papers, and just like those file folders, the folders on your computer hold data that's grouped together in a logical way.

Windows has several folders ready for you to use: Desktop, Documents, Downloads, Music, Pictures, and Videos.

- **Subfolders:** These are folders within other folders.

  A folder can contain any number of subfolders and files. You create subfolders to organize your data, which you then place in folders.

- **Libraries:** These are virtual collections of folders on your computer.

  Libraries aren't actual folders, although they may appear to be. Instead, libraries hold references or shortcuts to files or folders that are stored elsewhere. Windows 10 has several default libraries for you to use: Documents, Music, Pictures, Saved Pictures, Cameral Roll, and Videos. You can also create your own libraries.

Open File Explorer

You can start File Explorer many ways in Windows 10, but here's a list of the most common ones:

- On the taskbar, click the icon that looks like a folder.
- Click the Start button to access the Start Menu. When it appears, click the File Explorer shortcut (see Figure 6-1).
- Press Windows+E on your keyboard.

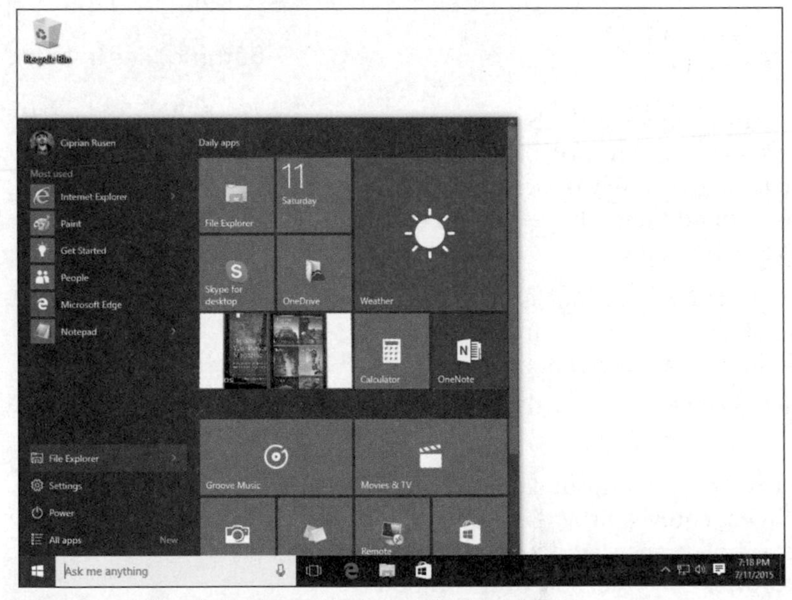

Figure 6-1: The File Explorer shortcut in the Start Menu.

- Right-click the Start button; then click the File Explorer shortcut.
- Click in the search bar on the taskbar, type **file explorer**, and press Enter on your keyboard or click the File Explorer search result.

Navigate File Explorer

When you start File Explorer, the Quick Access view is shown, which contains a list of the folders you browse most frequently and the files that you recently opened. This list changes as you use different folders, and you can customize it by pinning folders and libraries that you'd like to access as quickly as possible. Figure 6-2 shows the Quick Access section in File Explorer. (Chapter 7 shows how to pin items to Quick Access.)

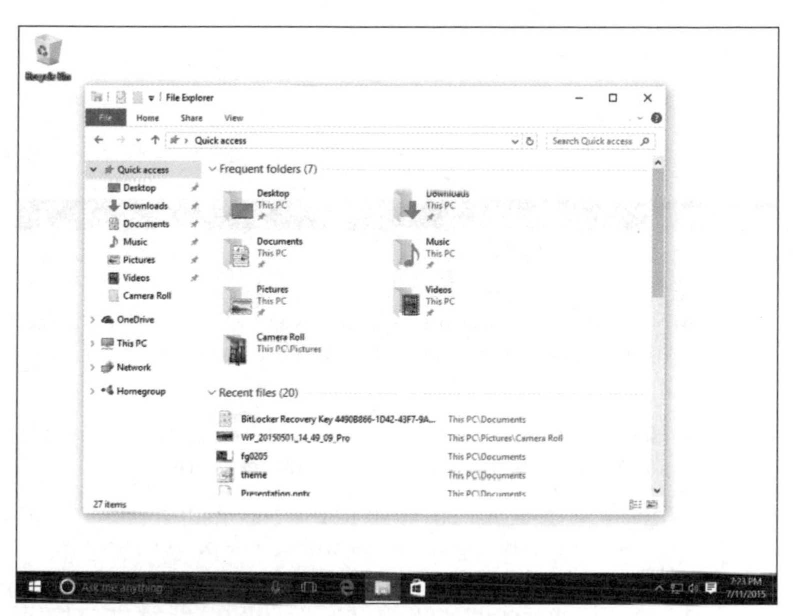

Figure 6-2: The Quick Access section in File Explorer.

On the left side of the File Explorer window, you find the Navigation pane, which is a column with several shortcuts. When you open File Explorer, you see these shortcuts in the Navigation pane:

- **Quick Access:** Shortcuts to the folders you frequently access and the files you opened recently.
- **OneDrive:** Files and folders that are stored on your OneDrive.
- **This PC:**
  - Your user folders (Desktop, Documents, Downloads, Music, Pictures, and Videos)

- Devices and drives that are available on your computer (see Figure 6-3)
- Network locations

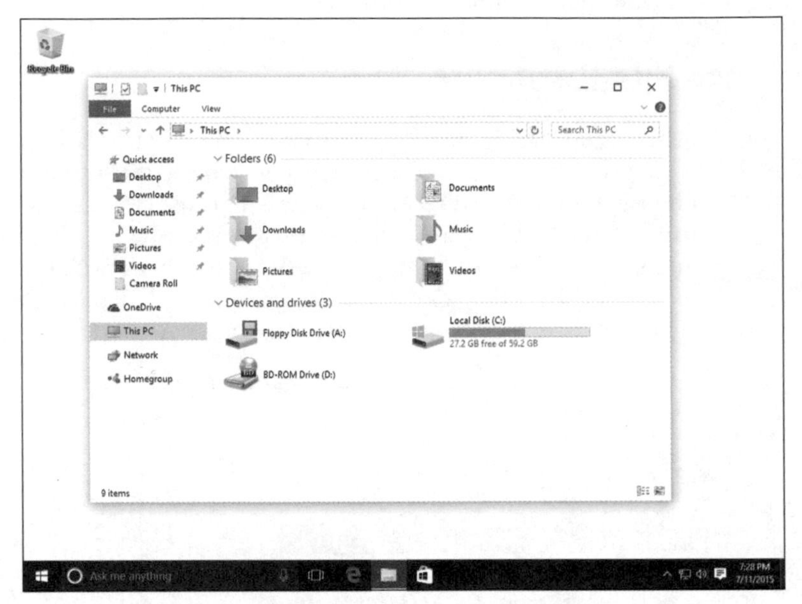

Figure 6-3: This PC in File Explorer.

- **Network:** Other computers and devices that are connected to the network. If they have shared files and folders, you can access those as well.
- **HomeGroup:** Members of your HomeGroup. If they have shared files and folders, you can access those, too.

When you click any shortcut in the Navigation pane, its contents are shown on the right side of the File Explorer window. To open a file or folder shown on the right, double-click it. As soon as you start navigating your Windows computer or device, the Back, Forward, Recent Locations, and Up buttons are activated, as well as the Address bar (see Figure 6-4).

Here's how to use these buttons and the Address bar to browse your computer:

1. **Open File Explorer.**
2. **Click OneDrive.**

   The OneDrive folder and its contents are shown.
3. **Click the Back button.**

   You're taken right back to the Quick Access screen.
4. **Click the Forward button to go to your OneDrive folder again.**

Figure 6-4: Back, Forward, Recent Locations, Up, and Address bar.

5. **Click the Recent Locations button.**
6. **In the menu that appears, click Quick Access.**

   You return to the Quick Access screen.
7. **Click This PC.**
8. **Double-click Documents.**

   As you open a new folder, its shortcut is added in the Address bar. If you click on any of the elements in the Address bar, you're taken to them.
9. **In the Address bar, click This PC.**

   File Explorer quickly jumps from the current folder to This PC.
10. **Click the Back button to go back to the previous folder.**
11. **Close File Explorer.**

Navigate the File Explorer Ribbon

File Explorer uses a graphical user interface feature called the *Ribbon* that runs across the top of the File Explorer window. The Ribbon comprises several tabs, such as File, Home, Share, and View. Depending on what you're browsing on your computer, additional tabs, such as Manage, may be displayed. Figure 6-5 shows the Ribbon in File Explorer.

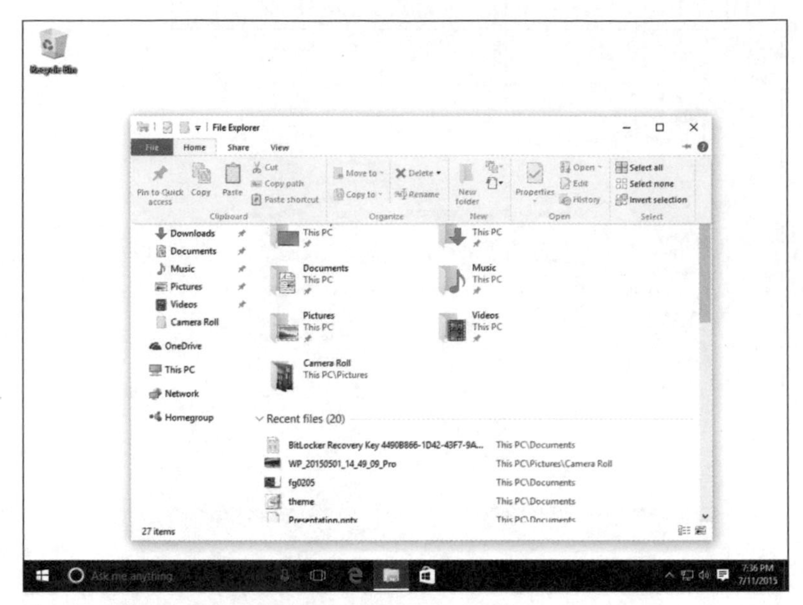

Figure 6-5: The Ribbon in File Explorer.

By default, the Ribbon is minimized, and you can see only the names of each tab. When you click a tab like Home, you see several buttons and options that are organized in logical sections.

Here's how to navigate the Ribbon in File Explorer:

1. **Open File Explorer.**
2. **Click This PC.**
3. **Click Documents.**

   The Documents folder and its contents are shown.
4. **Click the Home tab.**

   This tab includes tools for common operations such as Copy, Cut, and Paste, creating new folders and files, moving data, and deleting files and folders.
5. **Click the Share tab.**

   This tab includes tools for sharing files and folders with others through the network, the HomeGroup, email, or by burning your data to a disc.
6. **Click the View tab.**

   This is where you can change how files are displayed in File Explorer, and you can also enable or disable different user interface elements.

7. **In the Navigation pane, click This PC.**

   The ribbon is minimized again.

8. **Double-click the C drive, which is usually named Local Disk (C).**

   The Manage tab appears on the Ribbon.

9. **Click the Manage tab (see Figure 6-6).**

   Here you find contextual options for managing the C drive.

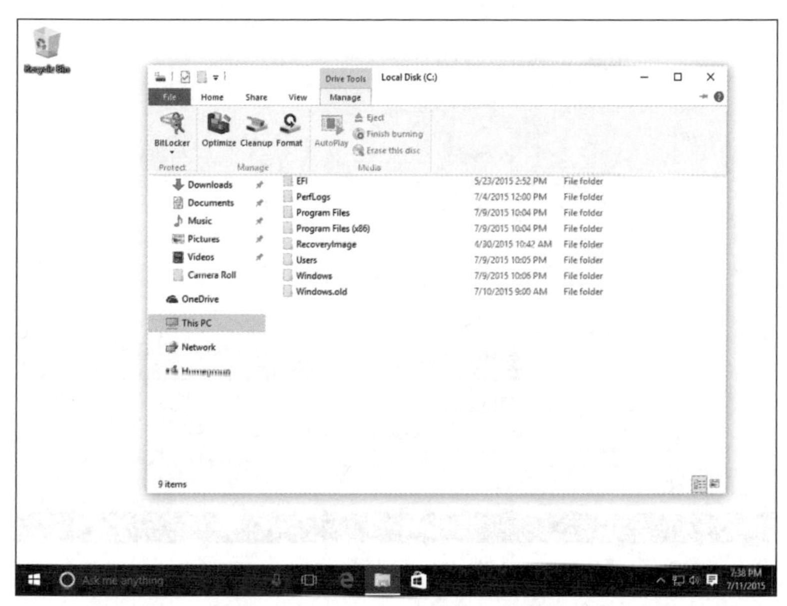

Figure 6-6: The Manage tab on the File Explorer Ribbon.

10. **Click File on the Ribbon.**

    A menu appears with options for opening a new File Explorer window, starting the Command Prompt and PowerShell, changing folder and search options, getting help, and accessing your most frequent places.

11. **In the File menu, click Close to exit File Explorer.**

Maximize or Minimize the Ribbon in File Explorer

By default, the Ribbon is minimized in File Explorer. If you find it useful and you often need to use it, you may want to maximize it all the time. Here's how to maximize and minimize the Ribbon in File Explorer:

1. **Open File Explorer.**
2. **Double-click the Home tab on the Ribbon.**

   The File Explorer window changes to make room for the maximized Ribbon (see Figure 6-7).

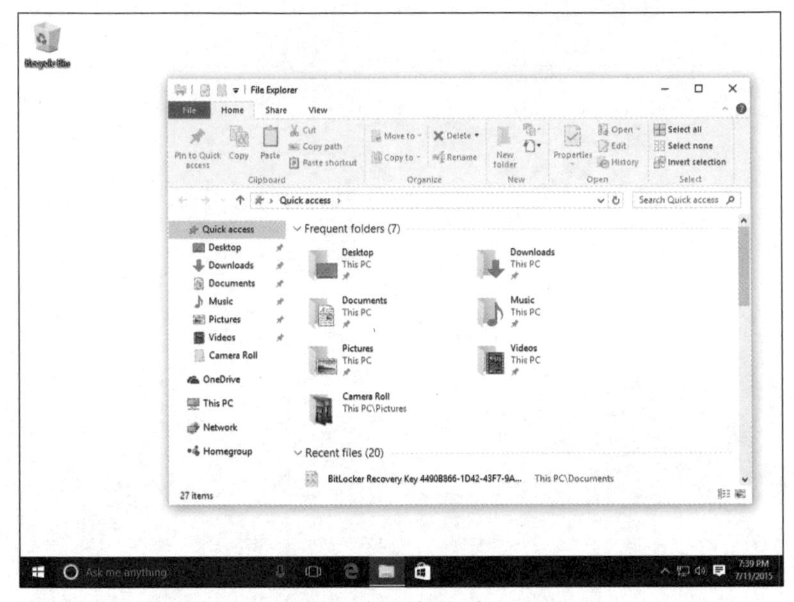

Figure 6-7: The Ribbon maximized in File Explorer.

3. **Close File Explorer.**
4. **To minimize the Ribbon, open File Explorer again.**

   From now on, the Ribbon is maximized each time you open File Explorer.
5. **Click the Share tab to open it.**

   The Share tab is shown on the Ribbon.
6. **Double-click the Share tab.**

   The Ribbon is minimized.
7. **Close File Explorer.**
8. **Open File Explorer again.**

   Now the Ribbon is minimized when you open File Explorer.

File Explorer remembers whether the Ribbon was minimized or maximized the last time you closed it and will open it that way the next time you open File Explorer.

Identify Common File Formats in File Explorer

You can open and view hundreds of file types on your Windows computer or device. The most common types of files are documents, music, pictures, videos, and executable files. You may also work with specialized files from third-party apps, such as PDF files, but usually the types of files you encounter are the common ones.

What File Explorer shows you depends on what you're doing on your computer. You see either several columns with information or a preview of each file. For example, when you open the Downloads folder, you see these columns: Name, Date Modified, Type, and Size (see Figure 6-8).

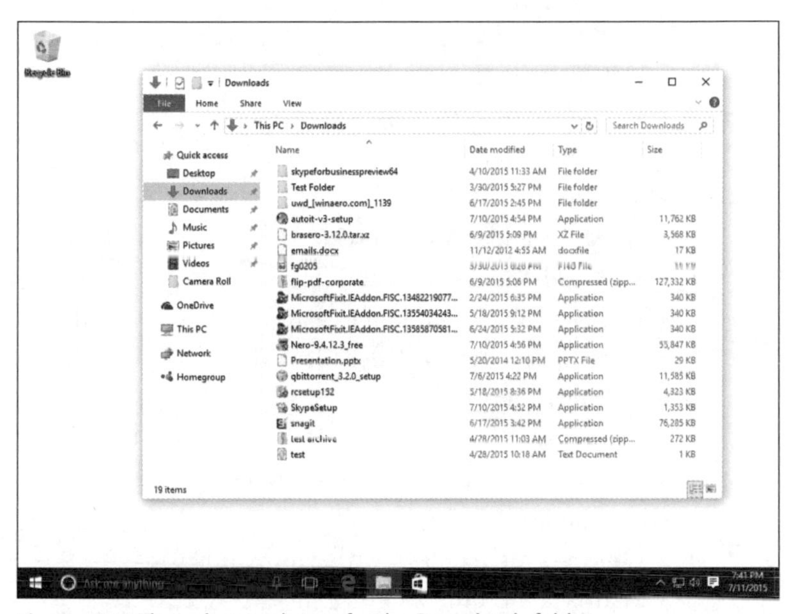

Figure 6-8: The columns shown for the Downloads folder.

For folders, the type is always File Folder. But if you're looking at previews of files, you really can't tell what kind of file you're looking at, so it's best to use the Details view, where you can get more useful information. (Turn to Chapter 7 to find out how to change the view in File Explorer.)

Here's how to identify the type of each file shown in File Explorer:

1. **Open File Explorer.**
2. **Click Downloads.**

   The Downloads folder and its contents are shown.
3. **Look at the first five to eight files and check their type in the Type column.**

Here are the most common types of files that you may encounter on your Windows 10 computer:

- **Microsoft Office files:**
  - Microsoft Word (.doc and .docx)
  - Microsoft PowerPoint (.ppt and .pptx)
  - Microsoft Excel (.xls and .xlsx)
  - Microsoft Publisher (.pub and .pubx)
  - Microsoft OneNote (.one)
- **Picture files:**
  - JPEG files (.jpg and .jpeg)
  - GIF files (.gif)
  - Bitmap files (.bmp)
  - PNG files (.png)
  - TIFF files (.tif and .tiff)
  - RAW files (.raw)
- **Music files:**
  - Windows audio files (.wav)
  - MP3 audio files (.mp3 and .m3u)
  - Windows Media audio files (.asx, .wm, .wma, and .wmx)
  - Free Lossless Audio Codec files (.flac)
  - AAC files (.aac)
- **Video files:**
  - Audio Video Interleaved files (.avi)
  - Motion JPEG files (.avi and .mov)
  - Windows Media files (.wm, .wmv, and .asf)
  - Matroska multimedia files (.mkv)
  - Apple QuickTime files (.mov and .qt)
  - MPEG Movie files (.mp4, .mov, .m4v, .mpeg, .mpg, .mpe, .m1v, .mp2, .mpv2, .mod, .vob, and .m1v)
- **Other types of popular files:**
  - *Application files* (.exe): Executable files that can run with a double-click
  - *Text documents* (.txt): Simple text documents without any kind of formatting
  - *Compressed* (.zip): Archives of other files and folders
  - *Portable Document Format files* (.pdf): A very popular type of file generally used for sharing non-editable documents that need to look the same on all devices, no matter what operating system you use

- *OpenOffice and LibreOffice documents* (.odt, .ott, .oth, and .odm): Documents created using free open-source productivity applications, such as OpenOffice and LibreOffice

By default, file extensions aren't shown in the lists you see while using File Explorer. Depending on the folder that you're viewing and its content, File Explorer may show a column named Type, where you can see the type of each file. (See Chapter 7 for more on changing how File Explorer displays data.)

Open a File in File Explorer

To open a file in File Explorer, browse the locations on your PC, find the file, and double-click it. An app, set by default for a file's type, automatically opens the file. To use another app to open a file type, start File Explorer and follow these steps:

1. **Browse to the location of the file that you want to open and select it.**
2. **Click the Home tab on the Ribbon.**

   The Home tab is displayed.
3. **In the Open section, click the down-pointing arrow beside the Open button.**

   The Open menu is displayed.
4. **In the Open menu, click the app that you want to use to open the file (see Figure 6-9).**

   Now the app you selected opens your file.

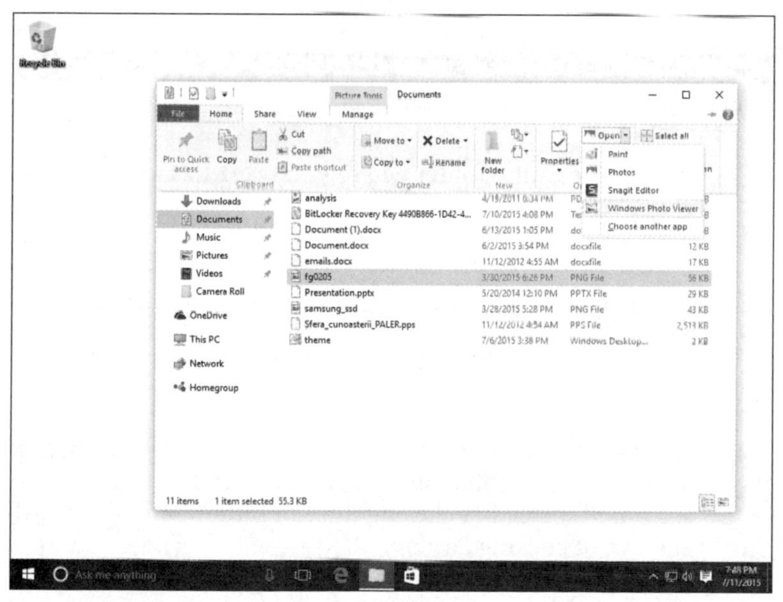

Figure 6-9: The Open menu in File Explorer.

Move a File or Folder in File Explorer

You can move one or more files or folders to another location several ways. One way is to use the Cut and Paste commands. To do so, open File Explorer and follow these steps:

1. **Browse to the file's or folder's location and select it by clicking on it.**
2. **Click the Home tab on the Ribbon.**

   The Home tab is displayed.
3. **In the Clipboard section, click the Cut button (see Figure 6-10).**

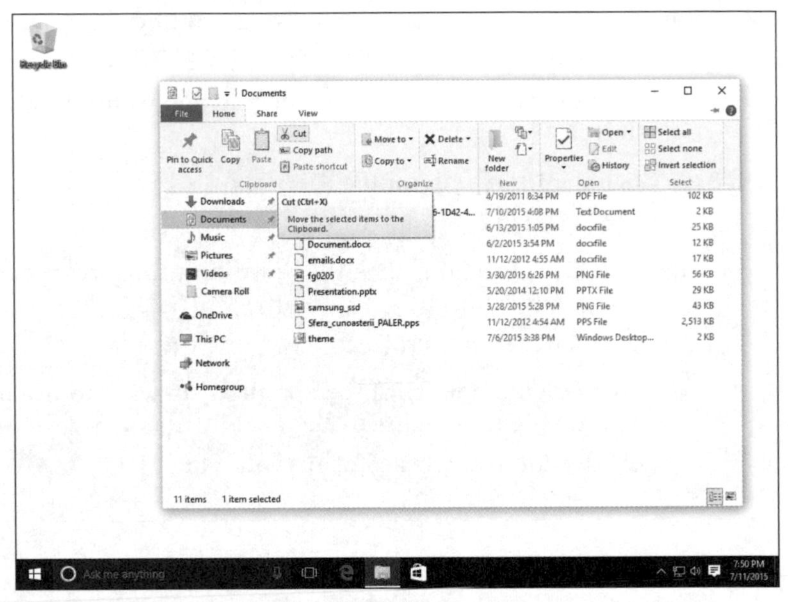

Figure 6-10: The Cut button in File Explorer.

4. **Browse to the folder where you want to move that file.**
5. **Click the Home tab on the Ribbon.**

   The Home tab is displayed.
6. **Click the Paste button in the Clipboard section.**

   The selected file is now in the new folder.
7. **Close File Explorer.**

Instead of using the mouse, you can also use the keyboard. Follow the preceding procedure and press Ctrl+X on your keyboard instead of clicking the Cut button, and press Ctrl+V instead of clicking Paste.

Another way to move a file or folder also starts on the Home tab of the Ribbon. Click the Move To menu in the Organize section, then click on the name of the folder where you want to move the selected item.

Rename a File or Folder in File Explorer

You can easily rename files and folders (unless they're system files that the operating system installs in folders, such as Windows and Program Files).

Don't fiddle with the files in folders such as Windows and Program Files because you could create problems that you might not be able to fix.

When it comes to your own files (such as documents, pictures, videos, and music), there's no stopping you from renaming files as you prefer. To rename a file or folder, open File Explorer and follow these steps:

1. **Browse to the file or folder that you want to rename.**
2. **Click the file or folder to select it.**
3. **Click the Home tab on the Ribbon.**

   The Home tab is displayed.
4. **In the Organize section, click the Rename button (see Figure 6-11).**

   You can now edit the name of the selected item.

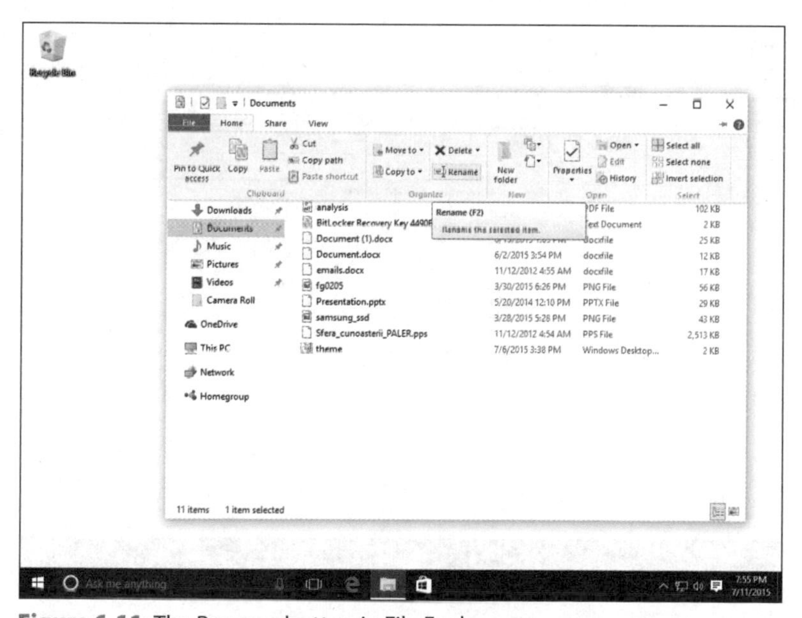

Figure 6-11: The Rename button in File Explorer.

5. **Type the new name.**
6. **Press Enter or click somewhere else in the File Explorer window.**

   The selected file or folder now has the name that you typed.

7. **Close File Explorer.**

The keyboard shortcut for the Rename command is F2.

Create a Folder in File Explorer

You can create as many folders as you want, either directly on a drive on your computer or within other folders. Using multiple folders enables you to better organize your files, so create as many as you need. To create a folder, open File Explorer and follow these steps:

1. **Go to the location where you want to create the folder.**

   It can be a drive on your computer or another folder.

2. **Click the Home tab on the Ribbon.**

   The Home tab is displayed.

3. **In the New section, click the New Folder button (see Figure 6-12).**

   A new folder is created with the name New Folder.

4. **Type the name that you want for the newly created folder.**

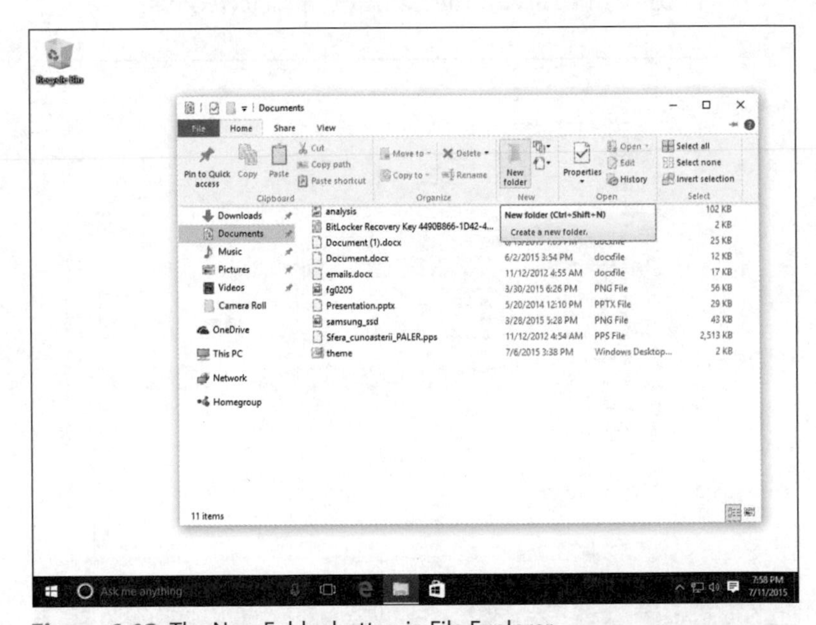

Figure 6-12: The New Folder button in File Explorer.

5. **Press Enter or click somewhere else in the File Explorer window.**

   The newly created folder now has the name that you typed.

6. **Close File Explorer.**

The keyboard shortcut for the New Folder command is Ctrl+Shift+N.

Create a File in File Explorer

You can create files in File Explorer. Actually, you can create them almost anywhere, except in system folders such as Windows and Program Files. When creating a new file, you first choose its type and then give it a name. To do so, open File Explorer and follow these steps:

1. **Go to the location where you want to create the file.**
2. **Click the Home tab on the Ribbon.**

   The Home tab is displayed.
3. **In the New section, click the New Item button (see Figure 6-13).**

   A menu appears with several types of files.

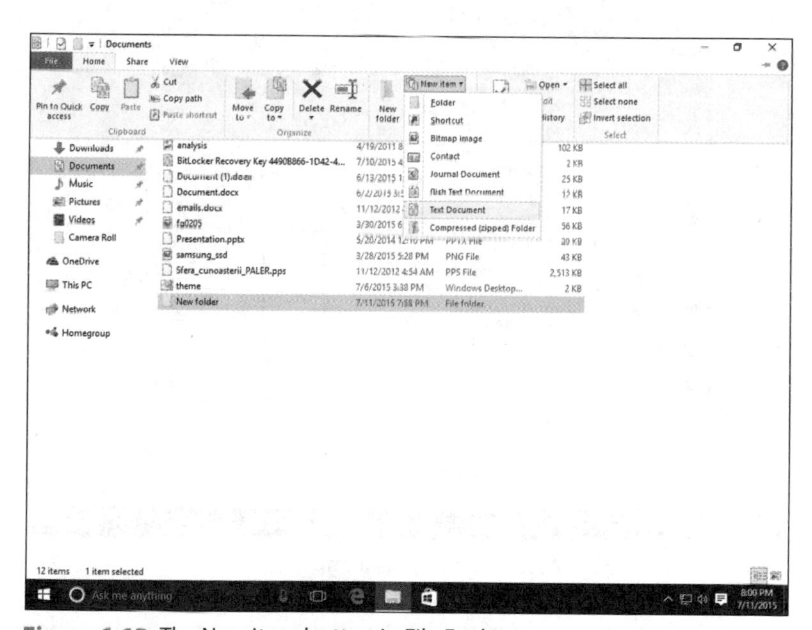

Figure 6-13: The New Item button in File Explorer.

4. **Click the type that you want, and the file is created.**
5. **Type the name that you want for that file.**

6. **Press Enter or click somewhere else in the File Explorer window.**
7. **Close File Explorer.**

The file that you created is an empty one. To add content to it, you must open it in an application that can edit that type of file and add the content that you want.

Save Your Files

Many apps work with all kinds of files and allow you to create files on your computer that you can use later. For example, you can use the Microsoft Word app to create documents and share them with your coworkers, or you can use Paint to create simple drawings and share them with your child. To save a file, you locate the Save button and click it. Some apps also offer a Save As button or menu so that you can choose between multiple file formats before saving a file. Figure 6-14 shows the Save As menu in Paint (the drawing app that's bundled with Windows 10). Paint enables you to select from among several image formats to save a drawing.

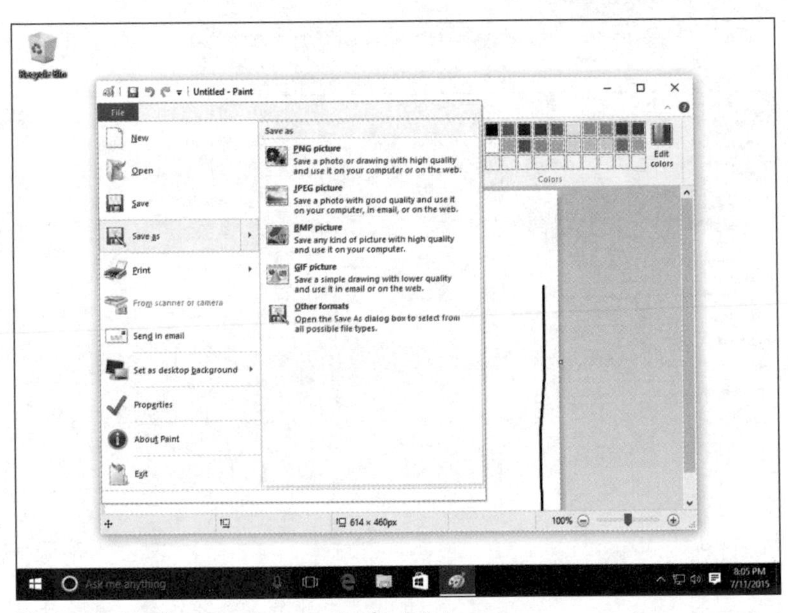

Figure 6-14: The Save As menu in the Paint app.

When you save a file, you're asked to select the folder where you want to save it, provide a name for the file, and select the type. To keep things organized, take advantage of the user folders and libraries that are available in Windows: Desktop, Downloads, Documents, Pictures, Music, and Videos.

Save your documents in the Documents folder, your pictures in the Pictures folder, your downloads in the Downloads folder, and so on. This way, you can easily find them when you need them.

Another advantage to using these user folders to store your files is that Windows 10 automatically indexes them, so you can easily search for and find everything that's stored in them. Searching for files stored in other locations takes much longer.

Here's an example of how to save files in Windows 10 desktop apps:

1. **Click inside the search bar on the taskbar and type** wordpad.

   A list of search results appears.

2. **Click the WordPad search result to create a new document.**

   The Document – WordPad window appears.

3. **Type** Hello!

4. **Click File.**

   The File menu appears.

5. **In the File menu, click Save.**

   The Save As window appears.

6. **Select the Documents folder in the column on the left (see Figure 6-15).**

7. **Type a name for the file; for example,** My Document.

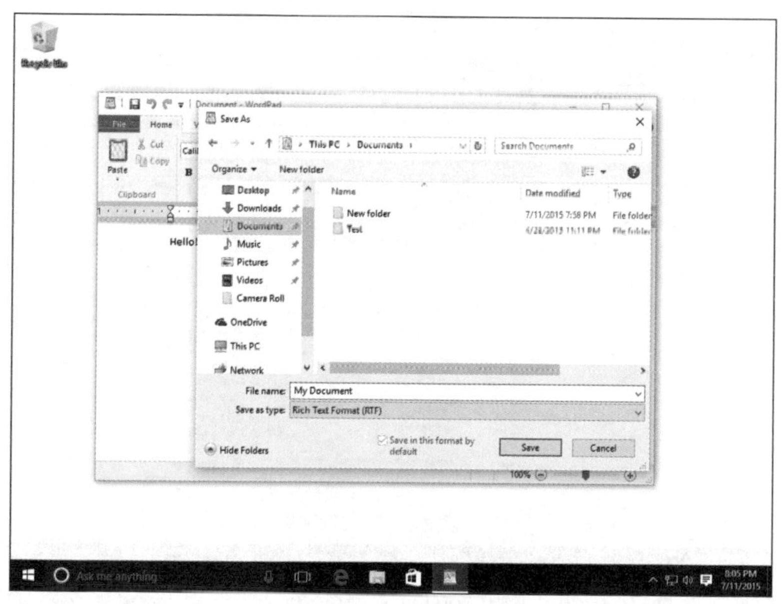

Figure 6-15: The Save As window.

8. **Click the Save As Type drop-down list.**
9. **Select the file type that you want to use.**
10. **Click Save.**
11. **Close WordPad.**

If you go to the Documents folder in File Explorer, you now see the file you just created.

Create a Shortcut to a File or Folder in File Explorer

You may want to create a shortcut to a file or folder and place it on the Desktop for quick access or in some other location that you go to frequently. To create a shortcut, open File Explorer and follow these steps:

1. **Locate the file for which you want to create a shortcut.**
2. **Right-click that file and, in the menu that appears, select one of these options (see Figure 6-16):**
   - *Click Create Shortcut.*

     This creates a shortcut in the folder where the file is found. You can then move the shortcut to another folder.
   - *Click Send To; then click Desktop (Create Shortcut).*

     This creates a shortcut to the file on the Desktop.

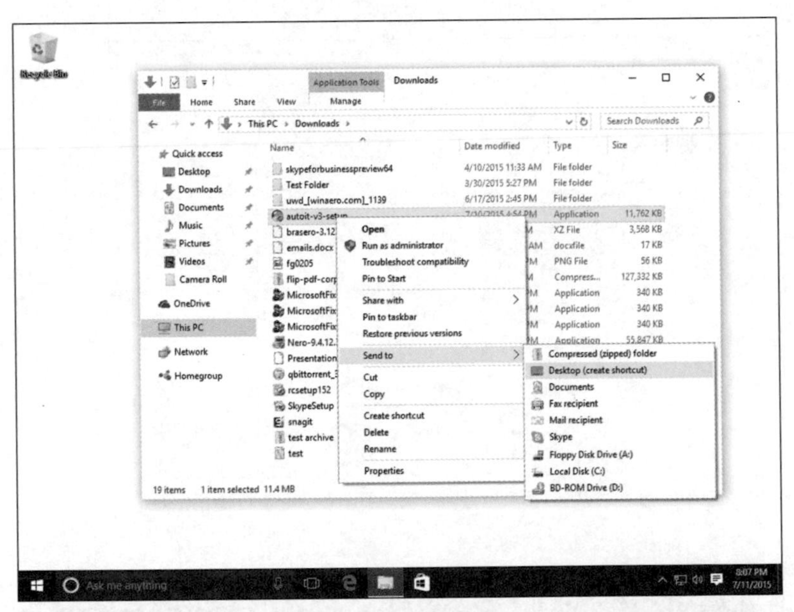

Figure 6-16: The right-click menu in File Explorer.

Shortcuts are references to the files and folders that they point to. When you delete a shortcut, the item it points to remains on your computer. On the other hand, if you delete or move the file or folder it points to, the shortcut doesn't work.

Select Multiple Files or Folders in File Explorer

When you're working with files and folders in File Explorer, sometimes you may want to select more than one item. For example, you may want to select a group of files and delete them or select multiple folders and move them to another folder.

Here's the quickest way to select items in File Explorer (also see Figure 6-17):

1. **Click the first file or folder that you want to select.**
2. **Press and hold the Ctrl key on your keyboard.**
3. **With the Ctrl key still pressed, click each file and folder that you want to select.**
4. **Release the Ctrl key after you select the items.**

   Each of the selected items is highlighted with a blue bar in File Explorer. Now you can apply commands like Cut, Copy, or Delete to all selected items.

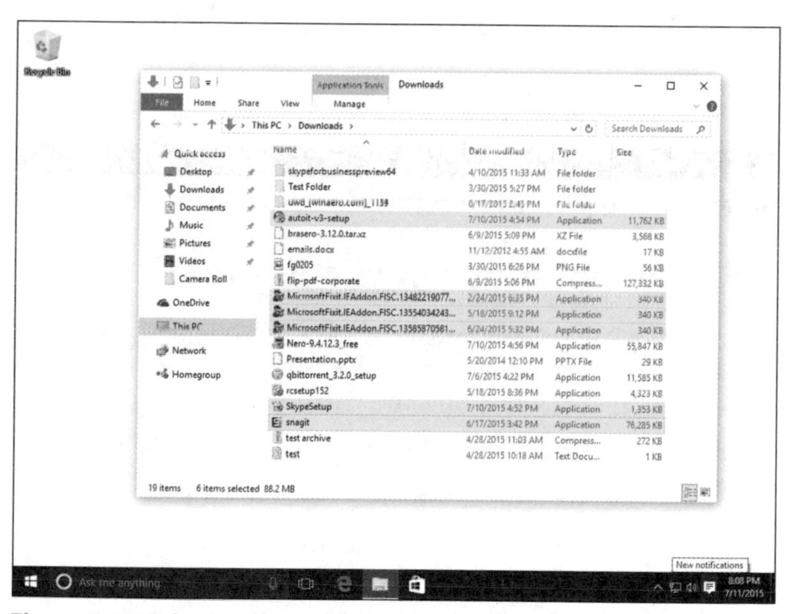

Figure 6-17: Selecting files and folders in File Explorer.

Another way to select files or folders in File Explorer is to use the Ribbon. Click the Home tab for access to the Selection section, as shown in Figure 6-18. Several options in the Selection section of the Home tab let you select and deselect groups of files:

- **Invert Selection:** Selects the currently unselected files and folders, and deselects the currently selected files and folders.

  Every time you click Invert Selection, the selected and deselected files and folders switch.

- **Select All**: Selects every file and folder.
- **Select None**: Deselects every file and folder.

TIP

The keyboard shortcut for the Select All command is Ctrl+A.

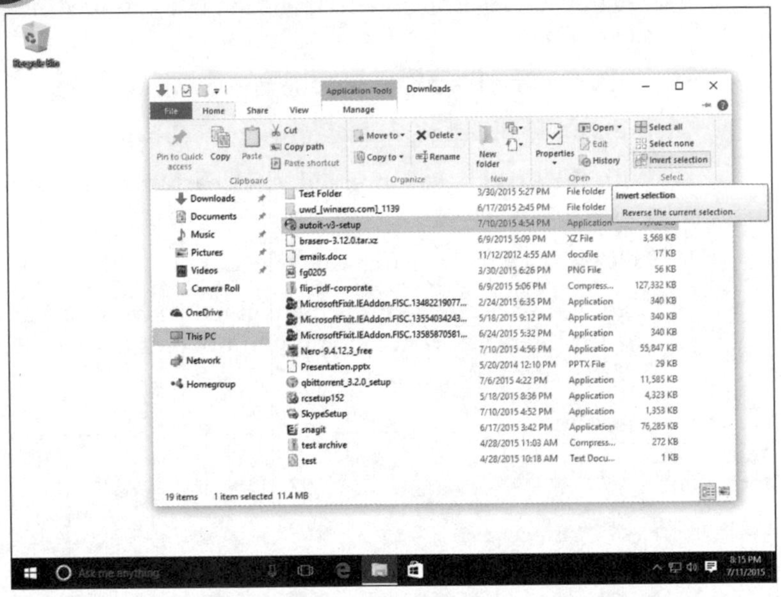

Figure 6-18: The options for selecting files using the Ribbon in File Explorer.

Delete a File or Folder in File Explorer

When you no longer need to use a file or folder, you can remove it from your computer to free up storage space. To do so, open File Explorer and follow these steps:

1. **Locate the file or folder that you want to delete.**
2. **Select that file or folder by clicking on it.**
3. **Click the Home tab on the Ribbon.**

   The Home tab is displayed.

4. **In the Organize section, click the Delete button (see Figure 6-19).**

   The selected item is moved to the Recycle Bin.

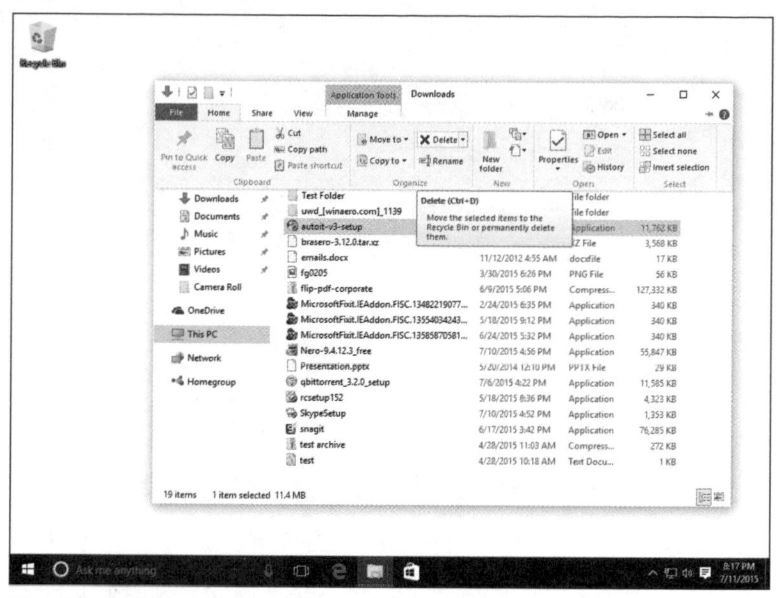

Figure 6-19: The Delete button in File Explorer.

You can use two keyboard shortcuts for the Delete command: Delete and Ctrl+D. Also, you can use Shift+Delete on your keyboard and delete files and folders without moving them to the Recycle Bin. When you do that, you can't restore them, because they are no longer stored in the Recycle Bin.

Restore Deleted Files and Folders

The files and folders that you delete without using the Shift+Delete keyboard shortcut are moved to the Recycle Bin. This is a folder that temporarily stores references to the items that you delete from your Windows 10 computer or device. The items in the Recycle Bin aren't fully deleted, even though they no longer show up in their original location. The data from the files and folders that you delete remain on your computer's hard drive until the Recycle Bin is emptied and other files write data on top of them in the same location on your hard disk.

Here's how to recover deleted files and folders from the Recycle Bin:

1. **Go to the Desktop.**
2. **Double-click the Recycle Bin shortcut.**

   You now see a list of deleted files and folders that you can recover.
3. **Select the item that you want to restore by clicking on it.**
4. **Click the Manage tab on the Ribbon (see Figure 6-20).**

   The Manage tab is displayed.

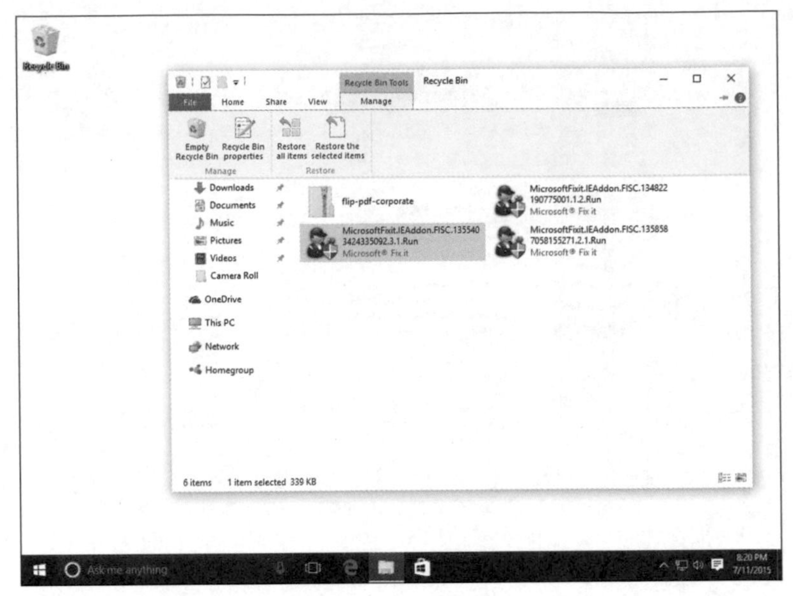

Figure 6-20: Restoring items in the Recycle Bin.

5. **In the Restore section, click the Restore The Selected Items button.**
6. **Close the Recycle Bin window.**
7. **Go to the original location of the selected item.**

   The item now appears there.

Items that are deleted using Shift+Delete aren't displayed in the Recycle Bin and can't be recovered using the preceding method. You have to use specialized third-party data recovery desktop apps (such as Recuva) to restore the items.

View the Properties of a File or Folder

When you use the default configuration of File Explorer, a lot of information about the properties of each file and folder is hidden from view. For example, the file extension is hidden by default, and you can't view when the file or folder was created or last accessed. If you want a complete overview of the properties of any file or folder, open File Explorer and follow these steps:

1. **Select the file or folder whose properties you want to see.**
2. **Click the Home tab on the Ribbon.**

   The Home tab is displayed.

3. **In the Open section, click the Properties button (see Figure 6-21).**

   The Properties window for the selected item appears. The available tabs (such as General Details) show information about that item.

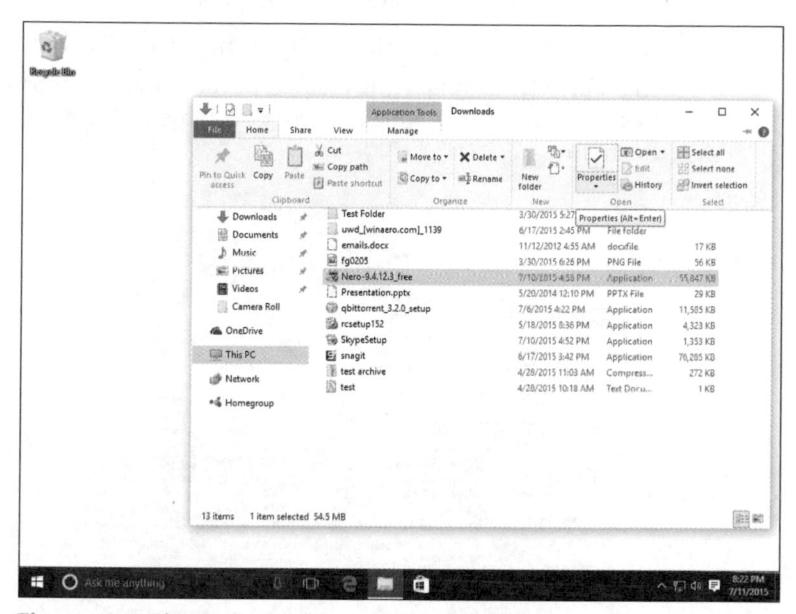

Figure 6-21: The Properties button in File Explorer.

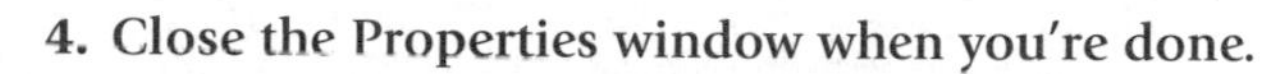

4. **Close the Properties window when you're done.**

You can use the Alt+Enter keyboard shortcut instead of the Properties button to open the Properties window for an item. You can also right-click a file or folder and click Properties.

Archive Files and Folders in a ZIP File

An archive is a file containing one or more files along with their data. You use archives to collect multiple files into a single file for easier portability and storage, or simply to compress files to use less storage space. Archives are also useful when you want to send multiple files to someone by email. Instead of attaching several large files, archive them into one file. That file takes less space than sending all the files separately, and it's easier to attach and send by email.

The most popular format for archiving files is .zip and Windows 10 can automatically work with this type of archive without having to install third-party apps. To archive several files and folders into a .zip file, open File Explorer and follow these steps:

1. **Select the files and folders that you want to archive.**
2. **Click the Share tab on the Ribbon.**

   The Share tab is displayed.
3. **In the Send section, click the Zip button (see Figure 6-22).**

   An archive is automatically created in the same folder as the files and folders that you selected. You can edit the name of the archive.

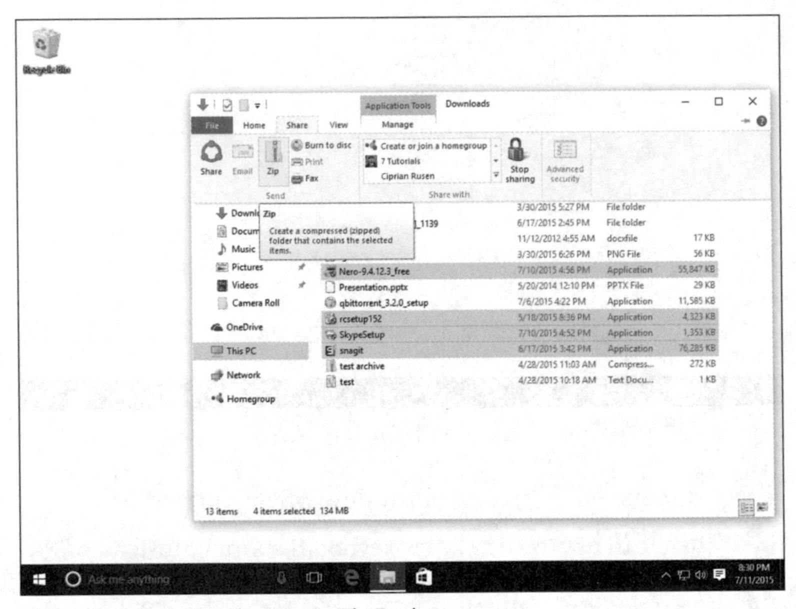

Figure 6-22: The Zip button in File Explorer.

4. **Type the name that you want for the archive file.**
5. **Press Enter or click somewhere else in the File Explorer window.**

   You can now use the newly created .zip archive and send it by email or store it where you want on your computer.

If you want to save space on your hard disk, it's a good idea to delete the files and folders that you placed in an archive, as you can always extract them from the archive, using the steps described in the next section of this chapter.

View and Extract the Contents of a ZIP File

When you receive an archive in the .zip format, you can view its contents and extract it in File Explorer. Here's how:

1. **Open File Explorer.**
2. **Go to the location of the archive file.**
3. **Double-click the file to view its contents.**
4. **Click the Extract tab on the Ribbon.**

   The Extract tab is displayed.
5. **Click the Extract All button (see Figure 6-23).**

   A wizard appears asking you to select where to extract the files.

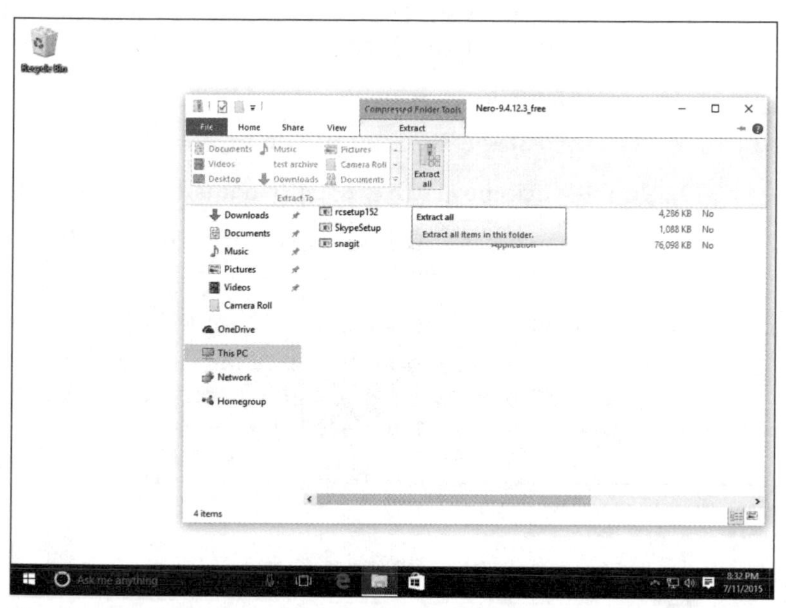

Figure 6-23: The Extract tab and the Extract All button in File Explorer.

6. **Click Browse.**
7. **Select where you want to extract the files.**
8. **Click Select Folder.**
9. **Click Extract.**

   The files are extracted. File Explorer opens the folder that you specified, where you can view all the files and folders that were in the archive.
10. **Close File Explorer and the archive you just extracted.**

The Extract tab on the File Explorer Ribbon also gives you options for extracting individual files to standard user folders like Documents, Pictures, and Downloads.

Find Files in File Explorer

The name of the search bar, which is located in the upper-right corner of the File Explorer window, always starts with "Search," followed by your current location in File Explorer. This search bar functions differently from the search bar found on the taskbar. First, you can use File Explorer's search bar only to search for files and folders. Also, the search is performed only in your current location. For example, if you're in Quick Access and you type the name of a file, Windows 10 searches for it only in the locations found in Quick Access. Similarly, if you go to the Pictures folder and you type the name of a file, Windows 10 searches for it only in the Pictures folder.

Here's an example of a search:

1. **Click the This PC shortcut in File Explorer.**
2. **Double-click the C drive, usually named Local Disk (C).**
3. **In the search bar at the top-right corner of the File Explorer window, type** notepad.
4. **Press Enter.**

   A progress bar appears at the top of the File Explorer window until the search finishes. The results returned are all from the C drive of your computer (see Figure 6-24).

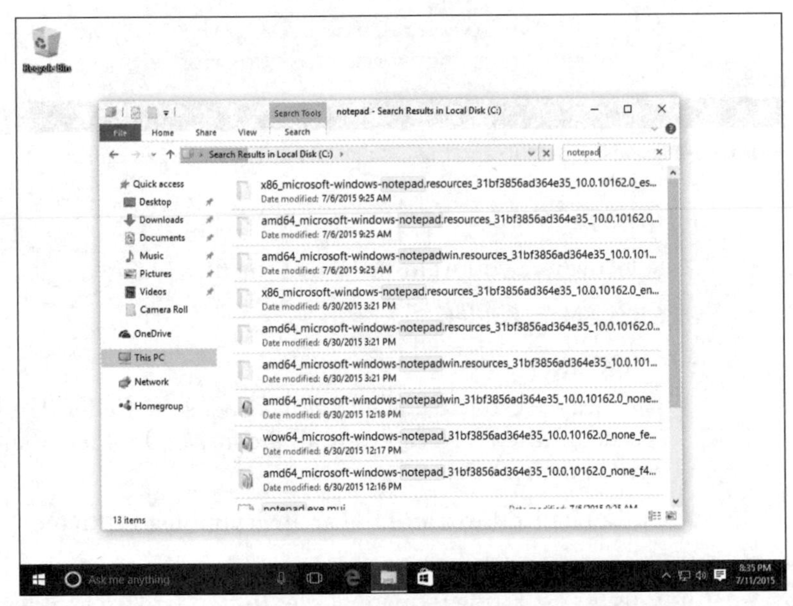

Figure 6-24: Search results returned by File Explorer.

5. **Click the Documents folder in the Quick Access section.**
6. **In the search bar, type a different filename, one that's found in your documents.**
7. **Press Enter.**

   The results returned are from the Documents folder, not from other locations on your computer. Also, because you're searching in a location that's indexed by Windows 10, you receive the results much faster than you did in the previous search.
8. **Close File Explorer.**

View or Hide Filename Extensions

By default, File Explorer hides the extensions of each file that it displays, which makes it hard to figure out the type of each file. I prefer to see the extensions of each file so that I'm not easily fooled by viruses and malware disguising themselves as something else. To view or hide filename extensions, open File Explorer and follow these steps:

1. **Go to a folder with lots of files, such as Documents.**
2. **Click the View tab on the Ribbon.**

   The View tab is displayed.
3. **In the Show/Hide section, select File Name Extensions (see Figure 6-25).**

   You can now see the file extension for each file.

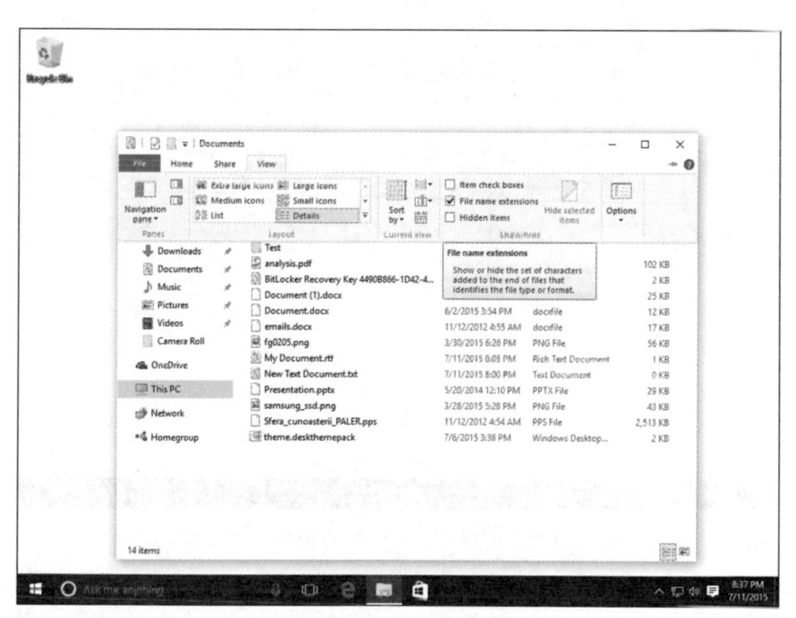

Figure 6-25: Reveal filename extensions in File Explorer.

To hide file extensions, click the View tab and uncheck File Name Extensions.

View or Hide Hidden Files or Folders

The Windows 10 operating system, as well as some apps, install folders and files that are hidden from File Explorer. They exist and can be used, but they aren't shown to you. Also, you can mark some files as hidden so that others can't see them. Luckily, File Explorer enables you to set whether to view or hide hidden items. Just follow these steps:

1. **In File Explorer, click This PC.**
2. **Double-click the C drive, usually named Local Disk (C).**

   A list of folders appears.
3. **Click the View tab on the Ribbon.**

   The View tab is displayed.
4. **In the Show/Hide section, select Hidden Items (see Figure 6-26).**

   More folders appear on the C drive. You should now see a new folder named ProgramData, which wasn't shown earlier. The number of hidden folders that you see depends on your device.

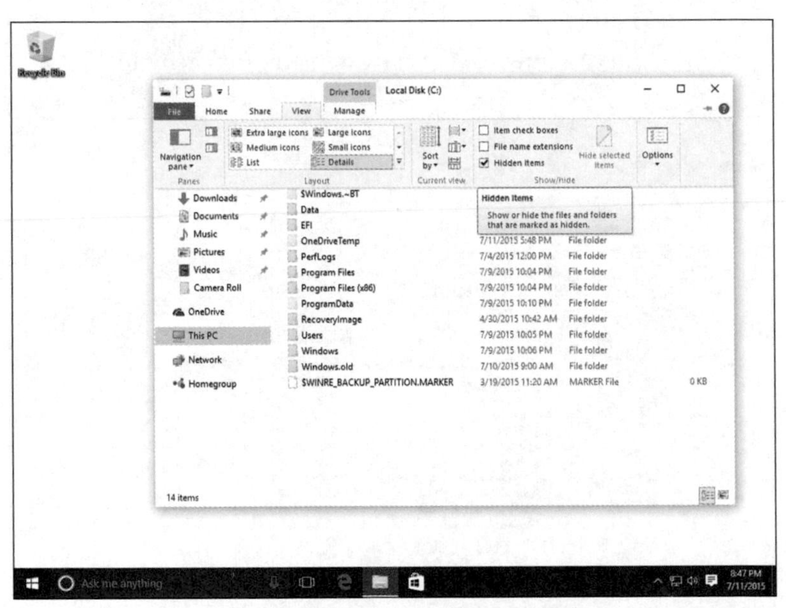

Figure 6-26: Showing or hiding hidden items in File Explorer.

To conceal the hidden items, click the View tab and uncheck Hidden Items.

Burn Files to a DVD or Blu-Ray Disc

If you have a DVD or Blu-Ray drive on your work computer with disc-burning capabilities, you can easily write your files to DVDs or Blu-Ray discs straight from File Explorer. Here's how:

1. **Insert an empty disc (DVD or Blu-Ray) into the disc-burning drive and wait for it to be detected.**
2. **Open File Explorer.**
3. **Click This PC.**
4. **Double-click the DVD or Blu-Ray drive.**

   The Burn a Disc wizard appears and you're asked how you want to use the disc.
5. **Type a title for the disc.**

   Make the title descriptive (don't use the default title proposed by Windows).
6. **Select Like a USB Flash Drive (see Figure 6-27).**

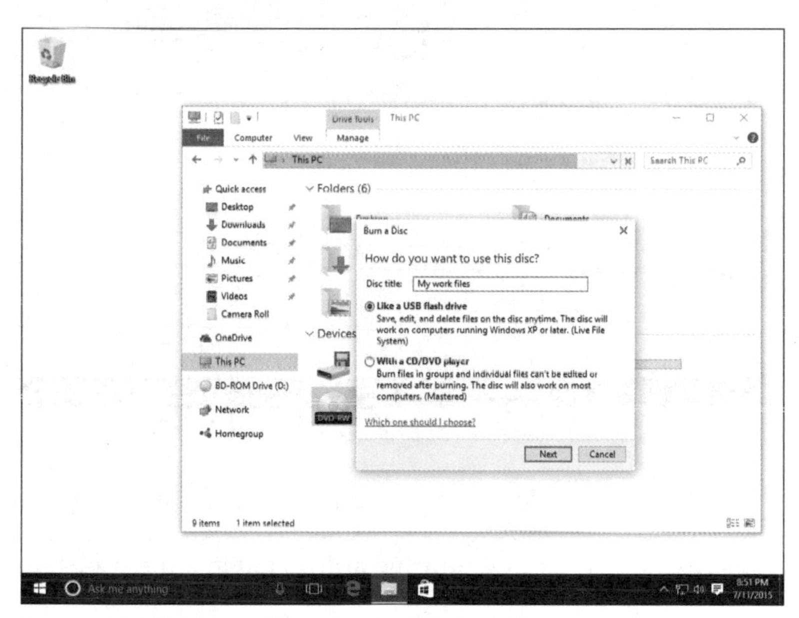

Figure 6-27: The Burn a Disc wizard in Windows 10.

7. **Click Next.**

   Windows spends some time formatting and preparing the disc.

8. **Double-click the DVD or Blu-Ray drive to open it.**
9. **Open another File Explorer window.**
10. **Copy the files that you want to burn to the disc, directly in the DVD or Blu-Ray drive, as you do when copying files to folders on your computer.**

    Wait for those files to be copied onto the drive.
11. **Click inside the window displaying the contents of the DVD or Blu-Ray drive.**
12. **Click the Manage tab on the Ribbon (see Figure 6-28).**

    The Manage tab is displayed.
13. **In the Media section, click Eject (see Figure 6-28).**

    Windows takes a few moments to eject your disc.
14. **Remove the disc from your computer.**

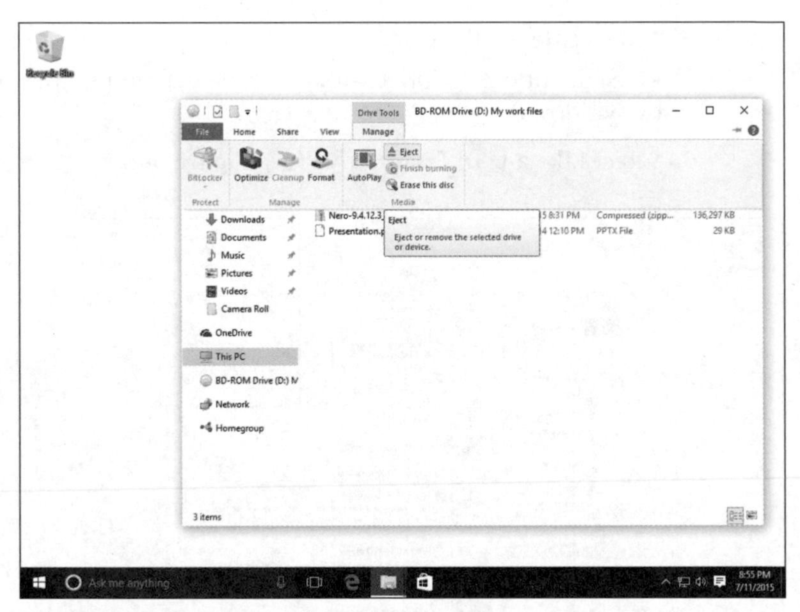

Figure 6-28: The Manage tab in File Explorer.

Don't try to add files that take up more space than is available on the disc because you won't be able to burn them onto the disc. Windows will copy only the files that fit into the available space onto the disc.

View What's Inside ISO Disc Images

Disk images are computer files containing all the content and structure of a storage device, such as a hard drive, CD, DVD, Blu-Ray, or USB flash drive. A disk image is a single file that faithfully

reproduces all the contents and capabilities of the storage device that it's cloning.

Think of a disk image as a clone of a DVD or some other device turned into a single file on your computer.

Disk images have specific file extensions, such as .iso, .bin, or .cue. The most popular format for disk images is ISO, and Windows 10 allows you to open them and view their contents directly from File Explorer. When you access an ISO file, it's mounted as though it were a drive on your computer. Here's how to view what's inside an ISO file:

1. **Open File Explorer.**
2. **Navigate to the ISO file that you want to mount.**
3. **Double-click the file to mount it in File Explorer.**

   File Explorer displays the contents of the ISO file.
4. **View the contents of the ISO file and copy and paste any files that you want to use on your computer, as you normally do (see Figure 6-29).**

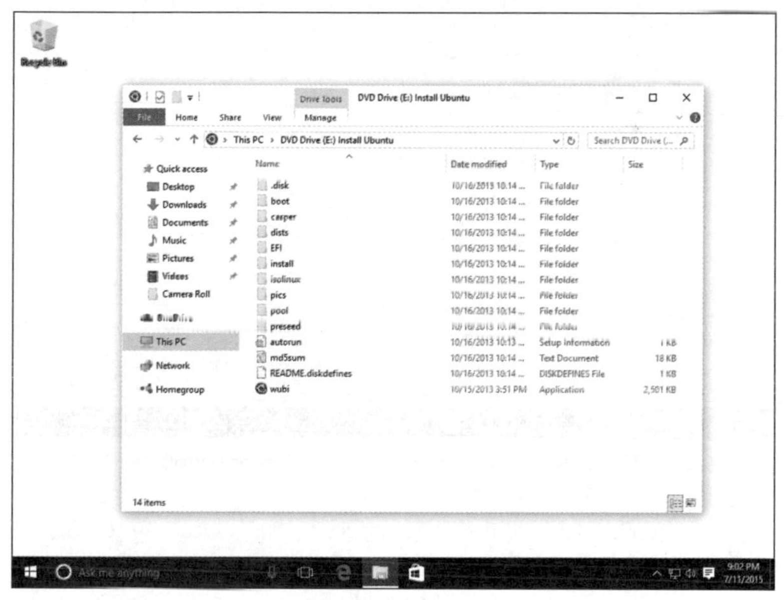

Figure 6-29: The contents of an ISO file that is mounted in File Explorer.

After you mount an ISO file, its contents are shown as a separate drive in File Explorer until you eject the ISO file. During the time it's mounted in File Explorer, you can't edit the ISO file, nor can you delete it or change its location.

Eject ISO Disc Images

In the previous section, you found out that ISO disc images remain mounted in File Explorer until you eject them. When you're done working with an ISO image, here's how to eject it:

1. **In File Explorer, click the This PC section.**
2. **In the Devices and Drives section, select the drive with the contents of the mounted ISO file by clicking on it.**
3. **Click the Manage tab on the Ribbon (see Figure 6-30).**

   The Manage tab is displayed.
4. **In the Media section, click Eject (see Figure 6-30).**

   The drive with the contents of the mounted ISO file no longer appears in your list of Devices and Drives.

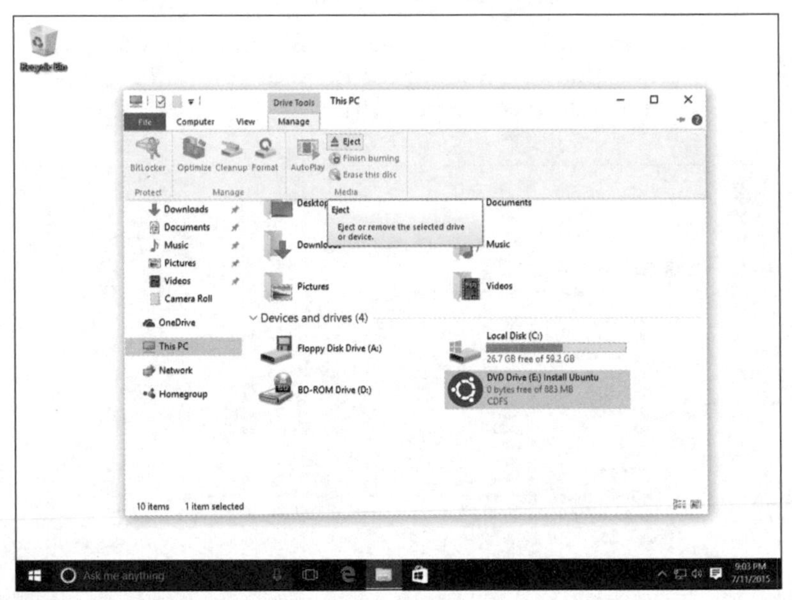

Figure 6-30: Shows the Manage tab on the File Explorer Ribbon.

You can achieve the same effect by right-clicking the drive in the Devices and Drives section and selecting Eject.

Change the Location of User Folders

Windows stores all your user files and folders in C:\Users, followed by your username. There, you see folders such as Desktop, Downloads, Documents, Music, and Pictures. In Windows 10, these folders also appear in File Explorer under This PC and Quick Access.

If your computer has multiple partitions, you may want to change the location of one or more of your user folders. For example, you might move the Downloads folder to another partition so that enough room is left on your Windows system drive. Doing so helps to ensure that your user folders and their contents are safe if Windows 10 fails and you need to reinstall it. If you have a solid-state storage device (SSD) with little space available, moving your user folders to another drive makes even more sense. This way, you can use the valuable space on the SSD for apps and games that benefit from the speed and performance of an SSD. Here's how to move a user folder, such as Downloads, to another location:

1. **Open File Explorer.**
2. **Click Quick Access if it isn't open.**
3. **Click the user folder that you want to change to select it.**
4. **Click the Home tab on the Ribbon.**

   The Home tab is displayed.
5. **In the Open section, click Properties.**
6. **In the Folder Properties window, click the Location tab (see Figure 6-31).**

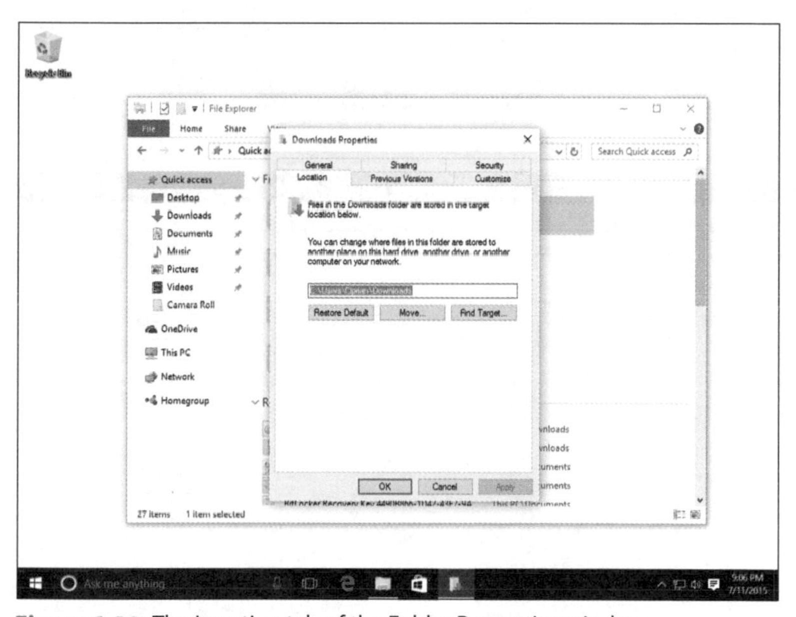

Figure 6-31: The Location tab of the Folder Properties window.

7. **Click Move.**
8. **Browse to the new location you want to use for this folder.**

9. **Click Select Folder.**
10. **Click OK.**

    You're asked to confirm that you want to move all files from the old location to the new location.
11. **Click Yes and wait for the files to be moved to the new location (see Figure 6-32).**
12. **Close File Explorer.**

    The next time you start File Explorer, the user folder will appear in the new location.

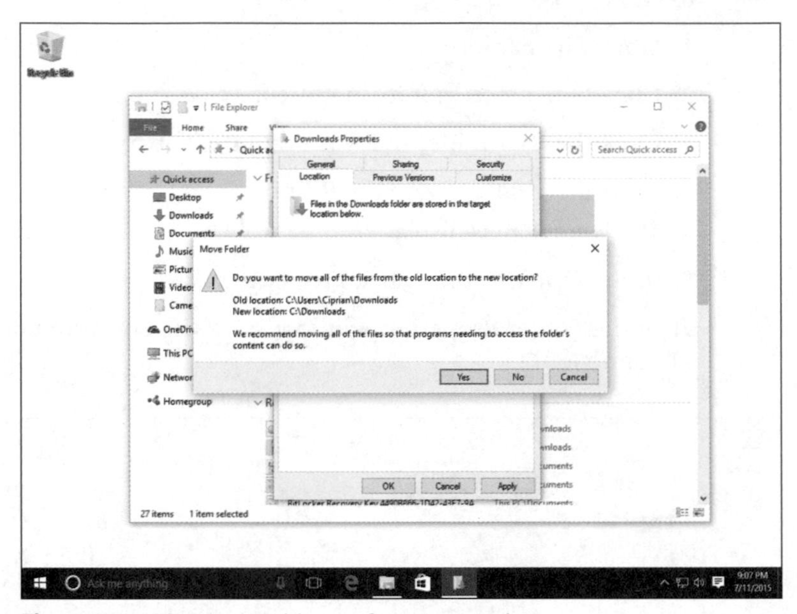

Figure 6-32: The Move Folder confirmation window.

CHAPTERSEVEN

Customizing File Explorer

When using Windows 10, you can customize in detail how File Explorer works, just like other Windows features. You may want to customize File Explorer in order to improve the way it works and be more productive when using it day by day. For example, you can add your own folders to Quick Access, enable libraries and make them easily accessible, or use check boxes to select files and folders.

This chapter is filled with many useful steps, such as how to change File Explorer's start location, how to enable or disable the different navigational elements, how to use the different Views that are available for an enhanced view of what's inside your folders, and how to use grouping and filtering options.

In This Chapter

- Changing the File Explorer start location
- Managing the files and folders in Quick Access
- Enabling or disabling panes
- Customizing the Quick Access Toolbar
- Using Views in File Explorer
- Grouping and sorting files and folders
- Improving how File Explorer works

Change the File Explorer Start Location

When you start File Explorer, by default, it opens Quick Access. You can change the start location to This PC by opening File Explorer and following these steps:

1. **Click the File tab on the Ribbon.**

   The File menu appears.

2. **Click Change Folder and Search Options.**

   The Folder Options window appears.

3. **In the General tab, click the Open File Explorer To drop-down list.**

   A list with two options is shown: Quick access and This PC.

4. **Select This PC (see Figure 7-1).**

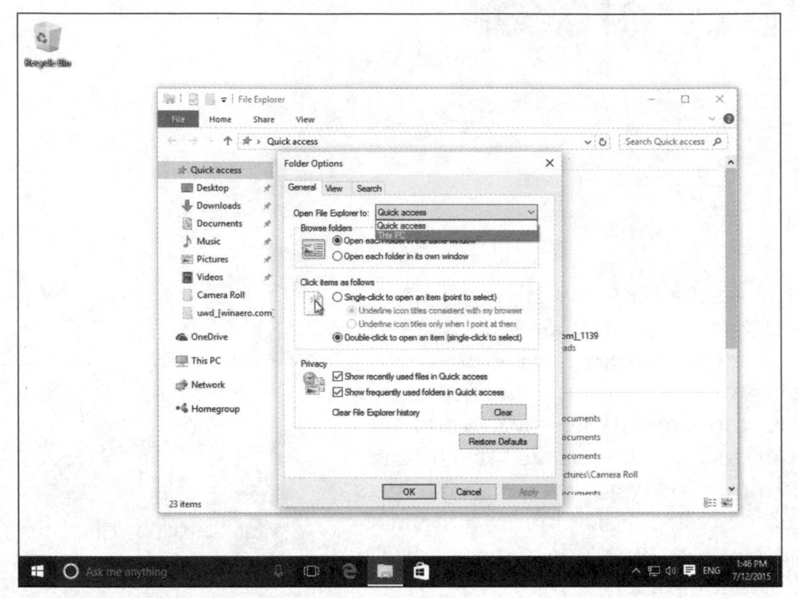

Figure 7-1: The Folder Options window.

5. **Click OK.**

6. **Close File Explorer.**

   The next time you open File Explorer, it displays This PC rather than Quick Access.

Pin Folders to Quick Access

As I mentioned in the previous section, when you start File Explorer, it displays Quick Access, where you see a list of the folders you browse most frequently and the files that you recently accessed. This list changes over time as you use different folders. You can always pin the folders and libraries that you want to access as quickly as possible to Quick Access. Here's how to do so:

1. **Open File Explorer.**

2. **Navigate to the folder that you want to pin to Quick Access.**

3. **Select that folder by clicking on it.**

4. **Click the Home tab on the Ribbon.**

   The Home tab is shown.

5. **In the Clipboard section, click the Pin to Quick Access button (see Figure 7-2).**

   The selected folder is now listed in Quick Access.

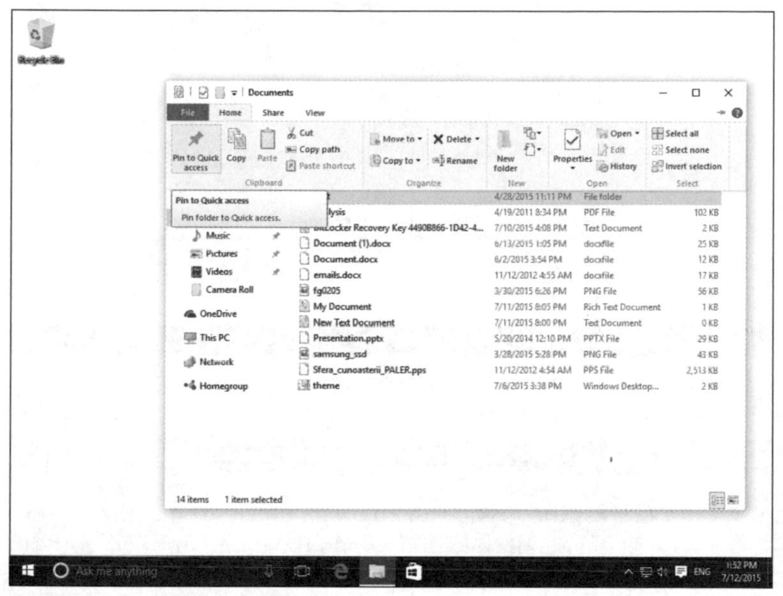

Figure 7-2: The Pin to Quick Access button in File Explorer.

You can also pin a folder by right-clicking it and selecting Pin to Quick Access in the right-click menu.

Unpin Folders from Quick Access

To unpin a folder from the Quick Access section, open File Explorer and follow these steps:

1. **Click the Quick Access section.**

2. **Right-click the folder that you want to unpin.**

   The right-click menu appears.

3. **In the right-click menu, click Unpin from Quick Access (see Figure 7-3).**

   The selected folder is no longer listed in Quick Access.

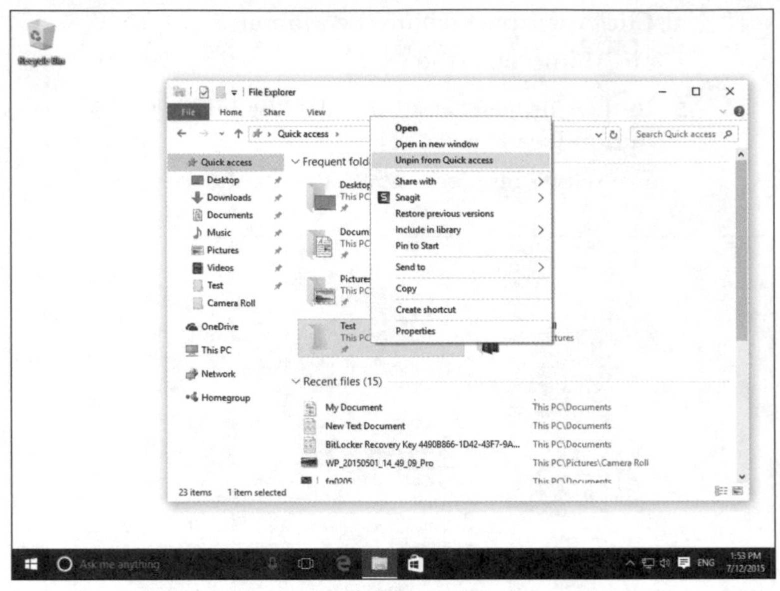

Figure 7-3: The Unpin from Quick Access option in the pop-up menu.

Enable and Use the Preview Pane

In File Explorer, you can enable a Preview pane that is shown on the right side of the window. As the name implies, you can use it to preview the contents of certain types of files. For example, if you select an image file in File Explorer, you can see a preview of it; if you select a text file, you can preview its contents. Figure 7-4 shows the Preview pane in File Explorer.

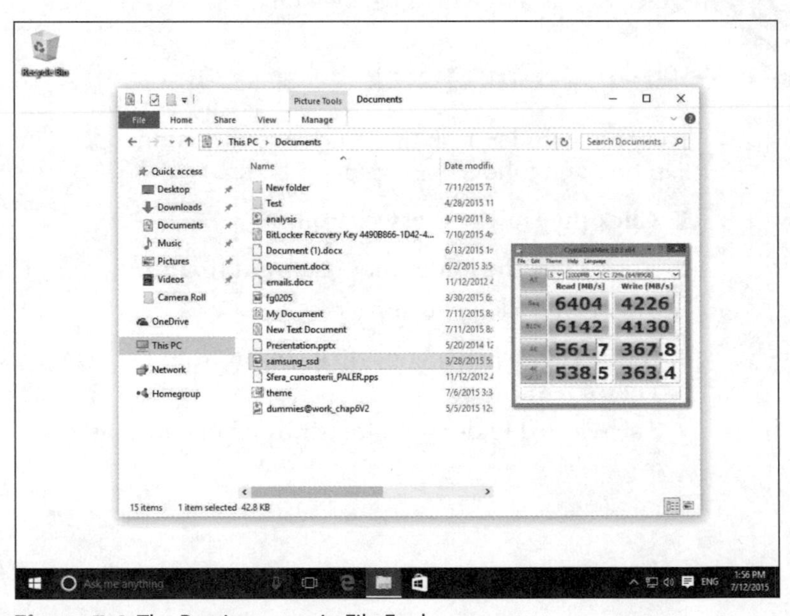

Figure 7-4: The Preview pane in File Explorer.

You can see previews of only certain file types: text, images, and videos.

To enable the Preview pane, open File Explorer and follow these steps:

1. **In the File Explorer window, click the View tab.**

   The View tab is shown.

2. **In the Panes section, click the Preview Pane button (see Figure 7-5).**

   The Preview pane is added to the right side of the File Explorer window.

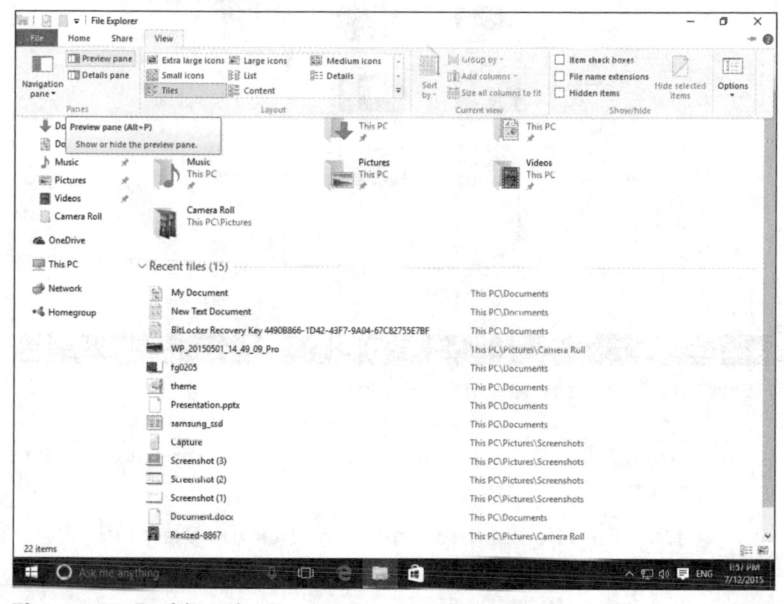

Figure 7-5: Enabling the Preview pane in File Explorer.

3. **Select several files one by one.**

   You can preview their contents in the Preview Pane, if they are text, images, or videos.

To disable the Preview pane, just follow the preceding steps.

You can also enable and disable the Preview pane in File Explorer by pressing Alt+P on your keyboard.

Enable and Use the Details Pane

In File Explorer, you can enable a Details pane that is shown on the right side of the File Explorer window (see Figure 7-6). As its name implies, you can use the Details pane to find more information about each file, such as its size, the date it was created, and the date it was last modified. The fields of data shown in this pane vary from file to file. For some files, such as pictures, you see lots of data; whereas for other files, such as PDF files, you see less data.

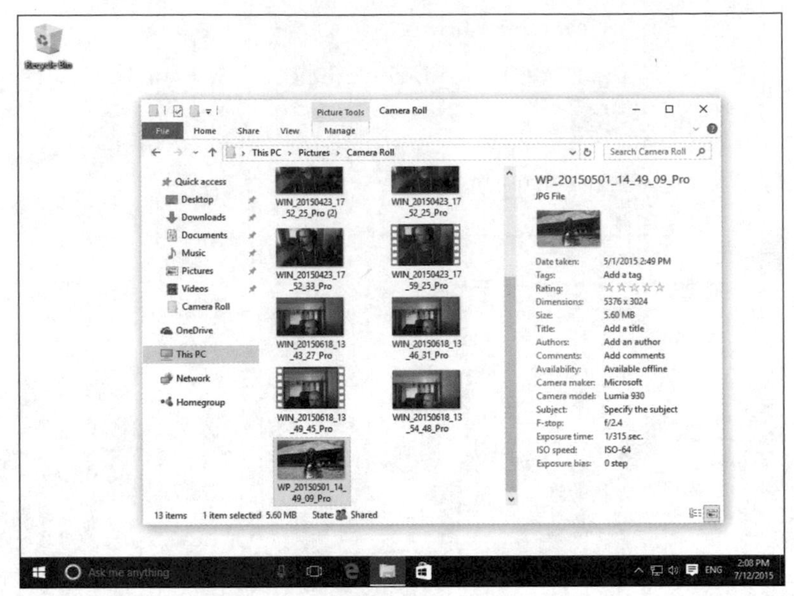

Figure 7-6: The Details pane in File Explorer.

To enable the Details pane, open File Explorer and follow these steps:

1. **In the File Explorer window, click the View tab.**

   The View tab is shown.

2. **In the Panes section, click the Details Pane button (see Figure 7-7).**

   The Details pane is added to the right side of the File Explorer window.

3. **To see a file's details, click it to select it.**

To disable the Details pane, just follow the preceding steps.

You can also enable and disable the Details pane in File Explorer by pressing Alt+Shift+P on your keyboard.

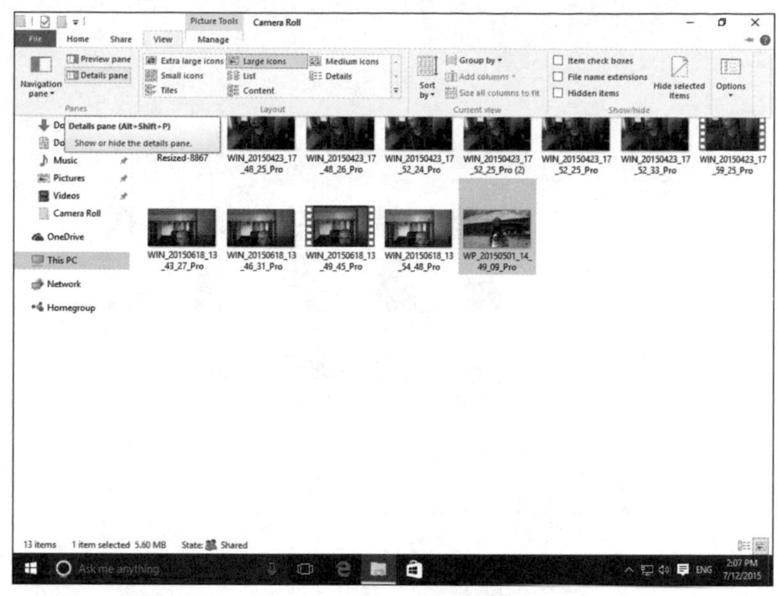

Figure 7-7: Enabling the Details pane in File Explorer.

Disable or Enable the Navigation Pane

In File Explorer, the Navigation pane is shown, by default, on the left side of the window. As the name implies, you can use it to quickly jump to different locations on your computer.

When the Navigation pane is disabled and you start File Explorer, either Quick Access or This PC is loaded, depending on your start location for File Explorer.

I don't recommend disabling the Navigation pane because doing so makes navigation more difficult.

If you decide to disable the Navigation pane, follow these steps:

1. **Open File Explorer.**
2. **Click the View tab.**

   The View tab is shown.
3. **In the Panes section, click the Navigation Pane button.**

   The Navigation Pane menu appears.
4. **In the menu, click Navigation Pane (see Figure 7-8).**

   The Navigation pane no longer appears at the left side of the File Explorer window.

To enable the Navigation pane, follow the preceding steps.

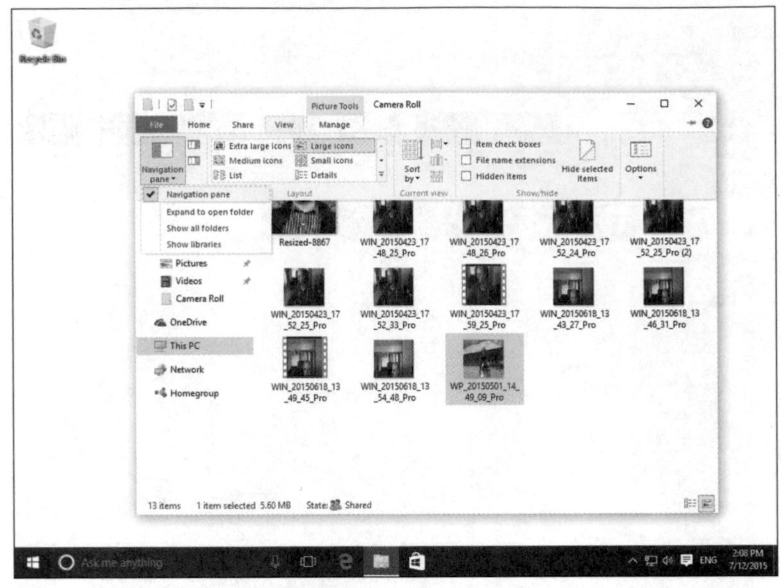

Figure 7-8: Disabling the Navigation pane in File Explorer.

Enable the Libraries Section in the Navigation Pane

By default, the Navigation pane doesn't show the Libraries in Windows 10, as it did in Windows 7. Fortunately, the libraries aren't gone; they're just hidden. To enable and use the libraries in Windows 10, open File Explorer and follow these steps:

1. **In the File Explorer window, click the View tab.**

   The View tab is shown.

2. **In the Panes section, click the Navigation Pane button.**

   The Navigation Pane menu appears.

3. **In the menu, click Show Libraries (see Figure 7-9).**

   The Libraries are now added to File Explorer.

4. **Click the Libraries shortcut in the Navigation Pane to view your libraries.**

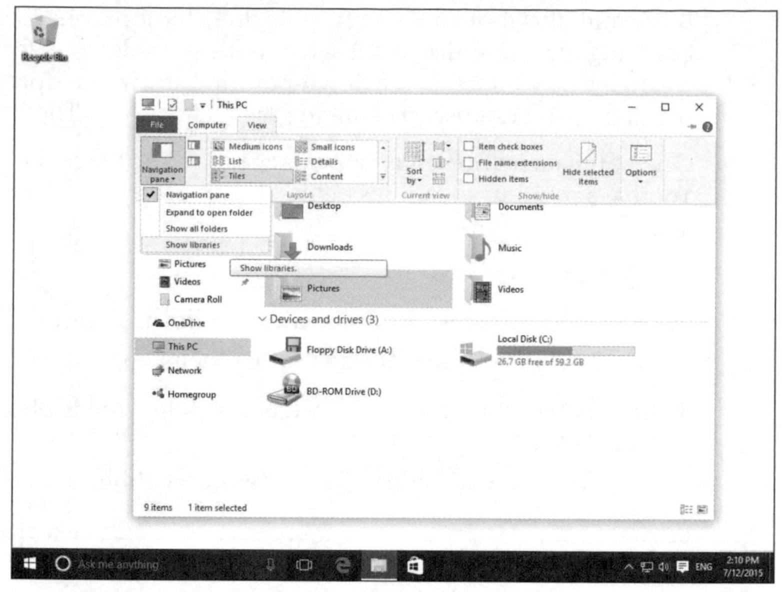

Figure 7-9: Enabling the Libraries section in File Explorer.

Change the Position of the Quick Access Toolbar

The Quick Access Toolbar is located at the top-left corner of the File Explorer window. You can see it highlighted in Figure 7-10.

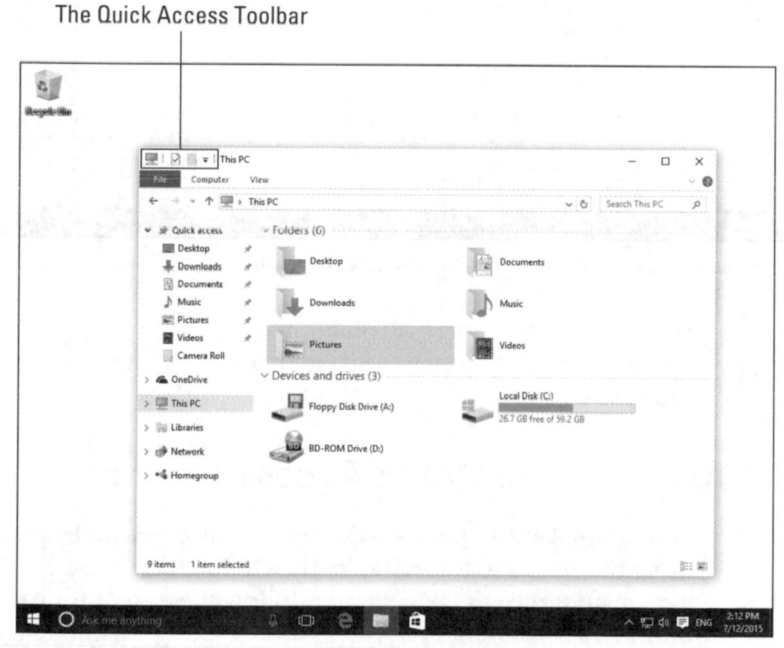

Figure 7-10: The Quick Access Toolbar.

By default, this toolbar contains only three buttons: one for accessing the properties of the selected file or folder, one for creating a new folder, and a down-pointing arrow that opens a menu that you can use to configure the Quick Access Toolbar.

One of the menu's options is to change the Quick Access Toolbar's position so that it's below the Ribbon rather than above it. Here's how:

1. **Open File Explorer.**
2. **In the Quick Access Toolbar, click the down-pointing arrow.**

   The Customize Quick Access Toolbar menu appears.
3. **In the menu that appears, click Show Below the Ribbon (see Figure 7-11).**

   The Quick Access Toolbar is now below the Ribbon.

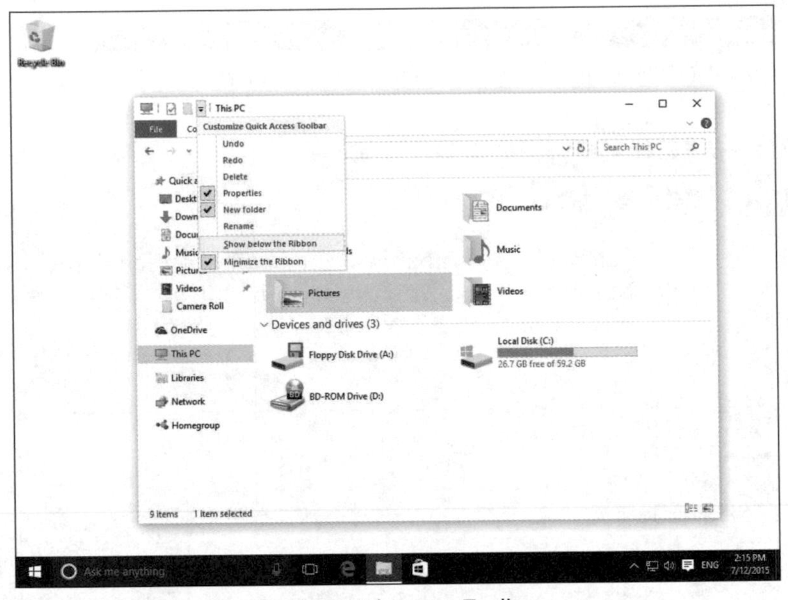

Figure 7-11: The menu for the Quick Access Toolbar.

To place the Quick Access Toolbar back at the top of the Ribbon, follow the preceding steps and, at Step 3, click Show Above the Ribbon.

Add Buttons to the Quick Access Toolbar

You can make the Quick Access Toolbar more useful by adding more buttons to it; for example, the Undo, Redo, Delete, and Rename buttons. In File Explorer, follow these steps for each new button that you want to add:

1. **In the Quick Access Toolbar, click the down-pointing arrow.**

   The Customize Quick Access Toolbar menu appears.

2. **In the menu that appears, click the function you want to add to the Quick Access Toolbar (such as Undo, Redo, or Delete; see Figure 7-12).**

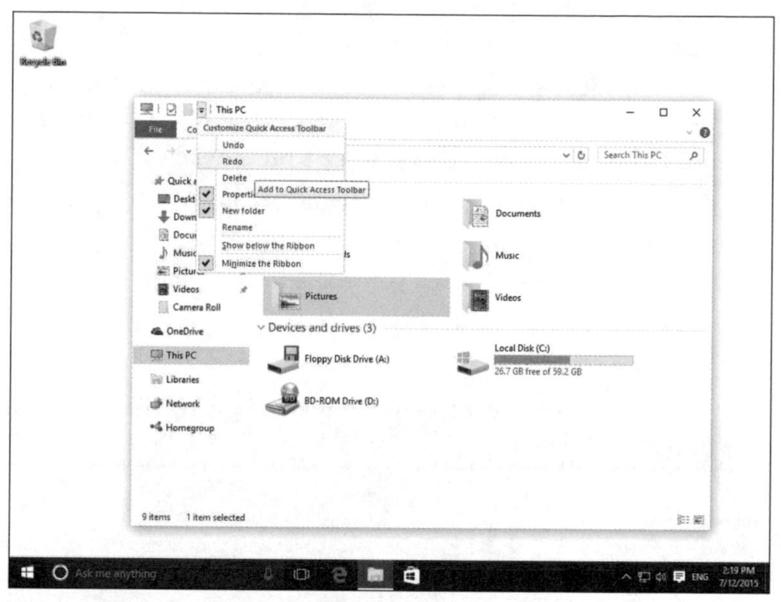

Figure 7-12: Adding buttons to the Quick Access Toolbar.

Use Views to Better Examine Your Folders' Contents

When you first browse a folder, File Explorer automatically applies a view that's optimized for the contents of that folder. However, the Ribbon has a multitude of view options in the Layout section of the View tab (as shown in Figure 7-13):

- **Details:** For each file and folder, the Details view shows several columns with information, such as Name, Date Modified, Type, and Size.

  Each file has its own small icon that represents the file type.

- **Content:** Each file and folder appears on a separate row, where you see detailed information about it, such as the date the file was last modified, its size, its author, and its length (for audio and video files).

  For picture and video files, you see a small preview of the content rather than a file icon.

- **List:** Displays a simple list of folders and files, each with an identifying icon.
- **Tiles:** Displays a medium-size icon representing each file and folder, along with information about their types and sizes.
- **Extra-large icons:** Displays extra-large icons that are representative of the contents of each file.

  For pictures and video, you see a preview of each file.
- **Large icons:** Displays large icons that are representative of the contents of each file.

  For pictures and video you see a preview of each file.
- **Medium icons:** Displays medium icons that are representative of the contents of each file.

  For pictures and video you see a preview of each file.
- **Small icons:** Displays small icons that are representative of the contents of each file.

You can easily switch between these views by clicking on them.

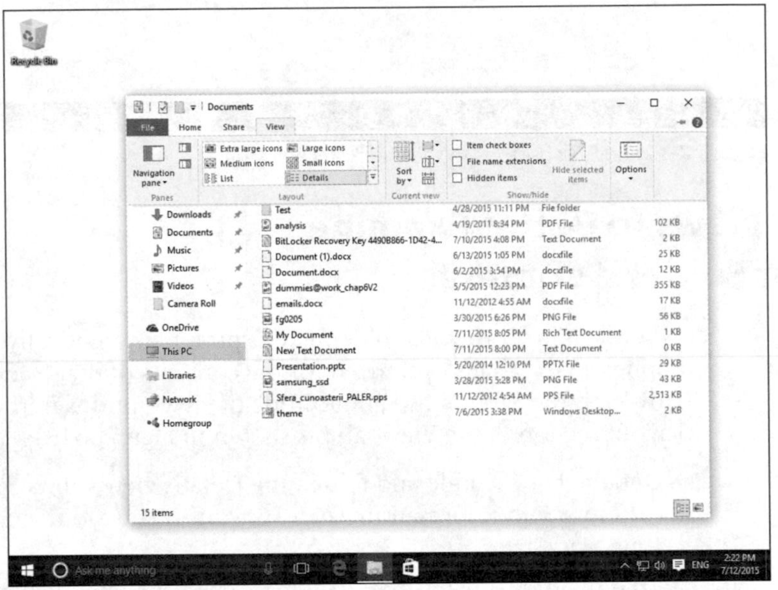

Figure 7-13: The Layout section of the View tab on the File Explorer ribbon.

File Explorer remembers the last view that you used for a folder and applies it the next time you open it.

Sort Files and Folders

File Explorer offers the Sort tool for sorting the files and folders that you're viewing based on criteria such as their name, type, size, authors, and more. To sort the files within a folder, open File Explorer and follow these steps:

1. **Navigate to the folder that you want to sort.**
2. **Click the View tab on the Ribbon.**

   The View tab is shown.
3. **In the Current View section, click the Sort By button (see Figure 7-14).**

   The Sort By menu appears.

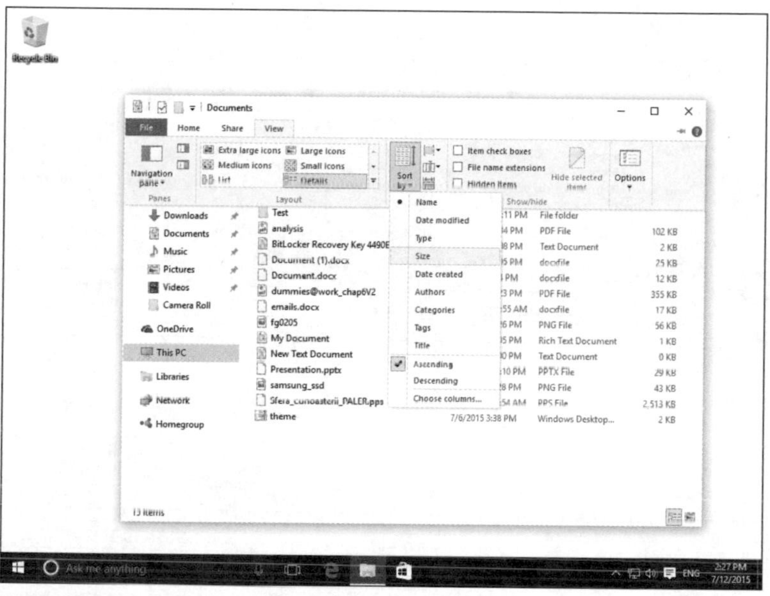

Figure 7-14: The Sort By menu in File Explorer.

4. **Click the sorting criteria that you want to use to apply it.**

   The files and folders for your current location are now sorted using the criteria you selected.

Group Files and Folders

With File Explorer, you can group the files and folders that you're viewing based on criteria such as their name, type, size, authors, and more. To group the files within a folder, open File Explorer and follow these steps:

1. **Navigate to the folder whose contents you want to group.**
2. **Click the View tab on the Ribbon.**

   The View tab is shown.
3. **In the Current View section, click the Group By button (see Figure 7-15).**

   The Group By menu appears.

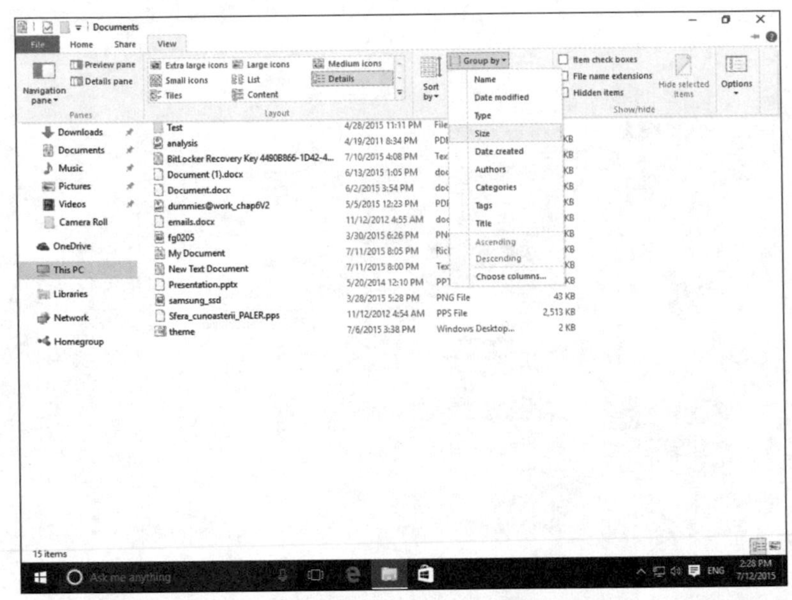

Figure 7-15: The Group By button and menu in File Explorer.

4. **Click the grouping criteria that you want to use to apply it.**

   The files and folders for your current location are now grouped using the criteria you selected.

Customize File Explorer with Folder Options

You can reconfigure certain ways that File Explorer works. All the configuration settings are in a window named Folder Options. This window has three tabs filled with settings. Here's how to access the Folder Options window, browse its settings, change them, and apply your desired configuration:

1. **Open File Explorer.**
2. **Click File.**

   The File menu appears.
3. **Click Change Folder and Search Options.**

   The Folder Options window appears at the General tab. Here are settings for browsing folders in File Explorer, opening an item in File Explorer, and whether to show recently used files and folders in Quick Access.
4. **In the General tab, change the settings that you're interested in.**
5. **Click the View tab (see Figure 7-16).**

   Here you find settings for viewing files and folders in File Explorer.

TIP

The list of settings is long. Browse through the list and read what they do. Each name is self-explanatory.

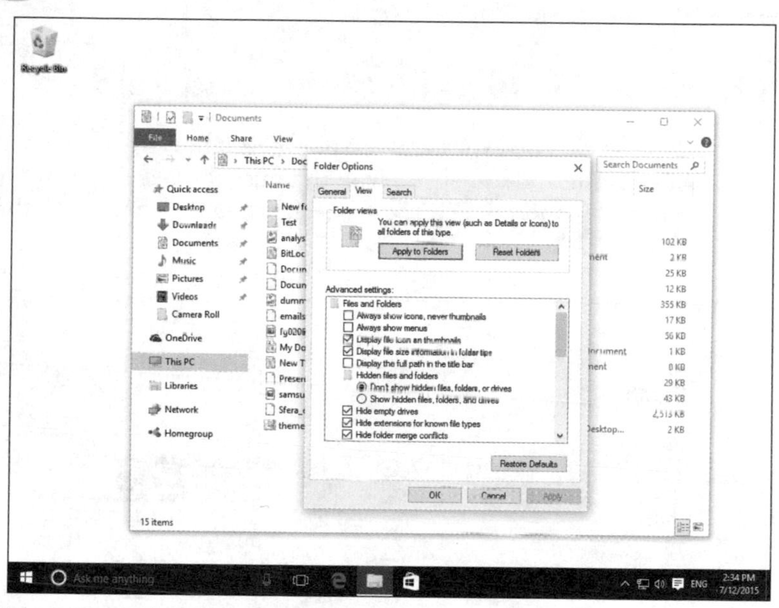

Figure 7-16: The View tab in Folder Options.

6. **Change any advanced settings that you want.**
7. **Click the Search tab (see Figure 7-17).**

   Here you find settings for using search in Windows 10 and in File Explorer.
8. **Change how search works.**
9. **To apply your settings, click OK.**

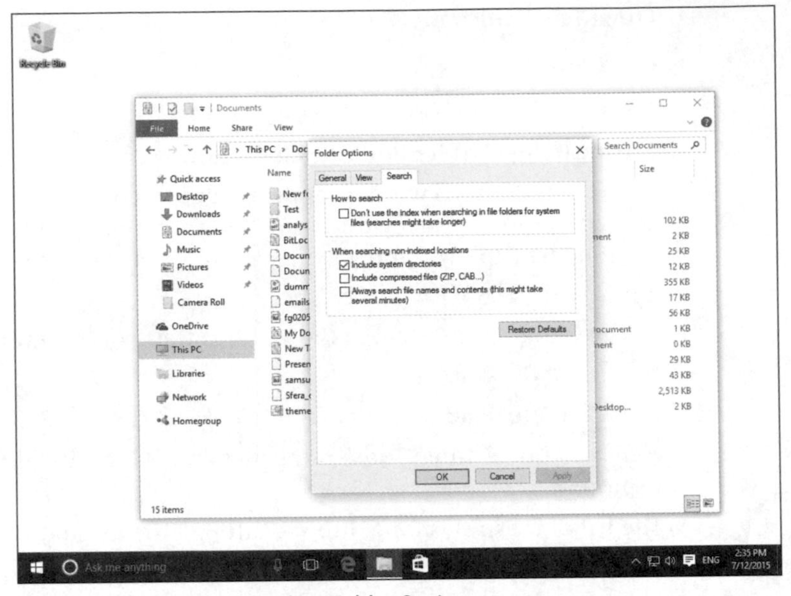

Figure 7-17: The Search tab in Folder Options.

Use Check Boxes to Select Files and Folders

You can set File Explorer to display check boxes near the name of each file and folder. You can then use these check boxes to select files and folders. These check boxes look similar to those in Figure 7-18.

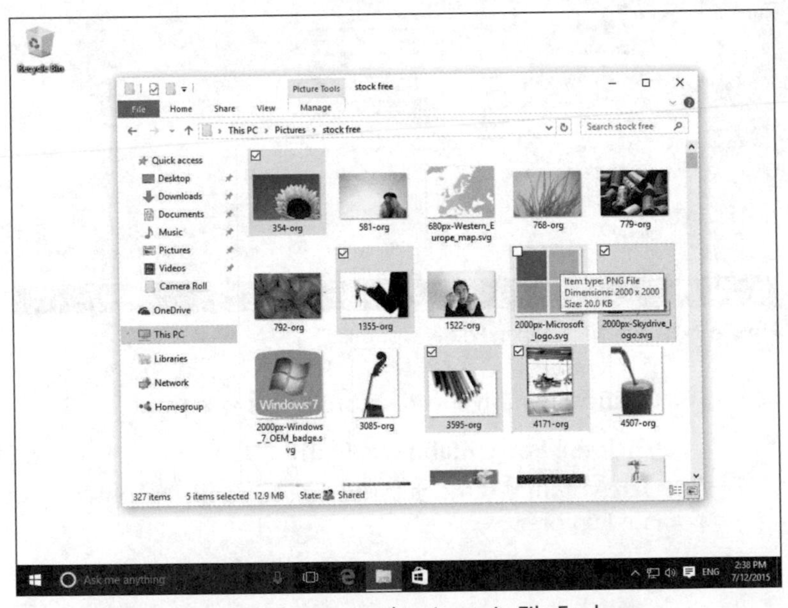

Figure 7-18: Using check boxes to select items in File Explorer.

To enable check boxes in File Explorer, follow these steps:

1. **Open File Explorer.**
2. **Click the View tab on the Ribbon.**

   The View tab is shown.

3. **In the Show/Hide section, click Item Check Boxes (see Figure 7-19).**

   Check boxes are now shown each time you move your cursor on top of a file or folder. Click the check box to select that item.

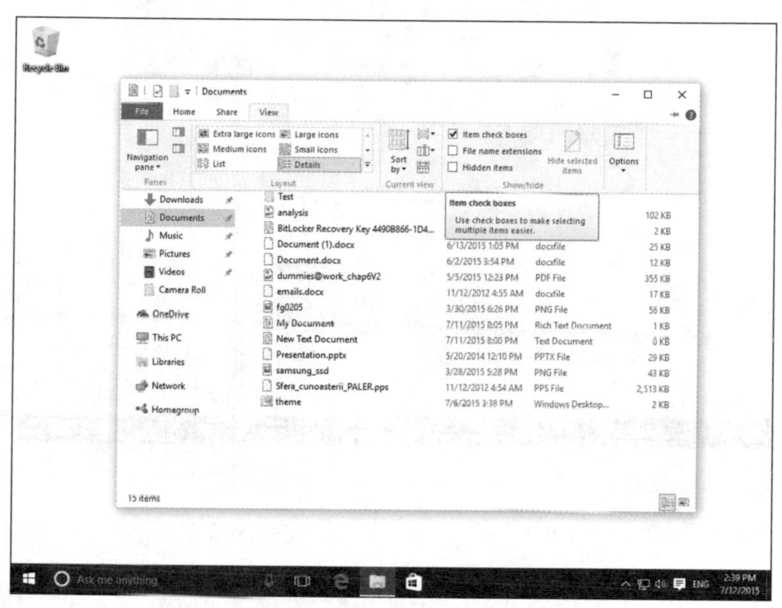

Figure 7-19: How to enable Item Check Boxes in File Explorer.

4. **Close File Explorer.**

To disable the check boxes, follow the preceding steps.

Clear File Explorer's History of Recently Used Files and Folders

By default, File Explorer remembers all the files and folders that you've accessed and displays them in different places, like in Quick Access. If you want to clear your history of accessed files and folders, open File Explorer and follow these steps:

1. **Click File.**

   The File menu appears.

2. **Click Change Folder and Search Options.**

   The Folder Options window appears.

3. In the General tab, look for the Privacy section.
4. Click the Clear button (see Figure 7-20).
5. Click OK.
6. Close File Explorer.

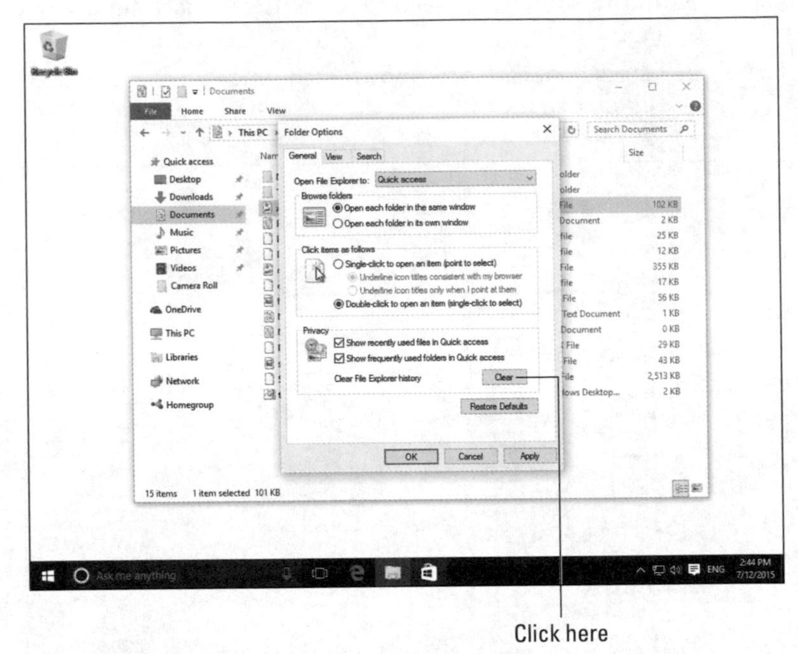

Figure 7-20: The Clear button in the Folder Options window.

CHAPTER EIGHT

Customizing Windows 10

This chapter focuses on customizing how Windows 10 looks and works, especially on how to customize the appearance of the operating system. I show you how to customize the desktop background, the colors Windows 10 uses, the theme, the icons that are displayed, the screen resolution, and the mouse pointer size and color. You also find out how to customize the Lock Screen, what it looks like and the information it displays. You discover how to customize the taskbar and how to change the sound volume.

This chapter also covers how to change the date and time, the time zone, and the country on Windows 10, which should be especially interesting to those of you who travel to other countries or work with different languages. You also find out how to add a new keyboard input language and how to download a language pack in Windows 10.

Finally, I show you how to set which Windows 10 settings are synchronized across your devices, which is handy if you use a Microsoft account on your work computers.

In This Chapter

- Changing the desktop background
- Changing the Windows theme
- Changing the resolution and the mouse pointer
- Customizing the Start Menu and the Lock Screen
- Customizing the taskbar
- Changing the sound volume
- Setting the date, time, time zone, and country
- Adding a new keyboard input language
- Downloading a language pack
- Tuning which settings get synchronized

Change the Desktop Background

Windows 10 allows you to change the desktop background to another picture that's bundled with the operating system or with a picture of your own. To change the desktop background, follow these steps:

1. **Open Settings.**
2. **Click Personalization.**

   All available personalization settings are shown.

3. **In the Background section, choose a picture from those included in Windows 10 by clicking on it (see Figure 8-1).**

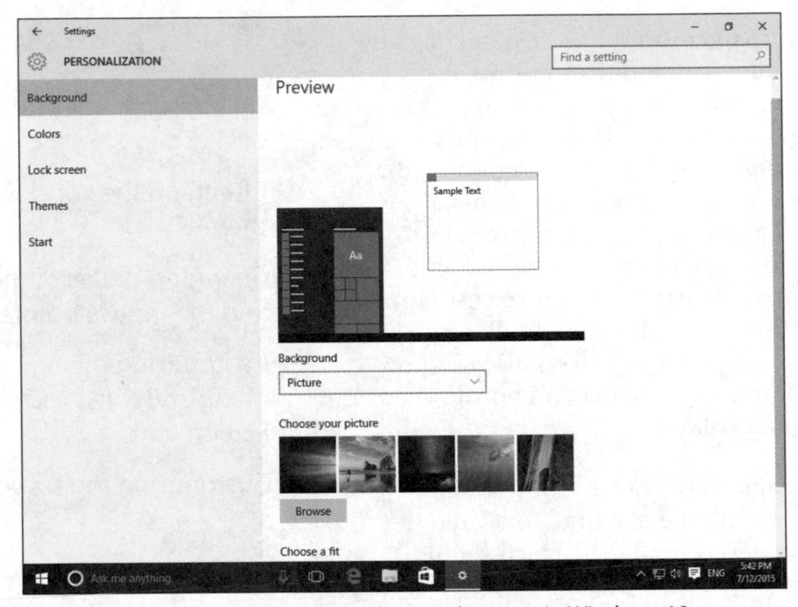

Figure 8-1: How to change the Background picture in Windows 10.

4. **Click the down-pointing arrow in the Choose a Fit drop-down list.**

   A list is shown with such choices and Fill, Fit, Stretch, Tile, Center, and Span.

5. **From the drop-down list, choose how you want the picture to fit your desktop.**
6. **Close the Settings window.**

If you want to use your own picture, at Step 3 click Browse, navigate to the picture that you want to use, and click Choose Picture; continue with Steps 4, 5 and 6.

Set a Slideshow of Pictures as the Desktop Background

You can use your Pictures folder (or any other folder with pictures) to create a "slide show" background on your desktop. When you do that, at regular intervals, Windows 10 automatically shows a rotating series of the pictures in your Pictures folder.

In order to create a slide show with your own pictures as the desktop background, follow these steps:

1. **Open Settings.**
2. **Click Personalization.**

   All available personalization settings are shown.

3. **Click the down-pointing arrow in the Background drop-down list.**

   A list is shown with such choices as Picture, Solid color, and Slideshow.

4. **In the drop-down list that appears, select Slideshow.**

   By default, the Pictures folder is used as the source for the slideshow (as shown in Figure 8-2).

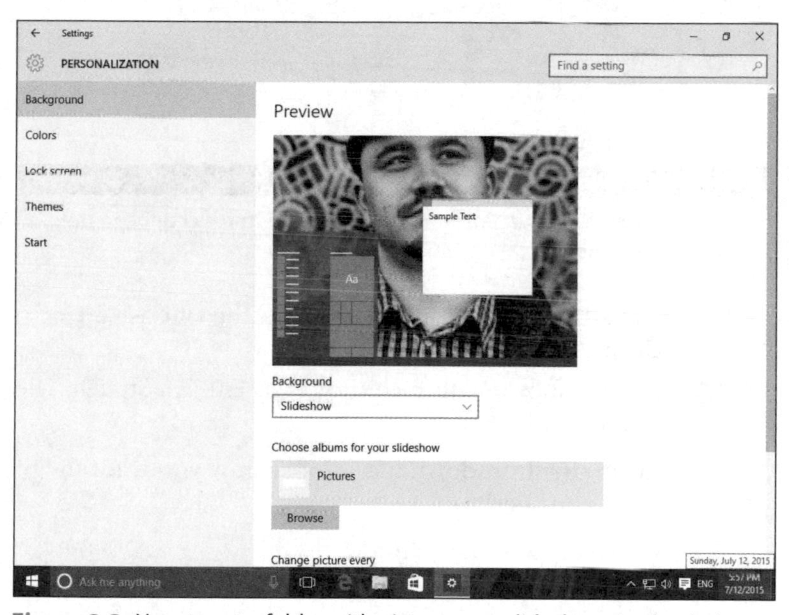

Figure 8-2: How to set a folder with pictures as a slideshow on the desktop.

5. **To choose another folder, click Browse.**

   The Select Folder window appears.

6. **Browse through the folders on your computer and select the one that you want to use; then click Choose This Folder.**

   The selected folder is used for the slide show.

7. **Click the down-pointing arrow in the Change Picture Every drop-down list.**

   A list is shown with several choices for the time interval at which the pictures should change.

8. **In the drop-down list that appears, select the time interval at which you want the pictures to change (see Figure 8-3).**

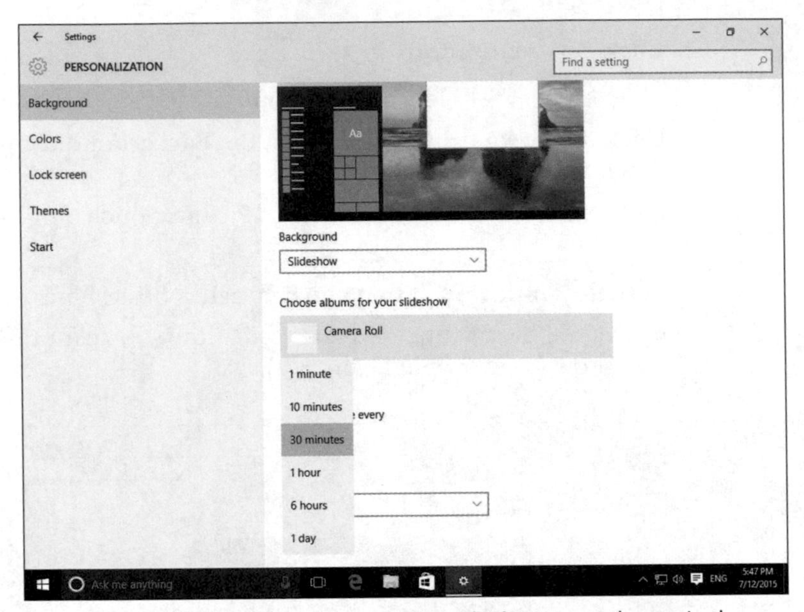

Figure 8-3: How to set the time interval at which pictures change in the slideshow.

9. **Click the down-pointing arrow in the Choose a Fit drop-down list.**

   A list is shown with such choices as Fill, Fit, Stretch, Tile, Center, and Span.

10. **From the drop-down list, choose how you want the picture to fit your desktop.**

11. **Close the Settings window.**

Set the Colors Used by Windows 10

Windows 10 allows you to change the main color that's used throughout the operating system. By default, this color is chosen from the desktop background. Windows 10 simply picks the desktop's accent color and uses it automatically. You can override this setting and choose your own accent color. Black is the default color for the Start Menu, the taskbar, and the Action Center. You can change this setting and have these elements use the accent color that you set. You can also make the Start Menu, the taskbar, and the Action Center transparent, so that you can see through them.

Here's how to change the color-related settings in Windows 10:

1. **Open Settings.**
2. **Click Personalization.**

   All the available personalization settings are shown.
3. **Click Colors.**

   The color-related settings are shown.
4. **To pick a custom accent color, set the Automatically Pick an Accent Color from My Background switch to Off; then choose your accent color from the list of options (see Figure 8-4).**

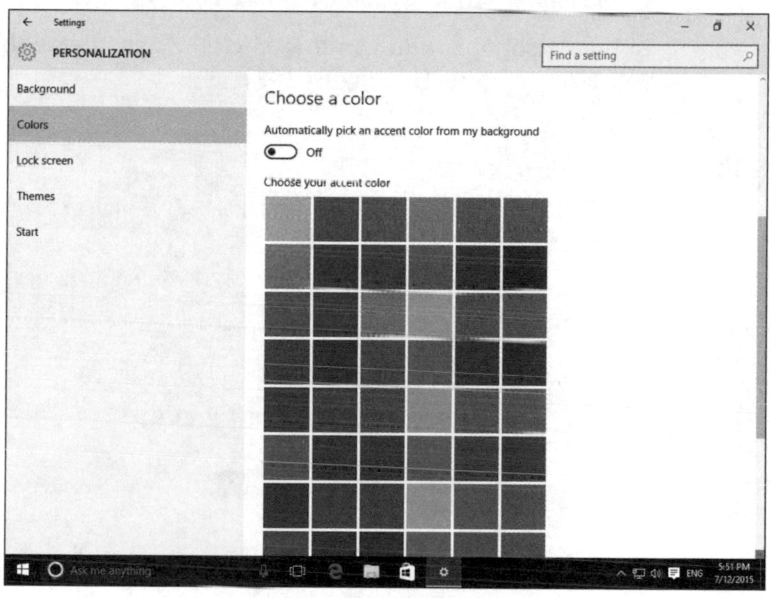

Figure 8-4: How to set the colors used by Windows 10.

5. **Set the Show Color on Start, Taskbar, and Action Center switch to On or Off, depending on what you want.**
6. **Set the Make Start, Taskbar, and Action Center Transparent switch to On or Off, depending on what you want.**
7. **Close the Settings window.**

Change the Windows Theme

A Windows theme includes the wallpaper used on the desktop as well as settings such as the standard desktop icons (for example, Computer, Network, and Recycle Bin), the visual styles applied to Windows and apps, the mouse cursors, the screensaver that runs when the computer isn't in use, and the sound scheme applied to the operating system. If you get bored with any of the items that are included in the theme, you can change the theme and freshen things up a bit.

To change the Windows theme, follow these steps:

1. **Open Settings.**
2. **Click Personalization.**

   All the available personalization settings are shown.
3. **Click Themes.**

   The themes-related settings are shown.
4. **Click Theme Settings.**

   The Personalization window opens (see Figure 8-5).
5. **In the Personalization window, click the new theme that you want to apply (see Figure 8-5).**

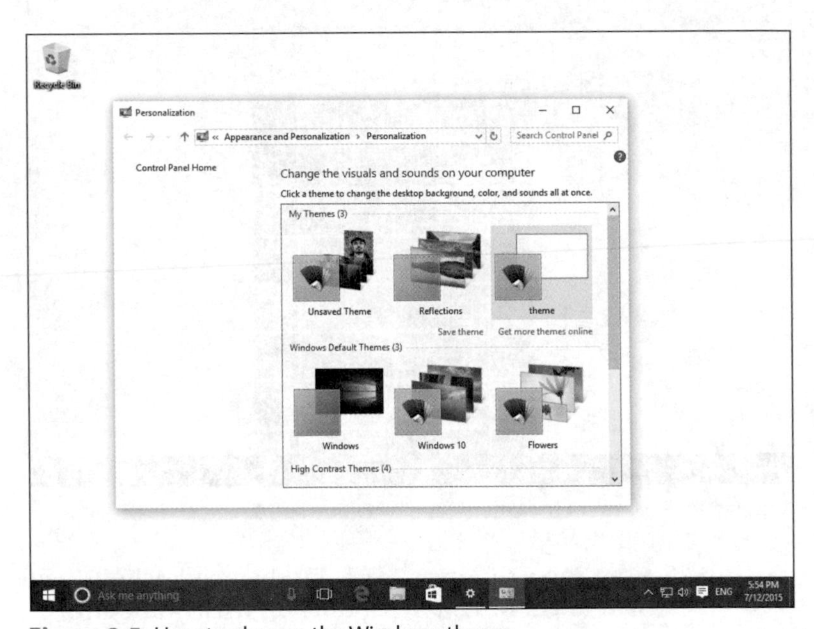

Figure 8-5: How to change the Windows theme.

6. **Close the Personalization window.**
7. **Close Settings.**

If you want access to more diverse Windows themes, try the gallery provided by Microsoft at `http://windows.microsoft.com/en-us/windows/themes`.

Change the Icons Displayed on the Desktop

You can change the icons shown on the desktop. For example, you can enable or disable any of the following icons: Computer, Users' Files, Network, Recycle Bin, and Control Panel. You can also create your own shortcuts on the desktop, just like in previous versions of Windows.

To enable or disable a standard icon on the desktop, follow these steps:

1. **Open Settings.**
2. **Click Personalization.**

   All the available personalization settings are shown.
3. **Click Themes.**

   The themes-related settings are shown.
4. **Click Desktop Icon Settings.**

   A window by the same name opens (see Figure 8-6).
5. **Check the desktop icons that you want to enable (see Figure 8-6).**

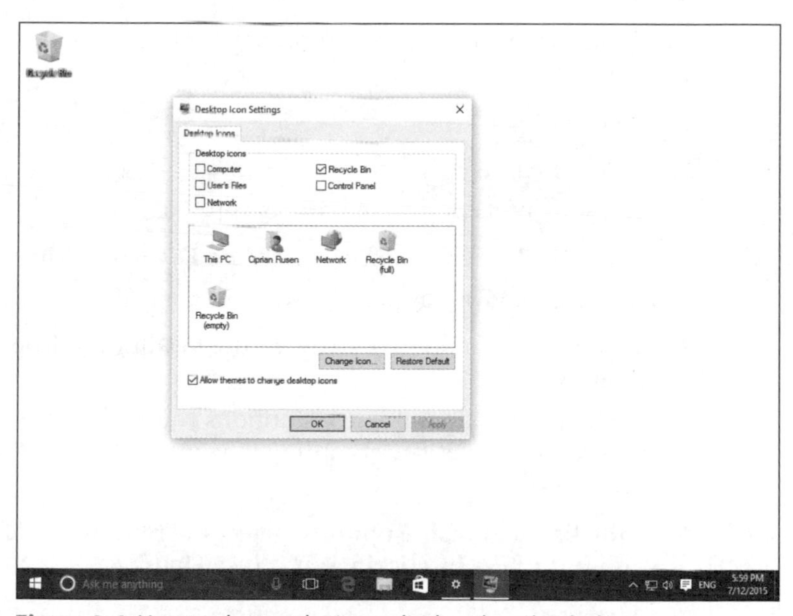

Figure 8-6: How to change the icons displayed on the desktop.

6. **Uncheck the desktop icons that you want to disable.**
7. **Click OK.**
8. **Close Settings.**

Change the Resolution of the Screen

Since the beginning of computers, resolution has been described by the number of pixels arranged horizontally and vertically on a monitor, for example 640 x 480 = 307,200 pixels. The choices were determined by the capability of the video card, and they differed from manufacturer to manufacturer. The resolutions built into Windows were very limited, so if you didn't have the driver for your video card, you were stuck with the lower-resolution screen that Windows provided. As monitor quality improved, Windows began offering a few more built-in options, but the burden was still mostly on the graphics card manufacturers, especially if you wanted a really high-resolution display.

The more recent versions of Windows, such as Windows 10, can detect the default screen resolution for your monitor and graphics card and adjust accordingly. This doesn't mean that what Windows chooses is always the best option, but now it works better than it did. As you expect, you can change the resolution manually. When you do that, you get a preview of what it looks like; you can decide whether you want to keep the new screen resolution.

Here's how to change the resolution of your screen, in Windows 10:

1. **Open Settings.**
2. **Click System.**

   The list of available system settings appears.
3. **In the Display section, click Advanced Display Settings.**

   The Advanced Display Settings window appears.
4. **Click the down-pointing arrow in the Resolution drop-down list.**

   A list appears with multiple resolutions you can choose from. Your options vary according to your display's size and specifications.
5. **In the list of available options, select the resolution that you want to use by clicking on it (see Figure 8-7).**

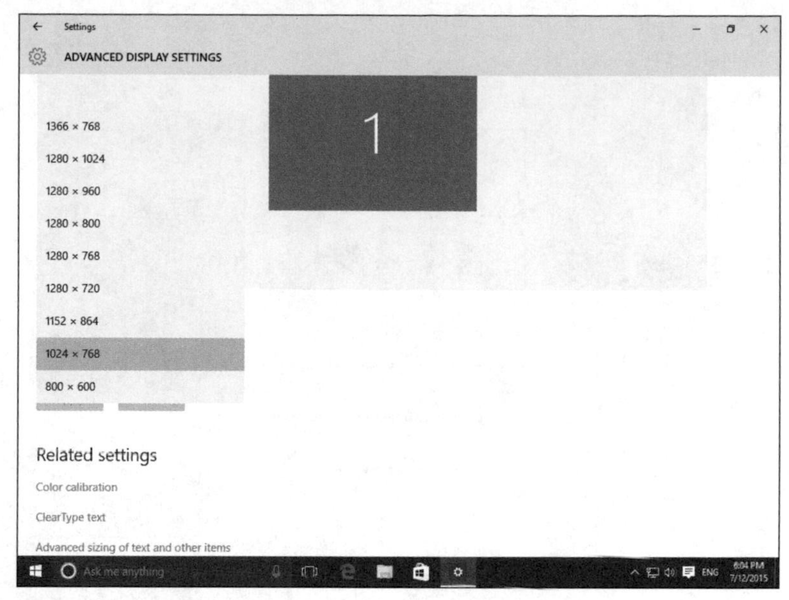

Figure 8-7: How to change the resolution in Windows 10.

6. **Click Apply.**

   The new resolution is applied. You're asked whether you want to keep these displayed settings.

7. **Click Keep Changes.**

8. **Close the Advanced Display Settings window.**

Change the Mouse Pointer Size and Color

If you want to, you can make the mouse pointer bigger and also change its color from white to black. Here's how:

1. **Open Settings.**

2. **Click Ease of Access.**

   The list of available ease of access settings appears.

3. **Click Mouse.**

   The available mouse-related settings appear (see Figure 8-8).

4. **In the Pointer Size section, click the size that you want to use (see Figure 8-8).**

5. **In the Pointer Color section, click the color that you want to use (see Figure 8-8).**

6. **Close Settings.**

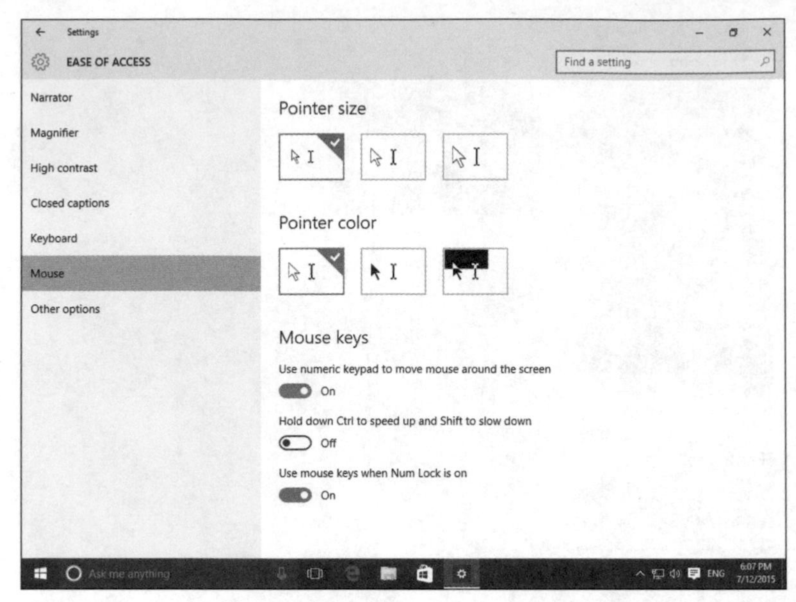

Figure 8-8: How to change the mouse pointer size and color.

Customize the Behavior of the Start Menu

The Start Menu is more customizable in Windows 10 than it was in Windows 7 and Windows XP. In Settings, there's a big section of settings that allow you to decide whether to

- Show your most used apps.
- Show your recently added apps.
- Use the full-screen Start Menu.
- Show recently opened items in Jump Lists on Start or on the taskbar.

Figure 8-9 shows the entire list of settings, which is mostly a list of simple switches that you can turn on or off. There's also a link that opens a new window where you can choose which folders appear on the Start Menu.

To access the settings that allow you to customize how the Start Menu works, follow these steps:

1. **Open Settings.**
2. **Click Personalization.**

   All of the available personalization settings are shown.
3. **Click Start.**

   The previous Start Menu customization options are shown.

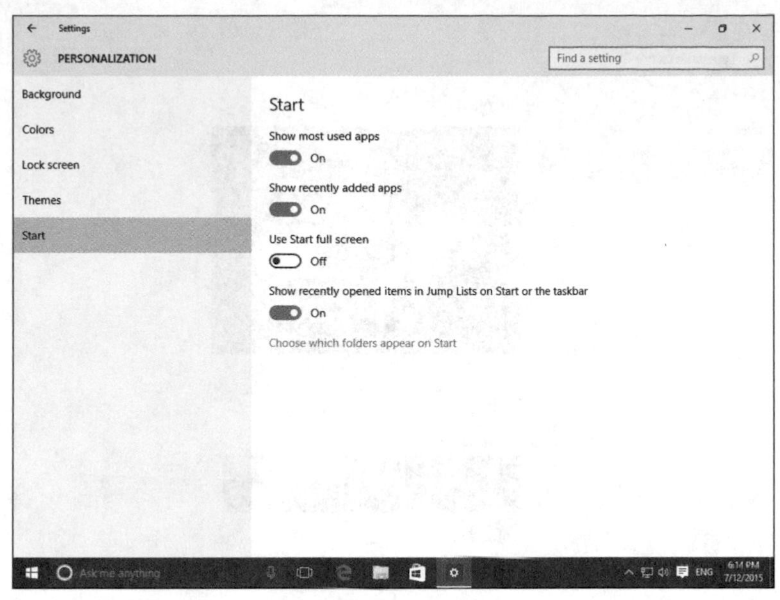

Figure 8-9: The Start Menu customization options.

4. **Set the Start Menu as you want it to behave, using the available switches.**
5. **When done, close Settings.**

If you want to set which folders appear on the Start Menu, start the preceding steps. At Step 4, click Choose Which Folders Appear On Start, then set the folders that you want to appear to On and those that you don't want to appear to Off.

Change the Picture Shown on the Lock Screen

If you're bored with the picture used for the Lock Screen in Windows 10, you can change it. Follow these steps:

1. **Open Settings.**
2. **Click Personalization.**

   All the available personalization settings are shown.
3. **Click Lock screen.**

   The lock screen-related settings are shown.
4. **In the Choose Your Picture section, select another picture from those that are included in Windows 10, by clicking on it (see Figure 8-10).**
5. **Close Settings.**

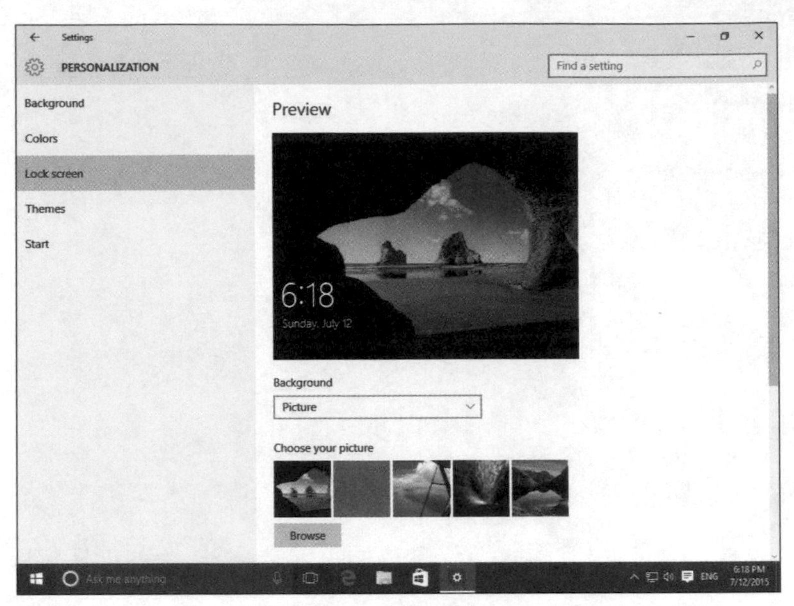

Figure 8-10: How to change the Lock Screen picture in Windows 10.

If you want to use your own picture, at Step 4, click Browse, navigate to the picture that you want to use, click on the picture, then Choose Picture.

Change the Apps That Show Their Status on the Lock Screen

You can set one app that shows its detailed status on the Lock Screen and seven other apps that show a quick status. To change which apps show their status on the Lock Screen, follow these steps:

1. **Open Settings.**
2. **Click Personalization.**

   All the available personalization settings are shown.
3. **Click Lock screen.**

   The lock screen-related settings are shown.
4. **Click the app icon shown in the Choose an App to Show Detailed Status section.**

   A list of apps appears.
5. **Click to select a new app from the list (see Figure 8-11).**

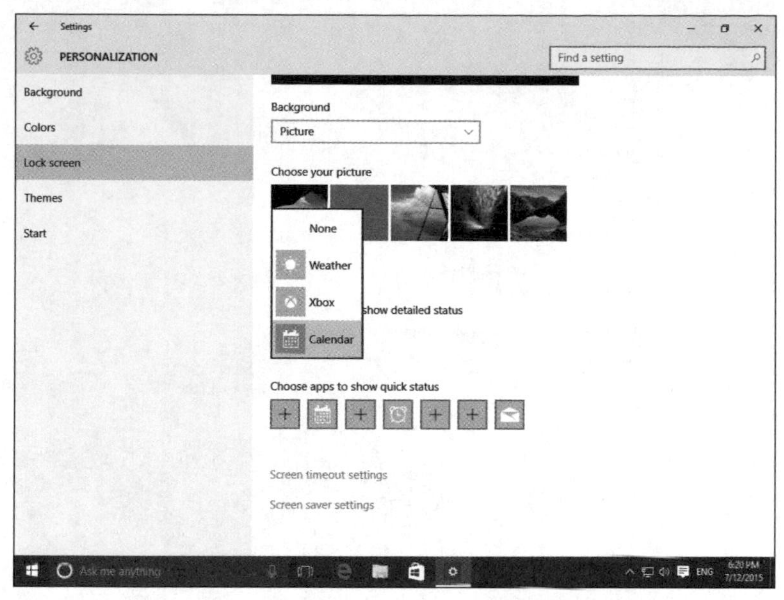

Figure 8-11: How to change the app showing the detailed status on the Lock Screen.

6. **In the Choose Apps to Show Quick Status section, click the icon of an app that you want to change.**

   A list of apps appears.

7. **In the app list, click the replacement app.**

8. **Close the Settings window.**

Customize the Taskbar

Just as in older versions of Windows, in Windows 10, you can customize the taskbar in the following ways:

- Lock the taskbar so that other users can't change it.
- Set the taskbar to auto-hide.
- Set the taskbar to use small buttons.
- Change the taskbar's location on the screen from the bottom to the top, or to the left or right of the screen.
- Set how taskbar buttons appear (either always combined with the labels hidden, or combined only when the taskbar is full, or never combined).
- Set whether to use the Peek feature to preview the desktop when you move your mouse to the Show Desktop button at the end of the taskbar.

Figure 8-12 shows all these settings.

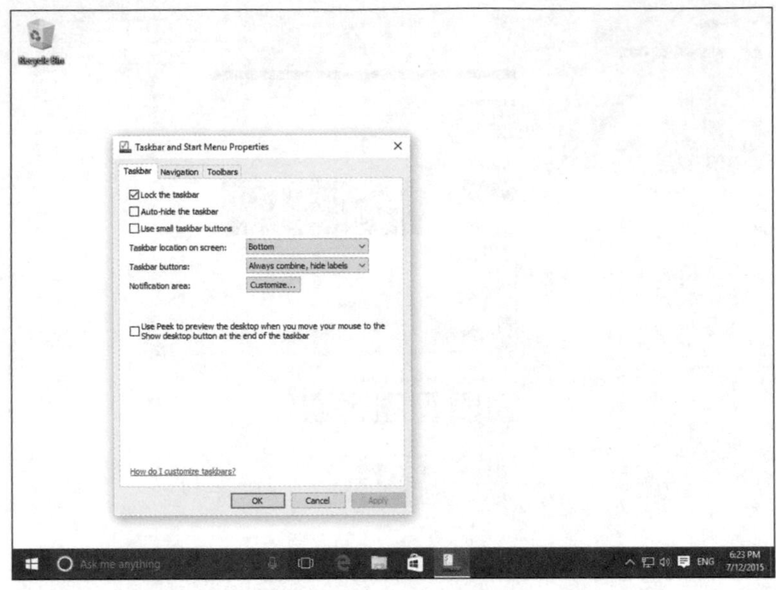

Figure 8-12: The settings for customizing the taskbar.

To customize the taskbar, follow these steps:

1. **Right-click the taskbar.**

   The right-click menu appears.

2. **Click Properties.**

   The Taskbar and Start Menu Properties window appears.

3. **In the Taskbar tab, set how you want the taskbar to behave by checking the available settings.**

4. **Click OK.**

Set Which Icons Appear on the Taskbar

You can customize the settings to show more or fewer icons on the right side of the taskbar. Here's how:

1. **Open Settings.**

2. **Click System.**

   The list of available system settings appears.

3. **Click Notifications & Actions.**

   The settings for notifications and quick actions are shown.

4. **In the Quick Actions section on the Taskbar, click Select Which Icons Appear.**

   A long list of icons is shown. Each has a switch to turn it On or Off.

5. **In the list of icons that appears, set the icons you want displayed to On and the icons you don't want displayed to Off.**

   The icons that you set to On are immediately shown in the Taskbar.

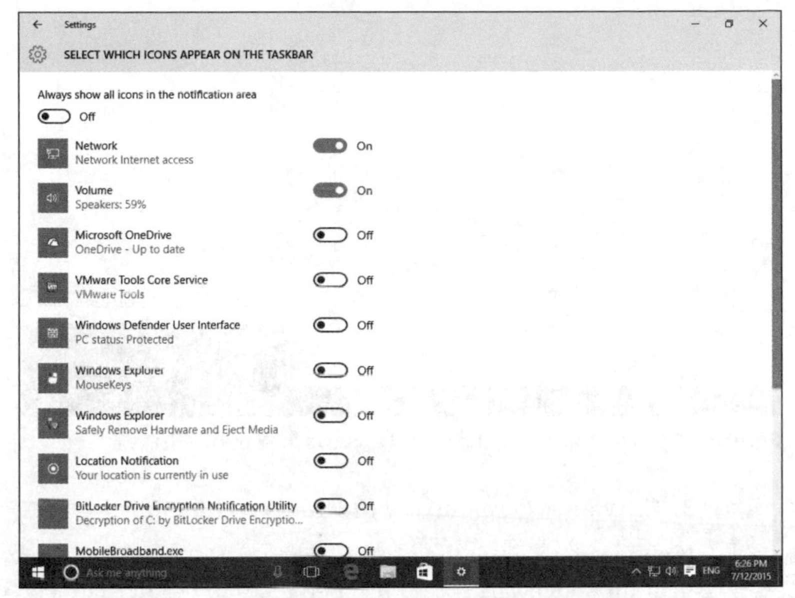

Figure 8-13: How to select which icons appear on the taskbar.

6. **Click the left-pointing arrow (the Back arrow) to go back.**

   The settings for notifications and quick actions are shown.

7. **Click Turn System Icons On or Off, in the Quick Actions section.**

   A list of system icons is shown.

8. **In the list of icons that appears, set the icons you want displayed to On and the icons you don't want displayed to Off.**

   The icons that you set to On are shown in the Taskbar immediately.

9. **Close the Settings window.**

Change the Sound Volume

If you want to change the volume of the speakers to be louder or softer, follow these steps:

1. **Click the Volume icon at the right side of the taskbar.**

   A volume slider appears above the taskbar.

2. **With the mouse, set the slider to the desired sound level (see Figure 8-14).**

Figure 8-14: How to change the sound volume in Windows 10.

3. Click anywhere outside the slider to hide it.

If you want to mute the sound, click the Volume icon shown near the slider. The sound level changes to 0. Alternatively, you can move the volume slider to 0.

Set the Date and Time Manually

Windows 10 automatically sets the date and time with servers on the Internet or on your company's network, depending on how it's set. However, you can also manually change the date and time, like this:

1. **Open Settings.**
2. **Click Time & Language.**

   The list of time- and language-related settings appears.
3. **In the Date & Time section, set the Set Time Automatically switch to Off and click Change.**

   The Change Date and Time window appears.
4. **Set the date and time you want to use; then click Change (see Figure 8-15).**
5. **Close the Settings window.**

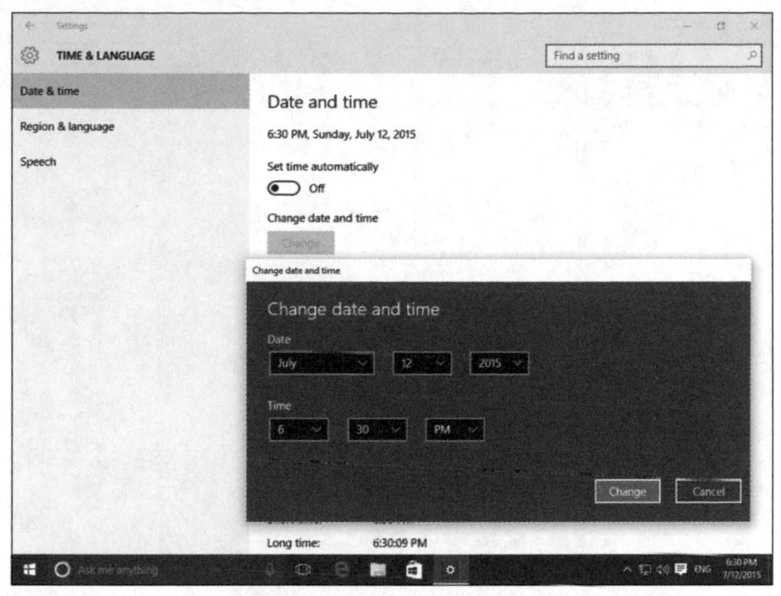

Figure 8-15: How to change the date and time in Windows 10.

Set the Time Zone

If you travel a lot, you can change the time zone when you arrive in a new country or in an area with a different time zone than your usual one. To change the time zone, follow these steps:

1. **Open Settings.**
2. **Click Time & Language.**

   The list of time and language related settings appears.
3. **In the Date & Time section, click the down-pointing arrow in Time Zone drop-down list.**

   A list appears with all the time zones.
4. **Click the time zone that you want to use.**

   The time zone is now changed.
5. **Close the Settings window.**

When you get back home, change the time zone again so that Windows and its apps use and display the correct time.

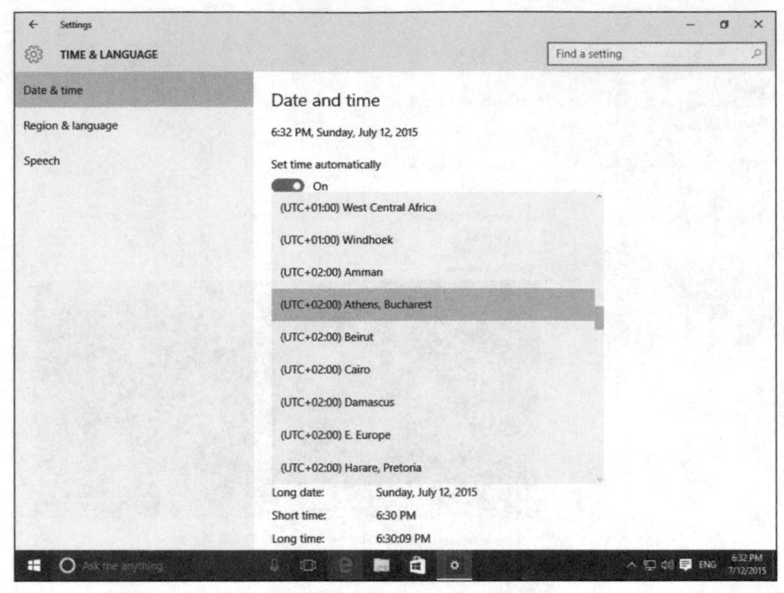

Figure 8-16: How to set the time zone in Windows 10.

Set the Country You're In

Some Windows apps might use your country or region to display local content that's personalized for you. For these apps to display the correct content, you need to set the country you're in. Follow these steps:

1. **Open Settings.**
2. **Click Time & Language.**

   The list of time- and language-related settings appears.
3. **Click Region & Language.**

   The settings for configuring the country, region, and languages are shown (see Figure 8-17).
4. **Find the Country or Region section and click the down-pointing arrow in the box labeled Window and Apps Might Use Your Country or Region to Give You Local Content.**

   A list of all the countries in the world appears.
5. **Click the country that you're in.**
6. **Close the Settings window.**

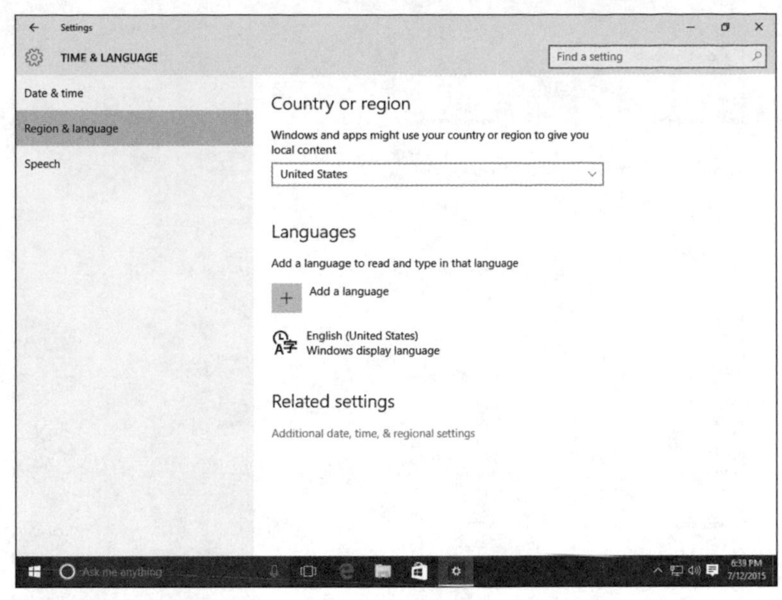

Figure 8-17: How to change the country you're in.

Add a Keyboard Input Language

If you frequently work with multiple languages, you may want to add a keyboard input language or two. To add a keyboard input language, follow these steps:

1. **Open Settings.**
2. **Click Time & Language.**

   The list of time- and language-related settings appears.
3. **Click Region & Language.**

   The settings for configuring the country, region, and languages are shown
4. **In the Languages section, click the + button beside Add a Language.**

   The Add A Language window appears, showing all the available languages.
5. **Scroll the list of languages until you find the one that you're looking for.**
6. **Click the language that you want to add.**

   A list with multiple dialects of that language appears.

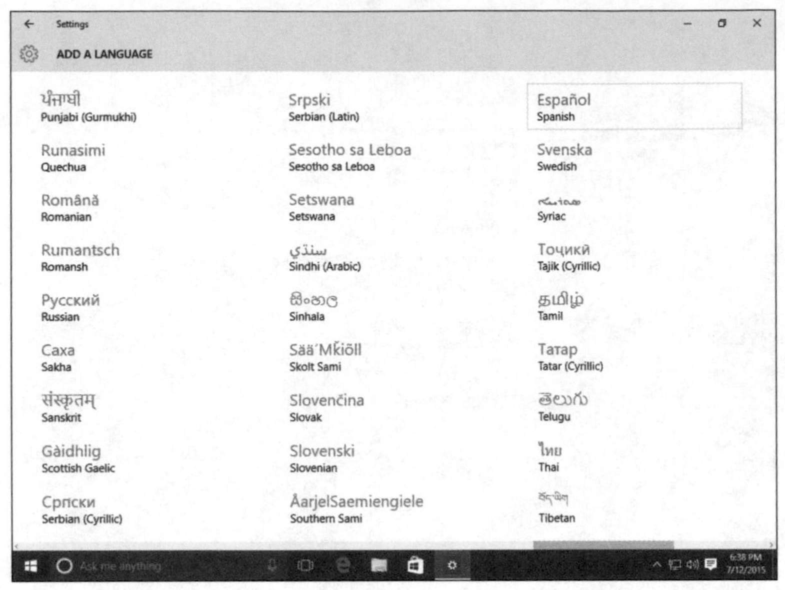

Figure 8-18: How to add a keyboard input language.

7. **Click the dialect that you want to add.**

   You're informed that a new feature is added to Windows. The language is downloaded in the background; you can resume using Windows.

8. **Close Settings.**

   Now you can use the added keyboard input language.

Download a Language Pack

Using Windows Update, you can install a language pack for languages other than your own. After you download a language pack and activate it, the Windows 10 operating system is translated into that language. Depending on the language, either the entire operating system is translated or only part of it. When no translation is available, Windows 10 uses English to display the elements that haven't been translated by Microsoft.

In order to install a language pack, you need to first install the keyboard input language using the procedure in the preceding section of this chapter. Once the keyboard input language is installed, you can use only the new language to type. In order to translate the entire operating system, follow these steps to install the language pack:

1. **Open Settings.**
2. **Click Time & Language.**

   The list of time- and language-related settings appears.

3. **Click Region & Language.**

   The settings for configuring the country, region, and languages are shown

4. **Click the language for the language pack you want to install.**

5. **Click Options (see Figure 8-19).**

   A new window appears with several language options.

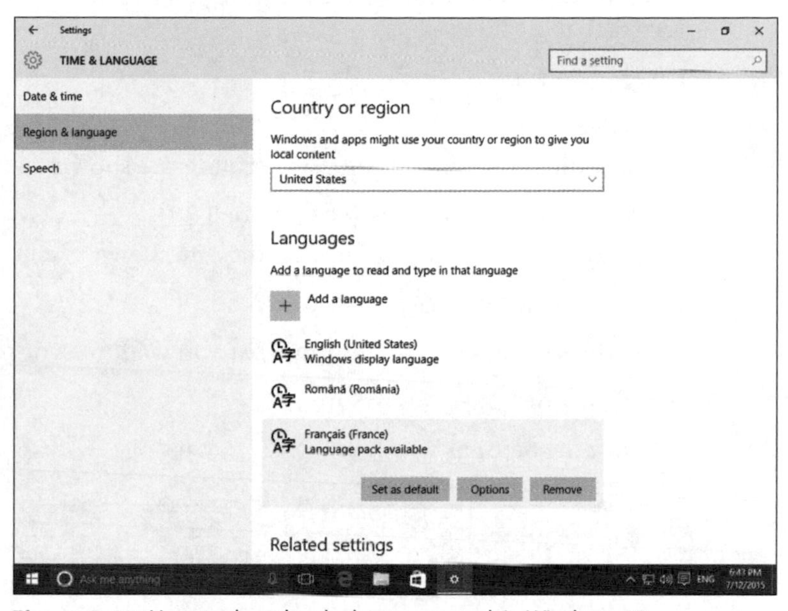

Figure 8-19: How to download a language pack in Windows 10.

6. **Find the Download button in the Language Options section.**

7. **Click the Download button to begin the installation.**

   Be patient, as the download takes a while.

   When the install is complete, you receive a message to that effect.

8. **Close the Settings window.**

At Step 4, the languages which have a language pack available to download and install are marked by a line of text that says: "Language pack available". If a language pack isn't mentioned as being available for a particular language, then you can't download a language pack for it. You can use that language only as a keyboard input language, not as a display language.

Set Which Settings Are Synchronized

If you're using a Microsoft account, you can customize Windows 10 to automatically synchronize settings for you across all your Windows 10 devices. By default, Windows 10 synchronizes the following elements: the Windows theme, the web browser settings for Internet Explorer and Microsoft Edge, your passwords, language preferences, ease of access settings, among others.

You can adjust settings to sync with your other Windows 10 devices. Follow these steps:

1. **Open Settings.**
2. **Click Accounts.**

   The settings for configuring user accounts are shown.
3. **Click Sync Your Settings (see Figure 8-20).**

   The available synchronization settings are shown.
4. **Set the Sync Settings switch to On.**
5. **Set the switches for the settings that you want to sync to On.**
6. **Set the other switches to Off.**
7. **Close the Settings window.**

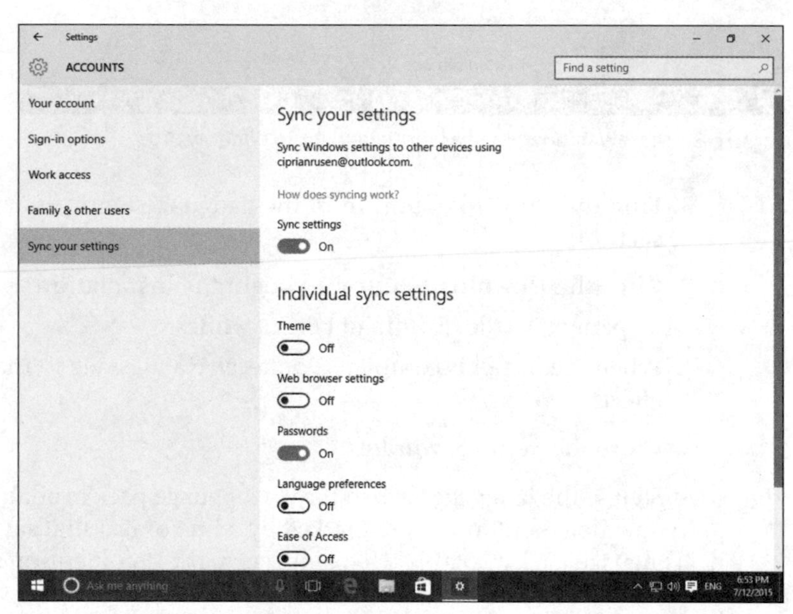

Figure 8-20: How to customize settings that Windows 10 synchronizes.

CHAPTERNINE

Using Mail and Calendar

The Mail and Calendar apps in Windows 10 have been completely redesigned since Windows 8. Personally, I like the new apps a lot more. They work better, and they're easier to use. If your company has chosen to use them as the default email and calendar apps, your email account is preconfigured on them. That's why, in this chapter, I don't show you how to set up your email account; instead, I get right into using these apps. If the Mail app isn't already configured and you're asked to use it as your email client, ask your company's IT support department or the network administrator for help.

You also find out how to create and send an email message with the Mail app, how to attach a file to your message, how to reply to emails, and how to forward them. Then you see how to switch between folders in the Mail app and how to quickly search for an email message without having to scroll a lot.

Finally, I cover the new Calendar app from Windows 10 and show you how to browse and add new events to your calendar.

In This Chapter

- Creating and sending emails with the Mail app
- Attaching files to your emails
- Replying to emails
- Forwarding emails
- Navigating your email's account folders
- Using search to find an email message
- Browsing your Calendar
- Adding a new event to the Calendar app

Create and Send an Email Message

In order to create an email message and send it with the Windows 10 Mail app, follow these steps:

1. **Click the Windows logo (Start button).**

   The Start Menu appears.

2. **Click All Apps.**
3. **In the list that appears, click Mail.**

   The Mail app window appears.

4. **Click the + button (known as the New Email button) located at the top-left corner of the Mail app window, just to the left of the Inbox column.**

   The tools for writing a new message are loaded on the right side of the Mail app window.

5. **In the To field, type the email address of the person you're sending the email to.**
6. **In the Subject field, type the subject of the email message.**
7. **In the body of the email, type your message.**
8. **Click Send (see Figure 9-1).**

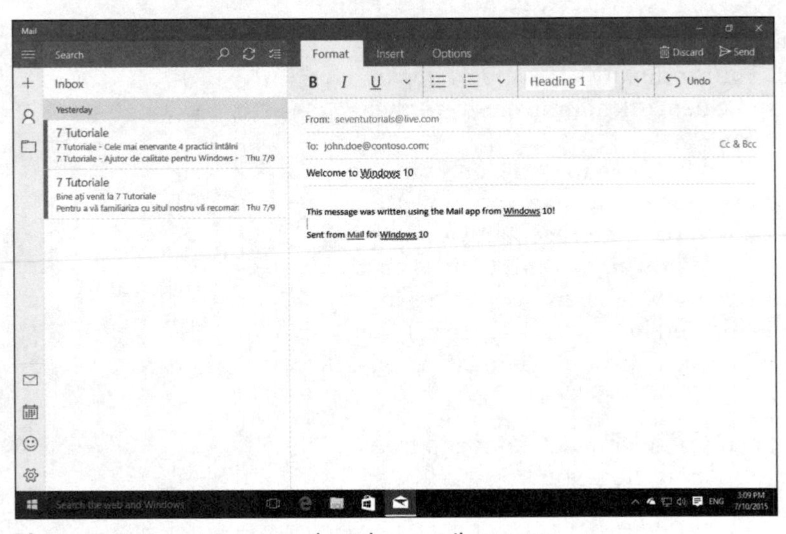

Figure 9-1: How to create and send an email message.

You can type more than one email address, separated by semicolons, in the To field.

Attach a File to an Email Message

As with any email program, you can attach files to your email messages in the Windows 10 Mail app. Here's how it works:

1. **Create a new email message.**
2. **Complete the email address of the person you want to send it to, as well as the subject and the message, as in the previous section.**
3. **Click the Insert tab (see Figure 9-2).**

   The Insert tab appears with all its options.

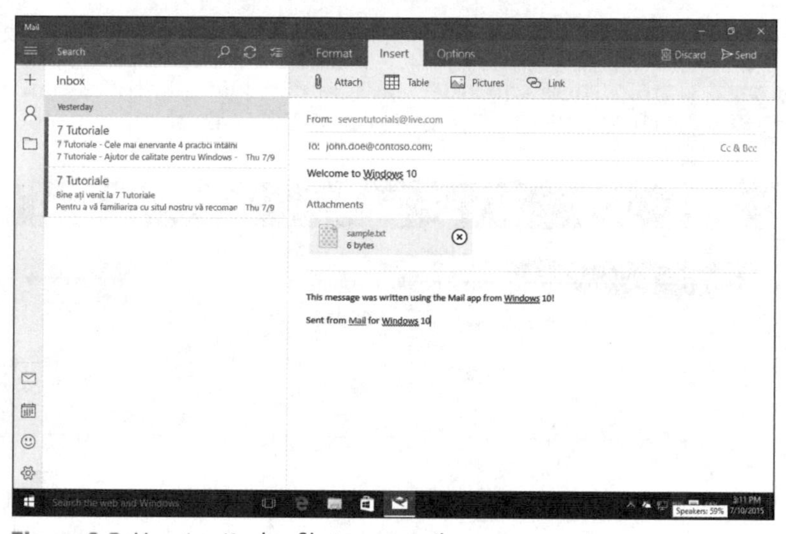

Figure 9-2: How to attach a file to an email message.

4. **Click Attach.**

   The Open window appears. It lists files from your computer.
5. **Browse your PC to find the file that you want to attach.**
6. **Select that file; then click Open.**
7. **Click Send.**

You can attach more than one file to the same email message. Either repeat the preceding steps for each file or press and hold the Ctrl key while you click each file you want to attach.

Reply to an Email Message

When you receive a message from someone, you often want to send a reply. If the email was sent to more than one person, you can opt to reply to everyone who received the email, not only the person who sent it.

Here's how to reply to an email message from the Mail app:

1. **Open the email message that you want to reply to by clicking it.**
2. **On the top-right corner of the Mail app window, click the Reply button (see Figure 9-3).**

If you want to reply to all the recipients of the email, click Reply All instead of Reply. But be very sure you want to do this. There's no faster way to annoy a lot of people than by clicking Reply All when you really meant to click Reply.

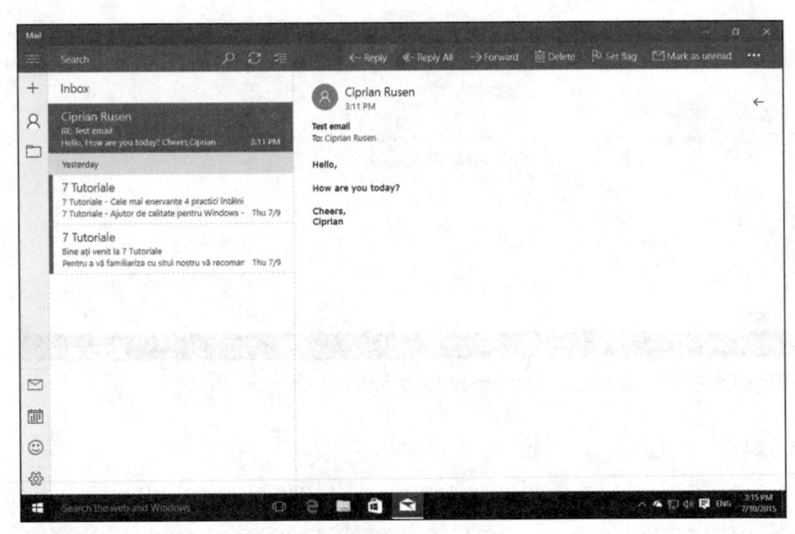

Figure 9-3: How to reply to an email message.

3. **Type your reply.**
4. **Click Send.**

Forward an Email Message

You may receive a message that you want to forward to a colleague. If so, follow these steps:

1. **Open the email message that you want to forward by clicking it.**

2. **On the top-right corner of the Mail app window, click the Forward button (see Figure 9-4).**

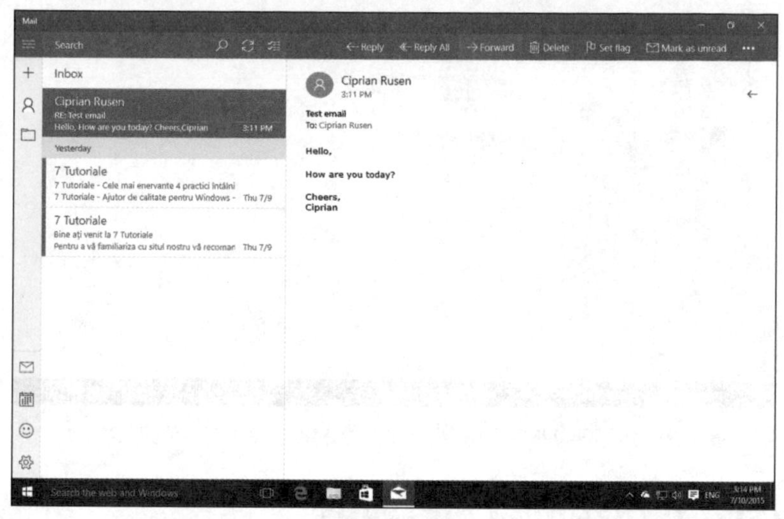

Figure 9-4: How to forward an email message.

3. **In the To field, type the email address of the person you want to forward the email message to.**
4. **If you want to add a message with the forwarded email, type it in the body of the message.**
5. **Click Send.**

Change the Folder You're Viewing in Mail

When you open the Mail app, it automatically shows your Inbox. If you want to navigate to another folder, such as your Sent folder, follow these steps:

1. **Open the Mail app.**
2. **Click the All Folders button on the left side of the Mail app window (see Figure 9-5).**

   This button is shaped like a folder.

3. **Click the folder that you want to use.**

To get back to the Inbox, repeat the preceding steps and, at Step 3, click Inbox.

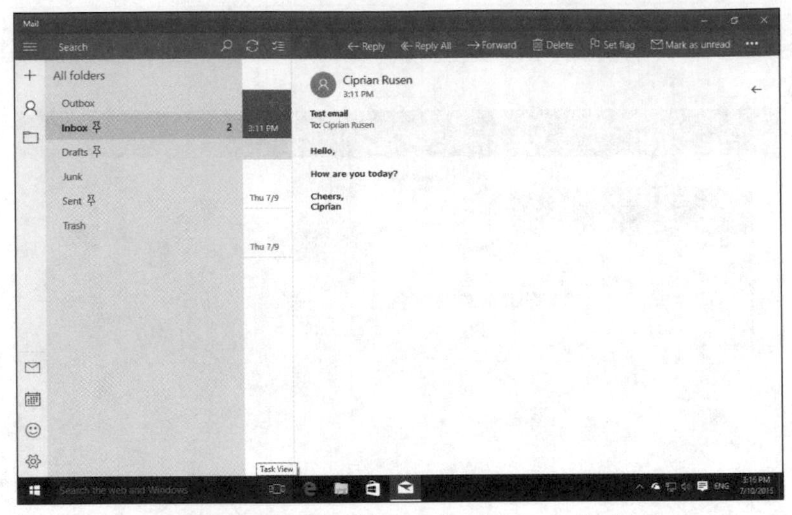

Figure 9-5: How to change the folder you're viewing in the Mail app.

Search for an Email Message

If you need to find an older message and don't want to scroll through your Inbox to find it, you can use search, like this:

1. **Open the Mail app.**
2. **Click inside the Search box at the top of the Mail app window.**
3. **Type the keyword(s) that you want to use to find the older message.**
4. **Click the Search button or press Enter on your keyboard (refer to Figure 9-6).**

   The list of search results appears.

5. **Click the email that you want to open.**

   The email's contents appear on the right side of the Mail app window.

To get back to your Inbox, click the X button alongside the Search box.

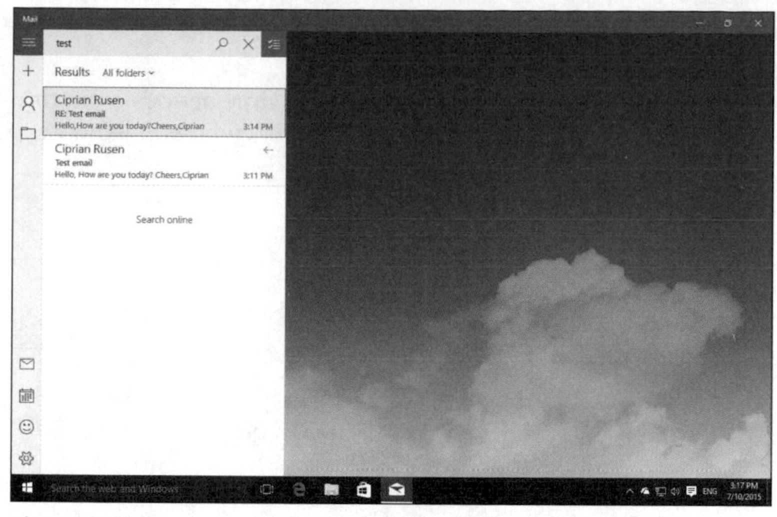

Figure 9-6: How to search for an email message in the Mail app.

Browse the Calendar

You can access the Calendar app from the Mail app by clicking the Switch to Calendar button (it looks like a calendar) or by starting from the Start Menu, just like you do with the Mail app. Once you open the Calendar, you can browse your meetings and events. The default Calendar view is by Month. The app shows you all the events that are scheduled during the current month (see Figure 9-7).

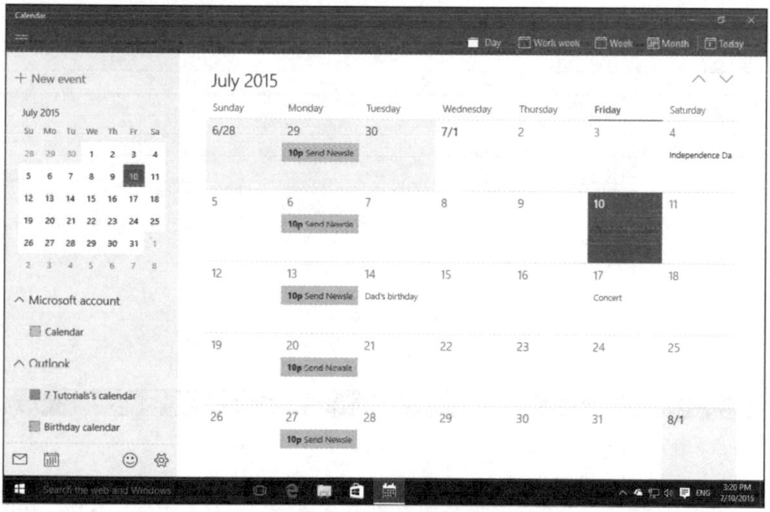

Figure 9-7: The Calendar displays your events during the current month.

To instantly see today's schedule, go to the toolbar and click Today.

To divide the Calendar into specific time periods, click one of the available buttons at the top of the Calendar app window to show your schedule by either

- Day (single day)
- Work week (Monday to Friday)
- Week (Sunday to Saturday)
- Month

Add a New Event to Your Calendar

To add a new appointment to your Calendar, follow these steps:

1. **Open the Calendar app.**
2. **Click the New Event button at the upper-left side of the Calendar app window.**

   The New Event button is preceded by a + sign (refer to Figure 9-7).
3. **In the Event Name field, type the name of the event (see Figure 9-8).**

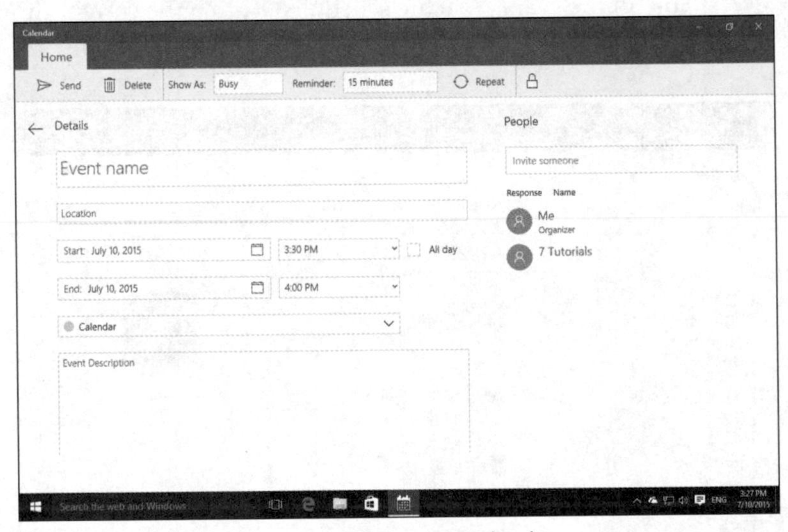

Figure 9-8: How to add a new event to your Calendar.

4. **If the event takes place in a specific location, type that information in the Location field.**
5. **Set the Start date and time.**

6. Set the End date and time.
7. In the Event Description field, type the description of the event.
8. In the People field, enter separately the email addresses of the people you want to invite.
9. In the Reminder field, select when you want to be reminded about the event.
10. Click Send.

CHAPTERTEN

Using Skype

Skype is the world's best-known application for making audio and video calls from computers and all kinds of mobile devices via the Internet. With Skype, you can send instant messages, exchange files, create conference calls, and speak with people all over the world. You can also use it to call landline and mobile phones, but this feature is available only if you purchase Skype Credit or a subscription to Office 365.

Skype is available for free in Windows 10. This chapter covers the free version, which you can use for such tasks as starting conversations, audio and video calls, group calls, and transferring files. However, many companies use Skype for Business. This is an improved version of Skype that's designed for business users, and it's integrated with Office. With Skype for Business, you can find anyone in your company, schedule meetings in Outlook, have meetings of up to 250 people instead of the usual 25, and benefit from enterprise-grade security and management of employee accounts. However, because Skype for Business isn't bundled by default with Windows 10, this chapter covers only the free version.

In This Chapter

- Starting and using Skype
- Sending, editing, and removing instant messages
- Transferring files via Skype
- Starting audio and video calls
- Starting group calls
- Sharing your screen in calls
- Improving the way Skype works

Start Skype

There are many ways to start Skype in Windows 10, and by default, a Skype shortcut appears on the Start Menu. If, however, you don't find Skype there, here's a way to start it no matter how your Windows 10 computer or device is set up:

1. **Click Start to open the Start Menu.**
2. **Click All Apps.**
3. **Scroll down the alphabetized list of apps to find the Skype folder (see Figure 10-1).**

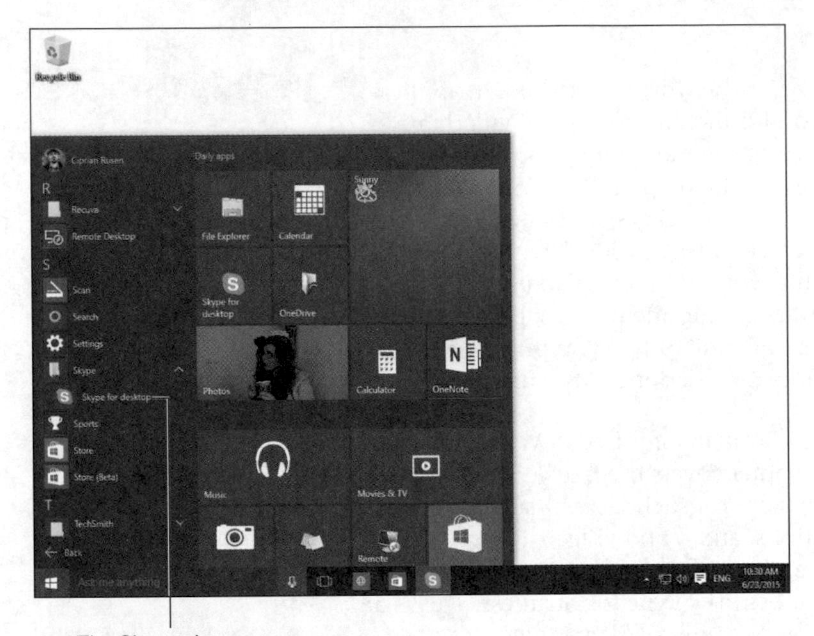

Figure 10-1: The Skype shortcut.

4. **Click this folder.**
5. **Click the Skype for desktop shortcut.**

You can also start Skype using the Search feature. In the search box on the Windows 10 taskbar, type **Skype** and then click the appropriate search result.

Navigate the User Interface

When you start Skype, you have to sign in to your Microsoft or Skype account. Once that's out of the way, you can start using the app. The Skype window has these interface elements:

- **A toolbar on the top.** The toolbar on top of the Skype window has shortcuts to these menus: Skype, Contacts, Conversation, Call, View, Tools and Help.
- **A column on the left side.** The left-side column of the Skype window has these shortcuts:
  - Your Skype account
  - A search box
  - The shortcut for the Home screen
  - A shortcut for calling phones and your list of contacts, split in two: all your contacts and your recent contacts (meaning the people that you have recently talked to)
- **A column on the right side.** The right-side column of the Skype window shows the content of what you select in the left-side column. For example, if you click your Skype account, it shows details about your account, including your Skype credit and subscription. If you click on a contact, it shows you the conversation you last had with that person, and so on.

Figure 10-2 shows the Skype app window.

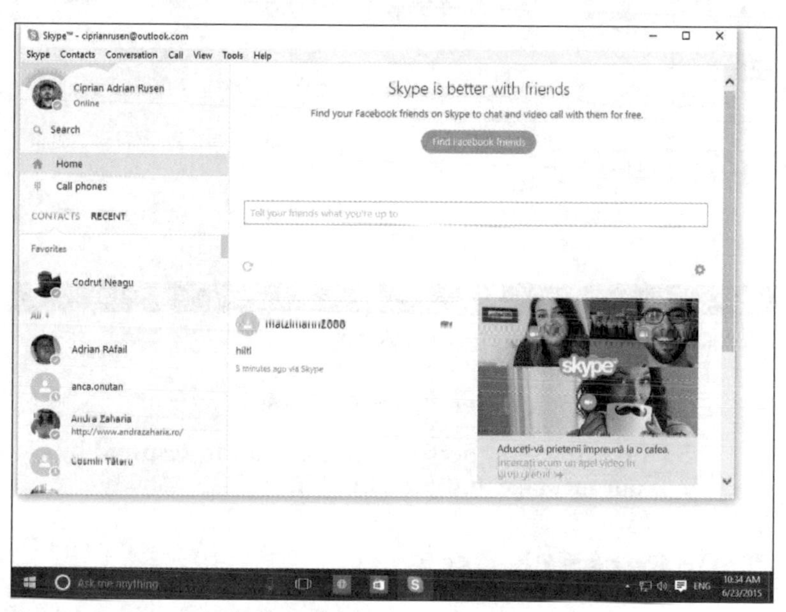

Figure 10-2: The Skype app window.

If you marked some contacts as favorites, your list of contacts will include a Favorites section. Also, near Contacts, there's a button named Recent. If you click on it, you see only the contacts that you have recently talked to.

Microsoft offers also a web version of Skype. You can access it at `https://web.skype.com`.

Chat on Skype

Starting a chat on Skype is really easy. Follow these steps:

1. **Start Skype and sign in to your account.**
2. **Go to your list of contacts and click the name of the person you want to talk to.**

   The chat window opens on the right side.
3. **In the chat window, type your message.**

Figure 10-3 shows a happy user chatting with others on Skype.

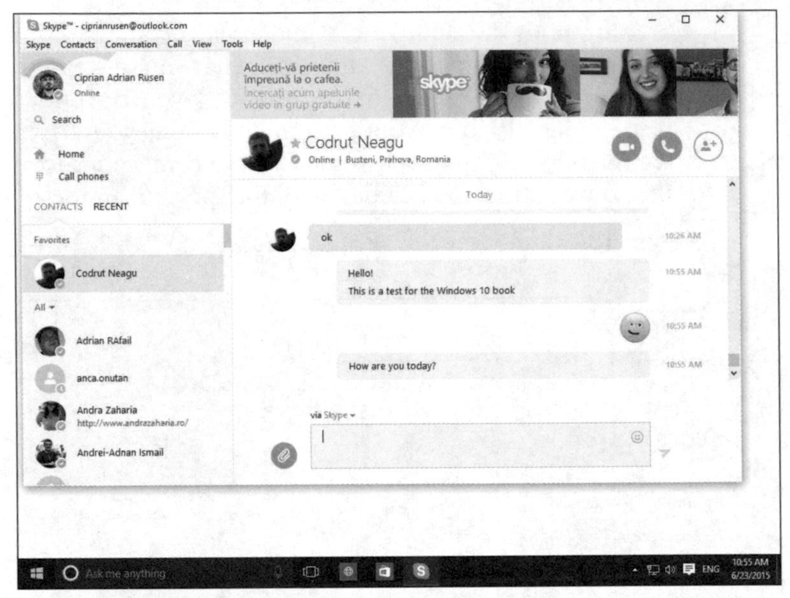

Figure 10-3: Chatting with others on Skype.

4. **Press Enter to send your message.**
5. **After the other person replies, you can respond by typing your message and pressing Enter.**

Edit Your Recent Messages

Skype allows you to edit or delete instant messages within 60 minutes after you send them.

You can edit or delete messages only from the computer or device that you used for sending the original message.

To edit a message that you sent recently over Skype, follow these steps:

1. **In the chat window, move your cursor over the message that you want to edit.**
2. **Right-click that message.**

   The right-click menu appears It contains several contextual options.
3. **In the right-click menu, click Edit Message (see Figure 10-4).**

   The message that you want to edit appears at the bottom of the chat window, where you type your messages.

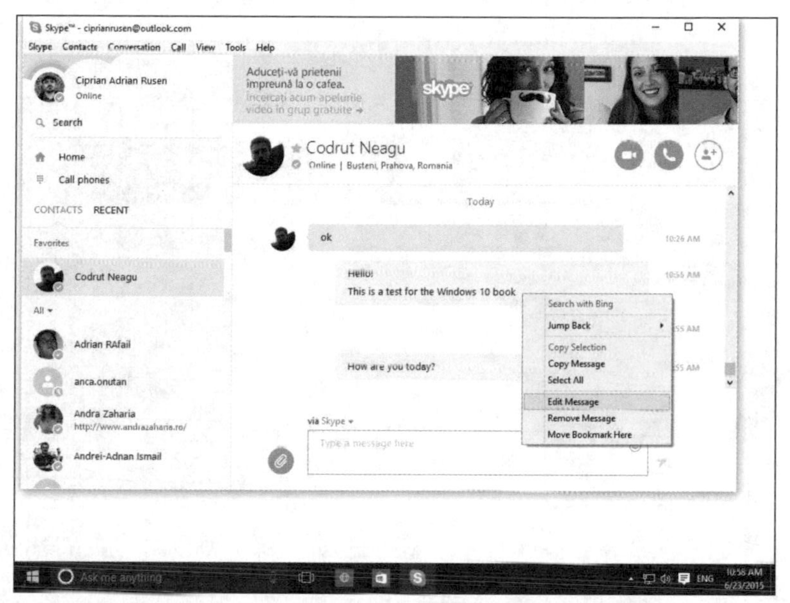

Figure 10-4: The menu for editing and removing recent messages.

4. **Edit the message.**
5. **Press Enter to send your edited message.**

   The previous message is changed according to your edits.

Remove Your Recent Messages

Skype allows you to delete an instant message within 60 minutes after you send it.

Permit me to repeat: You can do edits and deletions only from the computer or device that you used for sending the original message.

To remove a message that you sent recently over Skype, follow these steps:

1. **In the chat window, move your cursor over the message that you want to delete.**
2. **Right-click that message.**

   The right-click menu appears. It contains several contextual options.
3. **In the right-click menu, click Remove Message (see Figure 10-5).**

   Skype issues a notification that the message will be removed. You need to confirm that you want this.
4. **Click Remove to confirm.**

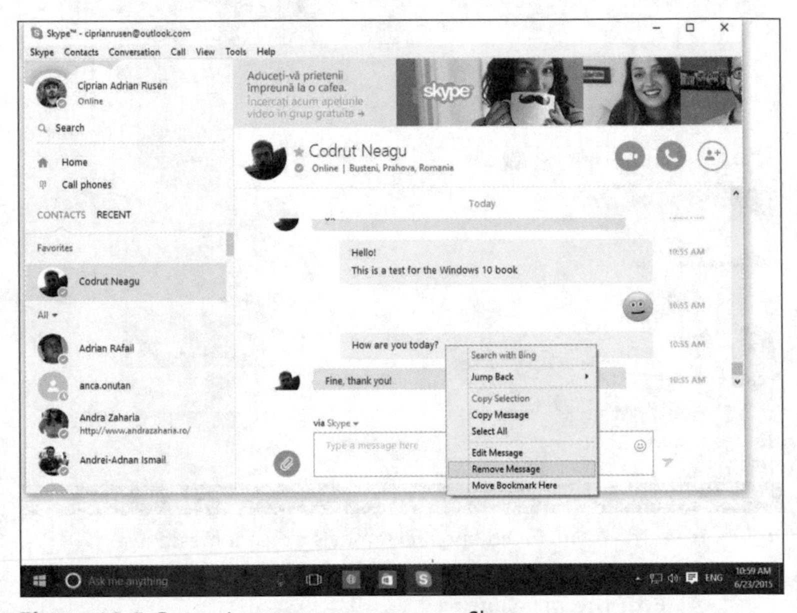

Figure 10-5: Removing recent messages on Skype.

Transfer Files

When communicating with others on Skype, you may need to transfer files. To send a file to the person you're talking to, follow these steps:

1. **In the chat window, click the Send Contacts and Media button.**

   The button is in the shape of a staple. It's on the left side of the box where you enter your messages when chatting with someone.

   A menu appears.

2. **In the menu that appears, click Send File (see Figure 10-6).**

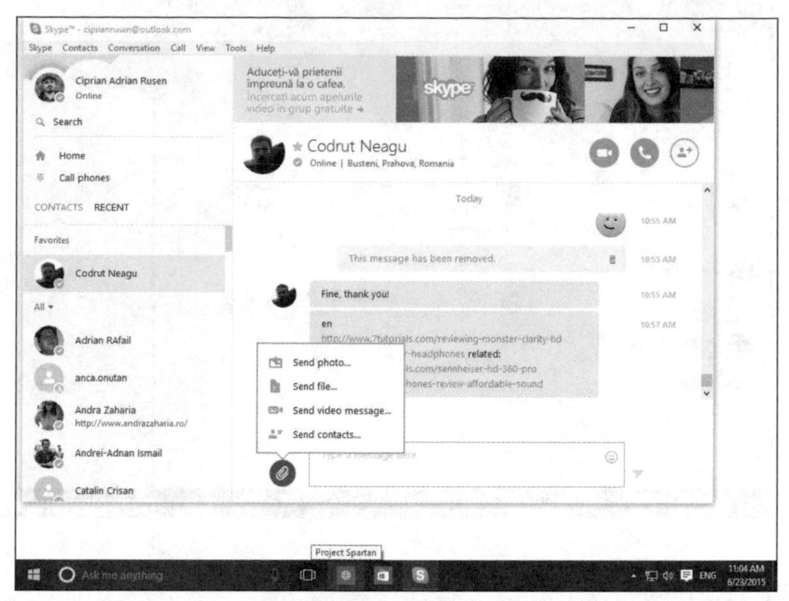

Figure 10-6: The Send File option in Skype.

3. **Browse to the file that you want to send, select it, and then click Open.**

   Now you just wait for the file to be accepted and downloaded by the other person.

Start an Audio Call on Skype

If you want to call somebody and have a verbal conversation using Skype, you need to connect a microphone or webcam to your Windows 10 device. Then you just follow these steps:

1. **Start Skype and sign in to your account.**
2. **Go to your list of contacts and click the name of the person you want to talk to.**

   The chat window opens on the right side.
3. **In the chat window, click the Call button (see Figure 10-7) and then click Call Skype.**
4. **When the other person answers the call, you start talking into your computer's microphone.**
5. **To close the conversation, move your mouse over the call window and click the red End Call button.**

   The button looks like a telephone handset that is ready to hang up.

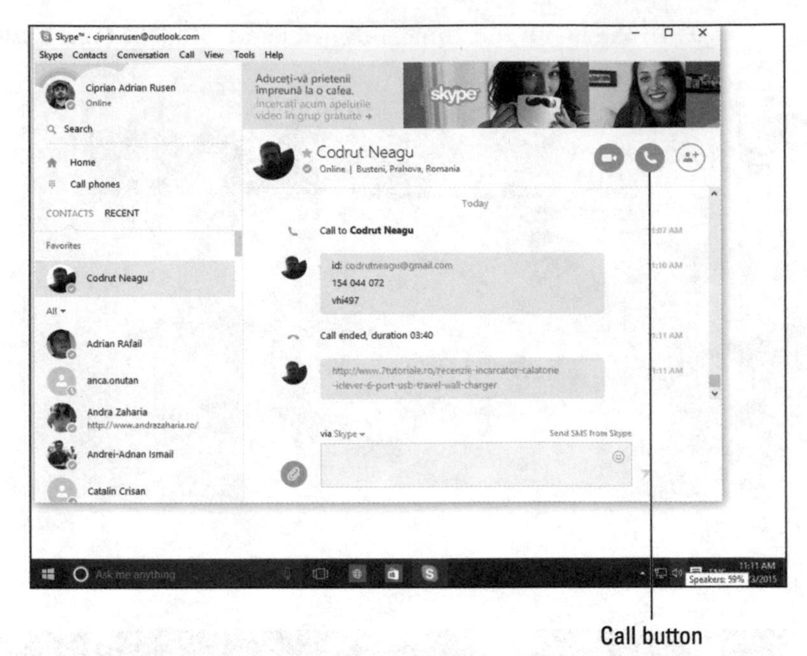

Figure 10-7: The Call button in Skype.

The person on the other end may pick up your call and answer with audio, or with video, or with both audio and video. However, you aren't streaming video to the other person. You're only using your microphone for a standard audio call. The other person may choose to turn off the video stream at any time.

Start a Video Call on Skype

If you have a webcam available on your Windows 10 computer or device, you can use it for video calls on Skype. To start a video call with another person, follow these steps:

1. **Start Skype and sign in to your account.**
2. **Go to your list of contacts and click the name of the person you want to talk to.**

   The chat window opens on the right side.
3. **In the chat window, click the Video Call button (see Figure 10-8).**
4. **When the other person picks up the call, start talking into your computer's microphone.**

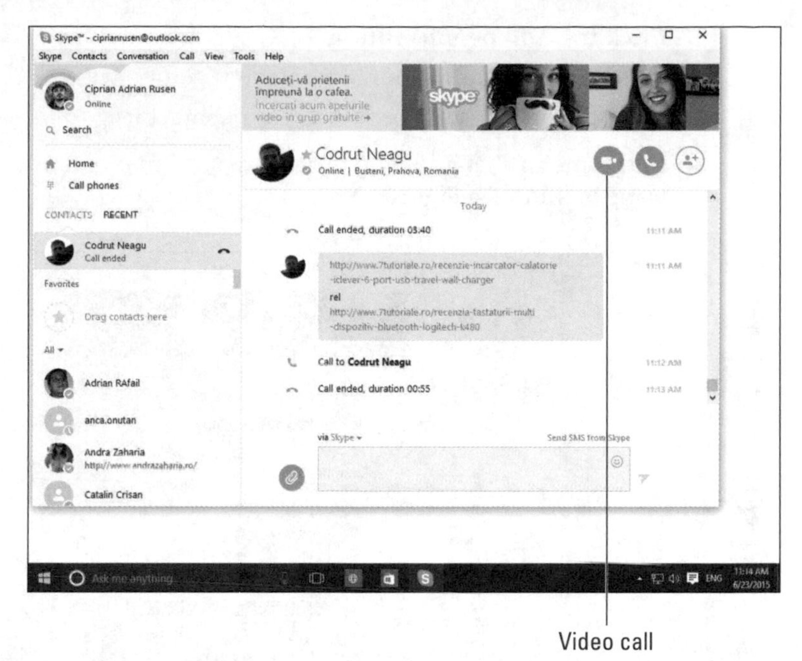

Figure 10-8: The Video Call button in Skype.

5. **To end the conversation, move your mouse over the call window and click the red End Call button.**

   The button looks like a telephone handset that is ready to hang up.

The person on the other end may answer with audio. The other person isn't obligated to use video to answer a video call. If you don't want to continue using video, you can turn it off by clicking the Video Call button. Then, until you press the End Call button, the conversation will continue using audio.

Start a Group Call on Skype

You can use Skype to make group calls of up to 25 people, for free. These calls can be audio or video or a mix of the two. For example, some people may join the group using only video, and others may use only audio. All parties can also type messages that are shown to all the participants in the group call.

To start a group call, follow these steps:

1. **Start Skype and sign in to your account.**
2. **Go to your list of contacts and click the name of the first person you want to talk to.**

   The chat window opens on the right side.

3. **Click the Add people button.**

   This button is the symbol of a person together with a + sign.

   A menu appears, with people in your contact list.

4. **In the menu that appears, select the participants that you want to add (see Figure 10-9).**

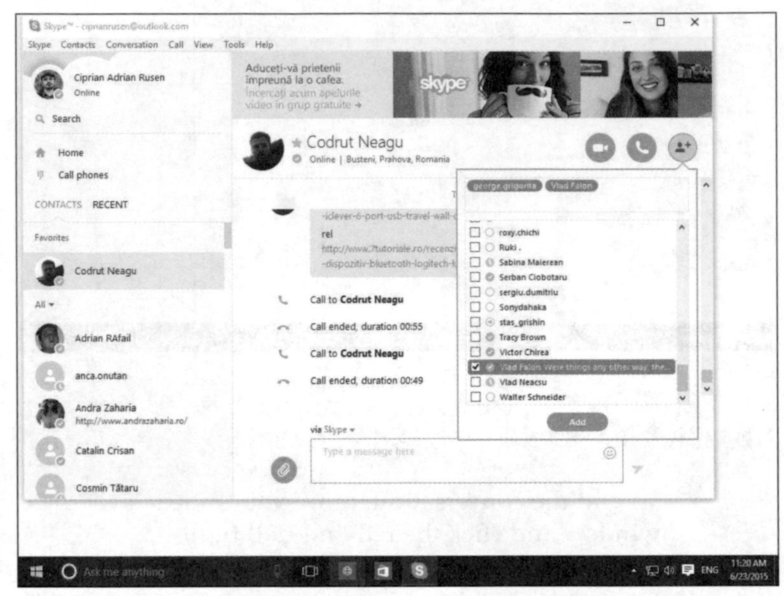

Figure 10-9: Selecting the participants to a Skype group call.

5. **Click Add.**

   You're on your way to a group text conversation.

6. **Start your call:**

   - To start a video call, click the Video Call button.
   - To start an audio call, click the Call Group button.

7. **When the other people pick up the call, start talking into your computer's microphone.**

8. **To end the conversation, move your mouse over the call window and click the red End Call button.**

   The button looks like a telephone handset that is ready to hang up.

Share Your Screen

When you're in an audio or video call with others, you can share your device screen with them.

Sharing is especially useful when you have to collaborate on a document or project with others. They can see what you're working on.

To share your screen on Skype, follow these steps:

1. **Start Skype and sign in to your account.**
2. **Start an audio call or a video call with another person or a group of people.**
3. **Move your mouse over the call window to bring up several buttons with actions that can be performed during the call.**
4. **Click the + button.**
5. **In the menu that is shown, click Share screens (see Figure 10-10).**

   You're asked to confirm that you want to share your screen and how you want to share it.

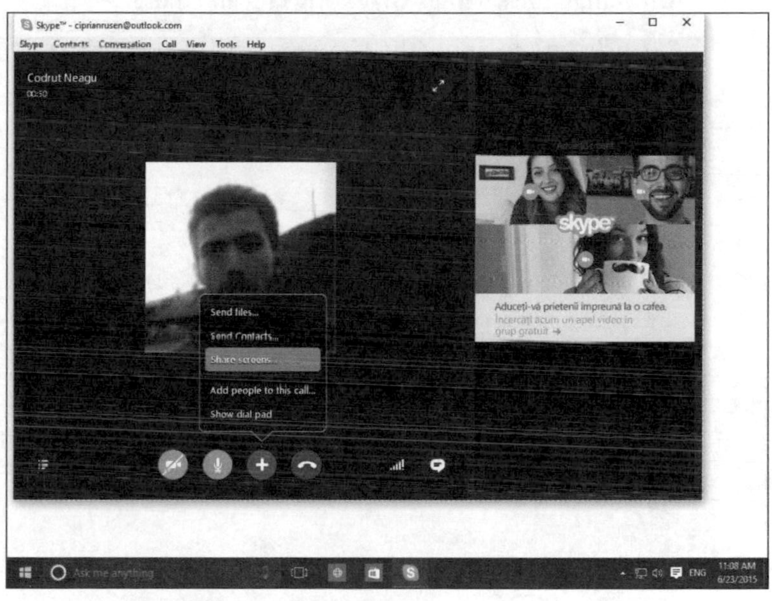

Figure 10-10: Sharing the screen in Skype.

6. **Click Start.**

   Your screen is now shared.

7. **When you want to stop sharing your screen, click the Stop sharing button shown in the top-right corner of the screen.**

Configure How Skype Works

Skype allows you to configure all kinds of aspects that are related to its functioning, such as how notifications are shown, which devices to use for the microphone and camera, your privacy, and how Skype gets updated. If you need to customize how Skype works, here's how to do so:

1. **Start Skype and sign in to your account.**
2. **In the toolbar on the top, click Tools.**

   The Tools menu appears.
3. **Click Options.**

   The Skype Options window appears.
4. **In the column on the left side of the window, click the group of settings where you want to make changes.**
5. **Click the type of settings that you want to change.**
6. **Change the settings that you want to change.**
7. **Click Save to apply the changes.**

   Figure 10-11 shows your Skype general settings.

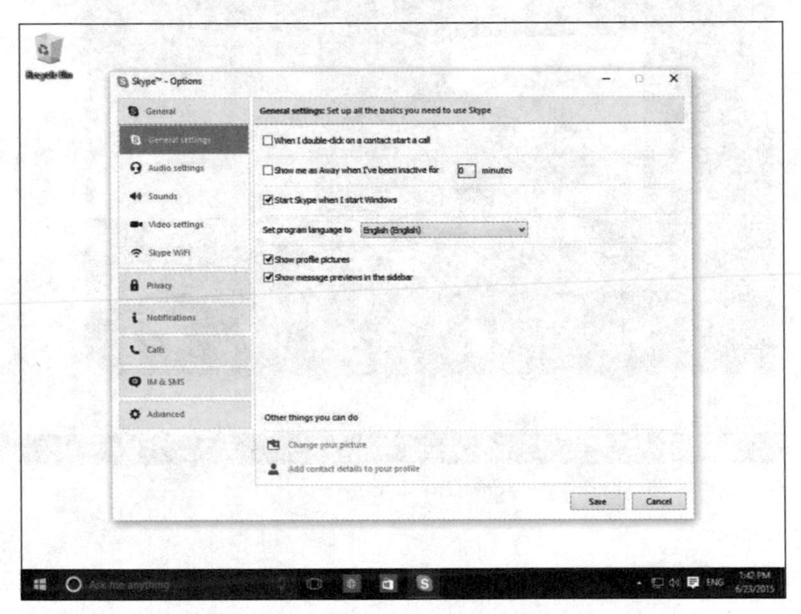

Figure 10-11: The list of Skype general settings.

Add a New Contact to Skype

You can add new contacts to Skype at any time. Follow these steps:

1. **Start Skype and sign in to your account.**
2. **Click inside the search box in the left column of the Skype window.**
3. **Type the name, email address, or Skype Name of the person you want to add as a contact.**
4. **Click Search Skype.**

   A list of search results appears.
5. **Click on the person that you want to add from the list of search results (see Figure 10-12).**

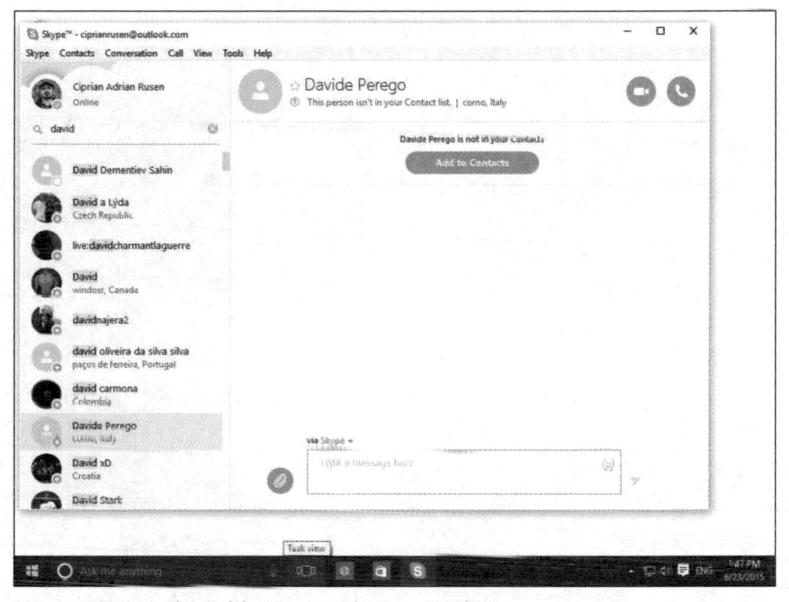

Figure 10-12: The Add a Contact button in Skype.

6. **Click Add to Contacts.**
7. **Wait for the other person to accept your invite.**

   When the other person has accepted your invite, he or she will show up in your list of contacts.

The other person will see your invite only when he or she is online.

CHAPTER ELEVEN
Using OneDrive

OneDrive is Microsoft's cloud storage solution. It's similar to products like Google Drive or Dropbox and is embedded in Windows 10. With OneDrive, you can synchronize your files and folders across all Windows devices as well as devices using Android or iOS. The files you store in your OneDrive folder are automatically uploaded to Microsoft's servers and then synchronized across all your devices on which OneDrive is installed and set up.

OneDrive offers 15GB of free storage space for every Microsoft account. You can add another 15GB of free space by turning on the camera upload on your smartphone and tablet. You can also purchase more storage or take advantage of offers like the 1TB of storage space available to Office 365 subscribers.

In this chapter, you find out how to use the OneDrive app that's bundled with Windows 10, which includes tasks such as uploading files, choosing which folders to synchronize, sharing files and folders with others, and fetching your files remotely.

In This Chapter

- Accessing your OneDrive files and folders
- Uploading files to OneDrive
- Choosing what folders synch via OneDrive
- Sharing via OneDrive
- Enabling and using remote Fetch
- Improving how OneDrive works
- Stopping OneDrive from starting automatically

Access OneDrive

You can start OneDrive and access your files in the cloud several ways. This one works on all Windows 10 devices:

1. **Click the Start button to open the Start Menu.**
2. **Click All Apps.**
3. **Scroll down the list of apps until you find those starting with the letter O.**
4. **Find and click the OneDrive shortcut (see Figure 11-1).**

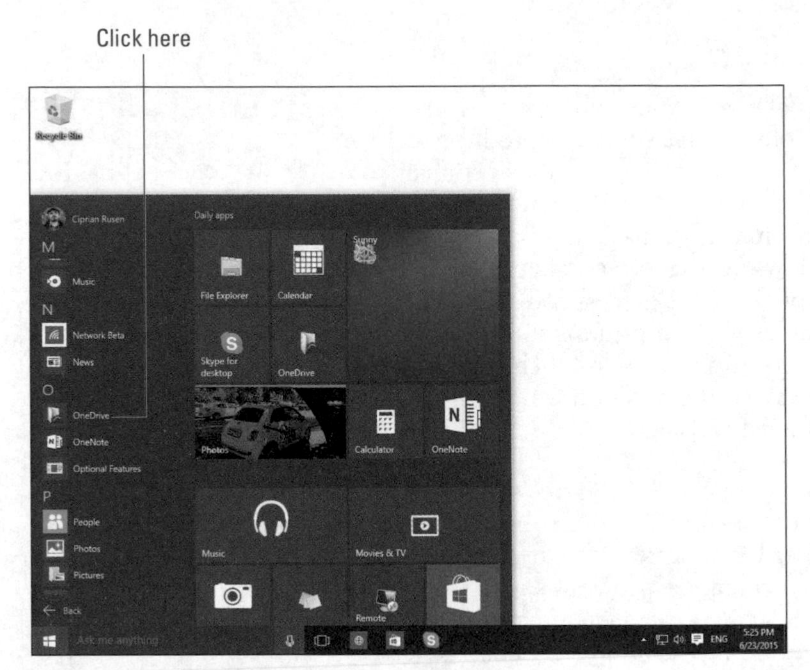

Figure 11-1: The OneDrive shortcut in the apps list.

Another easy way to start OneDrive is to use the Search feature. In the search box on the taskbar, type **OneDrive** and click the appropriate search result.

Upload Files

Uploading your files to OneDrive is as easy as copying them to the OneDrive folder. Here's what you do:

1. **Click the File Explorer icon on the taskbar.**
2. **Browse to the file that you want to upload to OneDrive.**
3. **Select the file and then click the Home tab on the Ribbon.**

4. **In the Clipboard section, click the Copy button (see Figure 11-2).**

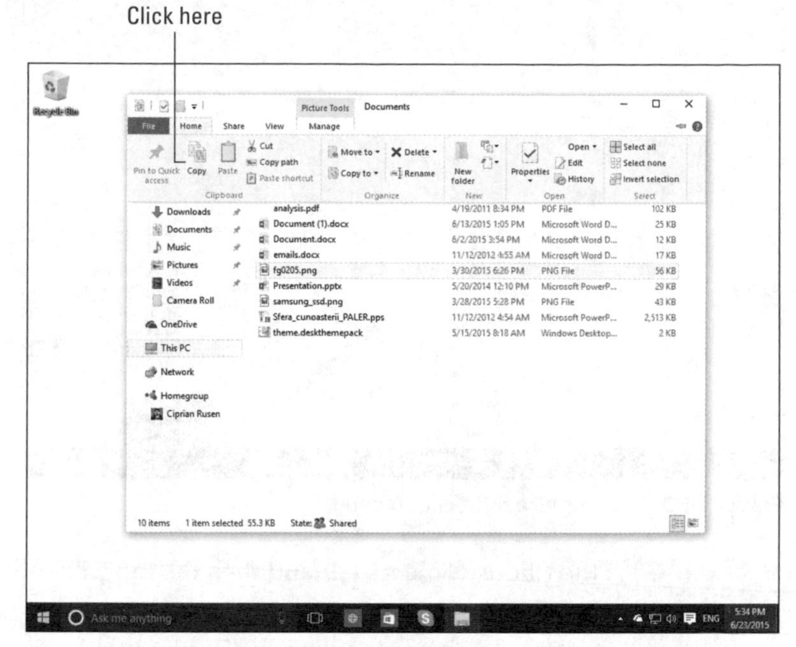

Figure 11-2: The Copy button in File Explorer.

5. **In the Navigation pane on the left side of the File Explorer window, click the OneDrive shortcut.**
6. **Navigate to the folder where you want to upload the selected file to OneDrive.**
7. **Click the Home tab and then click the Paste button in the Clipboard section.**

Choose Folders for Syncing

By default, OneDrive syncs all the folders you place in the OneDrive folder. Moreover, OneDrive enables you to choose what folders you sync on your Windows 10 computer or device. You can choose to sync only a subset of your OneDrive folders so that you don't waste storage space on your existing Windows 10 device. Here's how to select the folders that OneDrive syncs:

1. **On the taskbar, click Show Hidden Icons.**
2. **Right-click the OneDrive shortcut.**
3. **In the menu that appears, click Settings (see Figure 11-3).**

   The Microsoft OneDrive window appears.

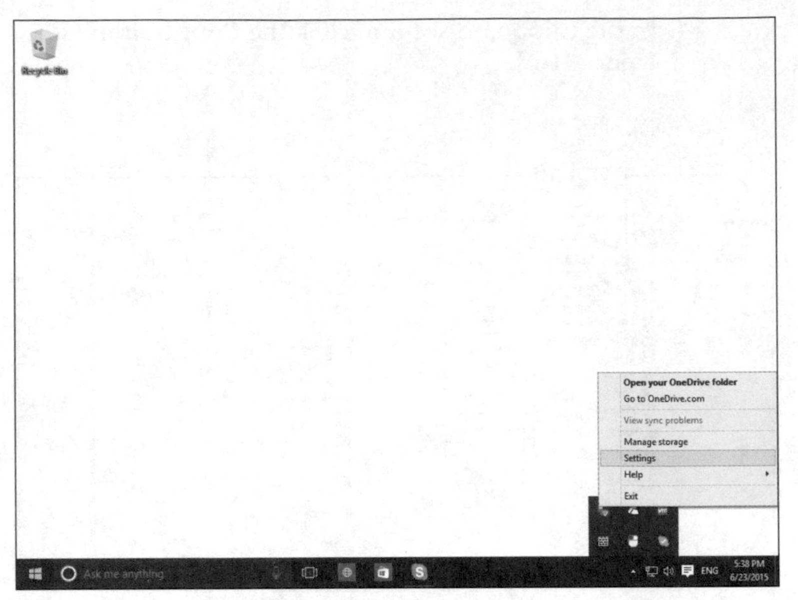

Figure 11-3: The OneDrive right-click menu.

4. **Click the Choose Folders tab and then the button with the same name.**

   You're asked to choose the folders that you want to sync.

5. **Select the folders that you want to sync.**
6. **Click OK twice to close the OneDrive settings.**

View a File or Folder on OneDrive.com

If you want to view the contents of a file or folder on the OneDrive website instead of viewing it locally, you can do so. Follow these steps:

1. **Open OneDrive.**
2. **Browse to the OneDrive file or folder that you want to view on the OneDrive website.**
3. **Right-click the file or folder you want.**

   The right-click menu appears.

4. **Click View on OneDrive.com.**

   The item loads into your default web browser (see Figure 11-4).

The options available on OneDrive.com for the selected item depend on whether it's a file or folder.

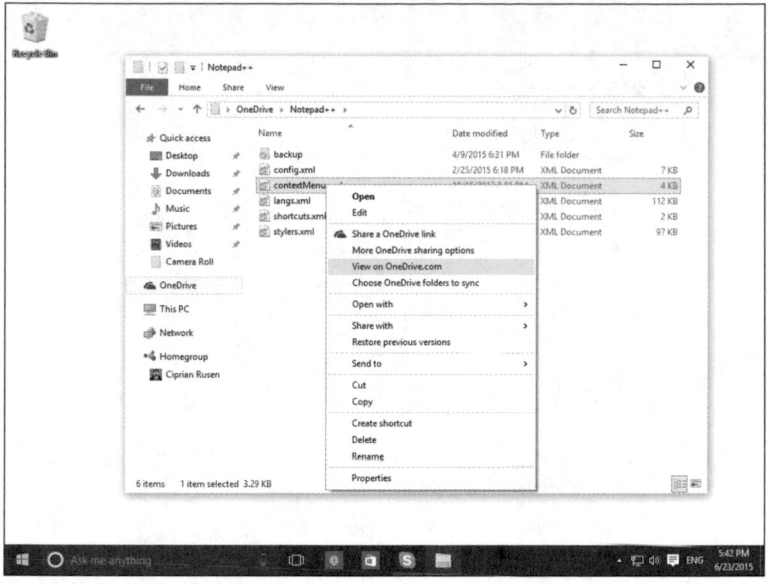

Figure 11-4: Viewing a file or folder on OneDrive.com.

Share a OneDrive Link

To share a file or folder with someone, you generate a sharing link on OneDrive. OneDrive automatically generates this link and stores it on the Clipboard. You can paste it anywhere you want; for example, in an email message, in a chat window on Skype, or on your favorite web browser.

If you share a file, anyone who receives the link can edit that file; if you share a folder, anyone who receives the link can view that folder.

Here's how to quickly generate a sharing link on OneDrive and share it with others:

1. **Open OneDrive.**
2. **Browse to the OneDrive file or folder that you want to share.**
3. **Right-click the file or folder you want to share.**

   The right-click menu appears.
4. **In the menu that appears, click Share a OneDrive link (see Figure 11-5).**

   A notification appears showing that the link is ready to paste.
5. **Open the app where you want to use this link.**
6. **Paste the link into that app and send the link to the intended person.**

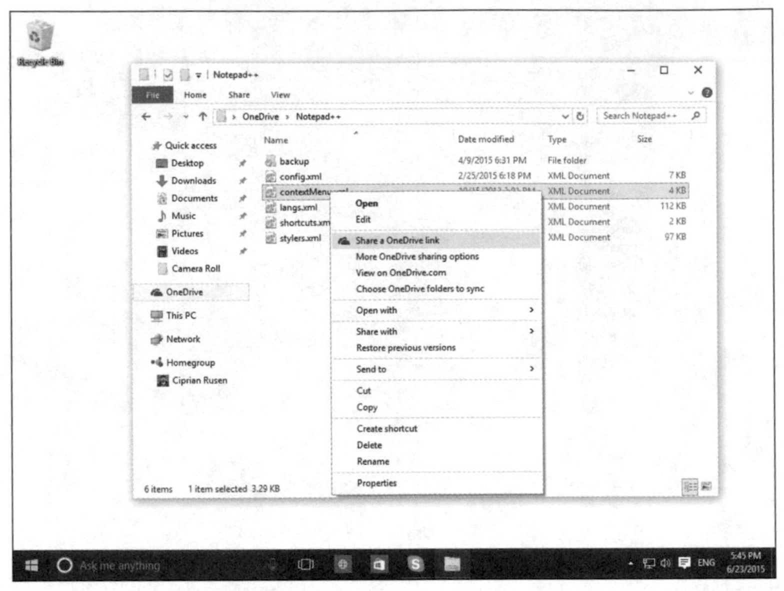

Figure 11-5: The Share a OneDrive link.

Share Files and Folders and Customize Permissions

If you want more control over how you share a file or folder via OneDrive, you can use the OneDrive website to invite one or more people to the shared item. In addition, you can set their permissions (view or edit) and select whether they need to sign in with a Microsoft account before accessing your shared item.

Here's how to use OneDrive's more advanced sharing options:

1. **Open OneDrive.**
2. **Browse to the OneDrive file or folder that you want to share.**
3. **Right-click the file or folder that you want to share.**

   The right-click menu appears.
4. **In the menu that appears, click More OneDrive Sharing Options.**

   The OneDrive website is loaded into your favorite web browser.
5. **Type the email address of the intended person and then type your message.**
6. **Click Recipients Can Edit.**

   Two selection lists are shown.

7. **In the first selection list, select the permissions that you want to assign to that person (edit or view).**
8. **In the second selection list, select whether the recipient(s) needs a Microsoft account to sign in.**
9. **Click Share (see Figure 11-6).**

   The selected item is shared.
10. **Click Close.**

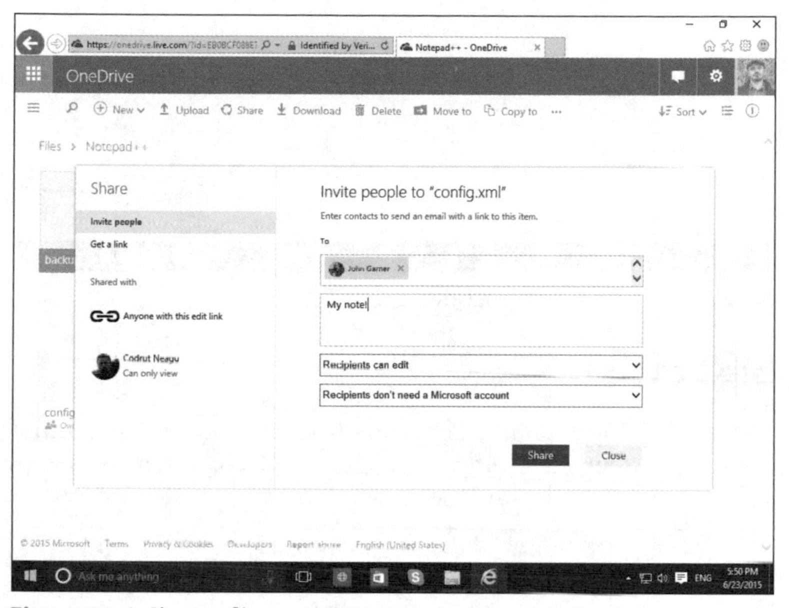

Figure 11-6: Sharing files on the OneDrive.com website.

Manually Force Your Files to Sync

You can force OneDrive to synchronize your files right away without waiting for it to discover your new files. To force OnDrive to manually sync your files, follow these steps:

1. **On the taskbar, click Show Hidden Icons.**
2. **Right-click the OneDrive shortcut.**

   The right-click menu appears.
3. **In the menu that appears, click Exit (see Figure 11-7).**

   Microsoft OneDrive is now closed.
4. **Start OneDrive.**

   When OneDrive starts, it automatically checks for newly added files and uploads them.

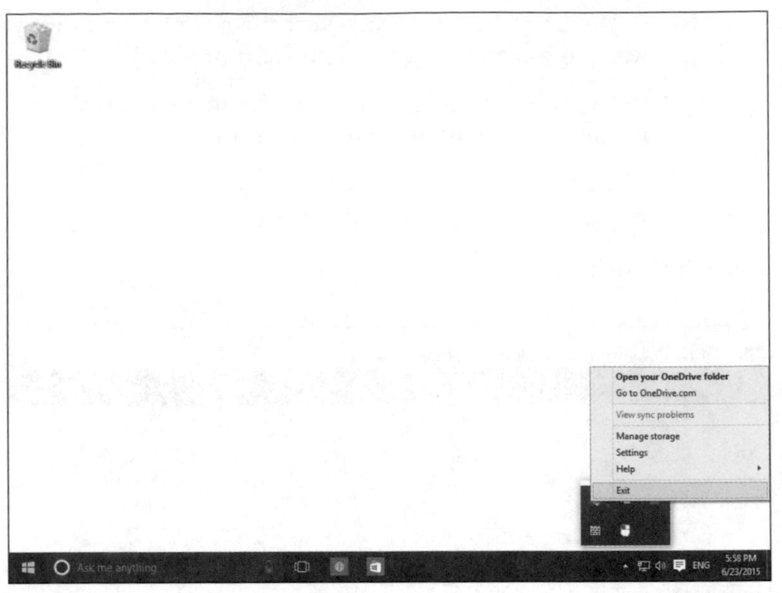

Figure 11-7: How to stop OneDrive.

Enable Fetch

OneDrive's remote Fetch files feature allows you to remotely access any file from your Windows 10 computer, as long as the file is synced with OneDrive and this feature is enabled.

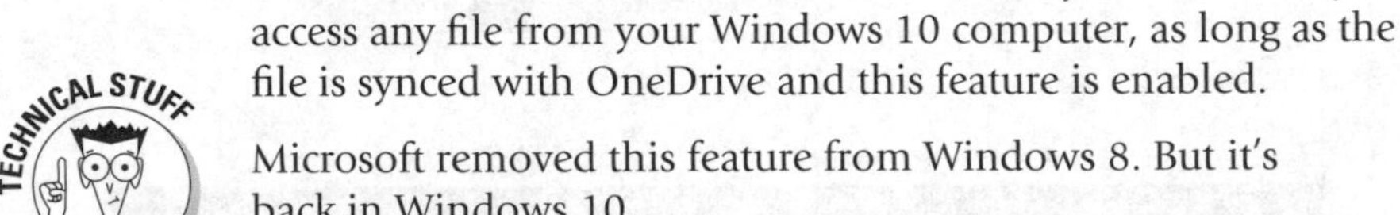

Microsoft removed this feature from Windows 8. But it's back in Windows 10.

Here's how to enable Fetch in OneDrive on Windows 10:

1. **On the taskbar, click Show Hidden Icons.**
2. **Right-click the OneDrive shortcut.**

   The right-click menu appears.
3. **In the menu that appears, click Settings.**

   The Microsoft OneDrive window appears.
4. **Click the Settings tab and find the General section.**
5. **In that section, select Let Me Use OneDrive to Fetch Any of My Files on This PC (see Figure 11-8).**
6. **Click OK.**

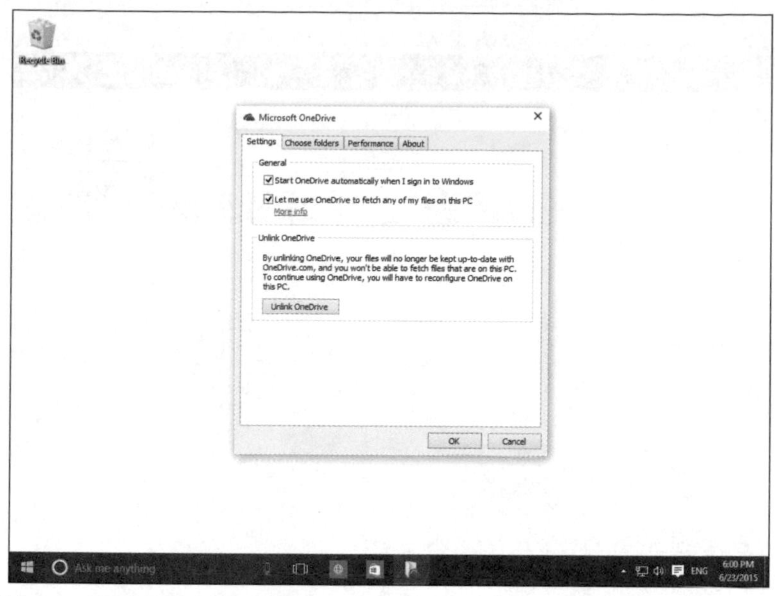

Figure 11-8: Enabling Fetch in OneDrive.

Fetch Your Files Remotely

If you want to Fetch your files remotely when you don't have access to one of your Windows 10 computers, you can use OneDrive to access them.

In order to remotely Fetch files from another computer, you must have enabled Fetch on the Windows computer whose files you want to access remotely.

Follow these steps to Fetch your files:

1. **Open a web browser.**
2. **Navigate to the `https://onedrive.live.com` website.**
3. **Sign in with your Microsoft account.**
4. **Click the burger button (three stacked lines, like a burger on a bun), at the top-left corner of OneDrive website.**
5. **In the PCs section, click the computer that you want to access remotely (see Figure 11-9).**

   Its files and folders are shown in a separate browser tab.
6. **Navigate to where the file that you want is located.**
7. **Select the file that you want to download remotely.**
8. **Click Download.**

   The Save As window appears.

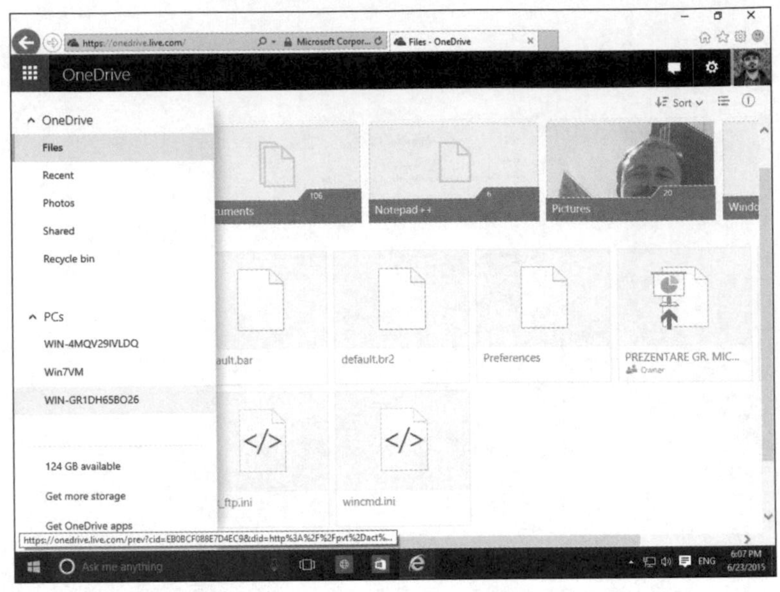

Figure 11-9: How to access a computer remotely with OneDrive.

9. **In the Save As window, select the folder where you want to download the file.**
10. **Click Save.**

    The file is now downloaded to your computer and you can use it once the download is finished.
11. **Sign out from the OneDrive website.**

Increase Your OneDrive Storage

If you don't have enough storage space left on OneDrive and want to increase the space, you can purchase an extension plan.

Purchasing an extension plan requires adding your payment details to your Microsoft account. You can use a credit card, a debit card, or a PayPal account.

Follow these steps to increase OneDrive storage:

1. **On the taskbar, click Show Hidden Icons.**
2. **Right-click the OneDrive shortcut.**

   The right-click menu appears.
3. **In the right-click menu, click Manage Storage (see Figure 11-10).**

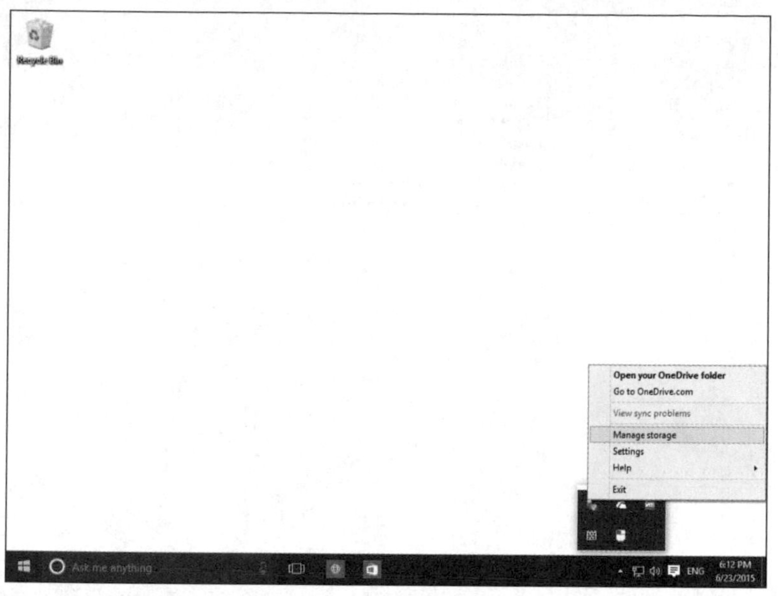

Figure 11-10: The Manage Storage link in the OneDrive pop-up menu.

The OneDrive website is loaded into your main web browser. Several storage related options are shown.

4. **Click Buy More Storage.**
5. **Select the plan that you want to buy.**
6. **Click Confirm to verify that you want to purchase the selected plan.**
7. **Once the purchase of the new plan is confirmed, close your web browser.**

Accelerate Uploads

If you aren't satisfied with OneDrive's uploading speed, you can set it so that it uploads faster. Here's how:

1. **On the taskbar, click Show Hidden Icons.**
2. **Right-click the OneDrive shortcut.**

   The right-click menu appears.
3. **In the right-click menu, click Settings.**

   The Microsoft OneDrive window appears.
4. **Click the Performance tab (see Figure 11-11).**

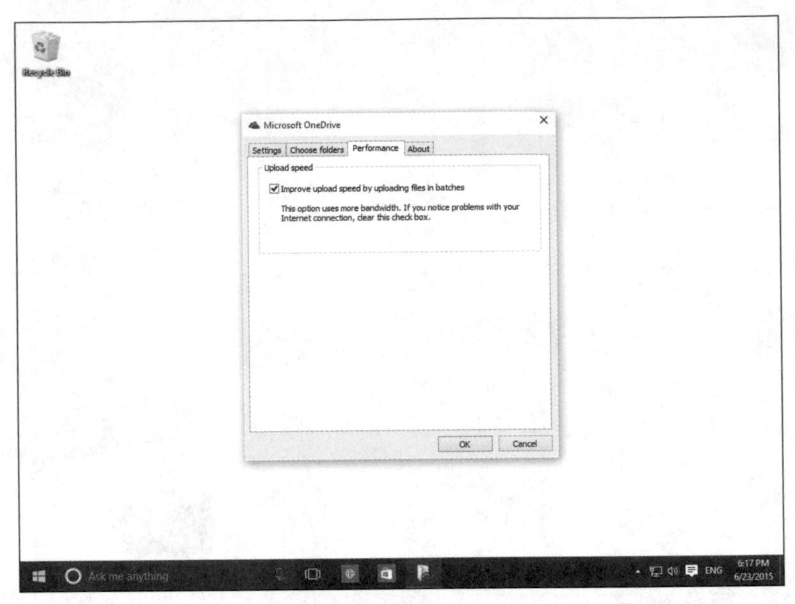

Figure 11-11: The Performance tab in OneDrive.

5. **Under this tab, select Improve Upload Speed by Uploading Files in Batches.**
6. **Click OK.**

If you still aren't satisfied with the speed of your OneDrive uploads, you may also want to try closing some of the programs that use your Internet connection, and free up some of your bandwidth that way.

Stop OneDrive from Starting Automatically

If you don't plan to use OneDrive regularly, you can stop it from running automatically each time you start and sign into Windows 10 starts and you sign in. Follow these steps:

1. **On the taskbar, click Show Hidden Icons.**
2. **Right-click the OneDrive shortcut.**

   The right-click menu appears.
3. **In the right-click menu, click Settings.**

   The Microsoft OneDrive window appears.
4. **In the Settings tab, find the General section.**
5. **Select Start OneDrive Automatically When I Sign In To Windows (see Figure 11-12).**
6. **Click OK.**

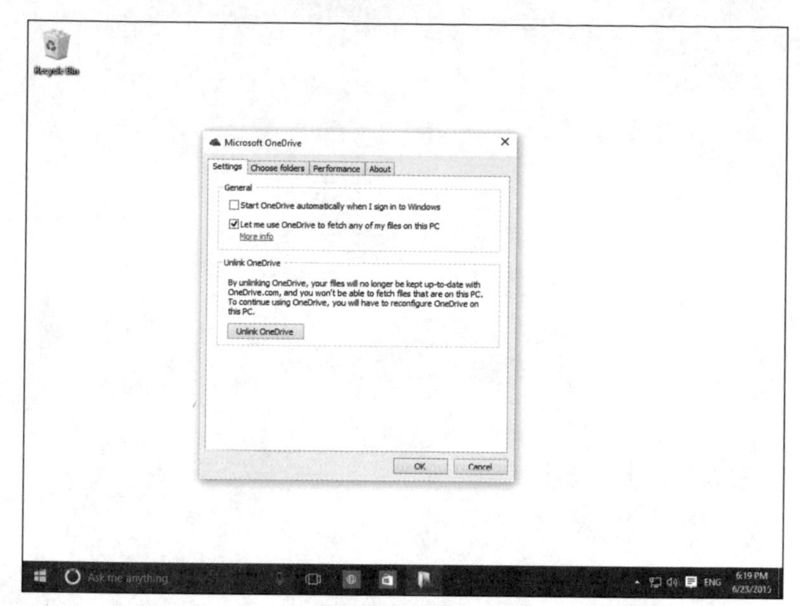

Figure 11-12: How to stop OneDrive from starting automatically.

CHAPTER TWELVE

Using OneNote

In This Chapter

- Starting and navigating the OneNote app
- Creating a new notebook
- Creating new sections and notes
- Organizing your notes
- Printing your notes
- Configuring the OneNote app

Windows 10 comes with the OneNote app installed by default. With this app, you can synchronize all kinds of notes across all your computers and devices, for free. Even though it's been included in the Microsoft Office suite for a long time, OneNote isn't as well-known as Evernote (a similar competing product that charges you for its services).

OneNote is very useful, especially when you use it at work. You can create quick to-do lists, keep track of them, and create meeting minutes. Moreover, it works well when using a mouse and keyboard, touchscreens, or styli. In the latter case, you simply draw or write your notes with your stylus and use them later on.

Start OneNote

You can start OneNote more than one way, but the following method works on all computers and devices with OneNote installed:

1. **Click Start to open the Start Menu.**
2. **Click All Apps.**
3. **Scroll down the list of apps until you find the OneNote shortcut, which is the second app under the letter O in Figure 12-1.**
4. **Click the OneNote shortcut.**

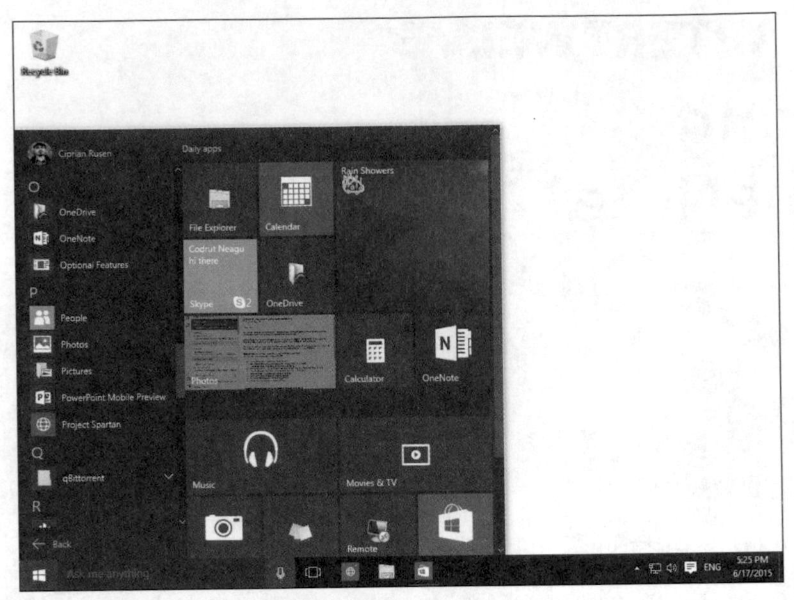

Figure 12-1: The OneNote app shortcut.

Just type **OneNote** in the search bar on the taskbar, and the first search result is the shortcut to OneNote.

Navigate the OneNote User Interface

The user interface offered by the OneNote app is straightforward. When you start OneNote for the first time, your notebook opens and automatically greets you with a sample of Quick Notes. These notes include a video that introduces OneNote and tells you what you can do with it. Figure 12-2 shows the OneNote user interface.

You see several tabs at the top of the OneNote window:

- **Home:** Includes basic text formatting tools such as Bold, Italic, and Underline. Here you can also add elements to an active note; for example, lists, to-do items, and pictures.
- **Insert:** Includes tools for adding tables, files, pictures, and links to an active note.
- **Draw:** Includes several drawing tools and options that are especially useful on devices with touch, pens, or styli.
- **View:** Offers several tools for viewing your notes, including zooming in or out. From here, you can also set rule lines and grid lines for your notes.

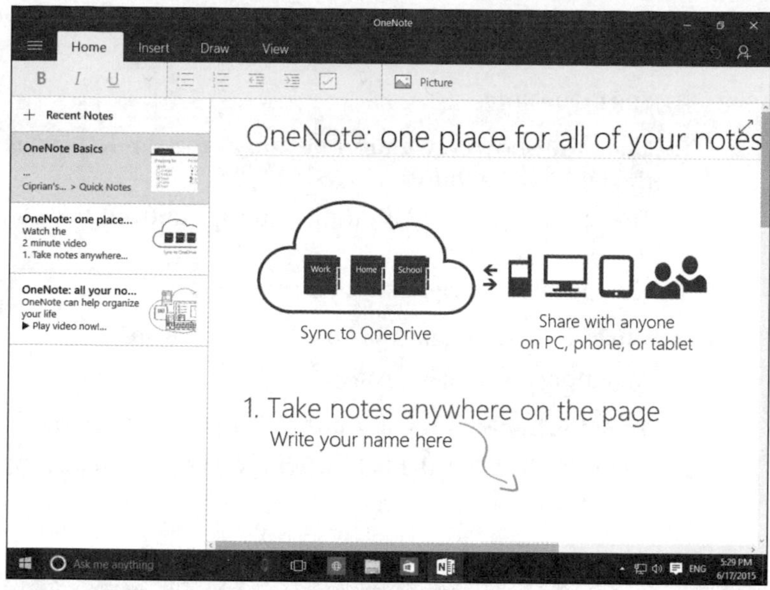

Figure 12-2: The OneNote user interface.

At the top left corner of the OneNote app window, you find a burger button (three stacked lines; they're to the left of the Home tab, as you can see in Figure 12-2). If you hover the mouse over this button, you see that it is named Show Navigation.

When you click the Show Navigation button, these options are available:

- **Recent Notes:** Click it, and you see a list of your recent notes.
- **Notebooks:** Displays your recently opened notebooks.
- You navigate to a different notebook by clicking on it, or by clicking More Notebooks and then clicking the one that you want to use.
- **Print:** Click it, and the Print dialogue box opens.
- **Settings:** Click it, and you see a list of settings for OneNote.

To fully utilize OneNote and all its features, you need to either use a Microsoft account or have your work account linked to a Microsoft account. Chapter 21 covers user accounts in detail.

Create a New Notebook

The main container for notes in OneNote is the notebook. By default, OneNote offers you a premade notebook with your name on it. In my case, it's Ciprian's Notebook. In your case, it might be John's Notebook or Tracy's Notebook.

If you use OneNote on a regular basis, you probably need your own notebooks. Here's how to create a new notebook:

1. **Start OneNote.**
2. **Click the Show Navigation button at the top-left corner of the OneNote window.**

   The Show Navigation button is a burger button (three stacked lines).

   The OneNote navigation menu appears.
3. **Click the + sign near the Notebooks section.**

   An empty text box appears.
4. **Type the name that you want for the new notebook.**

   Figure 12-3 shows the field where you type the name for the new notebook.

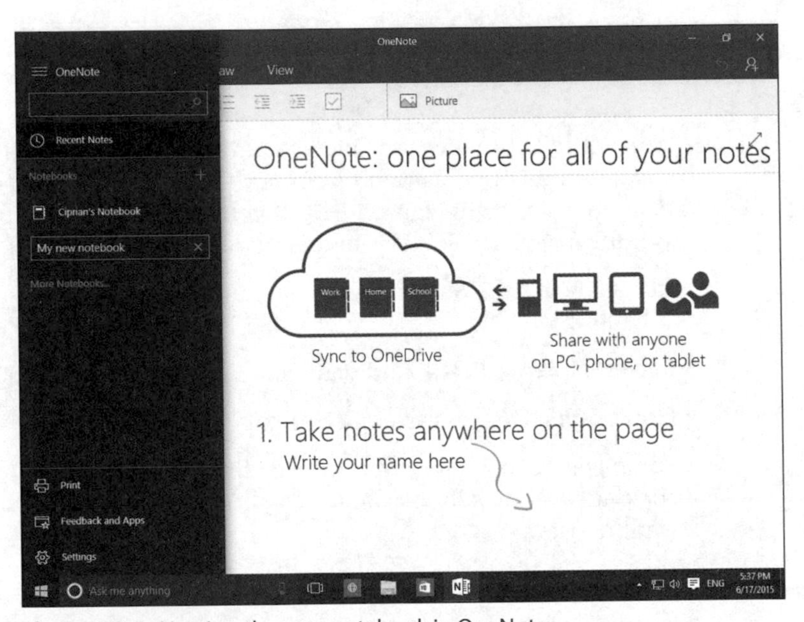

Figure 12-3: Naming the new notebook in OneNote.

5. **Press Enter or click somewhere else in the OneNote window to create the new notebook.**

The new notebook is created and displayed in OneNote. The new notebook contains one section named New Section 1 and one empty page named Untitled page.

Create a New Section in a Notebook

Notebooks are organized in sections. In a notebook, you can add as many sections as you want, and each section can have any number of pages. To create a new section in a notebook, follow these steps:

1. **Start OneNote.**
2. **Click the Show Navigation button at the top-left corner of the OneNote window.**

   The OneNote navigation menu appears.
3. **Click the notebook that you want to work with.**

   The selected notebook is shown.
4. **Click the + button at the right of the list with sections.**

   A new section is created; you can edit its name. By default, it's named New Section 1.
5. **Type a name for this section (see Figure 12-4).**

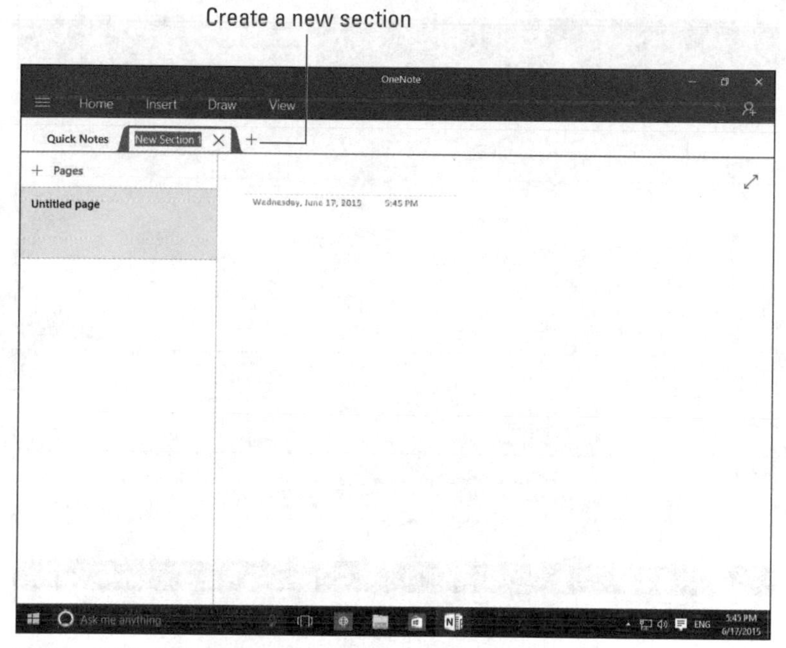

Figure 12-4: Adding a new section to a notebook.

6. **Press Enter or click somewhere else in the OneNote window to create the new section.**

A new section is created with an empty page named Untitled.

Create a Note

In OneNote, notes are organized in sections. In each section, you can create any number of notes. To create a new note, follow these steps:

1. **Start OneNote.**
2. **Click the Show Navigation button at the top-left corner of the OneNote window.**

   The OneNote navigation menu appears.
3. **Click the notebook that you want to work with.**

   The selected notebook is shown.
4. **Click the section where you want to create a new note.**

   The pages that are part of the selected section are shown.
5. **Click the + button at the left of the Pages list in that section (see Figure 12-5).**

   A new page is created, called Untitled page.

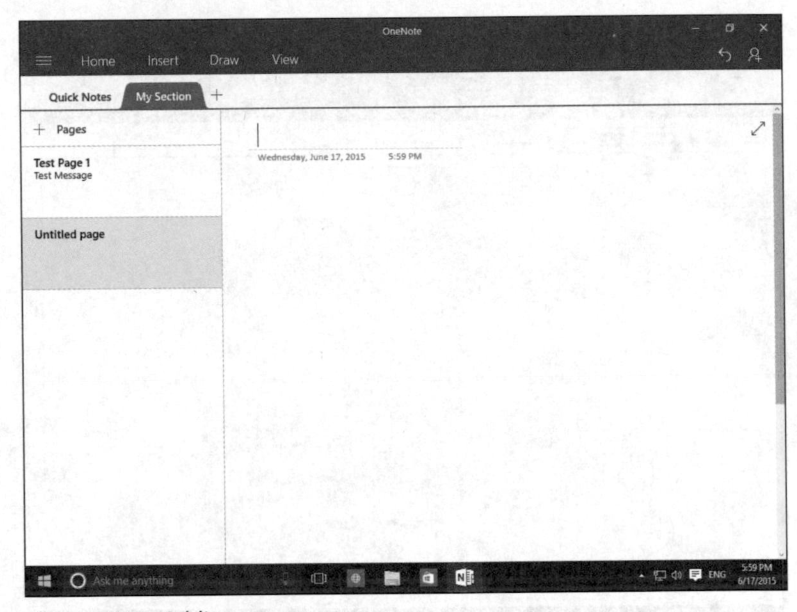

Figure 12-5: Adding a new note.

6. **Click in the title field on the right.**

   The mouse cursor flickers inside the empty title field.
7. **Type a name for this note.**

8. **Click in the body of the note.**

   The mouse cursor flickers inside the empty body of the page.

9. **Type the contents of the note.**

Organize Your Sections and Notes

You can easily change the order of the pages and sections that make up a notebook. Here's how it works:

1. **Start OneNote.**

2. **Click the Show Navigation button at the top-left corner of the OneNote window.**

   The OneNote navigation menu appears.

3. **Click the notebook that you want to work with.**

   The selected notebook is shown.

4. **Follow these steps to move a section:**

   a. *Click and hold the section that you want to move.*

   b. *With the left mouse still pressed, drag the section to where you want it in the list of sections (see Figure 12-6).*

   c. *Release the left mouse button when the section is in the desired position.*

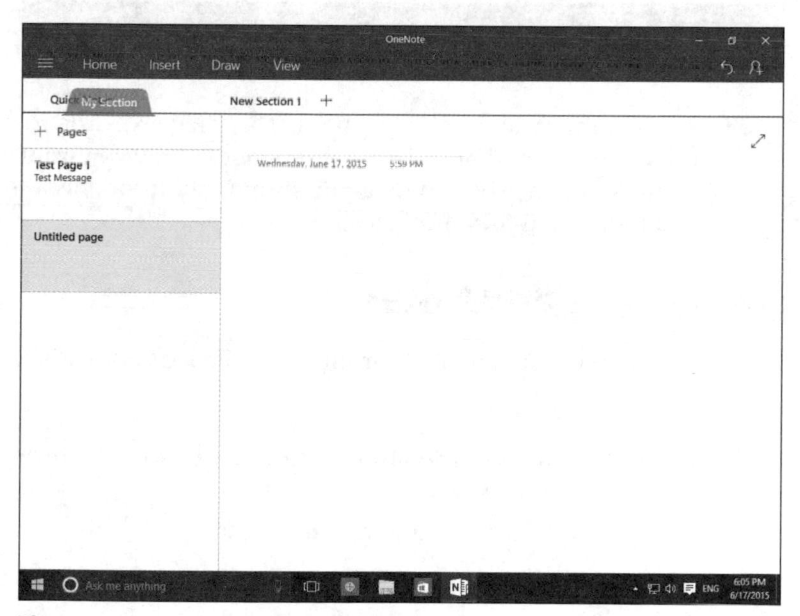

Figure 12-6: Moving sections in OneNote.

5. **Follow these steps to move a page:**
   a. *Click and hold the page that you want to move.*
   b. *With the left mouse button still pressed, drag the page to the position where you want it in the list of pages (see Figure 12-7).*
   c. *Release the left-click mouse button when you reach the desired position.*

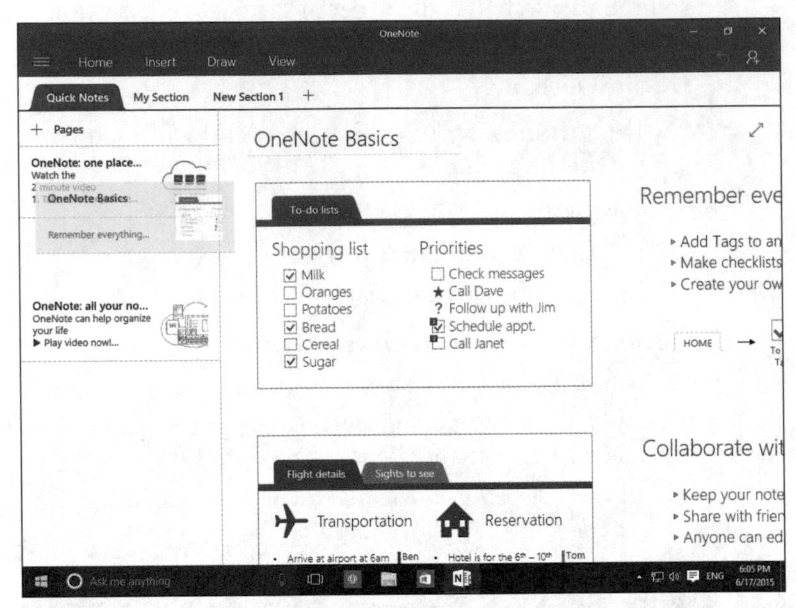

Figure 12-7: Moving pages in OneNote.

As you can see, all it takes is a traditional drag-and-drop to move things around and organize your notebooks how you want them. Similarly, you can drag-and-drop notes from one section to another, and they move accordingly.

Delete Sections and Notes

Deleting sections and notes from your notebooks is as easy as pie:

1. **Start OneNote.**
2. **Click the Show Navigation button at the top-left corner of the OneNote window.**

   The OneNote navigation menu appears.
3. **Click the notebook that you want to work with.**

   The selected notebook is shown.
4. **Follow these steps to remove a section:**
   a. *Right-click the section that you want to remove.*
   b. *Click Delete Section (see Figure 12-8).*

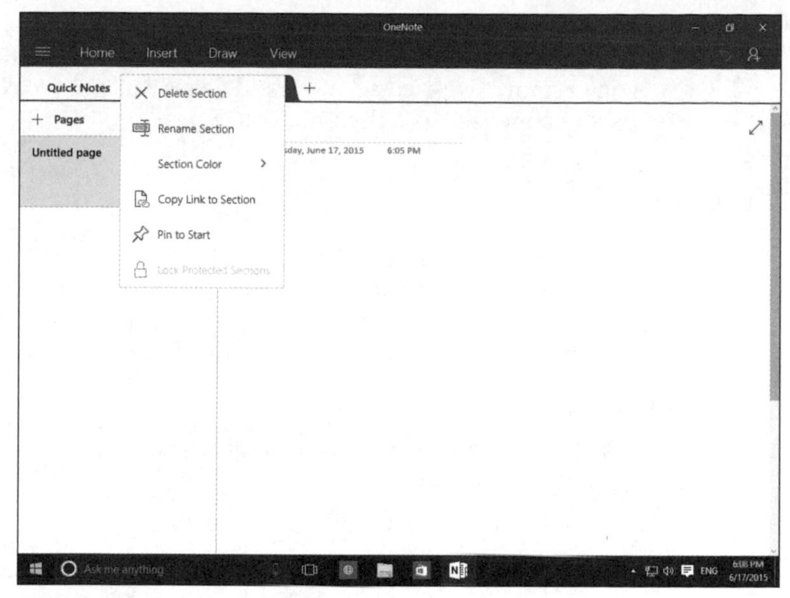

Figure 12-8: Deleting a section.

5. **Follow these steps to remove a note:**

   a. *Click the section with the note you want to delete.*

   b. *Right-click the note that you want to remove.*

   c. *Click Delete Page (see Figure 12-9).*

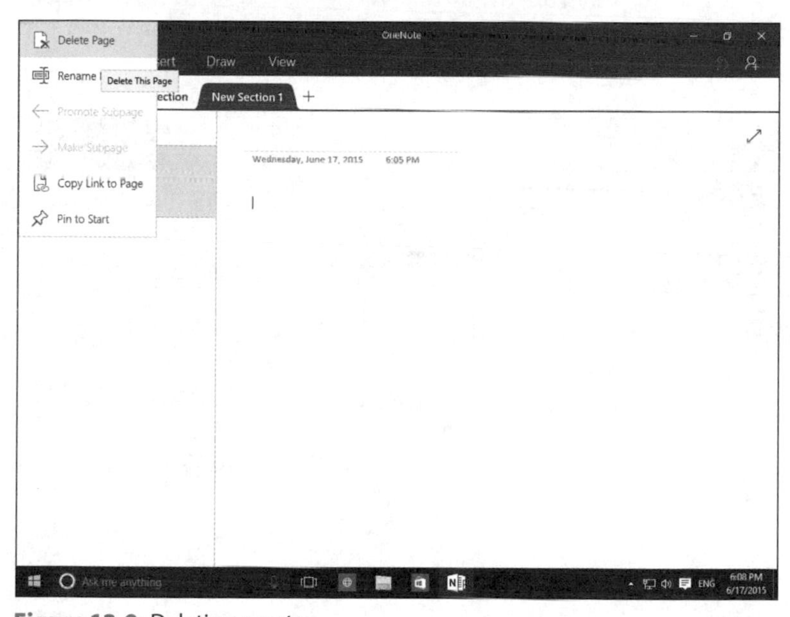

Figure 12-9: Deleting a note.

When you delete a section, all the pages that are inside it are lost. If you want to keep a page, first move it to another section that you won't remove. Deleted sections and pages can't be recovered after they're removed from the OneNote app.

Print Notes

Like any other app from the Microsoft Office suite, OneNote allows you to print your notes. (Of course, you need a printer installed and available for printing on your Windows 10 computer or device.) If you want to print a note, here's what you do:

1. **Start OneNote.**
2. **Click the Show Navigation button at the top-left corner of the OneNote window.**

   The OneNote navigation menu appears.
3. **Click the notebook; then click the section and page that you want to print.**
4. **Click the Show Navigation button.**

   The OneNote navigation menu appears.
5. **Click Print.**

   The Print window appears.
6. **In the Print window, select the printer that you want to use and configure how you want to print your note (see Figure 12-10).**

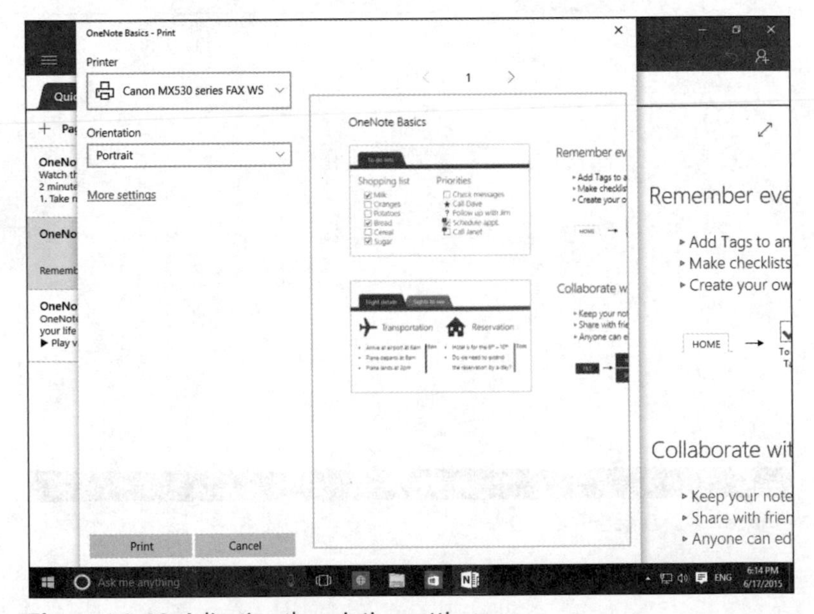

Figure 12-10: Adjusting the printing settings.

7. **On the left panel of the Print window, check whether the settings are accurate for printing your note.**

   If not, adjust the settings as you want.

8. **Click Print.**

Configure How OneNote Works

The OneNote app offers a few settings that allow you to adjust how it works. You can add new accounts and set whether you want to use touch to zoom; you can set it to sync notebooks automatically, to sync all files and images, and to choose the notebook for your quick notes.

To change how OneNote works, follow these steps:

1. **Start OneNote.**
2. **Click the Show Navigation button on the top-left corner of the OneNote window.**

   The OneNote navigation menu appears.

3. **Click Settings.**

   The Settings pane is shown on the right side of the screen.

4. **Click Options.**

   The list with configuration options appears.

5. **Adjust the settings that you want to change (see Figure 12-11).**

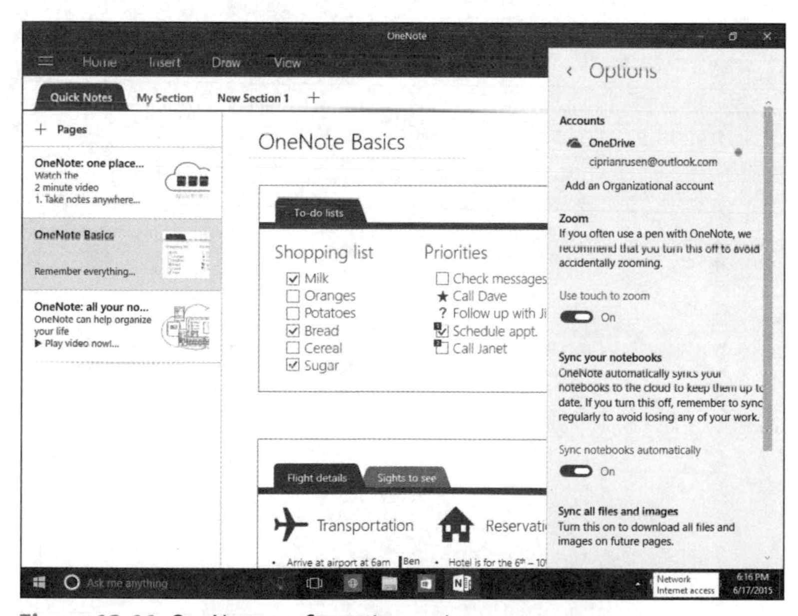

Figure 12-11: OneNote configuration options.

CHAPTER THIRTEEN

Using Office Online and Office Apps

In This Chapter

- Accessing Office Online
- Uploading documents
- Opening documents in Office Online
- Sharing your documents with Office Online
- Trying the free Office apps from the Windows Store

Shortly after the Windows 10 launch, Microsoft also launched Microsoft Office 2016. On top of that, Microsoft offers free Office apps for touch-enabled devices in the Windows Store, Google Play, and the Apple Store. Anyone can use them, for free.

This is a Windows book, so I don't cover the full versions of Microsoft Office. If you need help with a full version of Office, check out a *For Dummies* book for your version.

However, there may be times when you aren't at work and don't have Office available, but you need to get some work done. When you find yourself in such a situation, your best option is Office Online. This is an online Office suite that allows you to create and edit files using lightweight, web browser-based versions of Microsoft Office applications: Word, Excel, PowerPoint, OneNote, and Sway. You can use Office Online on all the PCs you want without paying anything. Because it's a web application that runs in your browser, Office Online runs on any kind of device; it doesn't require special plug-ins, and it works on all popular browsers.

In this chapter, I cover basic tasks; for example, how to access Office Online, how to upload your documents so that you can edit them in Office Online, and how to share them with others. You also find an introduction to the Office apps that are available in the Windows Store.

Access Office Online

To access Office Online, open a web browser and follow these steps:

1. **Navigate to** `https://office.live.com`**.**
2. **Click Sign In.**
3. **Type the email address of your Microsoft account.**
4. **Click Next.**
5. **You may be asked to enter your password or a security code (if you've enabled two-step verification). Enter the required details.**
6. **Click Submit.**
7. **Click the icon of the Office app that you want to use: Word Online, OneNote Online, PowerPoint Online, Excel Online, or Sway (see Figure 13-1).**

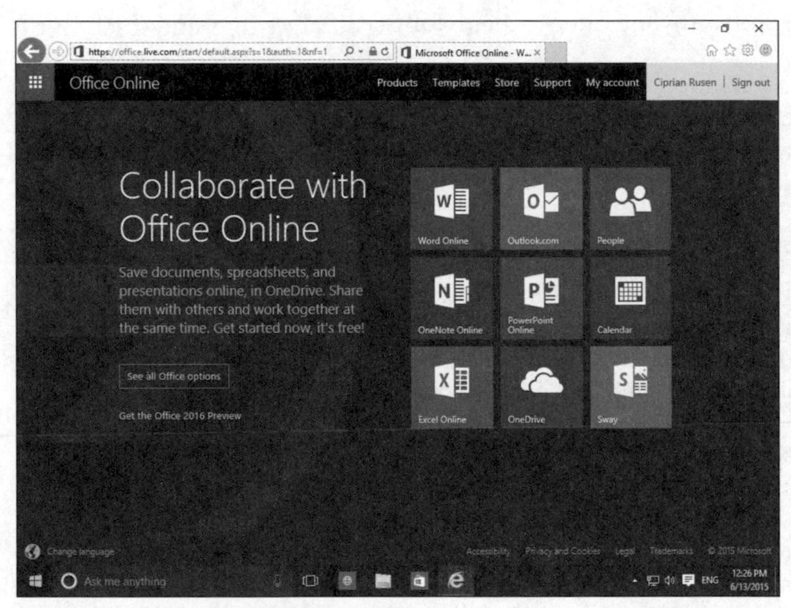

Figure 13-1: Accessing Office Online apps.

Office Online works with almost any web browser. You don't have to use Internet Explorer or Microsoft Edge in order to edit your documents online.

Upload Your Documents to Office Online

Once you open Office Online in your browser, you can use Office Online to open your documents, but only if they're uploaded to OneDrive or Dropbox. If you're using Dropbox, you must also connect your Office Online account with your Dropbox account. Here's how to upload a document to OneDrive, using your web browser:

1. **Sign in to Office Online.**
2. **Click OneDrive.**

   The OneDrive website is loaded in your web browser.
3. **Navigate to the folder where you want to store that document.**
4. **Click Upload.**
5. **In the Choose File to Upload window, navigate to the document that you want to upload (see Figure 13-2).**

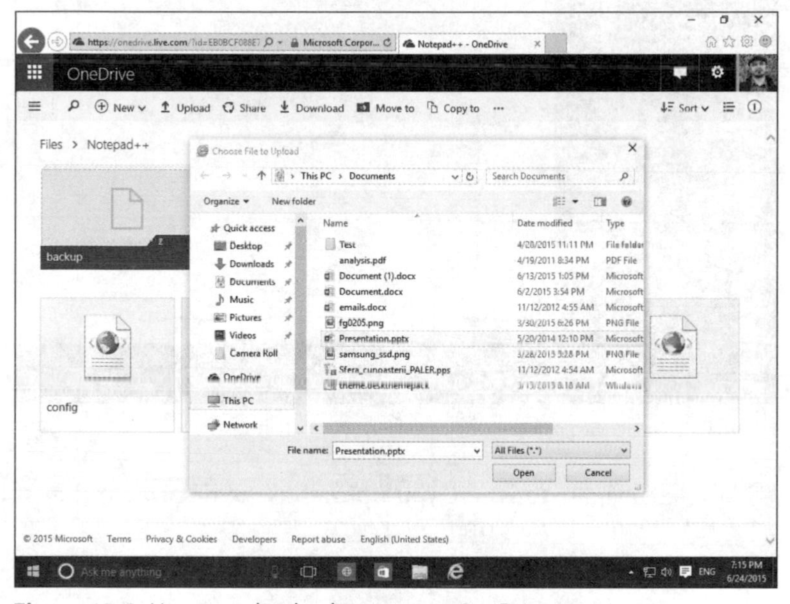

Figure 13-2: How to upload a document to OneDrive.

6. **Select the document.**
7. **Click Open to upload the document.**

Open Your Documents in Office Online

After the documents you want to work with are uploaded to OneDrive, you can access and work with them using Office Online in your web browser. Here's how to open documents in Word Online, after it's uploaded to OneDrive:

1. **Sign in to Office Online.**
2. **Click the Word Online app.**

   Word Online loads in your web browser.
3. **Click Open from OneDrive (see Figure 13-3).**

   The OneDrive website is loaded in your web browser.

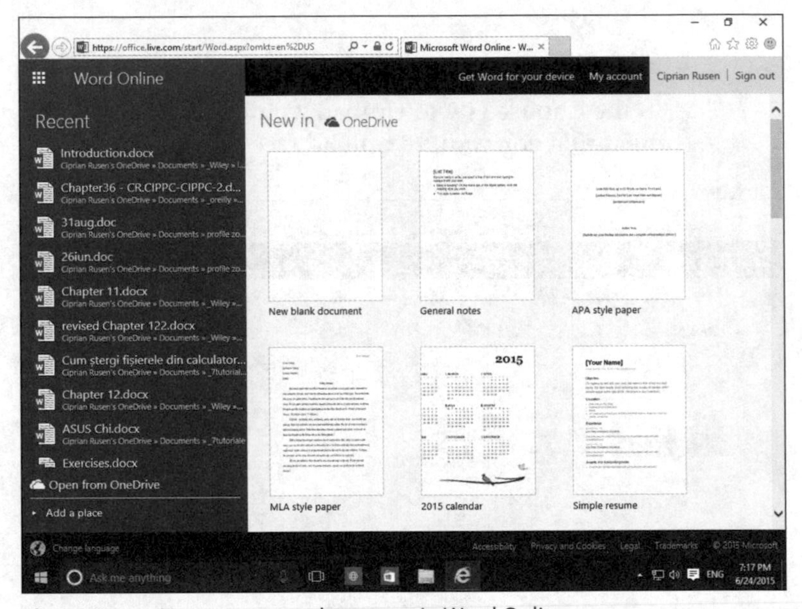

Figure 13-3: How to open a document in Word Online.

4. **Navigate to where you uploaded the document that you want to work on.**
5. **Click that document, and it opens in the appropriate Word Online app.**

For this exercise, I used Word Online for opening a Word document. However, the process is similar when using Excel Online and PowerPoint Online.

Share Your Documents with Office Online

While you're editing your documents and presentations in Office Online, you can share them with others in two ways:

- **Invite people to edit a document.** This involves completing a form with their email address and adding a quick note.
- **Get a link.** You can easily set the kind of permissions that are associated with the link and then copy and paste it anywhere you wish. Personally, I prefer this option.

Here's how to share a document with others from Office Online, using a link:

1. **Open the document that you want to share using the appropriate Office Online app.**
2. **Click Share.**

   A Share dialogue is loaded in your browser.
3. **Click Get a Link.**
4. **Click the down-pointing arrow under Choose an Option.**

   A drop-down list appears with sharing options.
5. **Select the permissions that you want to give to people receiving your link.**
6. **Click Create Link (see Figure 13-4).**

   The sharing link is generated and displayed.

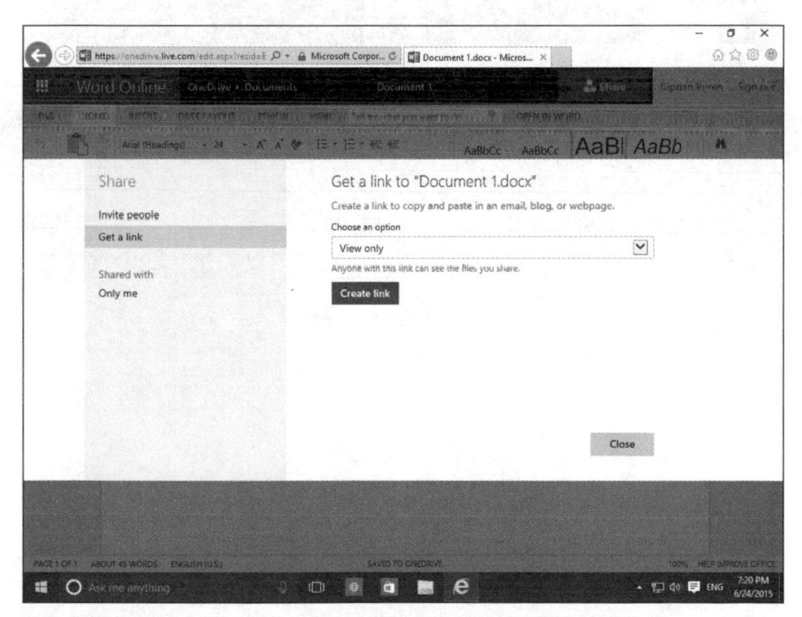

Figure 13-4: How to share a document using a link.

7. In the Share dialogue, click Shorten Link, to shorten it.
8. Copy the link.
9. Paste the link where you want to use it.
10. Click Close.

Avoid sharing by using public links, especially when sharing business documents. Others can easily find and use documents that are shared via public links. Also, give only the people you know and trust permission to edit your shared documents.

Use the Free Office Apps

Microsoft offers several free Office apps that are designed specifically for touch-enabled devices. Go to the Windows Store and search for Word, Excel, PowerPoint, and OneNote. Anyone can use these apps, even if they don't have an Office 365 subscription or have a desktop version of Microsoft Office installed. If you have a tablet or 2-in-1 device with Windows 10 or you don't have a full version of Office installed, give them a try.

You can install them easily on your Windows 10 computer or device (see, for example, Figure 13-5). And they're all free. So, try them out and use them when they come in handy.

Turn to Chapter 16 for details on finding and installing apps in the Windows Store.

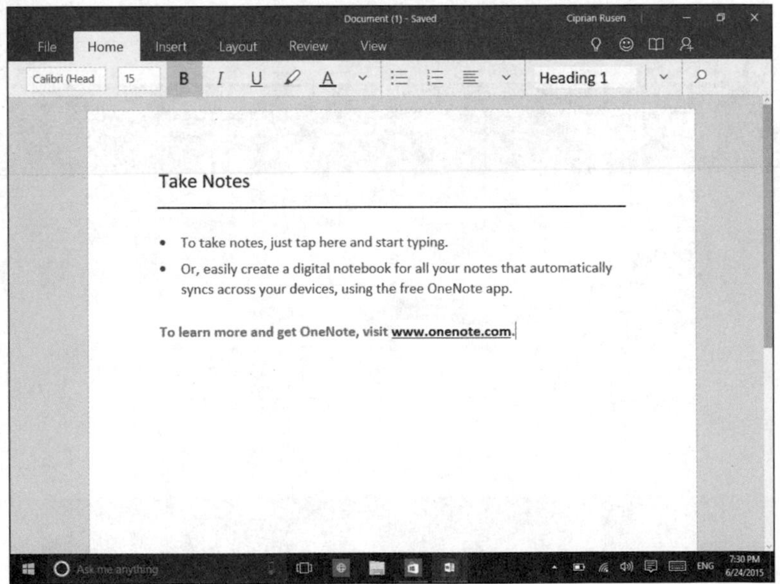

Figure 13-5: The Word app for Windows 10.

CHAPTERFOURTEEN
Using Cortana

Cortana is a voice-activated personal assistant that was first developed by Microsoft for its Windows Phone 8.1 mobile operating system. Since its launch in April 2014, Cortana has been improved and fine-tuned, and Windows 10 includes a more-advanced incarnation that can do a lot more than the original version. When Windows 10 was launched, Cortana was available in English, Mandarin Chinese, French, German, Italian, and Spanish. With time, Microsoft adds support for even more languages.

You can use Cortana on your Windows 10 devices, including computers, laptops, tablets, and smartphones. Once you set up Cortana on all devices, your data is automatically synced between them, and you can interact with Cortana on any of your Windows devices.

Cortana is named after an artificial intelligence character in Microsoft's *Halo* video game series. After talking to Cortana for a couple of weeks, my interactions were so personal and natural, that I stopped referring to her as "it." You may do the same after using Cortana for a while. But that's entirely your choice. Hopefully you won't mind me using the pronoun "her" instead of "it."

In This Chapter

- Setting up Cortana
- Starting Cortana
- Checking the weather
- Checking your calendar
- Setting appointments and reminders
- Adding notes
- Adding and removing places
- Configuring Cortana
- Discovering new commands

With Cortana, you can set reminders, check the weather, schedule appointments, set alarms, add notes, places, ask for directions, find songs, and so on. With each new iteration, she is capable of doing more and more. In this chapter, you find out how Cortana works, how you can use it at your workplace, and how to discover new commands that you can use to interact with it.

Set Up Cortana

Before you set up Cortana, you need a Microsoft account to use it. After you sign in with your Microsoft account, here's how to set up Cortana:

1. **Click in the search bar located near the Start button on the taskbar.**

   Cortana is loaded.

2. **Click I'm in!**

   You're asked if you want to let Cortana use your personal information, such as your location, contacts, voice input, and calendar.

3. **Click I agree to give Cortana permission to access them.**

   You may be informed that Cortana needs speech, inking, and typing personalization to be on. (If they're already on, skip to Step 5.)

4. **If prompted, click Yes to give Cortana permission to access speech, inking, and typing personalization.**

   You're asked if you would like for Cortana to listen when you say "Hey, Cortana".

5. **Click Yes please to confirm that you want Cortana to listen for "Hey, Cortana."**

   You're asked to enter your name or nickname.

6. **Type your name and click Use that (see Figure 14-1).**

   Cortana asks you to tell her to do something.

7. **Click the Microphone button on the bottom-right of the Cortana window.**

   Cortana is now listening.

8. **Say "Tell me a joke".**

   Cortana will tell you a joke.

9. **To close Cortana, click anywhere outside her Home screen.**

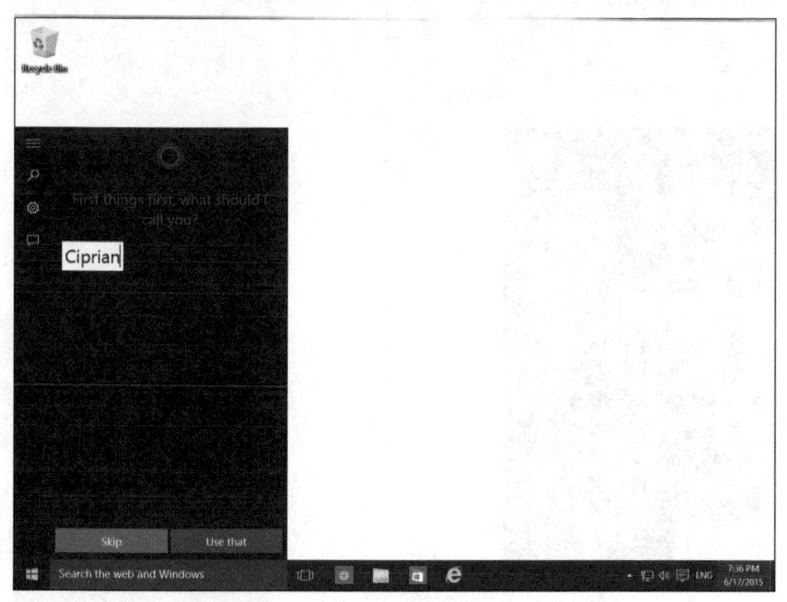

Figure 14-1: Entering your name when setting up Cortana.

From now on, each time you click in the search bar located on the taskbar and you're connected to the Internet, Cortana is loaded and it shows news and data based on your interests.

Enable Hey Cortana

When setting up Cortana, if you haven't enabled Cortana to start automatically when you say "Hey Cortana", you can enable this feature later. Here's how:

1. **Click in the search bar located on the taskbar.**

   Cortana appears.

2. **Click the burger button (three stacked lines, like a burger on a bun), at the top-left corner of Cortana.**

   A menu appears with several options.

3. **Click Settings.**

4. **Scroll down the list of settings until you find the Let Cortana Respond to "Hey Cortana" switch (see Figure 14-2).**

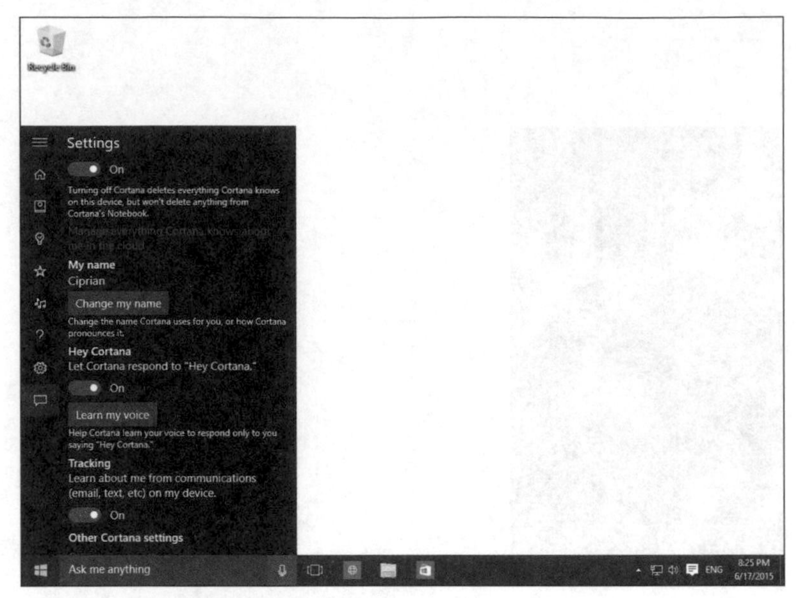

Figure 14-2: Enabling Hey Cortana.

5. **Set the switch to On.**
6. **Click anywhere outside Cortana to save this change.**
7. **Say "Hey Cortana" to confirm that this feature is turned on.**

If you want to disable Hey Cortana, follow the same steps and set the "Hey Cortana" switch to Off at Step 4.

Start Cortana

Once Cortana is set up, you can interact with her at any time. To start using Cortana, do one of the following:

- Click the microphone button found on the right side of the search bar.
- Say "Hey Cortana" if you enabled this feature in the previous section.

Figure 14-3 shows how to start Cortana.

Once Cortana is up and running, you can talk to her and give her voice commands, or if you prefer, you can type your commands in the search bar.

Figure 14-3: Start Cortana.

Check the Weather Forecast

One of the most popular ways to use Cortana is to check the weather forecast. To do so, you use the "What's the Weather" voice command, followed by the day or time period you're interested in.

- Ask "What's the weather today?" to check today's forecast.
- Ask "What's the weather tomorrow?" to check tomorrow's weather forecast.
- Ask "What's the weather this weekend?" to check this weekend's weather forecast.
- Ask "What's the weather on Friday?" to check this forecast for a specific day of the week.

Figure 14-4 shows Cortana's weather forecaster in action.

You can also add locations and days to your commands and check the weather in your destinations. For example, you can ask, "What's the weather in Los Angeles tomorrow?" or "What's the weather in Gainesville next Tuesday?" or "What's the weather in Pocatello on May 17?"

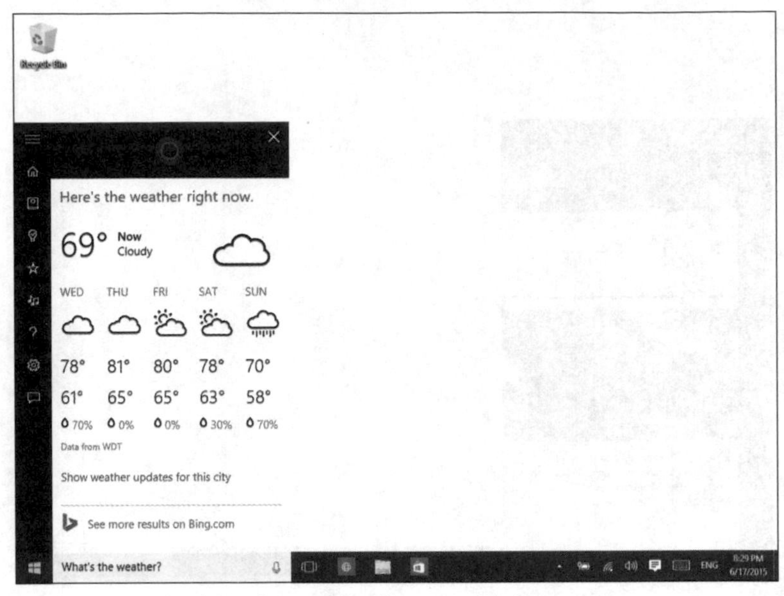

Figure 14-4: Checking the weather forecast with Cortana.

Check Your Calendar

You can ask Cortana to check your calendar and tell you what meetings you have scheduled. For example, if you want to find out what appointment you have next, start Cortana and ask, "What do I have next?" She will tell you the details of your next appointment.

You can also ask Cortana to check your schedule for a specific day or time period. For example, you can ask, "What am I doing tomorrow?" to learn your schedule for the next day. If you want to learn your schedule for an upcoming weekend, ask, "What am I doing this weekend?"

Schedule an Appointment

You can also use Cortana at work to schedule appointments. For example, to schedule a board meeting for tomorrow at 3 p.m., follow these steps:

1. **Start Cortana.**
2. **Say "Schedule a board meeting for tomorrow at 3 p.m."**

   Cortana shows you the details of the meeting and asks you to confirm that they are correct.

3. **Confirm the answer:**
   - If Cortana got it right, say Yes.
   - Say No if Cortana didn't get the message right.
   - When Cortana asks you to confirm a meeting that you want to add, and you say No, she asks you to say what you want to change about the meeting: the title or the time. Say what you want to change, then answer Cortana's questions to set up your event.
   - Say Cancel if you want to cancel the meeting and take it off your calendar.

Create a Reminder

Cortana is very good at working with reminders. You can set reminders that alert you on a specific date and time, when you get to a specific place, or when somebody calls. Here's how it works:

- To set a reminder for a specific day and time, say something like the following: "Remind me to email John tomorrow at 10" or "Remind me to print my report tomorrow."

  If you don't specify an exact time, Cortana asks for an exact time for the reminder. The time can be a specific hour or a time of day like noon, morning, or evening.

- To set a reminder of what to do when you get to a specific place, say something like this: "Next time I'm at work, remind me to call my manager" or "When I get home, remind me to prepare for tomorrow's presentation."

  These location-specific reminders work only if the locations you're referring to were added previously to Cortana. (See the "Add a New Place" section, later in this chapter, to find out how to add places to Cortana).

- To set a reminder to do something when a particular person calls, say something like this: "When Anna calls, remind me to say congratulations" or "When Dave calls, remind me to ask him about his project."

  This works only with people who are in your contact list and only on devices that have a SIM card, such as a Windows smartphone.

If you have a smartphone with Windows 10, all your data from Cortana is synced with your work computer or laptop. So, if you leave your desk and have your smartphone with you, you still receive your reminders via the smartphone.

Add Notes to Your Notebook

Cortana is also integrated with OneNote, so you can use Cortana to dictate your notes. All the notes that you add by speaking to Cortana, are stored in your personal notebook in OneNote, in the Quick Notes section. To dictate a note to Cortana, use one of the following options:

- Say "Note" or "Take a note," and Cortana responds that she will take a note and record everything you say.

  You aren't asked to give a name to your note. Just say what you want Cortana to store as a note; when you stop talking, Cortana saves that note for you. My experience is that this option works well.

- Say "Note" or "Take a note," followed immediately by what you want Cortana to note.

  My experience is that this option is more prone to errors.

Add a New Place

After you use Cortana for a while on your Windows 10 computer and/or tablet and smartphone, she's aware of the places you go most frequently and will ask if one place is your home, another is your work, and so on. However, you can manually add the places you most often go to. In this way, you're better able to use location-based reminders and other actions that involve use locations. To add a new place to Cortana's database, follow these steps:

1. **Click in the search bar on the taskbar.**
2. **Click the burger button (three stacked lines, like a burger on a bun), at the top-left corner of Cortana.**

   A menu with several options is shown.
3. **Click Places.**

   A list appears with the places that currently exist in Cortana's database (see Figure 14-5 for my "Favorite Places" example).
4. **Click Add.**

   You're asked to add a favorite.
5. **Type the exact address of the place that you want to add.**

   Cortana starts looking for addresses as you type.

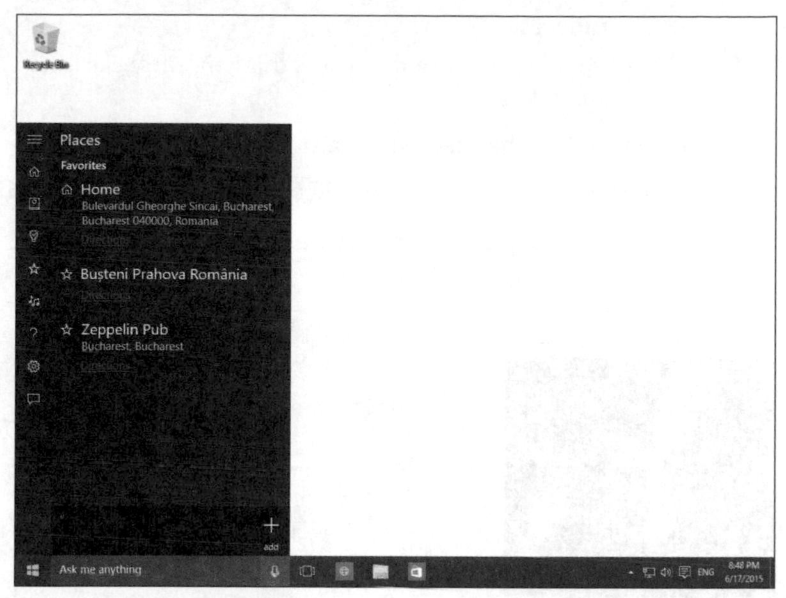

Figure 14-5: Favorite places known by Cortana.

6. **In the list of search results, click the address of the place that you want to add.**

   You're asked to enter a nickname.

7. **Type a nickname.**

8. **If the place you just added is your home, set the Set as Home switch to On. If it's your workplace, set the Set as Work switch to On.**

9. **Click Save.**

You and Cortana can now use the locations you add for location-based reminders and other location-based actions.

Remove a Place

Maybe you change jobs and no longer want Cortana to use your old work address. Or perhaps you move and don't want Cortana to use your old home address. In such cases, you can remove places from Cortana's database. Here's how:

1. **Click in the search bar on the taskbar.**

2. **Click the burger button (three stacked lines, like a burger on a bun), at the top-left corner of Cortana.**

   A menu with several options is shown.

3. **Click Places.**

   You're shown a list of the places that currently exist in Cortana's database.

4. **Right-click the place you want to remove.**
5. **In the menu that appears, click Delete (see Figure 14-6).**

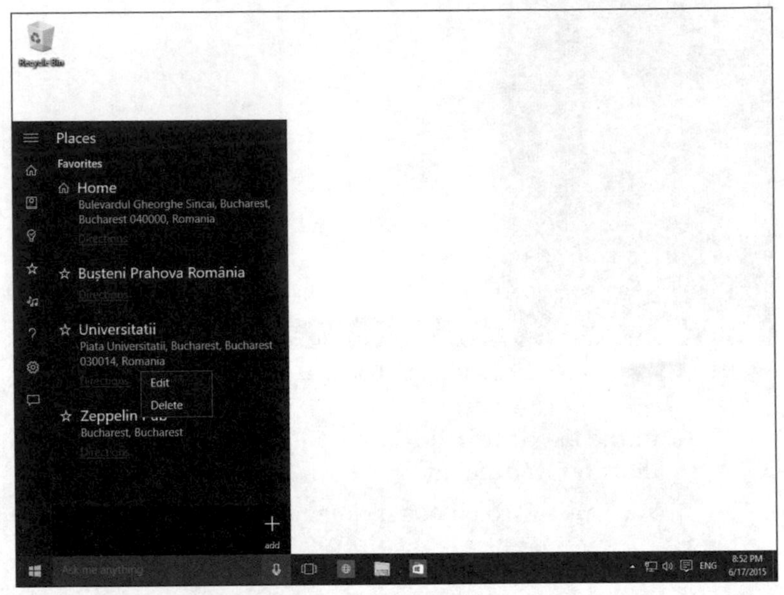

Figure 14-6: Removing a place from Cortana's database.

Configure How Cortana Works

You can change settings to maximize how Cortana works. For example, you can turn Cortana off entirely, change your name, change whether she calls you by name, delete her tracking information, enable or disable her ability to respond when you say "Hey Cortana." To change how Cortana works, follow these steps:

1. **Click in the search bar on the taskbar.**
2. **Click the burger button (three stacked lines, like a burger on a bun), at the top-left corner of Cortana.**

   A menu with several options appears.

3. **Click Settings.**

   You're shown a list of all the settings you can change.

4. **Change the settings you want (see Figure 14-7).**
5. **Click anywhere outside the list of settings to save your changes.**

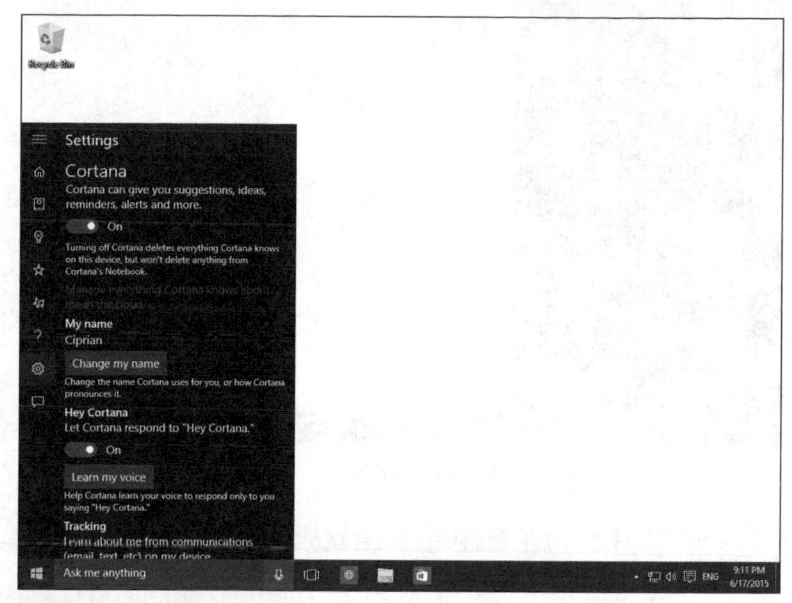

Figure 14-7: Cortana's settings.

Turn Cortana Off

If you don't like using Cortana, you can always turn her off. Just follow these steps:

1. **Click in the search bar on the taskbar.**
2. **Click the burger button (three stacked lines, like a burger on a bun), at the top-left corner of Cortana.**

   A menu with several options appears.
3. **Click Settings.**

   A list appears with all the settings that can be changed.
4. **The first switch in the list of settings is for enabling or disabling Cortana. Set it to Off (see Figure 14-8).**
5. **Click anywhere outside the list of settings to save your changes.**

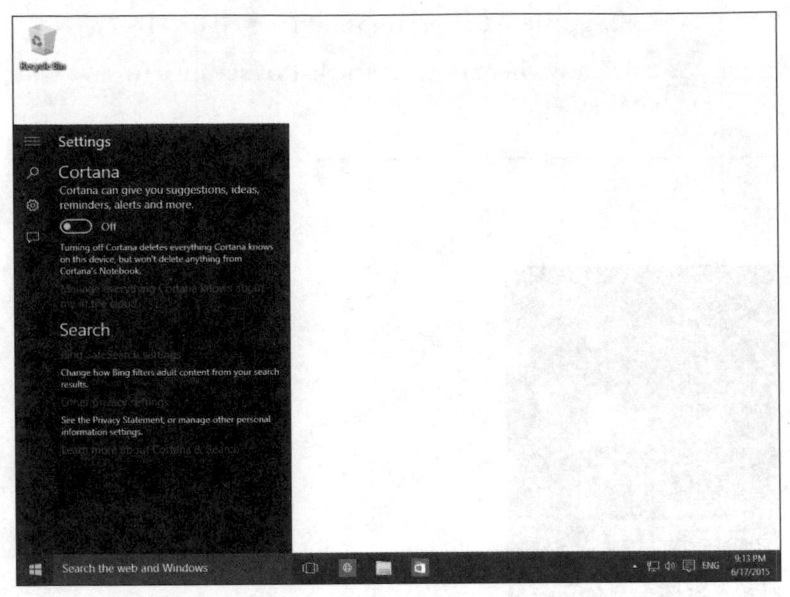

Figure 14-8: The switch for disabling Cortana.

Find New Cortana Commands

With each update of Cortana, Microsoft also updates her Help documentation so that you can use it to find the most important commands. Here's how to find most of the commands that you can use to interact with Cortana:

1. **Click in the search bar on the taskbar.**
2. **Click the burger button (three stacked lines, like a burger on a bun), at the top-left corner of Cortana.**

   A menu with several options is shown.
3. **Click Help.**

   You're shown a list of the tasks that you can perform with Cortana (see Figure 14-9).
4. **Click the task that interests you to learn more about it.**
5. **Navigate the examples shown by clicking them.**

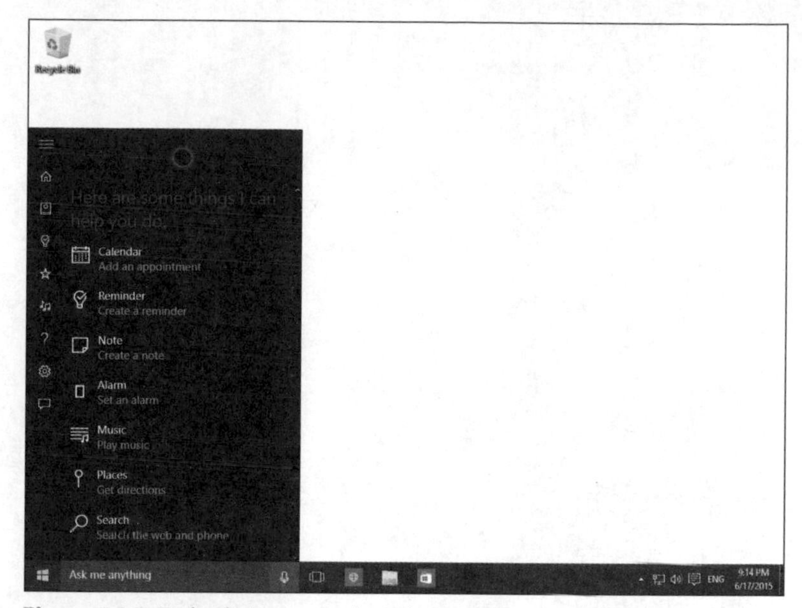

Figure 14-9: Tasks that you can do with Cortana.

CHAPTER FIFTEEN

Capturing Pictures, Screenshots, and Video

In the course of your work, you likely need to use all kinds of images. For example, you may need to take a quick screenshot and add it to a presentation or document. You may need to film a short video that showcases something you've worked on, or you might just want to take a picture for the fun of it. Hey, you may even want to take the occasional selfie and send it to a friend or coworker.

Windows 10 offers you the tools you need for taking pictures, for recording quick videos, and for taking screenshots. This chapter covers them in detail. As you can see in the following instructions, these tools are user-friendly and fun to use.

In This Chapter

- Starting the Camera app
- Taking pictures and recording video
- Viewing pictures and videos
- Configuring the Camera app
- Retuning the Camera app's settings
- Taking screenshots

Start the Camera App

If you have a webcam on your Windows 10 computer or device, you can use the Camera app to take pictures or record video. But, before you do that, here's how to start the Camera app in Windows 10:

1. **Click Start to open the Start Menu.**
2. **Click All Apps.**

   A list of all your apps appears.

3. **Scroll down the list to apps that start with the letter C and click the Camera app shortcut (see Figure 15-1).**
4. **If you're asked whether the Camera app can use your webcam and microphone, click Allow.**

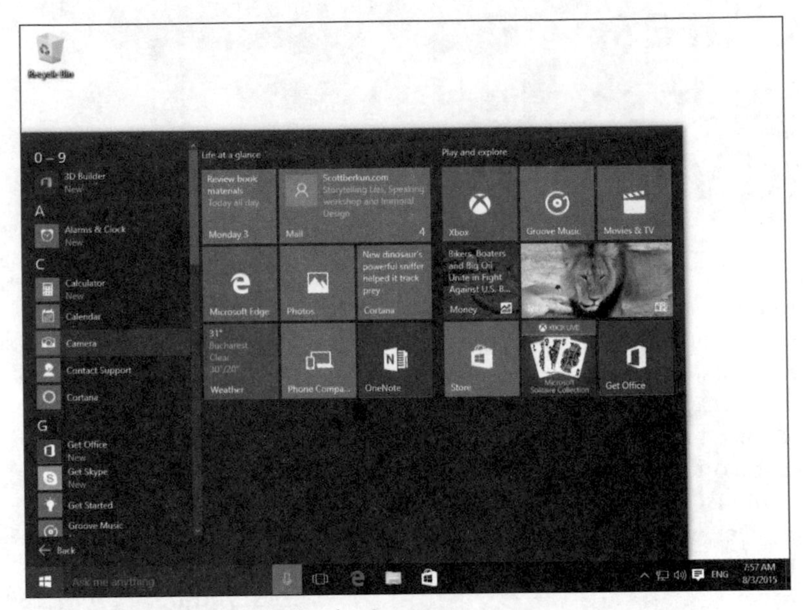

Figure 15-1: The shortcut for the Camera app.

Take a Picture

When you start the Camera app, it's already set to take pictures. To take a picture, just follow these steps:

1. **Start the Camera app.**
2. **Arrange the camera so that you capture the subject you're interested in.**
3. **When you frame the subject the way you want, click the button that looks like a camera (see Figure 15-2).**
4. **If you want to take another picture, click that button again.**

After taking your first picture, a picture icon appears in the upper-left corner of the Camera app window. You can use it to look at the pictures you take with the Camera app. Your pictures are stored as JPEG files in the Camera Roll folder located in your Pictures library/folder.

Figure 15-2: The button for taking pictures in the Camera app.

Record Video

You can also use the Camera app to record videos. Here's how:

1. **Start the Camera app.**
2. **Click the button that looks like a video camera (see Figure 15-3).**

   A timer appears at the bottom of the app window.
3. **Position the camera so you can record the subject you want.**
4. **Click the video camera button to start the recording.**

   The timer shows the progress of your recording.
5. **To stop the recording, click the video camera button again.**

Your videos are stored as MP4 video files in the Camera Roll folder located in your Pictures library/folder.

Use this button to record video

Figure 15-3: The Video button in the Camera app.

View Pictures and Videos

If you're using the Camera app and want to quickly view the pictures and videos you've just taken, follow these steps:

1. **In the Camera app, click the pictures icon in the upper-left corner of the app.**

   The Photos app window appears and shows the last picture or video taken.

2. **To navigate backward in the stored photos or videos, move the mouse cursor to the left corner of the app window and click the Back arrow (see Figure 15-4).**

3. **Click the Back arrow until you've looked at all the pictures and videos you're interested in.**

4. **To navigate forward, move the mouse to the right corner of the Photos app window and click the Forward arrow.**

Here are two other ways to view the pictures and videos you take with the Camera app:

- Using File Explorer, go to your Pictures library/ and find the Camera Roll folder, which, as I mentioned earlier, is where photos and videos are automatically stored.
- Open the Photos app and browse your collection of pictures and videos, which includes those taken with the Camera app.

Figure 15-4: The Back and Forward arrows in the Photos app.

Configure the Camera App

The Camera app allows you to configure such camera settings as the aspect ratio for your pictures, the resolution used for video, and the framing grids. The settings that are available also depend on your webcam model and its drivers. Some webcams have numerous configurable settings, whereas others have only a few. To access and configure the Camera app's settings, follow these steps:

1. **Start the Camera app.**
2. **Click the three dots on the top-right corner of the app window.**

   A pane with several options is shown on the right-side of the app window.
3. **Click Settings.**

   The available settings are shown (see Figure 15-5).
4. **Configure the settings that you want to change.**
5. **Click somewhere outside the list of settings.**

   Your settings are applied. The settings list is hidden automatically.

Figure 15-5: The available settings for the Camera app.

Capture Instant Screenshots

Capturing an entire screen in Windows 10 and saving it as a file is a one-step process. How you do it depends on whether your Windows 10 device has a keyboard:

- With a keyboard, press the Windows and PrtScn (Print Screen) keys simultaneously.
- Without a keyboard, press the Windows logo on your device and the Volume Down key at the same time.
- On a Windows 10 tablet, the Windows logo usually is on the screen, while the Volume Down key is on the side of the case.

Windows 10 creates a Screenshots folder in your Pictures library, and your screenshot is saved automatically using the PNG file format. Figure 15-6 shows the Screenshots folder.

The traditional way to take a screenshot in Windows is to press PrtScn (Print Screen) on your keyboard, paste the screenshot into an image-editing program such as Paint, and save the image as a file on your computer. While this method works in all versions of Windows (including Windows 10), it isn't the fastest way to take a screenshot in Windows 10. The preceding options are faster.

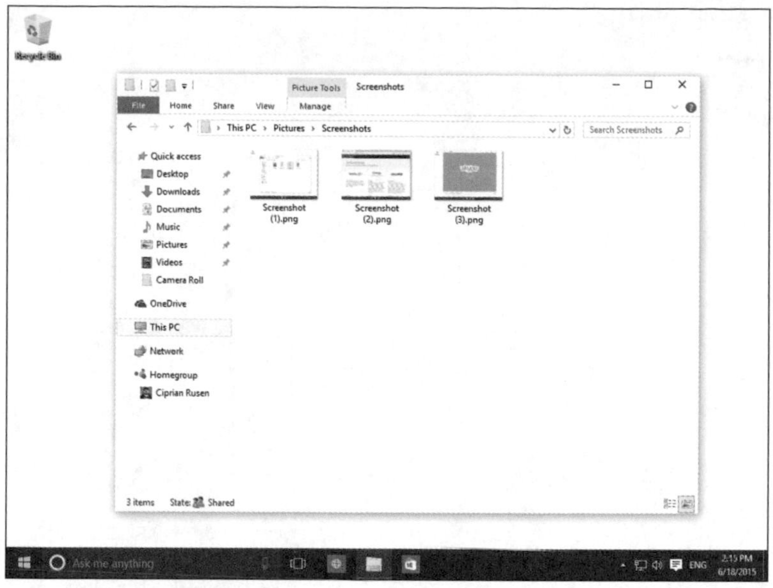

Figure 15-6: The Screenshots folder in Windows.

Capture Custom Screenshots with the Snipping Tool

If you have a desktop or laptop computer with Windows 10, the best tool for taking screenshots is the Snipping Tool. With the Snipping Tool, you can take full-screen screenshots, screenshots of a specific window, and rectangular or free-form screenshots. Once you've taken a screenshot, you can edit it and use tools such as pens, highlighters, and erasers. Here's how to use the Snipping Tool to take a screenshot of a specific app window:

1. **Open the app for which you want to take a screenshot.**
2. **In the search box on the taskbar, type the words** snipping tool.

   A list with search results appears.
3. **Click the Snipping Tool search result.**

   The Snipping Tool desktop app opens.
4. **In the Snipping Tool window, click the downward-pointing arrow, located near the New button.**
5. **In the menu that appears, click Window Snip.**

   Figure 15-7 shows the screenshot-taking tools available in the Snipping Tool.
6. **Click the app window that you want to capture.**

   The screenshot is loaded into the Snipping Tool.

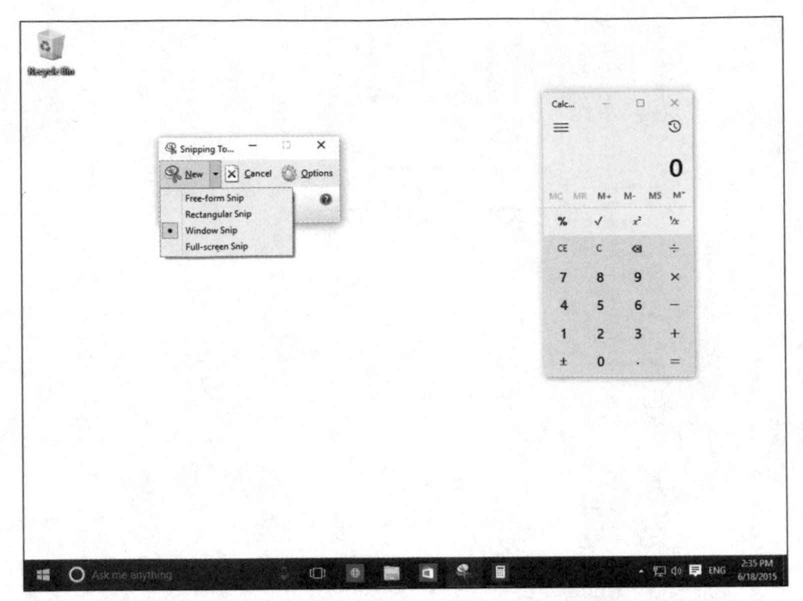

Figure 15-7: The screenshot-taking tools available in the Snipping Tool window.

7. **Click the Save button in the Snipping Tool window.**
8. **Type a name for this screenshot.**
9. **Select where to save the screenshot.**
10. **Click Save.**
11. **Close the Snipping Tool.**

CHAPTER SIXTEEN

Working with Apps

In This Chapter

- Using the Windows Store to find apps
- Installing apps from the Windows Store
- Manually updating apps from the Windows Store
- Uninstalling apps you no longer need
- Setting which apps get to show notifications
- Setting the default apps for Email, Calendar, Maps and others
- Snapping apps side by side
- Pinning apps to the taskbar

At work, you use many apps that come preinstalled on Windows, and I discuss several of those apps in previous chapters; for example, Skype, Mail, Calendar, and Internet Explorer. But I'm sure you also would like to install new apps from the Windows Store and other sources.

So, in this chapter, I focus first on using the Windows Store to find and install apps on your Windows 10 computer or device. I also tell you how to manually update and remove them from your computer. Then I show you how to set which apps are allowed to display notifications on the desktop and in the Notifications center and how to set your default apps for different kinds of tasks. Finally, I share some productivity tips for working with apps: how to snap apps side by side in Windows 10 and how to pin your most frequently used apps to the taskbar.

Browse the Windows Store

In your business environment, your company's IT department might choose to customize the Windows Store experience. Your company might choose to use only apps that are developed for internal use, or public apps from the Windows Store, or a mix of both. Therefore, the Windows Store may appear differently on your work computer than in the screenshots shown in this book. However, the procedures involved in browsing the Windows Store and finding apps remain the same.

Here's how to open the Windows Store and browse it in Windows 10:

1. **Click the Windows logo (Start button) on the taskbar.**

   The Start Menu appears.

2. **Click All Apps.**

3. **Scroll down the list of apps until you find Store and then click it.**

   The Windows Store is loaded.

4. **Click Apps to browse the apps that are in the Store.**

5. **Scroll down the list of apps (see Figure 16-1).**

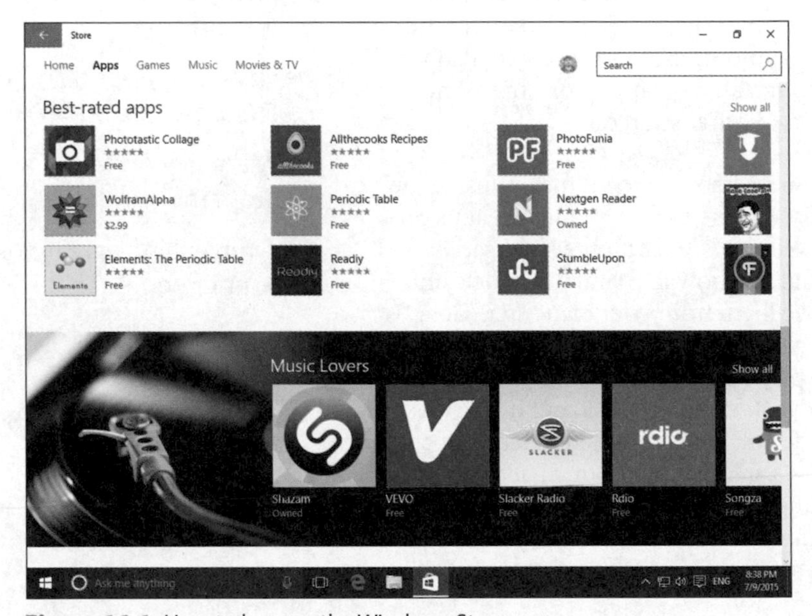

Figure 16-1: How to browse the Windows Store.

6. **To read an app's description, click it.**

7. **To get back to the list of apps, click the Back arrow on the top-left corner of the Store.**

8. **Continue browsing the Store by clicking on apps and categories to see what they offer.**

9. **Close the Windows Store when you're done.**

Search for Apps in the Windows Store

The fastest way to find an app in the Windows Store is to search for it. Here's how it's done:

1. **Open the Windows Store.**
2. **Click in the search box at the upper-right corner of the Windows Store.**
3. **Type the name of the app that you're looking for.**
4. **Click the Search button or press Enter.**
5. **In the list of search results that appears, click the app that you're interested in (see Figure 16-2).**
6. **When you finish using the Windows Store, close it.**

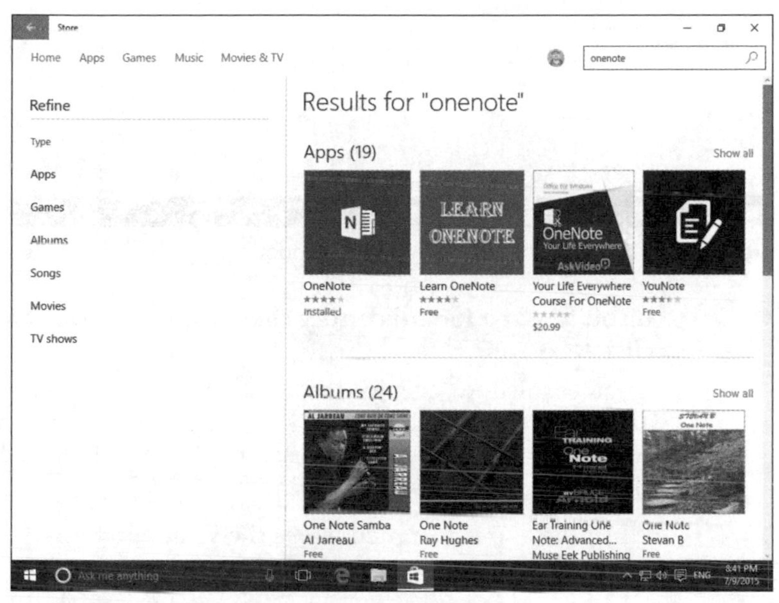

Figure 16-2: Search results in the Windows Store.

Install Apps from the Windows Store

Installing an app from the Windows Store involves just a few steps:

1. **Open the Windows Store.**
2. **Browse the Windows Store until you find the app that you're looking for or search for that app, using the steps in the preceding section of this chapter.**
3. **Click the app that you want to install.**

4. **Read the app's description to confirm it's the one you want.**
5. **Click the Install button to install the app (see Figure 16-3).**

   A progress bar appears below the app's name and description.

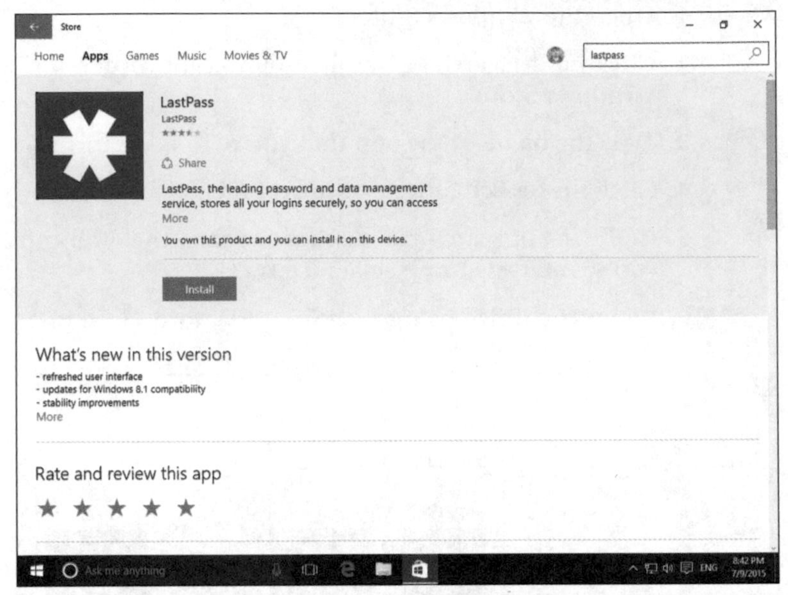

Figure 16-3: How to install an app from the Windows Store.

6. **If you're asked for an identity code, enter that code and click Next.**

   If you enabled two-step verification for your Microsoft account, you're asked to verify your identity by entering a code that can be sent to you in several ways (such as via SMS, email, or an Authenticator app).
7. **When the app is installed, close the Windows Store.**

At Step 5, if an app is a paid app, you don't see an Install button. Instead, you see a button with the app's price on it. Click it to purchase and install that app. Some apps offer a free trial so you can test them before purchasing. If you want to try an app before buying it, click Free Trial to install it.

Manually Update Apps from the Windows Store

The Windows Store is set in Windows 10 to handle app updates automatically. However, at times, you may want to force an app update rather than wait for the Windows Store to do so later.

To manually trigger an update for all your installed apps, follow these steps:

1. **Open the Windows Store.**

   The Windows Store appears. At its upper-right corner, you see the search bar.

2. **Click the second icon at the left of the search bar (it's a downward-pointing arrow with a number beside it).**

   A list of apps appears.

3. **Click Check for Updates (see Figure 16-4).**

   It takes the Windows Store a couple of seconds to find the available updates.

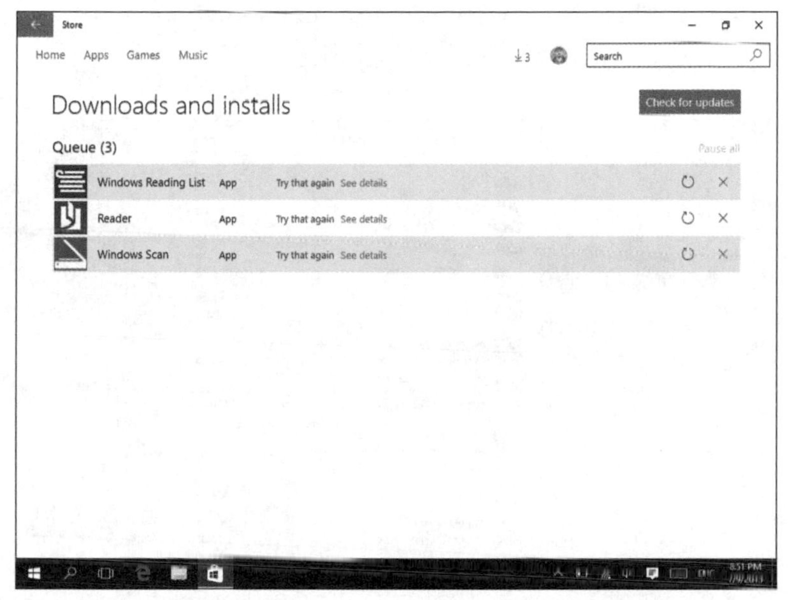

Figure 16-4: How to update apps in the Windows Store.

4. **To update individual apps, click their Download icon (a downward-pointing arrow), or click Update All to update all the apps.**

5. **When the update finishes, close the Windows Store.**

At Step 2, if you don't see a downward-pointing arrow with a number beside it, all your installed apps are up to date. You don't have to update any of them.

Uninstall Apps from the Windows Store

To remove an app from your Windows 10 computer or device, follow these steps:

1. **Open Settings.**
2. **Click System.**

   The list of system settings appears.
3. **Click Apps & Features.**

   A list with all installed apps appears.
4. **Scroll down the list of apps until you find the one you're looking for.**
5. **Click the app that you want to remove to select it.**
6. **Click Uninstall (see Figure 16-5).**

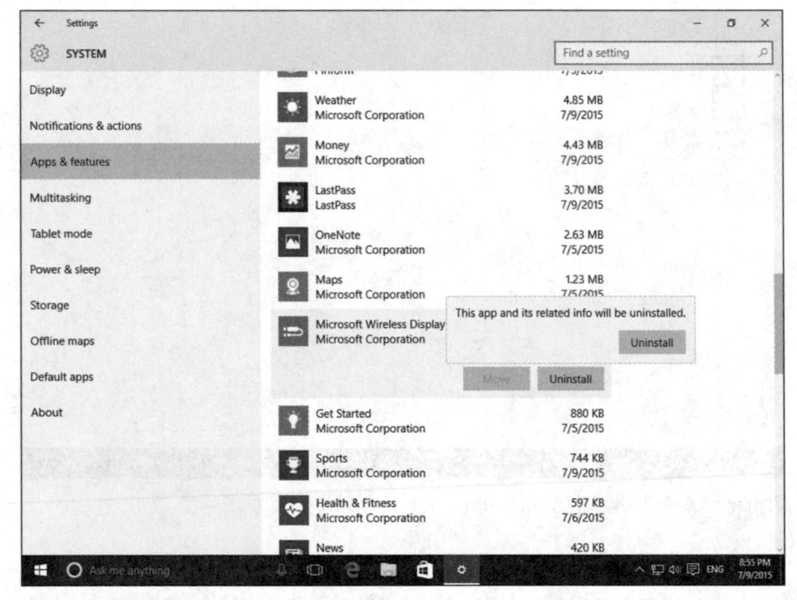

Figure 16-5: How to uninstall an app.

7. **Click Uninstall again to confirm your choice.**
8. **If you're asked for an administrator password, click Yes and go through the Uninstall wizard.**

   When you remove desktop apps, a UAC prompt appears. You must have the administrator password to remove the app. If you don't have the administrator password, you can't remove the desktop app from your computer. Your only choice is to click No and stop.
9. **When the app is uninstalled, close the Settings window.**

Set Which Apps Show You Notifications

While using Windows 10, you get notifications not only from the operating system but also from the apps that you're using. If you want to set which apps are allowed to show notifications, follow these steps:

1. **Open Settings.**
2. **Click System.**

   The list of system settings appears.
3. **Click Notifications & Actions.**

   A list of settings appears for configuring notifications and quick actions.
4. **Scroll down to the Show Notifications from These Apps section (see Figure 16-6).**

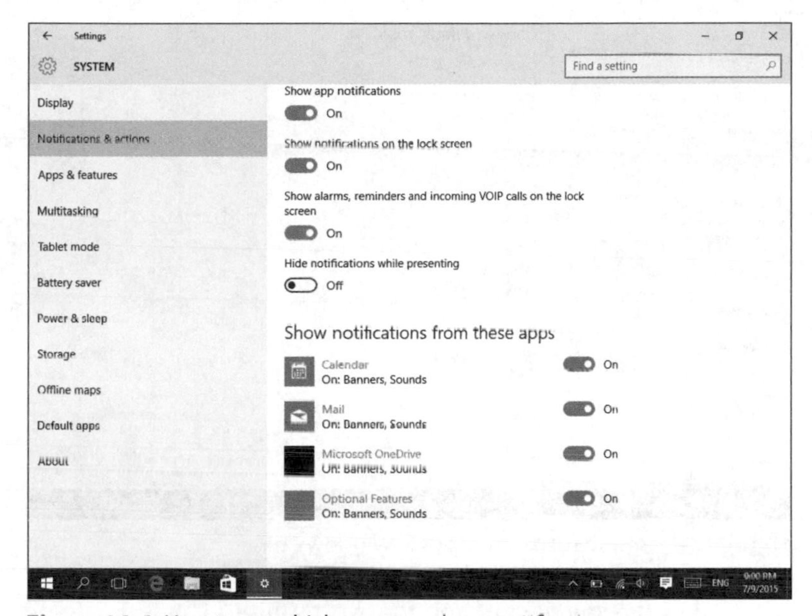

Figure 16-6: How to set which apps send you notifications.

5. **Set the switch to On for the apps that you want to show notifications.**
6. **Set the switch to Off for the apps that you don't want to show notifications.**
7. **Close the Settings window.**

Set the Default Apps

In Windows 10, you can set the default apps for functions like the Calendar, Email, Maps, playing music, and viewing pictures. If you prefer using something other than the apps Windows assigns for these tasks, you can switch to other apps by following these steps:

1. **Open Settings.**
2. **Click System.**

   The list of system settings appears.
3. **Click Default Apps.**

   The list of default apps appears (see Figure 16-7).

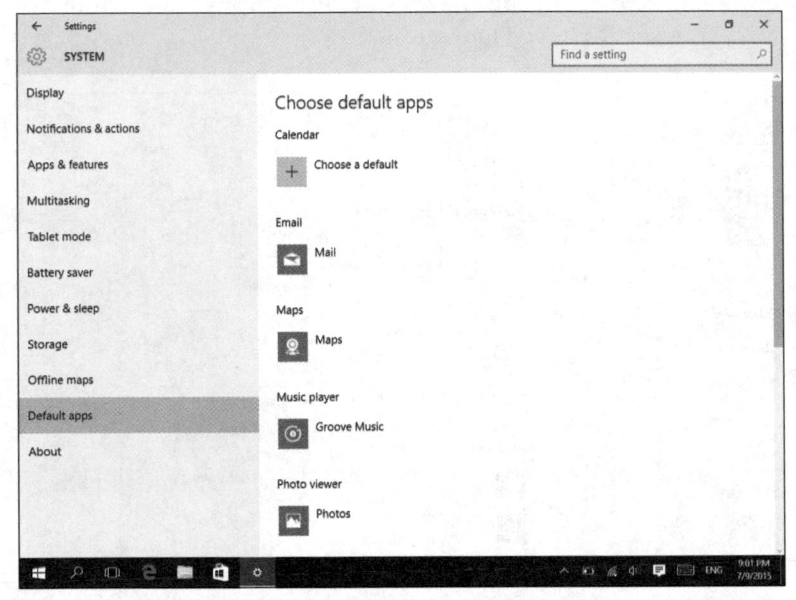

Figure 16-7: How to set default apps in Windows 10.

4. **Click the default app that you want to change.**

   A list shows other apps that you can set as the default.
5. **Click the new app that you want to set as the default.**
6. **Close the Settings window.**

Snap Apps Side by Side

If you need to work with two apps at the same time, it's a good idea to snap them side by side so that each consumes half of the screen. To snap one app to the left, use the mouse to drag the title bar of the first app to the left side of the screen. A trans-parent overlay appears, showing you where the window will be placed. Release the mouse button to snap the window there. Now, click the app that you want to see on the right side. You can see two apps, snapped side by side, in Figure 16-8.

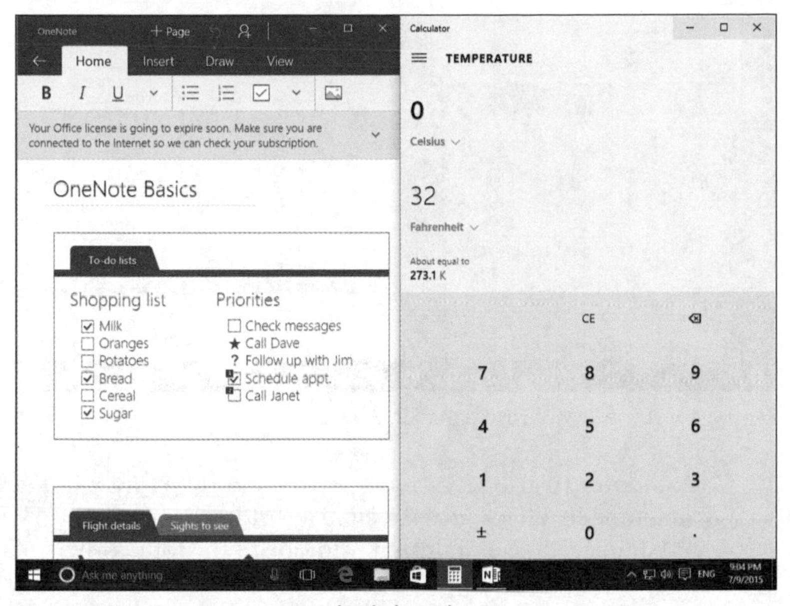

Figure 16-8: Two apps, snapped side by side.

When you snap an app with the mouse on Windows 10, the new Snap Assist feature pops up. Windows 10 displays a thumbnail list of your open windows. Click one thumbnail, and its app snaps to the unfiled side of the screen. It's faster and more intui-tive than the Snap feature on Windows 7 and 8. You can see the Snap Assist feature in action in Figure 16-9.

You can also press Windows+left arrow or Windows+right arrow to snap an app to the left or right half of your screen.

Windows 10 also adds support for vertical window snapping. For a reason known only to Microsoft, you can't do this with the mouse; you must use keyboard shortcuts:

- **Snap the current app to the top half of the screen:** Press Windows+up arrow.
- **Snap the current app to the bottom half of the screen:** Press Windows+down arrow.
- **Maximize the window:** Press Windows+up arrow twice.
- **Minimize the window:** Press Windows+down arrow twice.

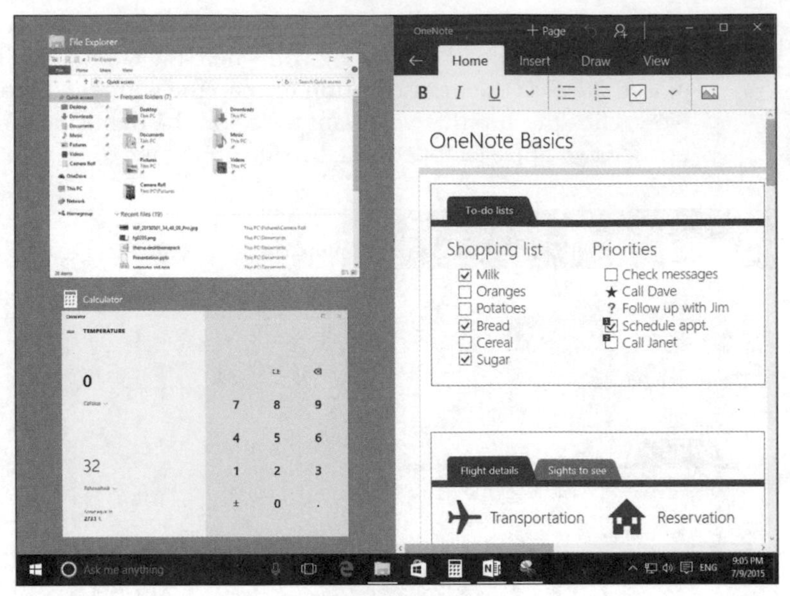

Figure 16-9: The Snap Assist feature in Windows 10.

Windows 10 also gives you the ability to snap four windows at a time in a 2 x 2 grid. To snap a window in a 2 x 2 grid with the mouse, drag and drop it into one of the four corners of the screen. Drag-and-drop several windows in this way to get your 2 x 2 grid of open windows. You can see the 2 x 2 grid in Figure 16-10.

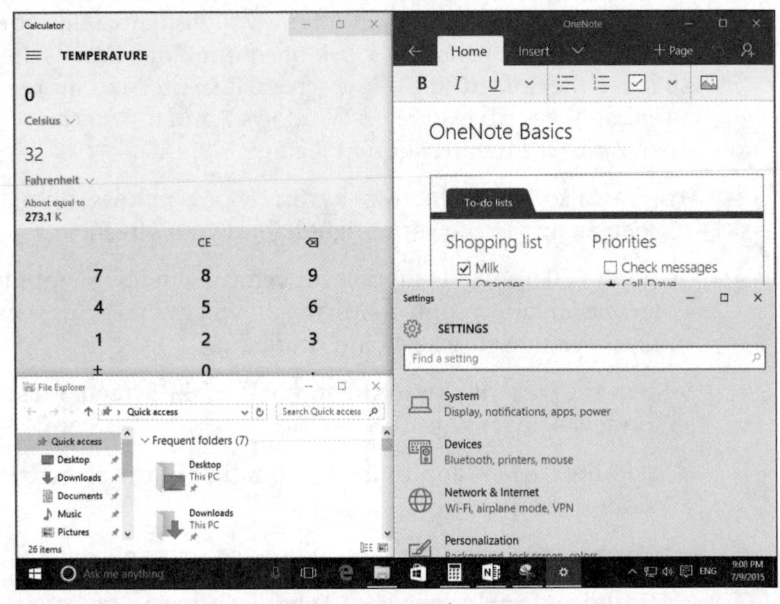

Figure 16-10: Snapping apps in a 2 x 2 grid.

You can combine the Windows+left/right/up/down arrows to snap a window into a quadrant of your screen. For example, press Windows+left arrow to snap a window into the left half of your screen; then press Windows+up arrow to snap it into the top-left quadrant.

You can use any layout up to 2 x 2. For example, you could have one tall window on the left and two short ones on the right. Or you could have one wide window on top and two narrow ones on the bottom.

Pin Apps to the Taskbar

If you use certain apps frequently, you may want to pin them to the taskbar so that you can access them as quickly as possible. Here's how to pin an app to the taskbar:

1. **Start the app that you want to pin.**
2. **Right-click the app's icon on the taskbar.**
3. **In the pop-up menu that appears, click to select Pin This Program to the Taskbar (see Figure 16-11).**

To unpin an app from the taskbar, at Step 3, select Unpin This Program from the Taskbar.

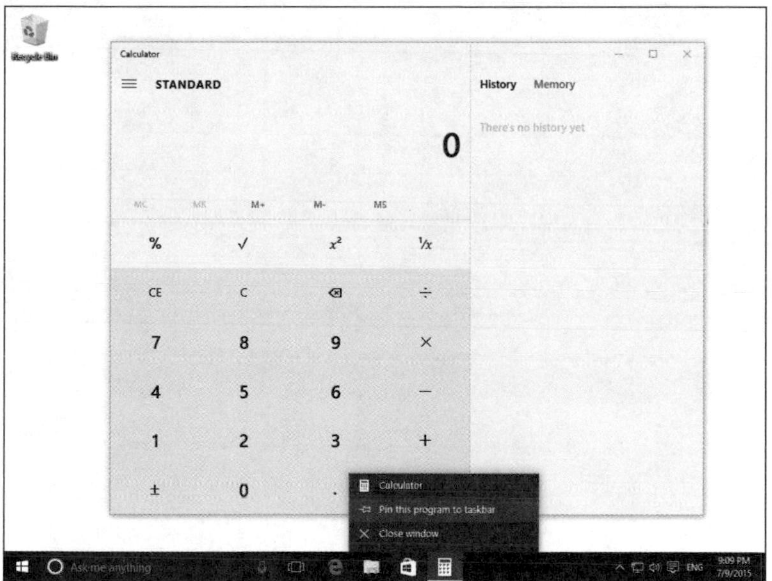

Figure 16-11: How to pin an app to the taskbar.

CHAPTERSEVENTEEN

Working with Devices

You may well have many devices connected to your computer at work or at home; for example, mice, keyboards, webcams, printers, and USB removable drives. That's why it's important to know how to manage hardware devices in Windows 10.

In this chapter, you first find out how to install drivers for your devices. Then you find out how to manage installed devices to get the most out of them.

In This Chapter

- Installing drivers for your hardware devices
- Managing installed devices
- Installing a network printer
- Installing Bluetooth devices
- Configuring your mouse and touchpad
- Setting which apps can access your webcam and microphone
- Setting AutoPlay defaults for media and devices
- Working with USB removable drives
- Understanding your PC's configuration

Install Drivers

Drivers are software components that enable operating systems, like Windows, to communicate with a hardware device (such as a printer, video card, mouse, or keyboard) that is part of your computer or device. Every device needs a driver in order to work. Many drivers, such as a keyboard driver, are built into Windows; some are offered as updates, through Windows Update, for devices you've installed.

When you plug a new device into your Windows 10 computer or device, the operating system spends some time detecting the device and tries to find the appropriate drivers for it and install them. In most cases, Windows 10 does a good job, and after it finishes the installation process, you can start using the device. However, there are cases in which Windows 10 isn't able to correctly identify a new device and you must install the drivers yourself.

When you purchase new hardware, you usually find its driver on a disc packaged with the hardware. You just insert the disc and install the driver according to instructions.

You can also go to the website of your device's manufacturer, where you can find the latest drivers for your device (plus, it's just good practice to check the manufacturer's website before you start using a new device). Find the Support or Downloads section, and then search for the exact model of the device that you're using. Before downloading drivers, make sure that they're for the version of Windows 10 that you're using; that is, 32-bit or 64-bit. Device drivers are operation-specific, and if you install the wrong one, your device may not behave properly or may not work at all.

In a locked-down business environment, you might not have permission to connect and install new devices on your work computer. In this case, if you must use a device on your computer, your only solution is to talk to the network administrator or the IT support department. They're the only ones who can help you.

View a List of Your Devices

Windows 10 offers you several lists of devices:

- All devices that are connected to your computer
- Installed printers and scanners
- Available Bluetooth devices in your area (if your device has Bluetooth)

To view the devices available in Windows 10 follow these steps:

1. **Open Settings.**
2. **Click Devices.**

   The settings related to devices are shown.
3. **Click Connected Devices.**

   A list appears showing all the devices that are connected to your Windows 10 computer or device (see Figure 17-1).
4. **Click Bluetooth, if it's available.**

   You see a list of Bluetooth devices that are available in the area. They may or may not be connected to your computer.

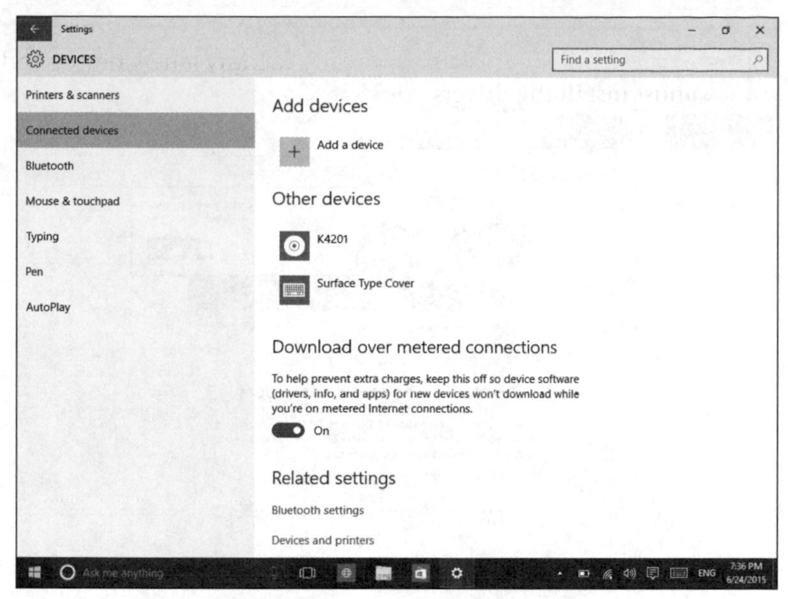

Figure 17-1: A list with connected devices in Windows 10.

5. **Click Printers & Scanners.**

   A list appears showing all the printers and scanners that are installed on your computer.

6. **Close Settings.**

Remove Installed Devices

If you no longer need to use a device, you can remove it. When you do so, your Windows 10 computer can't interact with the device until you connect and install it again. Here's how to remove connected devices from Windows 10:

1. **Open Settings.**
2. **Click Devices.**

   The settings for devices appear.

3. **Click the device type you want to remove (Connected Devices, Bluetooth, or Printers & Scanners).**

   The list of devices appears.

4. **Click the device that you want to remove to select it.**
5. **Click Remove Device.**
6. **Click Yes to confirm that you want to remove this device (see Figure 17-2).**
7. **Close Settings.**

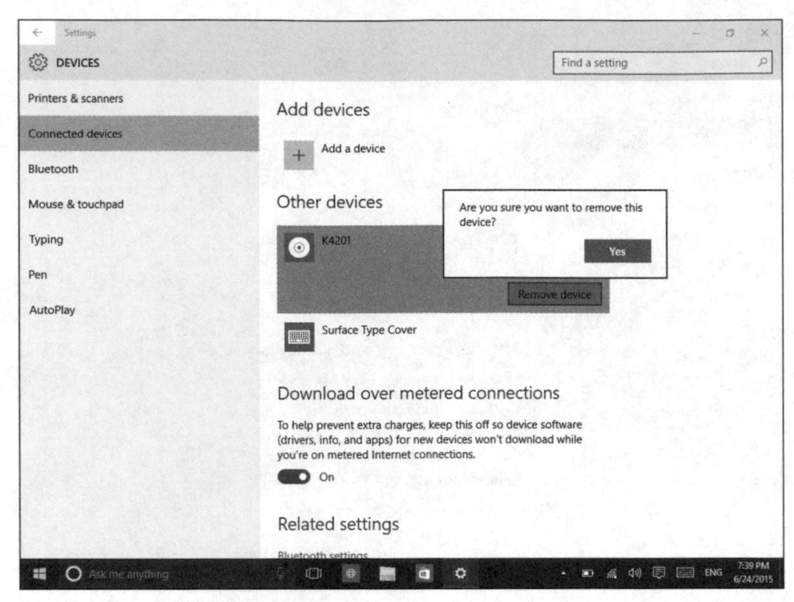

Figure 17-2: Selecting a device for removal.

Add the Windows Store App for a Device

After you install devices on your Windows 10 computer (for example, webcams, external hard disks, and printers), you may be able to find compatible apps for them at the Windows Store. Such apps can give you access to more options and features.

Here's how to get an app for a device that's connected to your Windows 10 computer:

1. **Open Settings.**
2. **Click Devices.**

   The settings related to devices are shown.
3. **Click the type of device you want to install (Connected Devices, Bluetooth, or Printers & Scanners).**

   The list of devices appears.
4. **Select the device that you're interested in.**

   If an app is available for the device, you see a Get App button alongside Remove Device.
5. **Click Get App, if this button is available (see Figure 17-3).**

   This takes you to the Windows Store, where the app for that device appears.

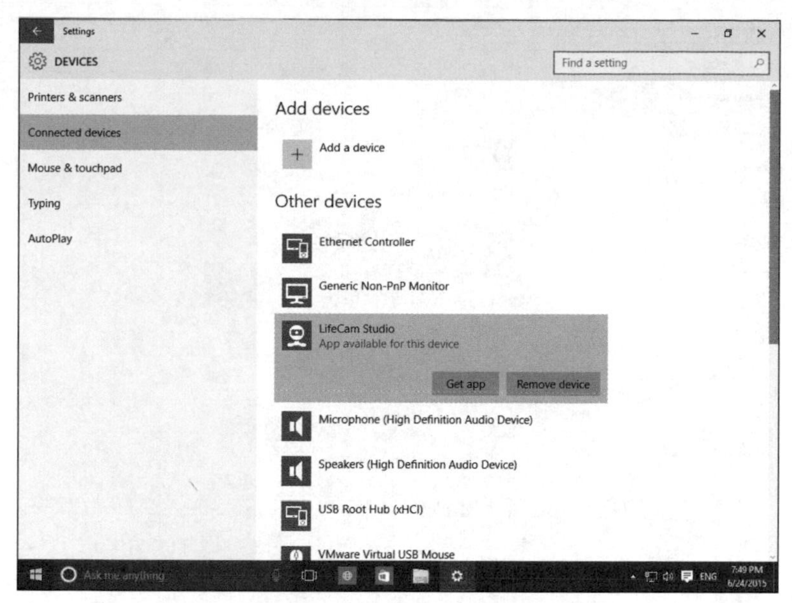

Figure 17-3: Getting the app available for a device.

6. **Click Install.**
7. **After the installation is finished, exit the Windows Store.**
8. **Close Settings.**

Connect a Network Printer

Windows 10 offers an easy way to install network printers on your computers and devices, including business network printers or wireless printers at home.

The procedure for installing them is easy and works the same for all printers and models. Just follow these steps:

1. **Open Settings.**
2. **Click Devices.**

   The settings related to devices are shown.
3. **Click Printers & Scanners.**

   A list with available printers and scanners appears.
4. **Click Add a Printer or Scanner.**
5. **Wait for Windows 10 to detect all the network printers that are available for installation.**
6. **When Windows 10 displays the printer that you want to install, click it to select it.**
7. **Click Add Device (see Figure 17-4).**

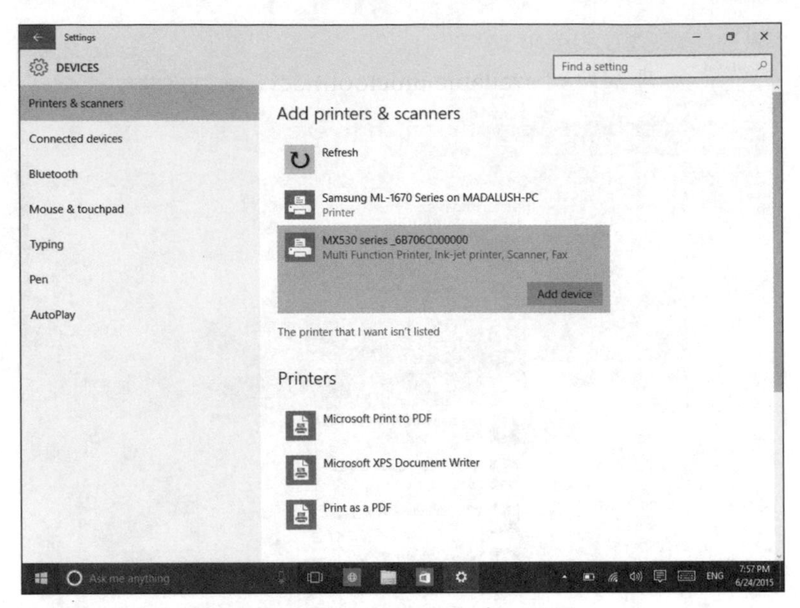

Figure 17-4: Adding a network printer in Windows 10.

8. **Wait for Windows 10 to install the printer and its drivers.**
9. **When Windows 10 notifies you that the printer is ready, close Settings.**

Now you can start using the printer the same way you use other printers.

Connect a Bluetooth Device

If you have a laptop with a Bluetooth chip or a 2-in-1 device like the Surface Pro 3, you can connect all kinds of Bluetooth devices, such as mice, keyboards, wearable devices, smartphones, and headsets.

Some Bluetooth devices, such as the Microsoft Sculpt Comfort mouse, have one button for turning them on and one for making them discoverable through Bluetooth. If that's the case for your device, press and hold, just for a couple of seconds, the button for making the device discoverable through Bluetooth. You must do this before beginning the following steps.

For example, here's how to install a Bluetooth mouse. Turn on the Bluetooth device that you want to install and follow these steps in Windows 10:

1. **Open Settings.**
2. **Click Devices.**

   The settings related to devices are shown.

3. **Click Bluetooth.**

   The list of available Bluetooth devices appears.

4. **Set the Bluetooth switch to On, if it's off.**
5. **Wait for Windows 10 to detect the Bluetooth devices that are available for installation.**
6. **Select the device you want to install by clicking it.**
7. **Click Pair (see Figure 17-5).**

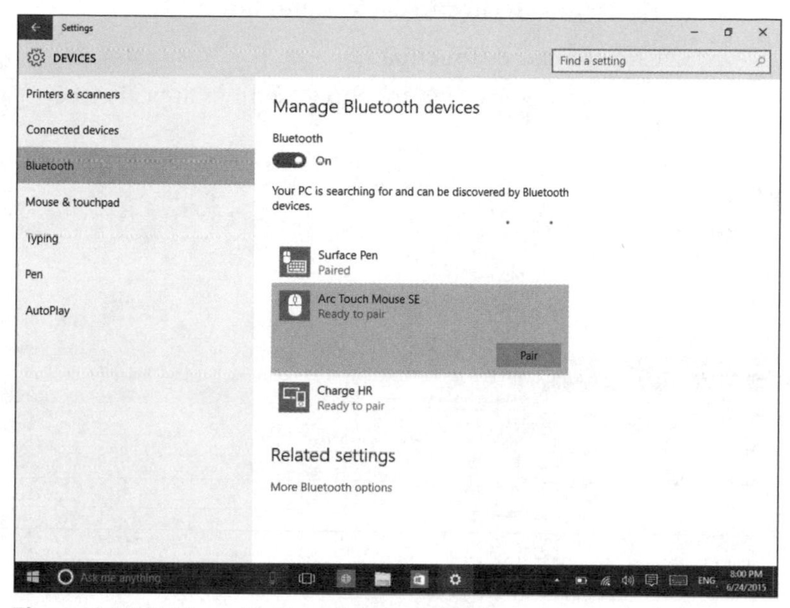

Figure 17-5: Pairing a Bluetooth device in Windows 10.

8. **Wait for Windows 10 to download and install the drivers for your Bluetooth device.**

   When the installation finishes, the device returns to the Connected status, and you can start using it.

9. **Close Settings.**

Configure the Mouse and Touchpad

If you have a mouse or touchpad (or both), Windows 10 offers settings that can help you configure how they work. When configuring the mouse, you can choose which is the primary button (left or right) and what happens when you scroll with the mouse wheel; you can choose how many lines to scroll at a time and whether you want to scroll inactive windows when you hover the mouse over them. When you configure the touchpad, you can turn it on or off and select whether you want it left on when a mouse is connected; you can change the cursor speed and allow gestures, double-taps, right-clicks, and more. The settings that are available depend on the mouse and touchpad models and their drivers.

In this section, you find out how to locate the mouse- and touchpad-related settings and how to customize them. You begin by configuring the mouse and touchpad:

1. **Open Settings.**
2. **Click Devices.**

   The settings related to devices are shown.
3. **Click Mouse & Touchpad.**

   The list of mouse and touchpad settings appears (see Figure 17-6).

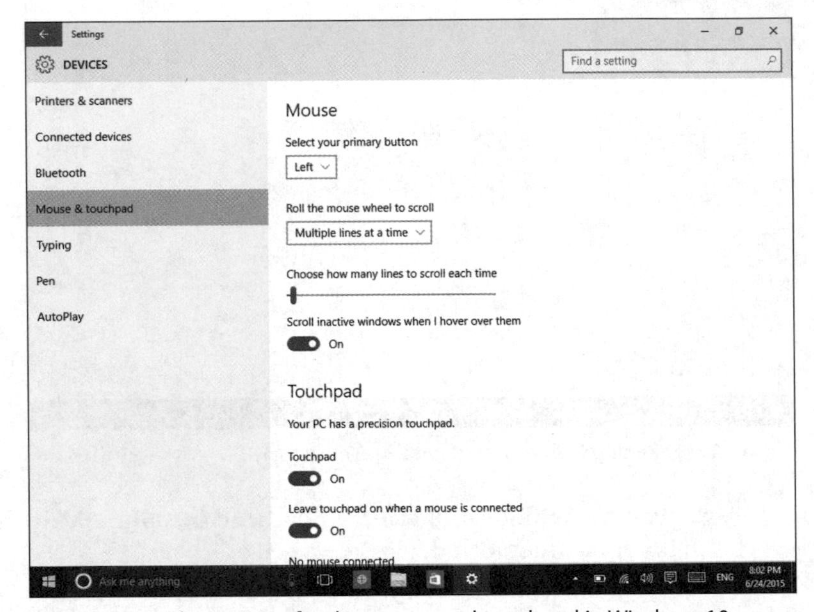

Figure 17-6: The settings for the mouse and touchpad in Windows 10.

4. **In the Mouse section, change the settings that you're interested in.**
5. **Scroll to the Touchpad section, if you want to configure it.**
6. **Change the touchpad settings that you're interested in.**
7. **Close Settings.**

It's a good idea to experiment with all the available mouse and touchpad settings, see what they do, and then configure them to work how you want them to. After a while, you'll notice a small, but useful, improvement in productivity when working on your computer or device.

Allow Apps to Access Your Webcam

Improvements in Windows 10 allow you to set whether apps can use devices like your webcam and which apps can or can't access your devices. You have more control over your privacy, and only approved apps can access your devices. Here's how to set which apps can access your camera:

1. **Open Settings.**
2. **Click Privacy.**

   The list of privacy related settings appears.
3. **Click Camera.**

   Your camera related settings are shown.
4. **To enable some apps to use your camera, set the Camera switch to On (see Figure 17-7).**

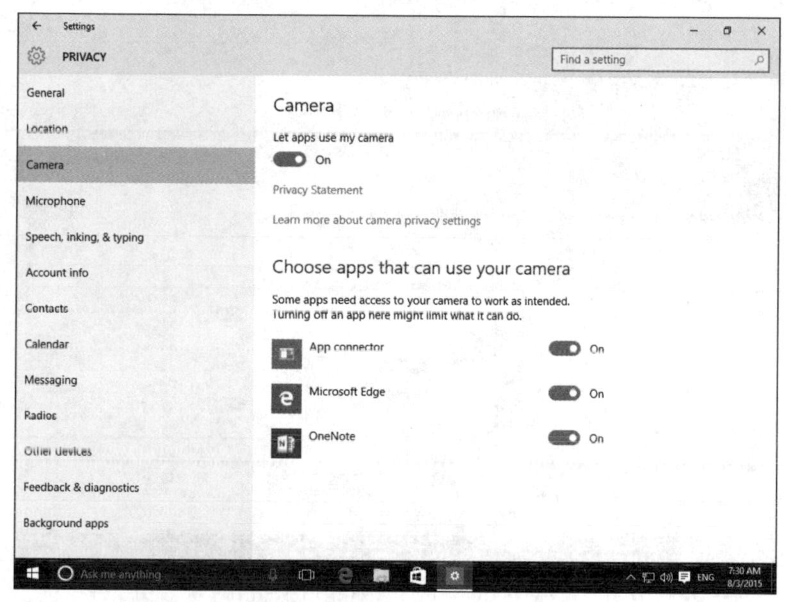

Figure 17-7: Setting which apps can use your camera.

5. **Go to the list of apps shown in the Choose Apps That Can Use Your Camera section.**
6. **Set the available switch to Off for the apps that you don't want to use your camera.**
7. **Set the available switch to On for the apps that you want to use your camera.**
8. **Close Settings.**

Allow Apps to Access Your Microphone

In Windows 10, you can set whether you want apps to access your microphone and which apps can or can't access it. It works whether your mic is connected directly to your computer or is built into a webcam.

Here's how to set which apps can access your microphone:

1. **Open Settings.**
2. **Click Privacy.**

   The list of privacy related settings appears.
3. **Click Microphone.**
4. **If you want some apps to use your microphone, set the Microphone switch to On (see Figure 17-8).**

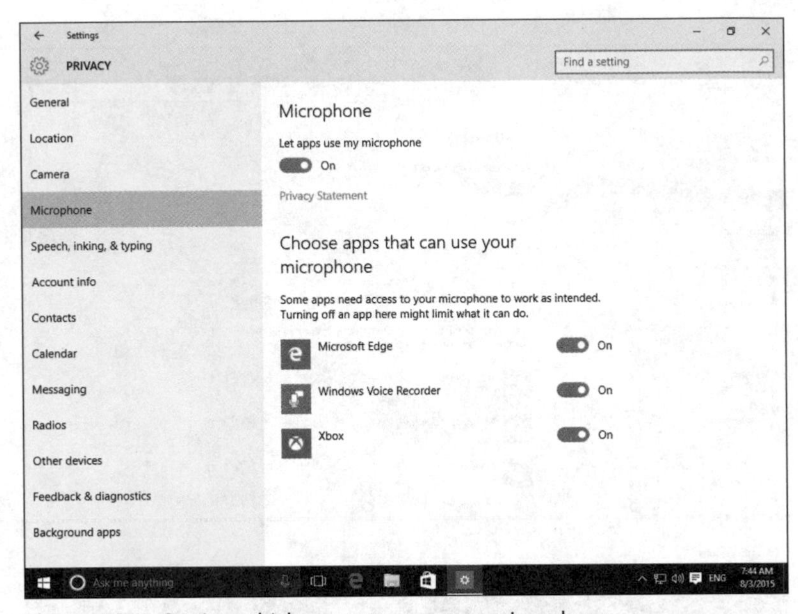

Figure 17-8: Setting which apps can use your microphone.

5. **Go to the list of apps shown in the Choose Apps That Can Use Your Microphone section.**
6. **Set the available switch to Off for the apps that you don't want to use your microphone.**
7. **Set the available switch to On for the apps that you want to use your microphone.**
8. **Close the Settings menu.**

Set the AutoPlay Defaults for Media and Devices

In Windows 10, you can set the AutoPlay defaults for media and devices. For example, you can set what happens each time you plug in a removable drive like a USB memory stick or a USB external hard disk. You can also set AutoPlay defaults for devices like memory cards and smartphones, such as the Windows 10 Mobile smartphone that you may have received at work. Here's how to change the AutoPlay defaults in Windows 10, for your media and devices:

1. **Open Settings.**
2. **Click Devices.**

   The settings related to devices are shown.
3. **Click AutoPlay.**

   Your AutoPlay settings are shown.
4. **To turn on AutoPlay for Media and Devices, set the AutoPlay switch to On (see Figure 17-9).**

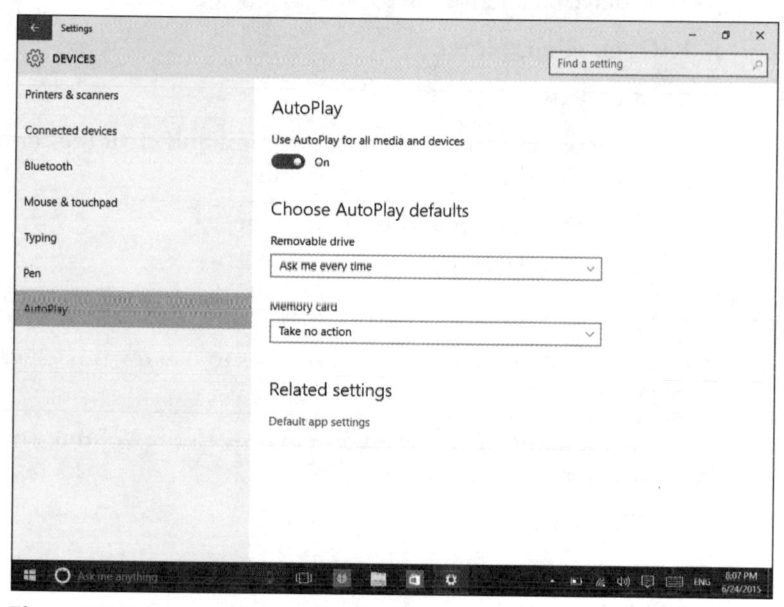

Figure 17-9: How to set AutoPlay for media and devices.

5. **Click the Removable Drive down-pointing arrow.**

   A drop-down list appears with several possible actions.
6. **From the list, select the default action that you want Windows 10 to perform each time you connect removable drives to your computer.**

7. **Do the same for the other types of devices that you're interested in.**
8. **Close Settings.**

The number of AutoPlay settings differs among computers depending on the number of devices installed on them. So you may not have the same number of AutoPlay defaults as shown in Figure 17-9.

Format a Removable USB Drive

When you first plug in a USB removable drive, such as a memory stick, you may need to format it so that you can use it. You may also need to format an old USB removable drive, if the data on it becomes corrupted and unusable or if you just want to delete everything that's on it.

The following process permanently deletes all data from the formatted device. If you need any data from the device, copy the data to another device before you begin the formatting steps.

To format a USB removable drive, plug in the device, wait for it to be detected and installed, and follow these steps:

1. **Open File Explorer.**
2. **Click This PC.**
3. **Go to the Devices and Drives section and click the removable drive that you want to format.**
4. **Go to the Ribbon and click Manage.**

   The Manage tab appears.
5. **Click Format.**
6. **Select the file system that you want to use for this drive (see Figure 17-10).**
7. **Type a name, if you want a new one, in the Volume Label field (see Figure 17-10).**
8. **Click Start.**

   You're warned that formatting will erase all data on this disk.
9. **Click OK.**
10. **Click OK again when the formatting is complete.**
11. **Close the Format window.**
12. **Close File Explorer.**

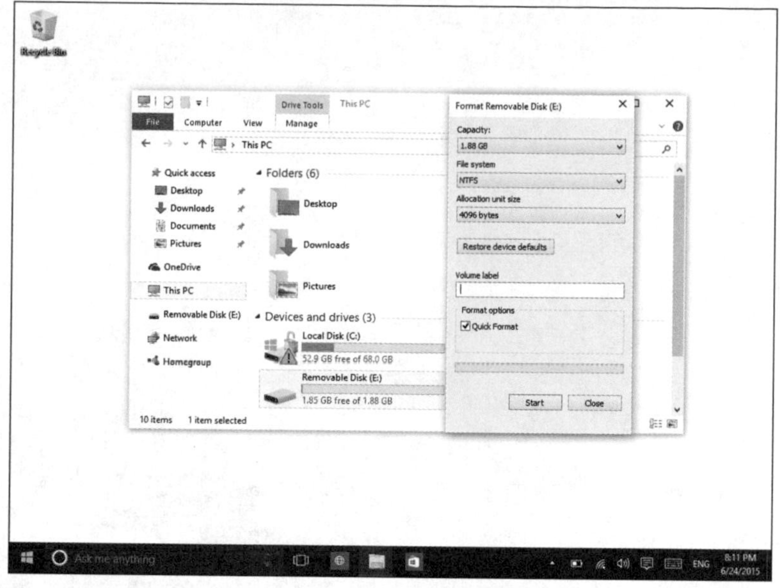

Figure 17-10: How to format a removable drive.

If you want to completely remove data on a USB removable drive and make sure that nobody can recover it, formatting won't help. You have to use specialized desktop apps like Eraser or File Shredder.

Safely Remove a USB Drive

During the course of your workday, you may use several removable drives, including USB memory sticks and USB external hard disk drives. If you have precious data on them, it's a very good idea to safely eject them from Windows, before physically ejecting the drives from your computer. Doing so ensures that all opened files are closed and that no data is written on the removable drive while you unplug it. Here's how to safely remove a drive from your computer, in Windows 10:

1. **With the removable drive still inserted, go to the Desktop.**
2. **Click the Show Hidden Icons arrow (the upward-pointing arrow on the right side of the taskbar).**
3. **Click the USB removable drive symbol (the one with a green check mark on it; see Figure 17-11).**

   A list of removable devices appears.
4. **Click the drive that you want to eject.**

   A Safe to Remove Hardware notification appears.
5. **Physically unplug the removable drive from your Windows 10 computer or device.**

Figure 17-11: How to safely eject a removable drive.

Find Your PC's Hardware and Software Configuration

With only a few clicks, you can find basic information about the hardware and software configuration of your Windows 10 computer or device. Just open the PC panel, where you can view information such as the processor (CPU) that's available, how much RAM memory is installed, the operating system type (32-bit or 64-bit), the PC name, and whether pen and touch input are available. Here's how to find the basic configuration of your Windows 10 computer:

1. **Open Settings.**
2. **Click System.**

   The list of available system settings appears.
3. **Click About (see Figure 17-12).**
   - The Processor entry shows what CPU is installed on your computer.
   - The Installed RAM entry shows how much RAM memory you have available.
   - Other entries show you more detail about your computer's configuration.
4. **When you finish, close Settings.**

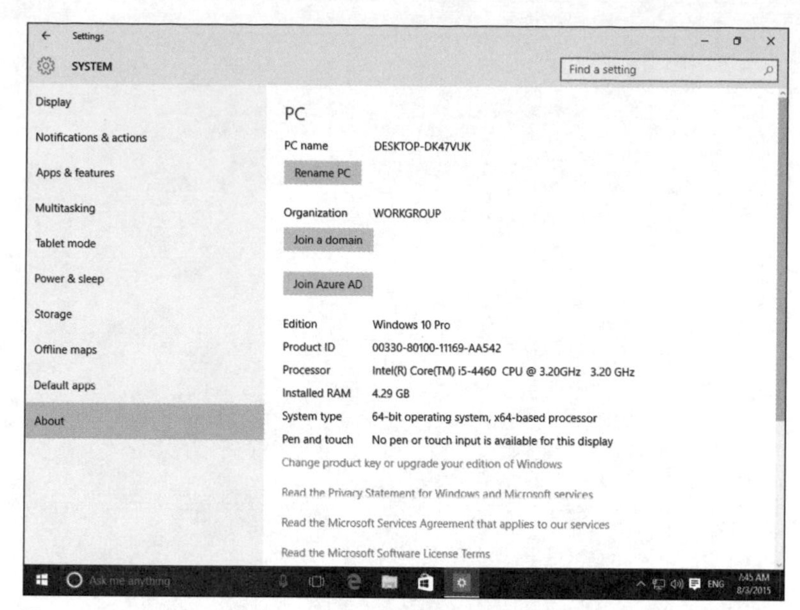

Figure 17-12: The hardware and software configuration of your PC.

CHAPTER EIGHTEEN

Working on the Road

In This Chapter

- Creating and using VPN connections
- Disconnecting or removing VPN connections
- Setting up Work Folders
- Using Work Folders
- Connecting remotely to another PC
- Using Airplane mode while flying
- Saving power while traveling

If you travel as part of your job, you probably need access to your company's network in order to do your work. That's where virtual private networks (VPNs) come in. VPNs establish secure connections to a company's private network. So I start this chapter by showing you how to work with VPN connections in Windows 10.

On the other hand, perhaps you work from home on your personal devices and need to access your files at work. This is where the Work Folders feature, which was first introduced in Windows 8, comes in. With the help of Work Folders, you can access your work on personal devices that are connected to the Internet. You don't have to take your work computer or laptop with you. You just need to set up Work Folders on your work computer and your personal devices; your work always is available, no matter which device you use. If this feature is available on your company's network, be sure to check out this chapter's discussion on how to use it from just about anywhere.

You may need to connect remotely to your work computer, either from home or from another location in your company's network. If so, this chapter shows how Remote Access works in Windows 10.

Traveling also means that you need as much battery power as possible. So, for example, if you're taking a long flight and need to do some work, you'll appreciate the new Battery Saver feature that's included in Windows 10. With this feature, you can squeeze in more time for work and also find out what's using up most of your battery. Also, this chapter explains how to further improve the use of your battery by manually adjusting Windows settings.

Create a VPN Connection

VPNs allow users to connect to private networks from the Internet in a secure manner. Many companies provide VPN services for their employees so that they can connect to the enterprises' networks as needed. If your workplace has this service, depending on how it's set up and implemented, you may be able to connect to the VPN service either straight from Windows 10, using the features offered by the operating system, or via a special VPN client app that's provided by your company.

If your workplace uses a special VPN client app, the network administrator or the IT department must provide you with the specific instructions for that app.

However, if you connect straight to the VPN service from Windows 10, you need information about your company's VPN. Depending on your company's setup, you may need to know the following details to connect with VPN:

- The VPN server name or address
- The VPN type (such as PPTP, L2TP/IPsec, SSTP, or IKEv2)
- The sign-in details (usually your username and password)

If your company uses Windows to create a VPN connection to the workplace network, here's what you need to do to connect to its VPN service:

1. **Click the Notifications icon on the right side of the taskbar.**

   The Action Center appears.

2. **Click VPN.**

   The Settings window appears.

3. **Click Add a VPN Connection (see Figure 18-1).**

   A window with the same name opens.

4. **Type the name that you want to use for the connection and the other required details (such as server name or address, VPN type, username, and password; see Figure 18-2).**

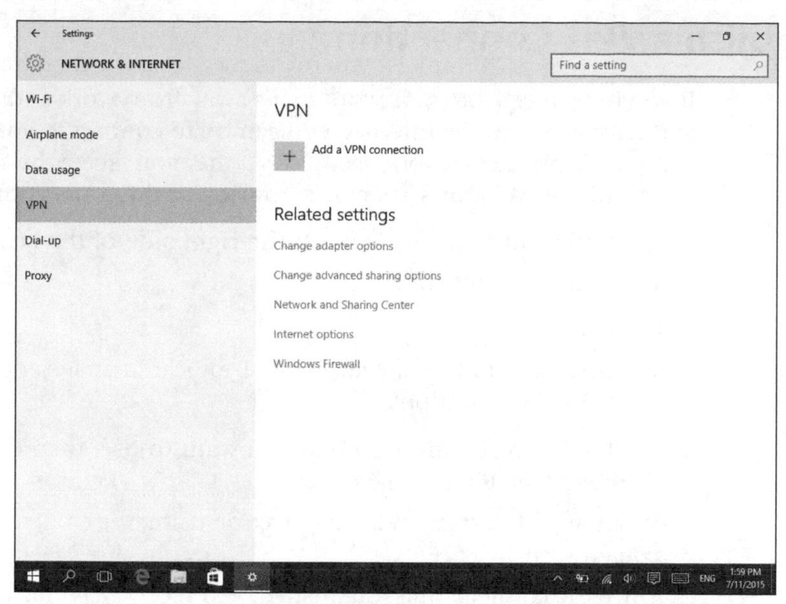

Figure 18-1: Adding a VPN connection.

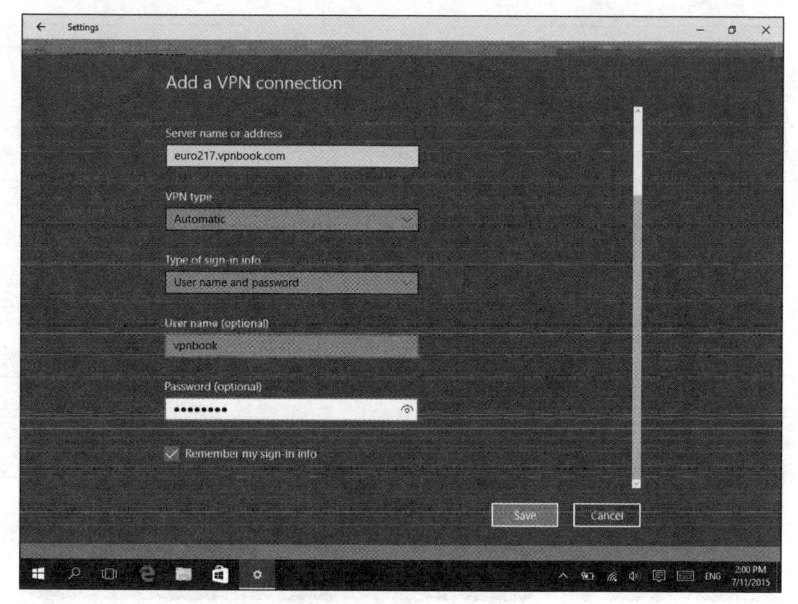

Figure 18-2: Entering the VPN connection details.

5. **When you finish, click Save.**

   The VPN connection is now added to your list of VPN connections.

Establish a VPN Connection

If you're connected to a network that's away from work and you have access to the Internet, you can try to connect to your company's private network using VPN. After you create the VPN connection in Windows 10, here's how to use the connection:

1. **Click the Notifications icon on the right side of the taskbar.**

   The Action Center appears.

2. **Click VPN.**

   The Settings window appears, where you can manage and create VPN connections.

3. **Click the VPN connection that you want to use; then click Connect (see Figure 18-3).**

   Windows 10 starts the VPN connection using the credentials you entered.

   Once the connection is established, you receive a confirmation from Windows 10.

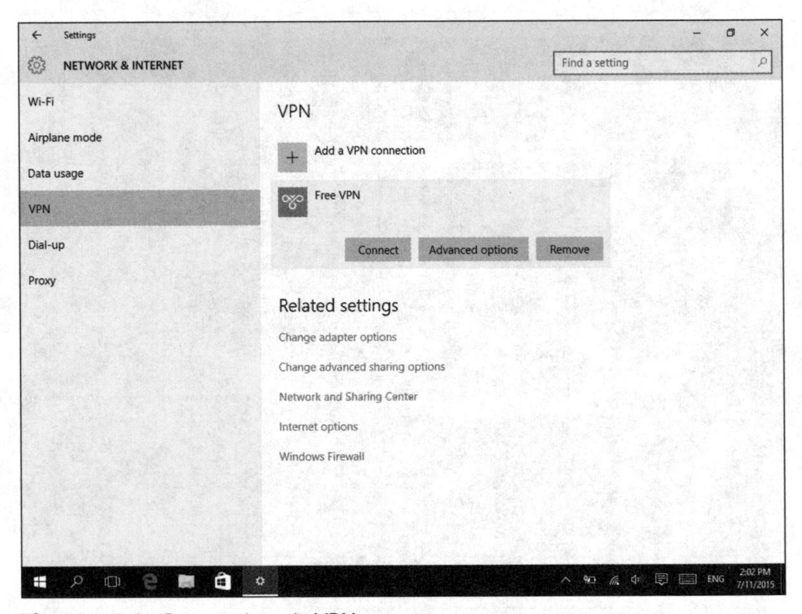

Figure 18-3: Connecting via VPN.

4. **Close the Settings window.**

   Now you can use your VPN connection when needed.

Not all public networks that have access to the Internet allow you to connect using VPN to your company's network. Some networks are configured so that they specifically block VPN connections of any kind. If that's the case for the network that you're connected to, your only solution is to change the network and try another one.

Disconnect from a VPN Connection

When you finish using your VPN connection, here's how to disconnect from it:

1. **Click the Notifications icon on the right side of the taskbar.**

   The Action Center appears.

2. **Click VPN.**

   The Settings window appears.

3. **Click the VPN connection that you want to disconnect from; then click Disconnect (see Figure 18-4).**

4. **Close the Settings window.**

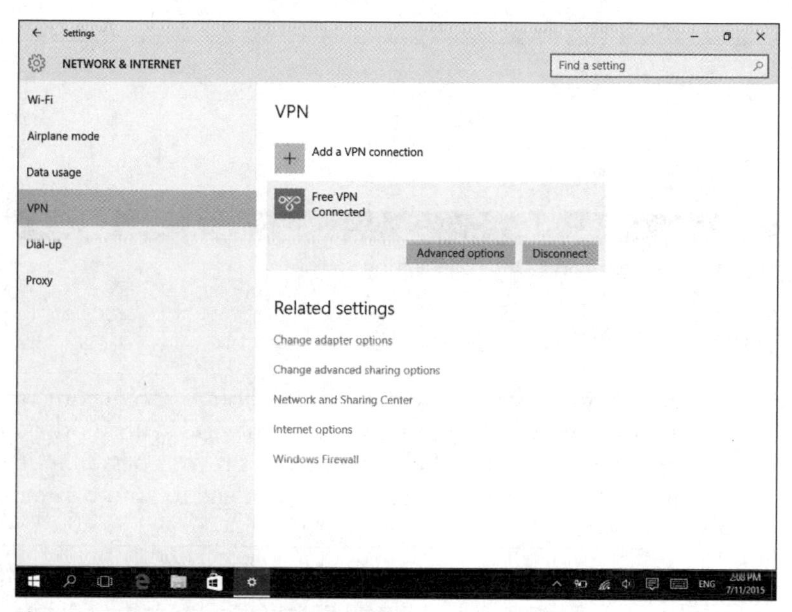

Figure 18-4: Disconnecting from VPN.

Remove a VPN Connection

If you no longer need to use a VPN connection that you created, you can remove it easily from Windows. Just follow these steps:

1. **Click the Notifications icon on the right side of the taskbar.**

   The Action Center appears.

2. **Click VPN.**

   The Settings window appears.

3. **Click the VPN connection that you want to delete; then click Remove (see Figure 18-5).**

4. Click Remove again to confirm your choice (see Figure 18-5).
5. Close the Settings window.

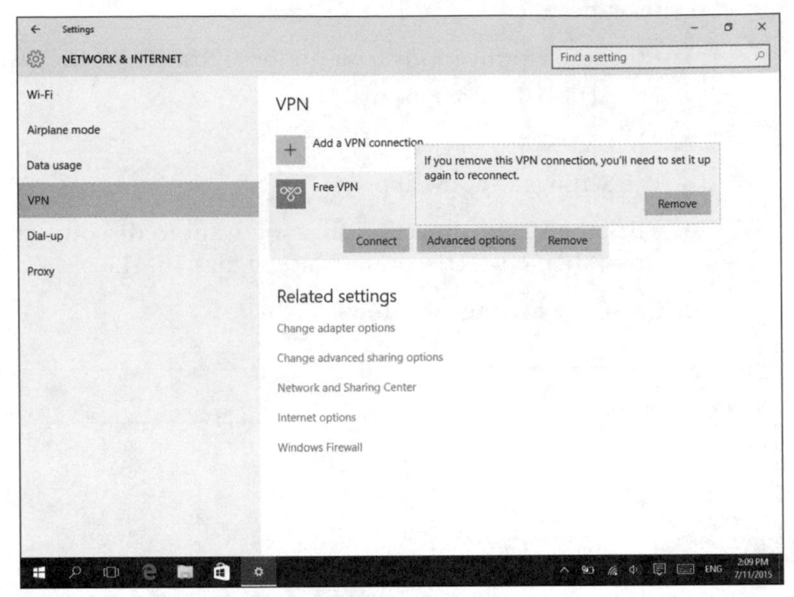

Figure 18-5: Removing a VPN connection.

Set Up Work Folders

Work Folders is a feature that enables you to access your work files from your personal computer or device. With Work Folders, you can keep copies of your work files on your personal devices and have them automatically synchronized to your company's datacenter.

Here's an example of how an information worker (I'll call her Alice) might use Work Folders to separate her work data from her personal data, while having the ability to work from any device:

Alice saves a document in the Work Folders directory on her computer at work. The document is synced to a file server controlled by her company's IT department. When Alice returns home that evening, she picks up her Microsoft Surface Pro 3 device, where the document is already synced because she previously set up Work Folders on that device. She takes her Microsoft Surface Pro 3 on a trip, and she doesn't have any Internet access while travelling. She works on the document offline, and when she returns home and an Internet connection is available, the document automatically is synced back with the file server from her company. The next day, she returns to her office and opens the document. All the changes that she made the previous evening are in her Work Folders directory on her work computer.

To set up Work Folders on your Windows 10 computer or device, follow these steps:

1. **Click the search bar on the taskbar.**
2. **Type** work folders.

   A list of search results appears.
3. **Click Work Folders.**

   The Work Folders window appears.
4. **Click Set Up Work Folders (see Figure 18-6).**

   You're asked to enter your work email address.

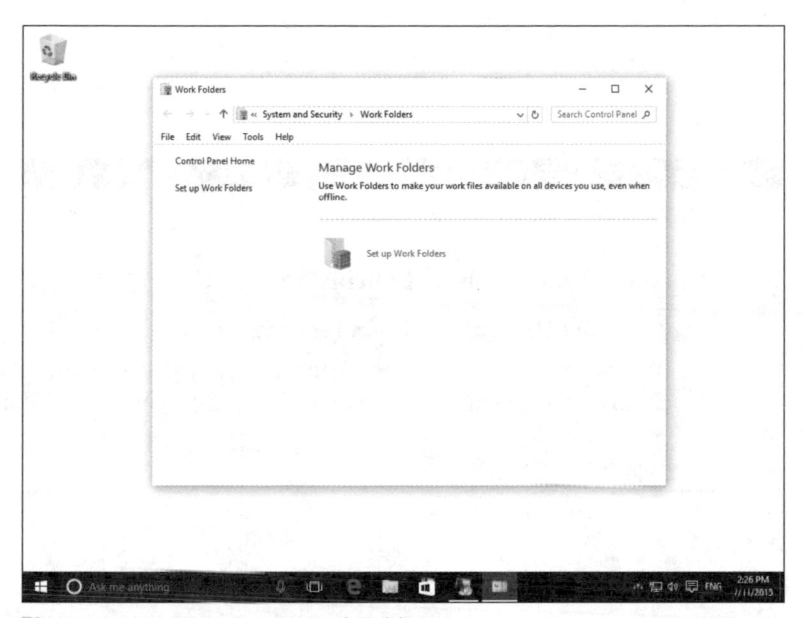

Figure 18-6: How to set up Work Folders.

5. **Type your work email address; then click Next.**

   You're asked to enter the username and password that you use on your company's network.
6. **Type the requested details and click OK.**

   You're asked to enter a Work Folders URL.
7. **Type the URL address of your company's Work Folders server (see Figure 18-7).**
8. **Click Next.**

   You see information about the Work Folders feature and where your files will be saved on your computer.
9. **Click Next.**

   The Accept Security Policies page appears.

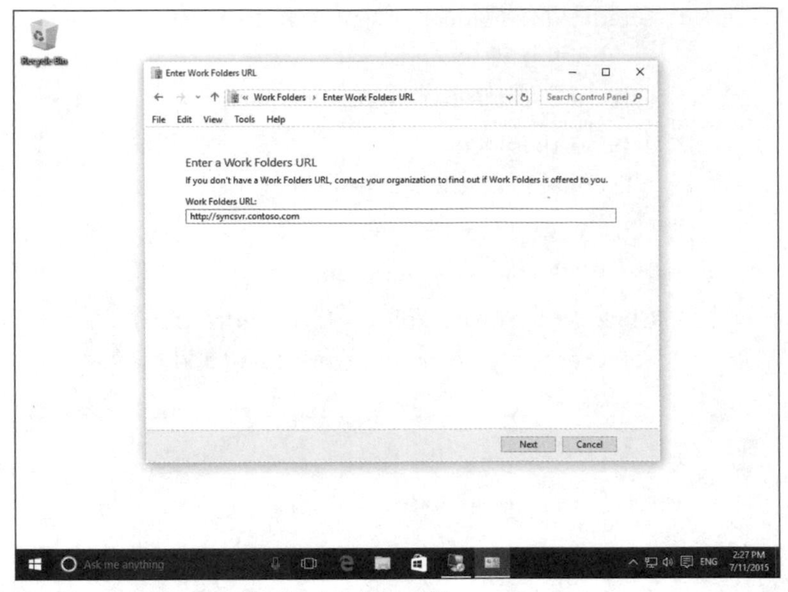

Figure 18-7: Entering the Work Folders URL.

10. **Select I Accept These Policies on My PC.**
11. **Click Set Up Work Folders (see Figure 18-8).**

    Windows 10 spends some time configuring this feature then sends a message informing you that Work Folders has started syncing with your PC.

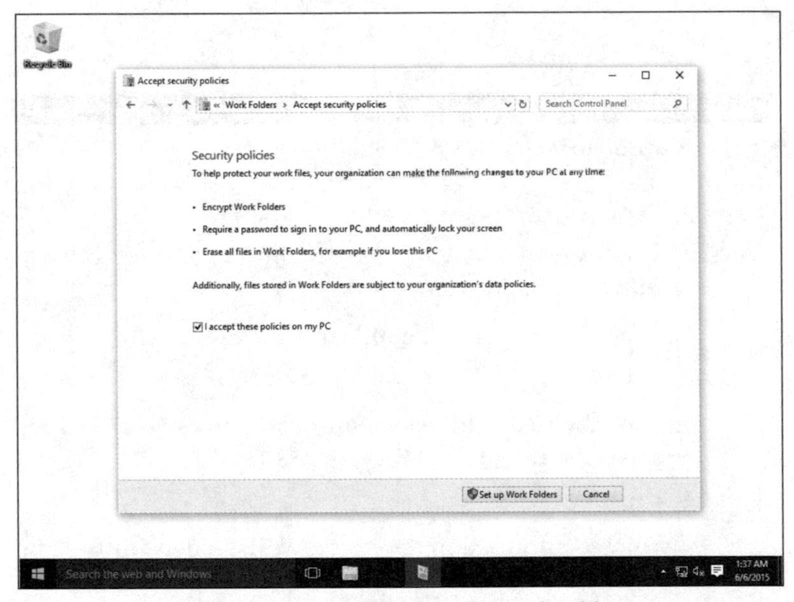

Figure 18-8: Accepting the security policies for Work Folders.

12. **Click Close.**

    You don't have to wait until syncing finishes. It runs automatically in the background.

Before setting up Work Folders on your devices and computers, you need to ask your company's IT department for the appropriate connection details. For example, you need to know the URL of the Work Folders server and the email address and password to use for this feature. If you're setting up Work Folders on your work computer, you may not have to go through Steps 6, 7, and 8. These steps are generally activated only when you set up Work Folders on your computers and devices from home.

Use Work Folders

In order to use the Work Folders service, all you need is an active Internet connection and File Explorer up and running. In File Explorer you find a new folder called Work Folders. Click it, and you see all the files that are synced by Work Folders. Every file that you add to this folder is automatically synced to your work computer and vice versa. Figure 18-9 shows the Work Folders folder in File Explorer.

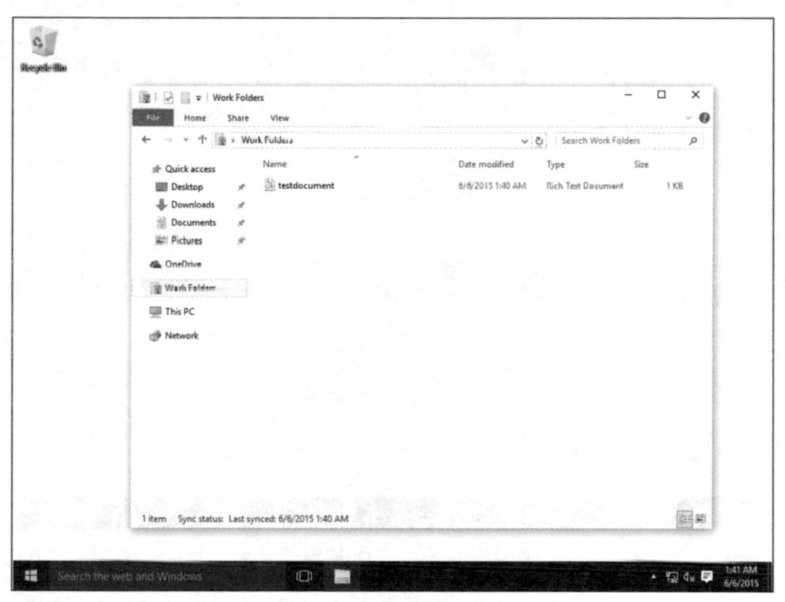

Figure 18-9: The Work Folders folder in File Explorer.

On the File Explorer status bar, you see the sync status and when Work Folders was last synchronized.

To manually sync a file in Work Folders, right-click it in File Explorer and, from the menu that pops up, select Sync Now.

Stop Using Work Folders

To stop using Work Folders on any of your Windows 10 computers and devices, follow these steps:

1. **Click the search bar on the taskbar.**
2. **Type** work folders.

   A list of search results appears.
3. **Click Work Folders.**

   The Work Folders window appears.
4. **In the column on the left, click Stop Using Work Folders.**

   You're asked to confirm that you want to stop using this feature.
5. **Click Yes (see Figure 18-10).**
6. **Close the Work Folders window.**

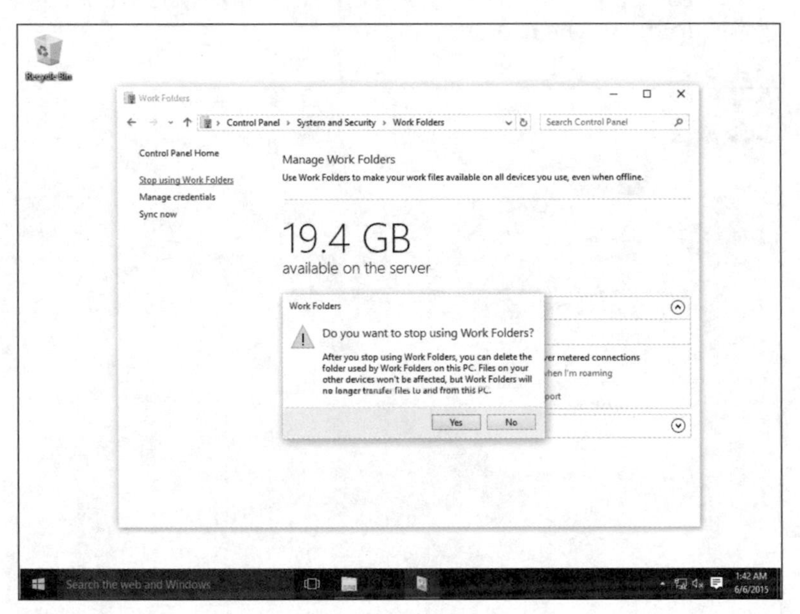

Figure 18-10: How to stop using Work Folders.

In the Work Folders window (opened in Step 3), you can see how much space is available on the Work Folders server, and you can also manage the credentials that you're using to log in to the Work Folders server.

Connect Remotely to Another Computer on the Network

The Remote Desktop Connection app allows you to connect to other computers or devices that are connected to your local network or that are on the Internet and have a public IP address. For example, you can use the Remote Desktop Connection app to connect to a colleague's computer from your desk or to your work computer when you're using some other computer or device.

Here's how to use Remote Desktop Connection to connect remotely to another device:

1. **Click the search bar on the taskbar.**
2. **Type** remote desktop.

   A list of search results appears.
3. **Click Remote Desktop Connection.**
4. **In the Remote Desktop Connection window, type the IP address or the name of the Windows device that you want to connect to; then click Connect (see Figure 18-11).**

Figure 18-11: The Remote Desktop Connection app.

   Windows initiates the remote connection; then you're asked to enter your credentials.
5. **Enter the username and password that you want to use on the computer you're connecting to; then click OK.**

6. **If you're informed that the remote computer couldn't be authenticated due to problems with its security certificate, click Yes to connect anyway (see Figure 18-12).**

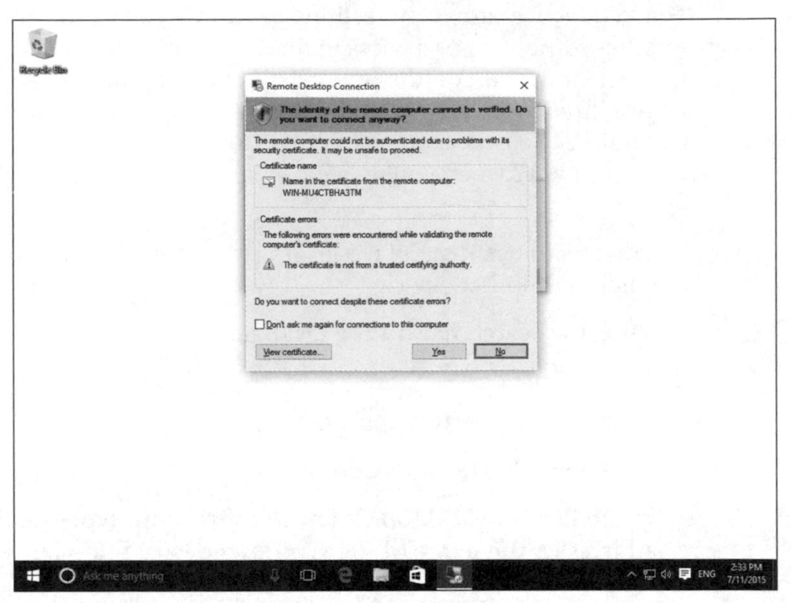

Figure 18-12: Problems with the security certificate.

You're now connected to the remote computer and can use it as though it were your local computer.

7. **When you finish using the Remote Desktop Connection, close the app by clicking the x button on the top of the window, then clicking OK.**

   The remote session is disconnected.

If Remote Desktop Connection says that it can't connect to the remote computer, check whether the remote computer is turned off, whether it isn't available on the network, or whether remote connections are disabled on it. The next section describes how to enable remote connections.

Allow Remote Access to Your Windows 10 Computer

By default, Windows 10 doesn't allow remote access to your computer or device. If you need this kind of access, you must manually enable it. Here's how:

1. **Click the search bar on the taskbar.**
2. **Type** remote desktop.

   A list of search results appears.

3. **Click Allow Remote Access to Your Computer.**

   The System Properties window appears.

4. **In the Remote tab, go to the Remote Desktop section and check the Allow Remote Connections to This Computer box (see Figure 18-13).**

5. **Click OK.**

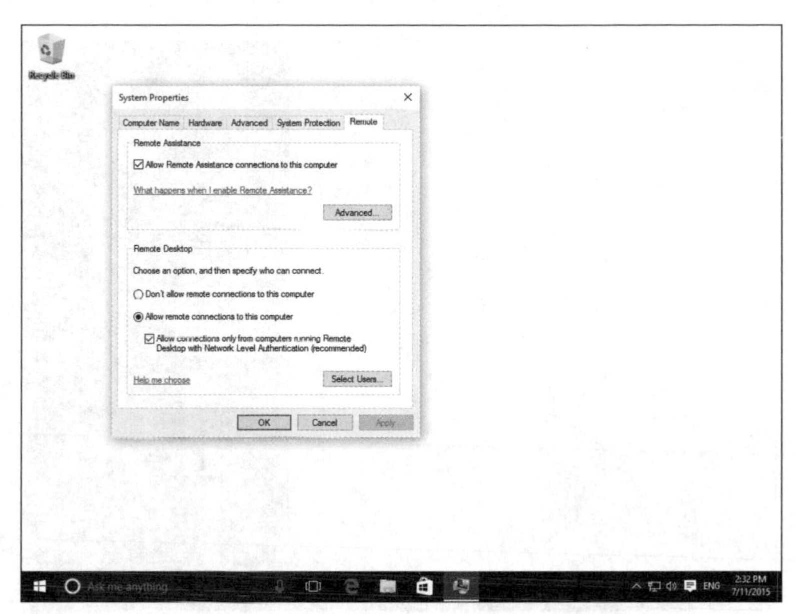

Figure 18-13: How to allow remote connections to your computer.

Use Airplane Mode

Airplane mode turns off all radio chips on your device. In Windows 10, when Airplane mode is turned on, wireless network cards, Bluetooth chips, and mobile data connections (3G and 4G) are turned off. You should turn on Airplane mode when you board a plane. After take-off, you can turn on the Wi-Fi or the Bluetooth, if you need to use one of them. However, you must turn them off again when the plane prepares for landing.

This feature also helps you save power. Because some of your device's components are turned off, they aren't used and don't consume any power. Therefore, you get slightly better battery life. This benefit alone makes Airplane mode useful, even when you're nowhere near a plane but want to save as much power as possible.

Here's how to enable Airplane mode in Windows 10:

1. **Go to the Notification area on the taskbar and click the wireless icon.**

   The Action Center appears.

2. **Click Airplane Mode (see Figure 18-14).**

   The wireless icon on the taskbar turns into an airplane icon.

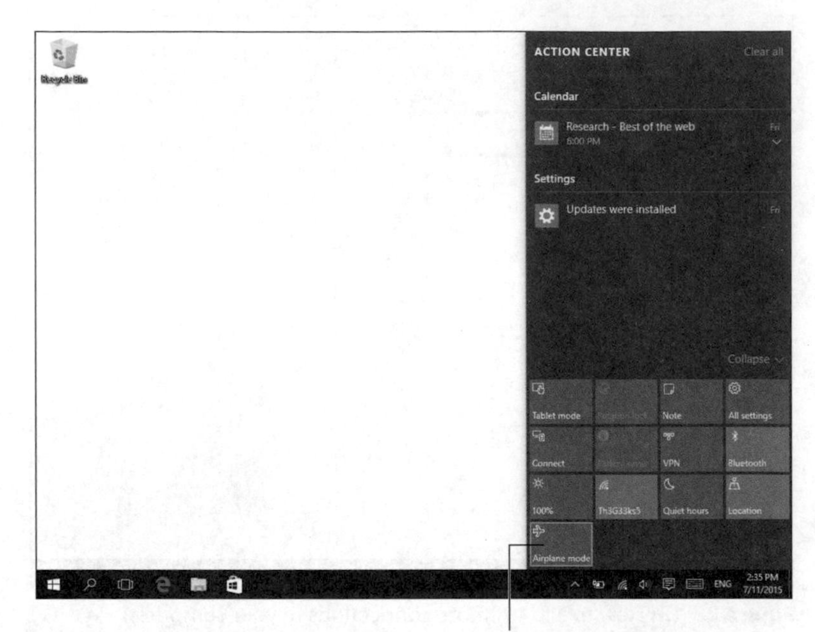

Figure 18-14: Turning on Airplane mode.

To disable Airplane mode, click the airplane icon and then click the Airplane Mode button.

Save Battery Power on the Go

Windows 10 introduced the Battery Saver feature. As its name implies, this tool allows you to improve battery life on mobile devices (such as laptops, Ultrabooks, tablets, and 2-in-1 devices). In Windows 10, Battery Saver does the following:

- Turns Battery Saver on automatically if the battery falls below a certain level.
- Controls which apps can run in the background while your battery is low.
- Controls which push notifications are allowed when the battery is low, and monitors what is using most of your battery.

Battery Saver automatically activates itself when your battery falls below 20 percent, but you can also enable the feature manually at any time. Here's how:

1. **Go to the Notification area on the taskbar and click the battery icon.**

   A pop-up appears with information about your battery.

2. **Click the Battery Saver button (see Figure 18-15).**

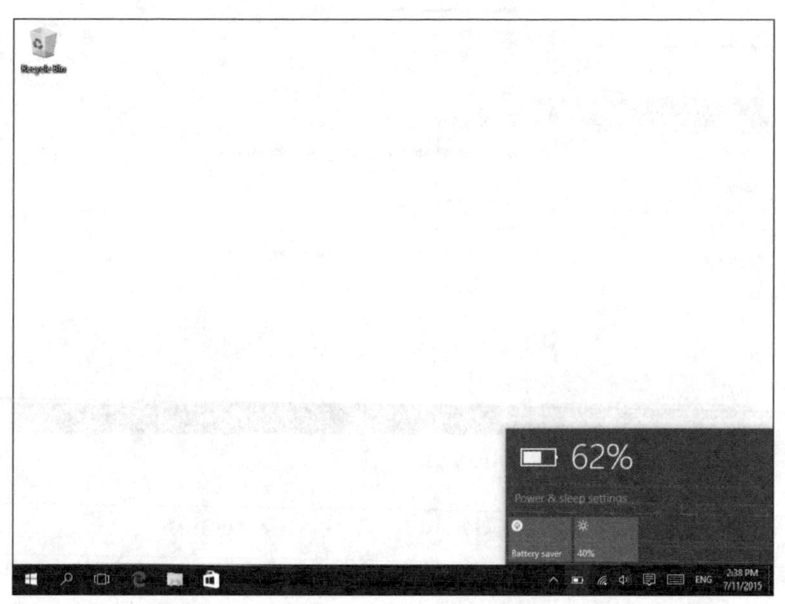

Figure 18-15: Manually turning on the Battery Saver.

   The battery icon changes to reflect that the Battery Saver feature is turned on.

3. **Click anywhere outside the pop-up with information about your battery to resume normal computing activities.**

To turn off the Battery Saver, just repeat the preceding steps.

See What's Using Your Battery Power

You can take steps to identify the services and features that eat up the most battery power. To check your battery use in Windows 10, follow these steps:

1. **Open Settings.**
2. **Click System.**

   A list with system settings appears.

3. **Click Battery Saver.**

   Here you see the percentage of Battery Life Remaining and the Estimated Time Remaining (see Figure 18-16).

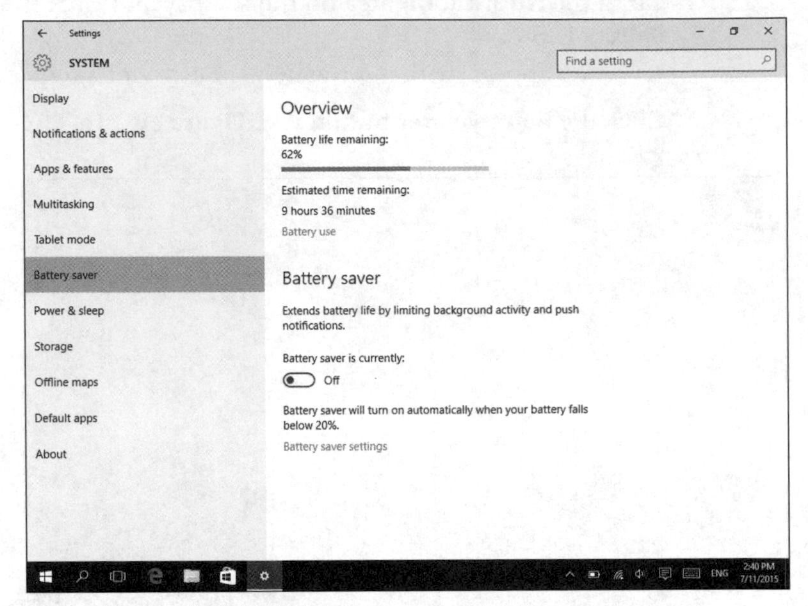

Figure 18-16: Checking battery use.

4. **Click Battery Use in the Overview section.**

   A list appears showing what is consuming most of your battery.

5. **When you finish, close the Settings window.**

Improve Your Power & Sleep Settings

When you're on the road and want to work productively, battery time can be very important. While the new Battery Saver feature can help you save some battery time, you can extend that time by manually editing the Power & Sleep settings that are available in Windows 10; for example, when Windows 10 turns off your computer and/or device's screens, when it goes into Sleep mode, and whether Wi-Fi remains connected while your device is asleep.

To extend your battery time by adjusting the Power & Sleep settings, follow these steps:

1. **Open Settings.**
2. **Click System.**

   A list with system settings appears.

3. **Click Power & Sleep.**

   The list of available power and sleep settings appears.

4. **In the Screen section, change when you want the screen to be turned off while on battery power.**

5. **In the Sleep section, change when your PC goes to sleep when it's running on battery power (see Figure 18-17).**

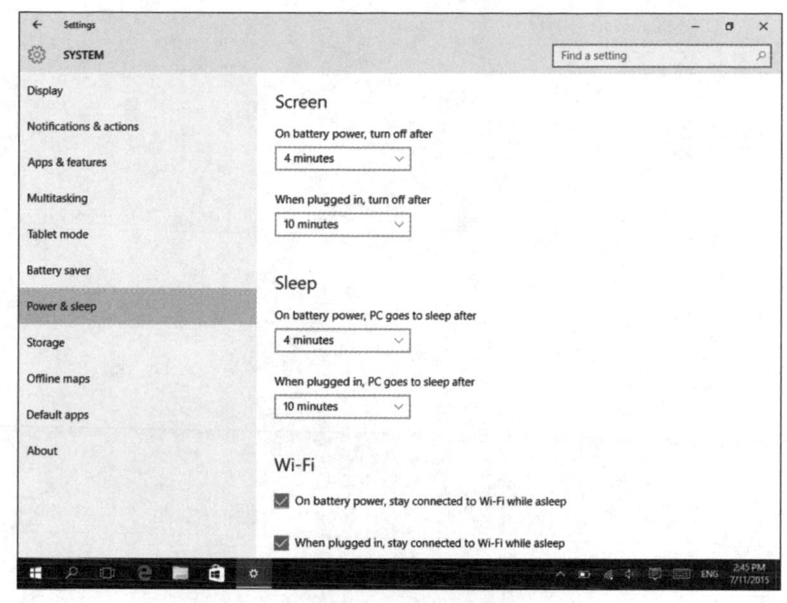

Figure 18-17: Improving your Power & Sleep settings.

6. **In the Wi-Fi section, change how the Wi-Fi behaves when on battery power.**

7. **Close the Settings window.**

CHAPTERNINETEEN

Doing Your Job in Windows 10

This chapter focuses on practical tasks that you may encounter in your work environment. For example, you find out how to connect your computer to a second display and project the image on it. You also find out how to use this second display with the Windows Mobility Center so that you can deliver presentations like a pro.

At work, you probably print and scan all kinds of documents, so I cover these tasks in this chapter, too.

Perhaps you work with multinational teams or use multiple languages at work. If so, you'll be glad to know that you can find some important details on those topics in this chapter. First, you see how to set and view the time in multiple locations across the world. Then you see how to switch between multiple keyboard input languages when you type, as well as how to switch between multiple display languages.

Lastly, I cover a tool that is surprisingly useful: the new Calculator app from Windows 10. You never know when you might need to do some quick calculations, and in such cases, this app will come in handy.

In This Chapter

- Projecting the image to a second display
- Delivering presentations with the Windows Mobility Center
- Printing documents
- Scanning documents
- Setting and viewing the time in multiple locations
- Switching between multiple keyboard input languages
- Switching between multiple display languages
- Making complex calculations with the Calculator

Project to a Second Display

In the business world, it's customary to project your work on a second display so that others can see it. For example, you might connect a projector to your laptop, you might connect a large TV in a meeting room, or you might connect some other kind of display. To project your work to another display, you first must connect that display to your Windows 10 computer or device, which you do though a port such as VGA, DVI, HDMI, or Mini DisplayPort, depending on how current your computer and the second display are. After you connect the second display, the simplest way to project an image to the display is to press Windows+P on your keyboard and then select how you want to project the image (see Figure 19-1).

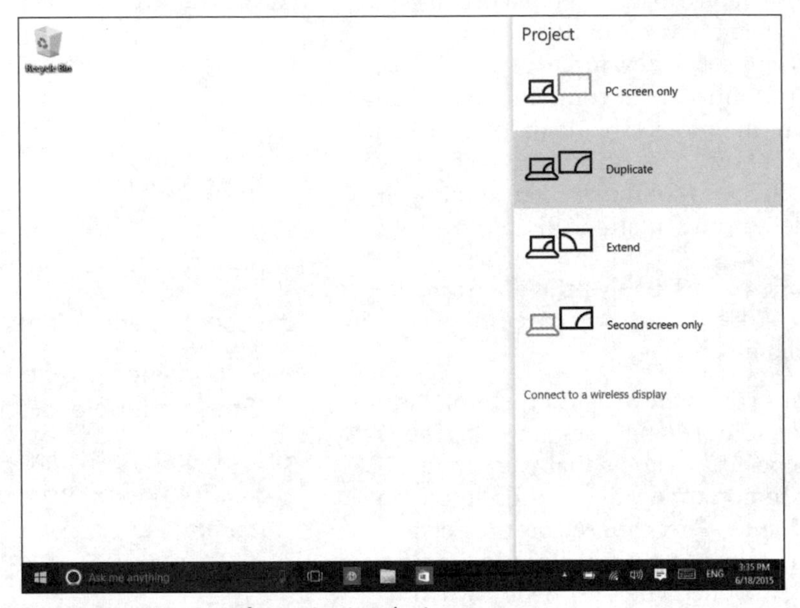

Figure 19-1: Options for projecting the image.

As you can see in Figure 19-1, here are your options:

- **PC Screen Only:** Displays the image on your main display; it ignores the second display.
- **Duplicate:** Shows the same image on both displays.
- **Extend:** Extends the image on the second display; you can use both displays like one single desktop. You can move windows from one display to the other.

- **Second Screen Only:** Displays the image only on the second display.

  To bring the image back to the main display, either disconnect the second display or press Windows+P again and select PC Screen Only.

Another way to project to a second display is to use search. Here's how it works:

1. **Click in the search box on the taskbar.**
2. **Type** Project.

   A list with search results appears.
3. **Click the Project to a Second Screen search result.**
4. **Click the option you want for projecting the screen.**

Deliver Presentations with the Windows Mobility Center

The Windows Mobility Center centralizes information and settings most relevant to mobile computers and devices such as laptops, netbooks, Ultrabooks, and 2-in-1s.

The Windows Mobility Center isn't available on desktop computers.

Windows Mobility Center's role is to help you be mobile and to enable you to take quick actions, such as the following:

- Change the brightness of the screen.
- Change the sound volume.
- Change the active power plan.
- Connect or disconnect external displays.
- Set synchronized partnerships with such devices as portable music players and USB removable drives.
- Set the Presentation mode to either On or Off.

If you're a typical business user, you're likely to find that the most useful features of the Windows Mobility Center are the ability it gives you to connect external displays and to turn on Presentation mode. These settings are especially useful when you must switch your presentation from room to room and connect your device to different kinds of external displays. However, before you start using the Windows Mobility Center for presentations, make sure that you connect a second display, as shown in the previous section.

Here's how to start the Windows Mobility Center and use it to turn on Presentation mode:

1. **Click in the search box on the taskbar.**
2. **Type** mobility.

   A list with search results appears.
3. **Click the Windows Mobility Center search result.**

   The Windows Mobility Center window appears.
4. **Review all the settings that you're interested in.**
5. **In the Presentation Settings section, click the Turn On button (see Figure 19-2).**

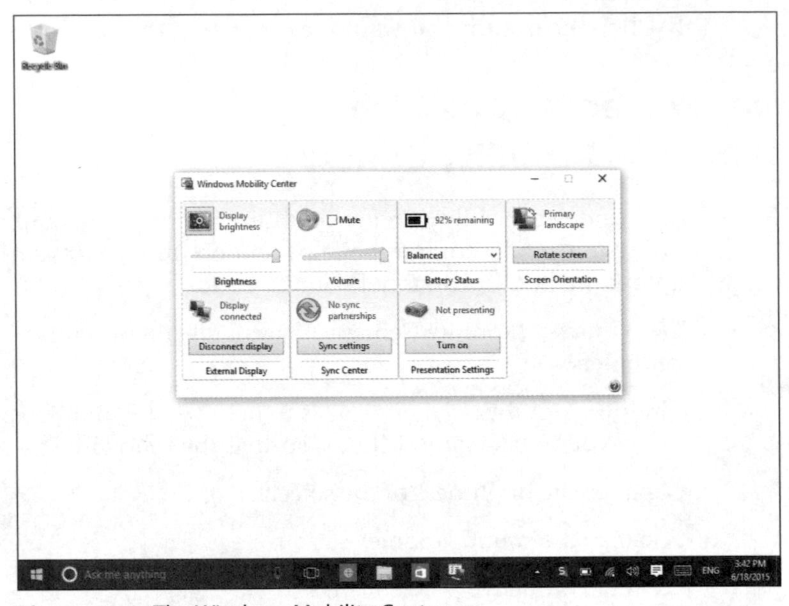

Figure 19-2: The Windows Mobility Center.

6. **Minimize Windows Mobility Center.**
7. **Deliver your presentation.**
8. **When you finish the presentation, click Turn Off in the Presentation Settings section.**
9. **Close the Windows Mobility Center.**

Print Your Documents and Presentations

To print the documents and presentations you create, you, of course, need to install a printer. (Refer to Chapter 17 if you need a refresher on installing a printer.) Once you install a printer, you need to access the Print menu. Here, you select the printer you want to use, set up how items are printed, and then click the Print button. The universal keyboard shortcut for printing in Windows 10 is Ctrl+P, and this command accesses the Print window in most apps. However, you can also use clicks and taps to print.

As an example, here's how to print a document from the Word app:

1. **Start the Word app.**
2. **Open a document that you want to print.**
3. **Click File.**

   The File menu appears.
4. **Click Print.**

   The Print dialog box appears (see Figure 19-3).

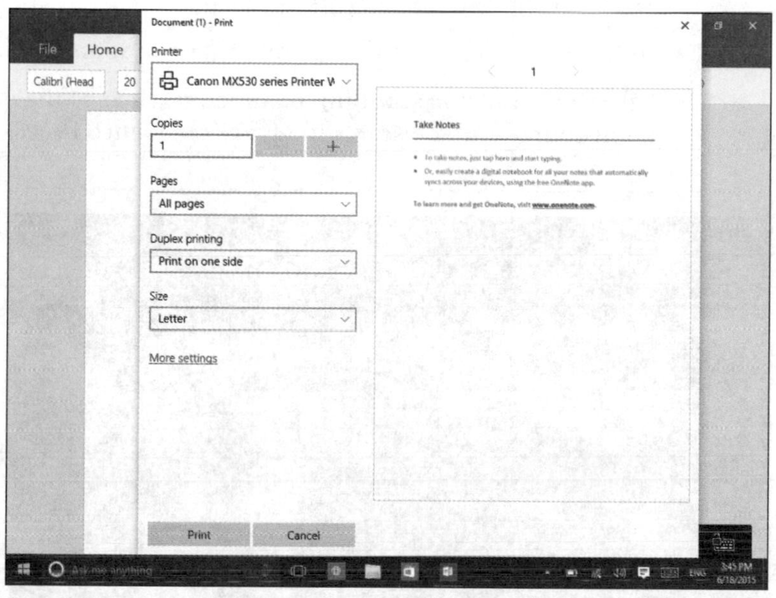

Figure 19-3: Printing a document from the Word app.

5. **Select the printer that you want to use.**
6. **Configure how you want to print the document.**
7. **Click Print.**
8. **After the document prints, close the Word app.**

The process for printing documents is similar in all Microsoft Office apps.

Scan Documents

Windows 10 offers an improved Scan app that you can use to quickly scan and save documents to your computer. To use this app, you must first install a scanner on your computer. Many modern printers are multifunctional and include both printing and scanning features so that you can use one device for both tasks.

Before scanning a document, insert it in the scanner and then follow these steps:

1. **Click in the search box on the taskbar.**
2. **Type** scan.

   A list with search results appears.
3. **Click the shortcut for the Scan app.**

   The Scan app window appears.
4. **In the Scan app, select the scanner that you want to use.**
5. **Select the available scanning parameters, such as the document source and the scan's file type (see Figure 19-4).**

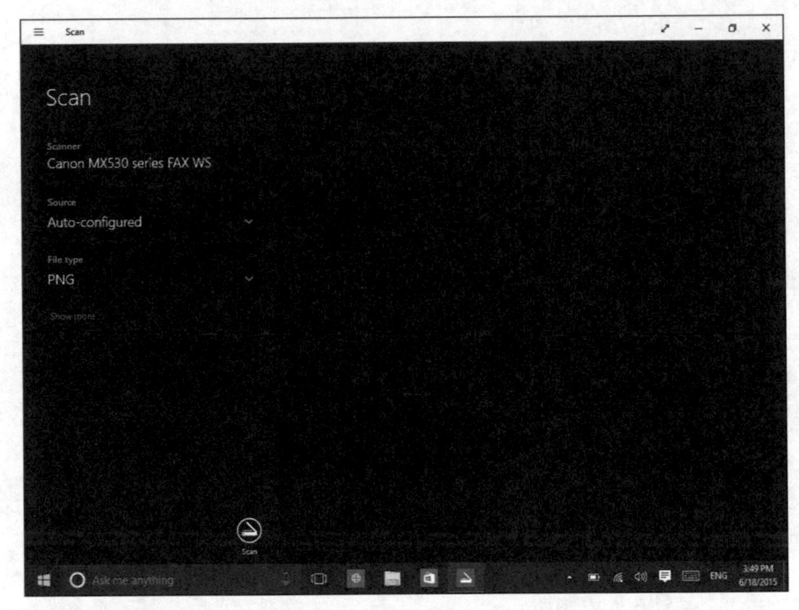

Figure 19-4: Scanning a document.

6. **Click Scan.**

   After the Scan app does its job, you're informed that the scan was saved to the Scans folder on your computer.
7. **Click View to view your scan.**

8. **If you're satisfied with the end result, close the document you just scanned.**

9. **Close the Scan app.**

The Scans folder is in your Pictures library or your User folder.

View Time Around the World

These days it's becoming common to be part of a multinational project team that spans continents and multiple time zones. If that's your case, you surely want to use the Windows 10 Alarms & Clock app. With this app, you can set alarms and timers and use the stopwatch. Most importantly, you can set and view the time in multiple locations across the world, and here's how to do so:

1. **Click Start.**
2. **Click All Apps.**

   The list of installed apps appears.

3. **Click Alarms & Clock.**
4. **Click World Clock (see Figure 19-5).**

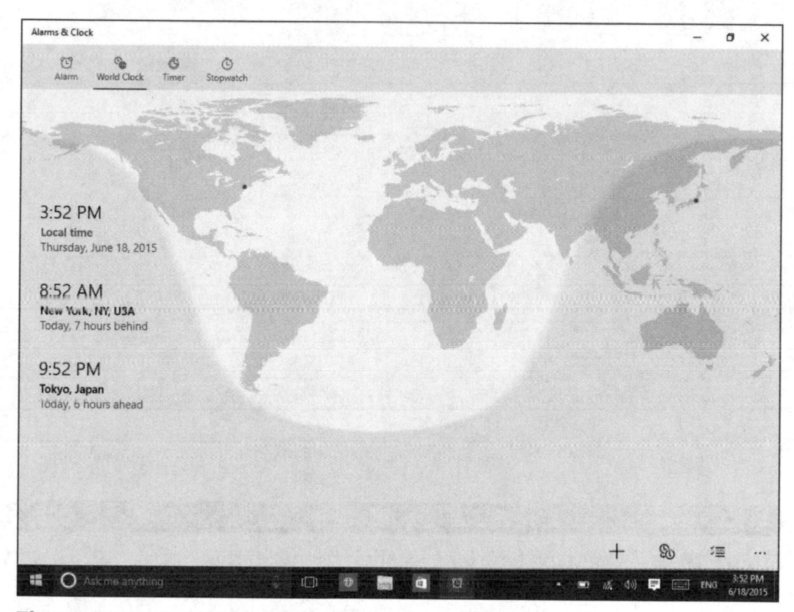

Figure 19-5: The Alarms & Clock app.

5. **Click the + button at the bottom of the app window.**
6. **In the search field that appears, type the name of the city whose time you want to find.**
7. **Click the search suggestion that fits that city.**

8. **View the time in the newly added location.**
9. **Close the Alarms & Clock app.**

Add all the cities where your teammates work so that you can easily keep track of the time in their location and schedule meetings and conference calls at times that work best for all of you.

Add Multiple Time Zones to the Start Menu

To check the time quickly in multiple locations across the world, you can pin the locations that you add in the Alarms & Clock app to the Start Menu. Here's how:

1. **Start the Alarms & Clock app.**
2. **Click World Clock.**

   The time appears in the cities that you have added to this app.
3. **Right-click the city that you want to pin.**
4. **Click Pin to Start (see Figure 19-6).**

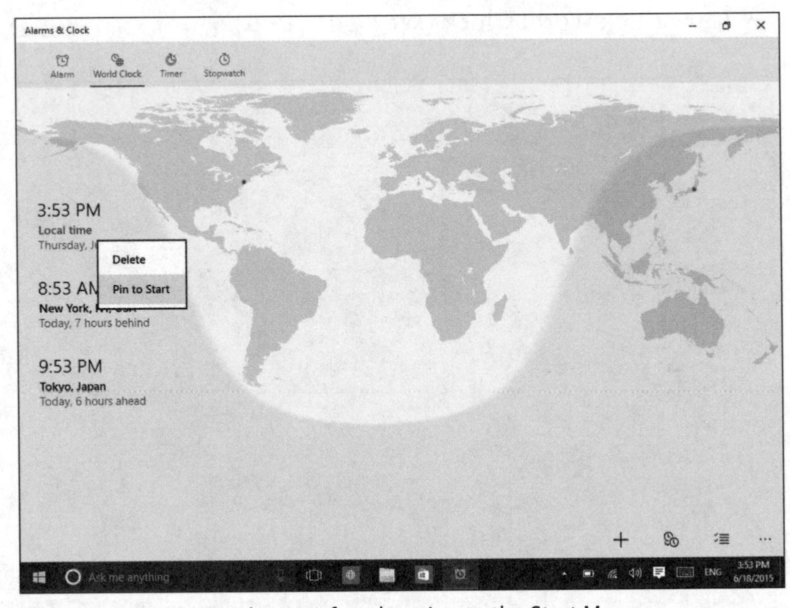

Figure 19-6: Pinning the time for a location to the Start Menu.

5. **Close the Alarms & Clock app.**
6. **Click Start to see the time shown for the location that you just pinned to the Start Menu.**

You can pin as many locations as you want.

Switch Between Keyboard Input Languages

If you type in multiple languages, then you've installed more than one keyboard input language, and you need to quickly switch between languages as you type. The quickest way is to press the Windows+Space keys on the keyboard. This keyboard shortcut switches to the next available keyboard input language. Press these keys again, and you switch to the next language. However, you can also change the keyboard input language by using the mouse, like this:

1. **On the right side of the taskbar, click the Input Indicator that displays the current keyboard input language.**

   For example, this button says ENG when the English keyboard language is active.

   A list appears showing all the available languages (see Figure 19-7).

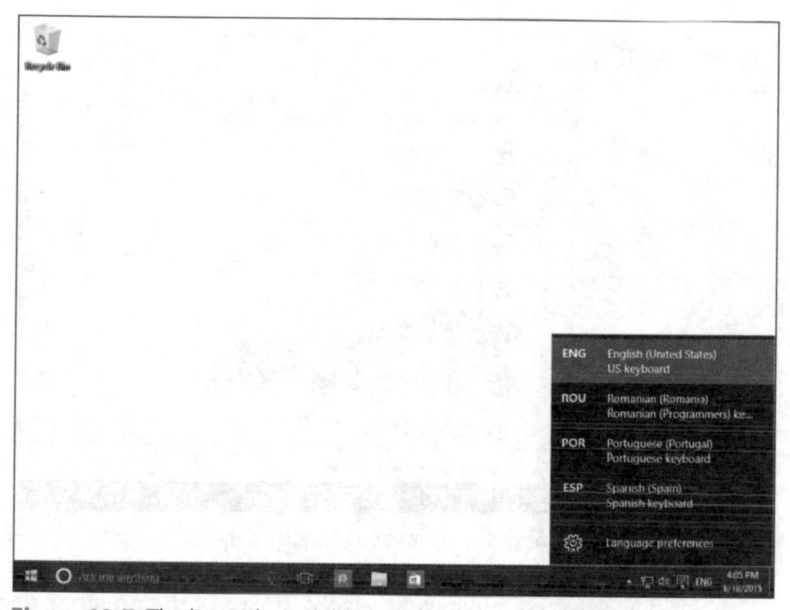

Figure 19-7: The list with available keyboard input languages.

2. **Click the language that you want to use.**

   The language Input Indicator changes, now showing the language you just selected.

3. **Start typing, using the newly selected language.**

Before you can switch to a new keyboard input language, you need to install it. Refer to Chapter 8 to find out how to add a keyboard input language.

Switch Between Display Languages

In addition to keyboard input languages, Windows 10 allows you to install and use multiple display languages. Here's how to set up your operating system to translate in a different language:

1. **Open Settings.**
2. **Click Time & Language.**
3. **Click Region & Language.**
4. **In the Languages section on the right, select the language that you want to use for Windows 10.**
5. **Click the Set as Default button for that language (see Figure 19-8).**

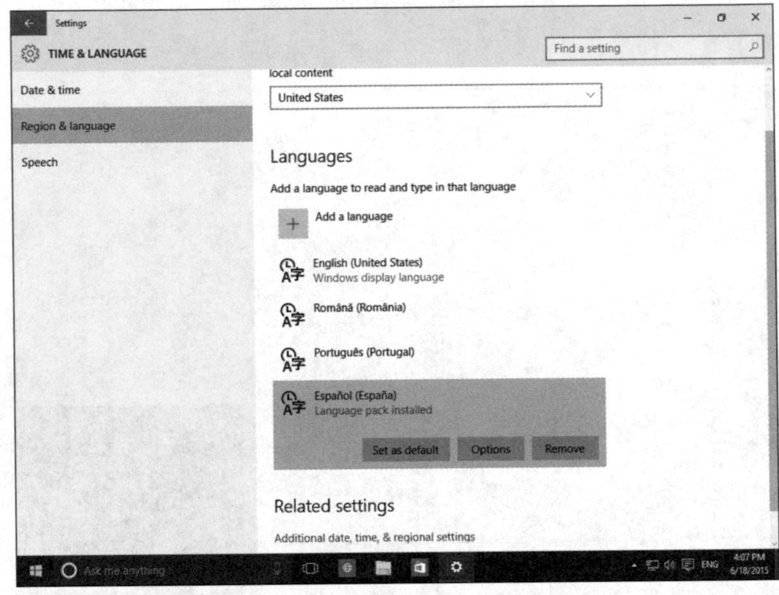

Figure 19-8: Setting a new display language as the default.

The selected language is placed ahead of the previous display language, and you're told that the selected language will be used the next time you sign in.

6. **Sign out of Windows 10.**
7. **Sign in to Windows 10 using your user account.**

   The operating system now uses the language that you selected.

Before you can switch to a new display language, you need to install it (refer to Chapter 8 for more on this topic). To revert to the previous display language, follow the same procedure and select the previous display language at Step 4.

Make Complex Calculations

Windows 10 includes a new, improved, touch-friendly Calculator app. With this app, you can do these calculations:

- **Standard mathematical calculations:** You can do simple calculations, such as addition, subtraction, and multiplication.
- **Scientific calculations:** You can work with advanced scientific values, such as degrees, radians, and grads.
- **Programmer calculations:** You can use functions that are useful to software developers.
- **Conversions:** You can make all kinds of conversions: volume, length, weight and mass, temperature, energy, area, and speed.

Figure 19-9 shows the Calculator app in Windows 10 and the options you have for standard mathematical calculations.

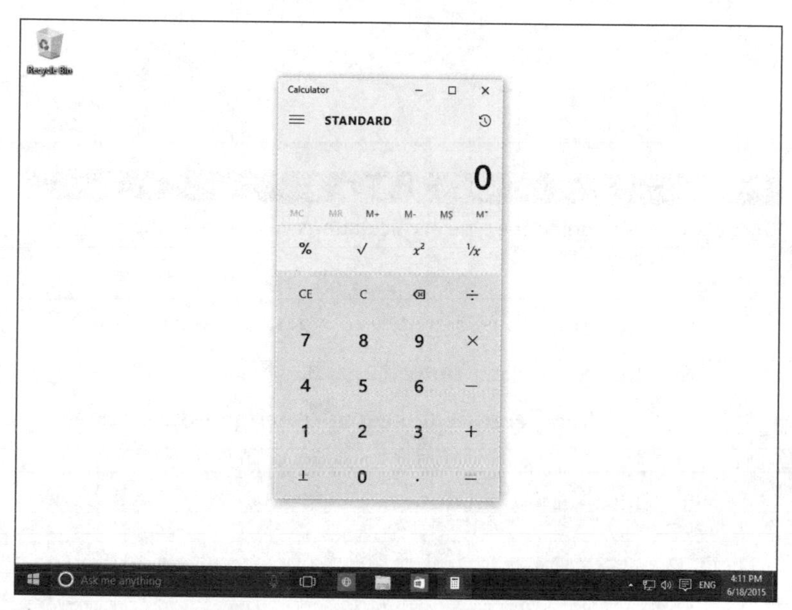

Figure 19-9: The Calculator app in Windows 10.

Here's how to start the Calculator app and switch between different types of calculations and conversions:

1. **Click Start to open the Start Menu.**
2. **Click All Apps.**

   The list with available apps appears.
3. **Click Calculator to open the app.**

   The Calculator app appears.

4. **Click the burger button (three stacked lines, like a burger on a bun), at the top-right corner of the Calculator app (see Figure 19-10).**

   A menu appears with several options.

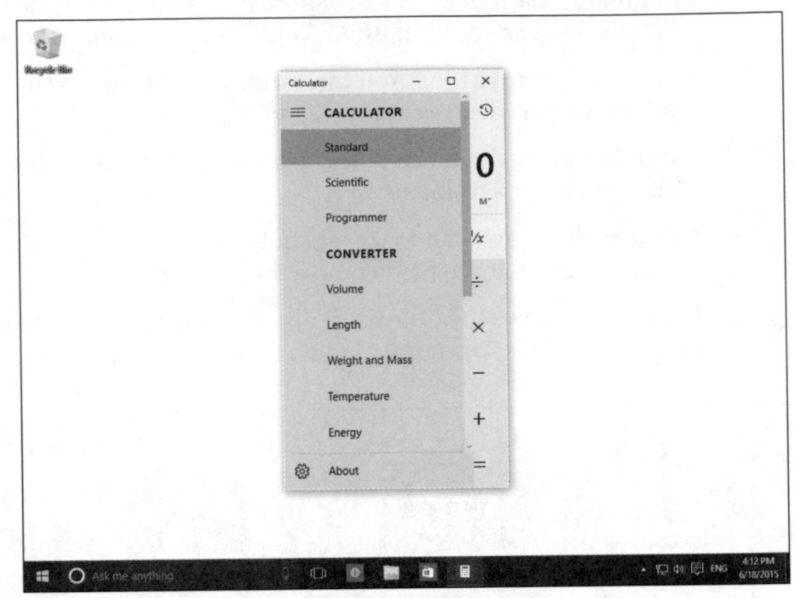

Figure 19-10: Changing the type of calculations you make in the Calculator app.

5. **Click Scientific to switch to scientific calculations.**
6. **Click the burger button again.**
7. **Click Temperature to switch to temperature-related conversions.**
8. **Close the Calculator.**

CHAPTER TWENTY
Protecting Your Data

Many companies use encryption to ensure the security of the data stored on their devices. If a business laptop is stolen or a USB memory stick with company data is lost, it's important that the stored data isn't accessible to the wrong people. In such cases, encryption is the only solution to ensure that the data is accessed only by people with the appropriate access keys and passwords. Some businesses also have policies that forbid the distribution of company data on removable media such as USB memory sticks. Be sure you comply with such policies. However, if you need to have important business data on a mobile device when you're away from the office and you won't break any company policies by doing so, use encryption. It's the only sensible solution to the challenge of protecting your data.

This chapter starts by demonstrating how to use BitLocker. It's the built-in encryption solution that's available with Windows 10. BitLocker is available only for the business editions of Windows 10 (Windows 10 Pro and Windows 10 Enterprise). That's why it's very likely that you use it only on your work computers. In addition, it works only on computers with Trusted Platform Module (TPM) chips. These chips can store the cryptographic keys that BitLocker and other encryption solutions use. TPM chips are included in most business computers but not in computers sold to consumers and home users.

In This Chapter

- Encrypting the operating system drive with BitLocker
- Encrypting removable drives with BitLocker
- Unlocking encrypted removable drives
- Decrypting encrypted drives
- Backing up data with File History
- Configuring File History
- Turning off File History

This chapter shows you how to encrypt drives with BitLocker, how to unlock encrypted drives, and how to decrypt a drive when you no longer need it encrypted. This chapter also covers File History. It creates automated backups of your important user data. Once you set up File History, you leave it turned on and forget about it. This feature can back up all your data so that you can recover it whenever you need to.

Encrypt the Operating System Drive with BitLocker

Encrypting the operating system drive with BitLocker (or any other encryption software) takes significant time and involves setting a password to use before starting Windows and using an encrypted drive.

It's important to remember this password. Without it, you can't access the encrypted drive. To prevent you from completely losing access to the encrypted drive, the encryption process includes a step to save a backup recovery key. You can use the recovery key if you forget your password and need to recover the encrypted data. You can save the recovery key automatically to your Microsoft account (if you log on to Windows 10 with a Microsoft account), to a file on a USB memory stick, or on a different drive. (Of course, you can write it down on paper, too.)

Before the encryption process begins, you're asked whether you want to encrypt only the used disk space or the entire drive:

- If you have a newer computer with a fresh installation of Windows, I recommend encrypting only the used disk space.
- If your computer is a long-serving veteran, I recommend encrypting the entire drive, which takes longer.

Here's how to encrypt the operating system drive with BitLocker:

1. **In the search bar on the taskbar, type** bitlocker.
2. **In the search results that appear, click Manage BitLocker.**

   The BitLocker Drive Encryption window appears.
3. **In the BitLocker Drive Encryption window, find the operating system drive and click the Turn on BitLocker button (see Figure 20-1).**

   You're asked to enter an encryption password.
4. **Set the encryption password that you want to use by typing it twice in the appropriate fields; then click Next.**

   You're asked where you want to back up your recovery key. You can use it if you forget your password.

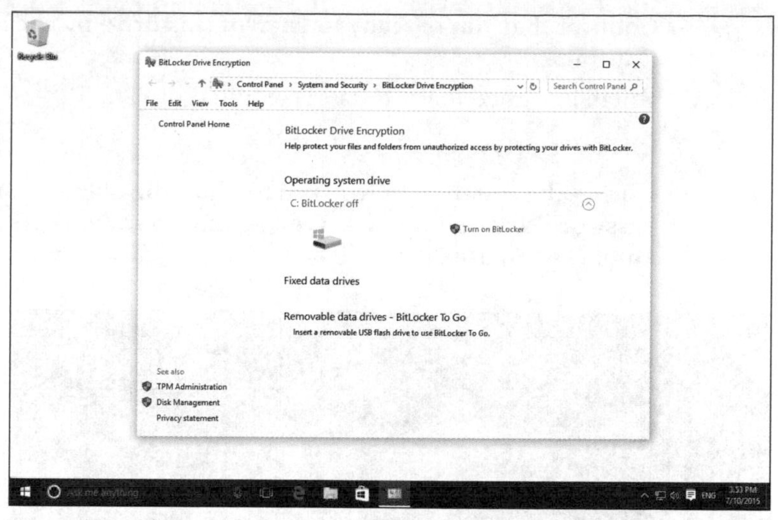

Figure 20-1: Turning on BitLocker for the operating system drive.

5. **Select where you want to back up your recovery key by clicking the option you prefer; then click Next (see Figure 20-2).**

   You're asked to choose how much of your drive you want to encrypt and given two options: encrypt the used disk space only or encrypt the entire drive.

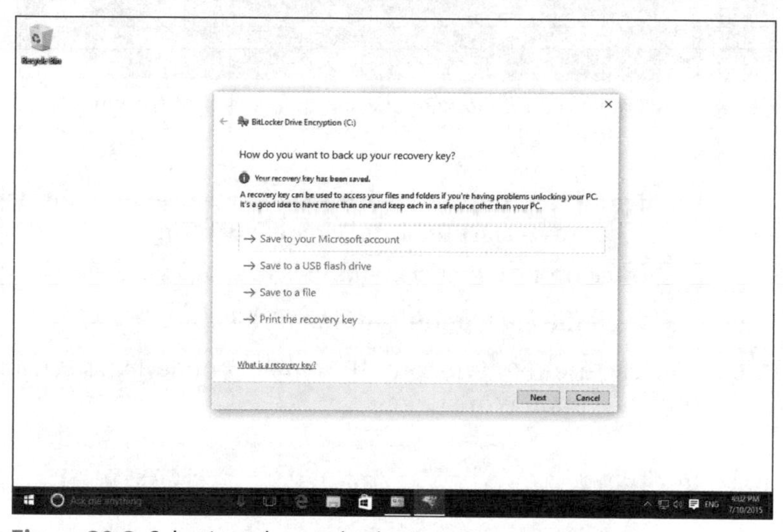

Figure 20-2: Selecting where to back up your recovery key.

6. **Choose how much of your drive to encrypt; then click Next.**

   You're asked whether you're ready to encrypt the selected drive.

7. **Confirm that you're ready to encrypt this drive by clicking Continue.**

   You're informed that a restart is required.

8. **Click Restart now.**
9. **During the restart, you're asked to enter the encryption password that you just set. Type the password and press Enter (see Figure 20-3).**

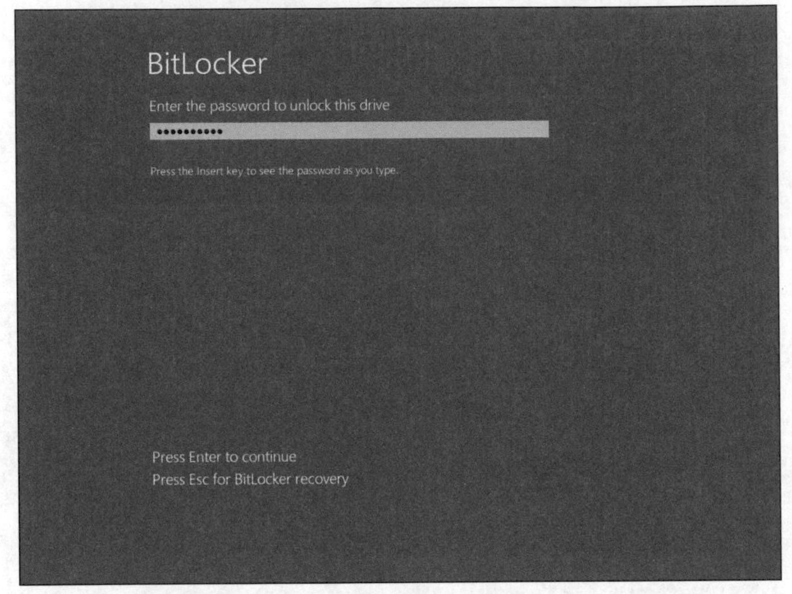

Figure 20-3: Entering the BitLocker password to unlock the operating system drive.

10. **Sign in to Windows 10 using the same user account that you used to start the BitLocker encryption.**

    You're notified that encryption is in progress.

11. **When the encryption is done, click Close.**

You can use your Windows 10 computer or device as usual while the encryption is in progress.

Encrypt a Removable Drive with BitLocker

Encrypting a removable drive such as a USB memory stick doesn't take long, and it involves fewer steps than encrypting the operating system drive. After the encryption process ends (as described in the preceding section), each time you plug your device into a Windows computer, File Explorer shows the device with a lock icon, which signals that the device is encrypted. To access its content, you must enter the password set during the encryption process.

To encrypt a USB memory stick or an external hard drive, follow these steps:

1. **In the search bar on the taskbar, type** bitlocker.

   A list of search results appears.

2. **Click Manage BitLocker.**

   The BitLocker Drive Encryption window appears.

3. **In the BitLocker Drive Encryption window, find the removable drive that you want to encrypt and click it.**

   A list with options appears.

4. **Click the Turn on BitLocker button for that drive (see Figure 20-4).**

   You're asked to choose how you want to unlock this drive.

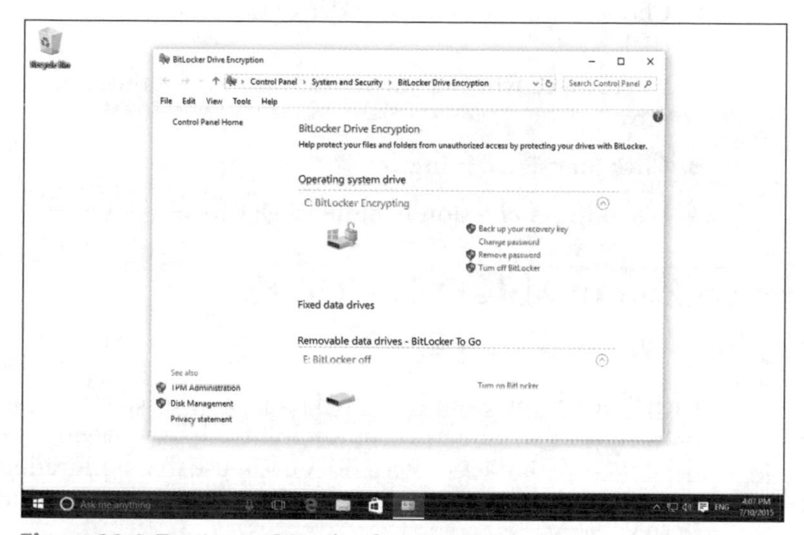

Figure 20-4: Turning on BitLocker for a removable drive.

5. **Select Use a Password to Unlock the Drive.**

   The fields for entering the password and confirming it now are editable.

6. **Type the password in the appropriate fields; then click Next (see Figure 20-5).**

   You're asked where you want to back up your recovery key.

7. **Click the option you prefer; then click Next.**

   You're asked to choose how much of your drive you want to encrypt and given two options: encrypt the used disk space only or encrypt the entire drive.

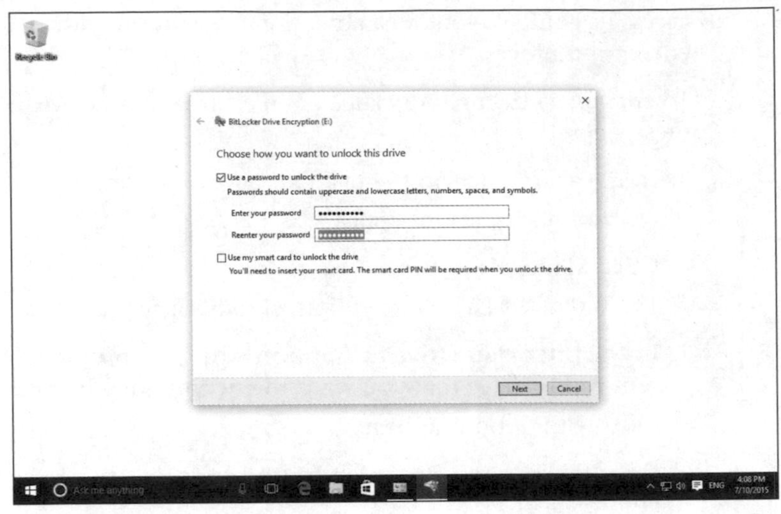

Figure 20-5: How you want to unlock the removable drive.

8. **Choose how much of your drive you want to encrypt and click Next.**

   You're asked whether you're ready to encrypt the selected drive.

9. **Click Start Encrypting.**
10. **When the encryption is done, click Close.**

Unlock a Removable Drive That's Encrypted with BitLocker

Each time you plug the encrypted removable drive into a computer running Windows 10, a notification appears saying that the drive is BitLocker-protected. You can use that notification to unlock the drive at that time, or you can do so later and follow these steps:

1. **Open File Explorer.**
2. **Click This PC.**

   A list with your folders, devices, and drives appears.

3. **Double-click the removable drive.**

   A BitLocker prompt appears asking for the password to unlock the drive.

4. **Type the password (see Figure 20-6).**
5. **Click Unlock.**

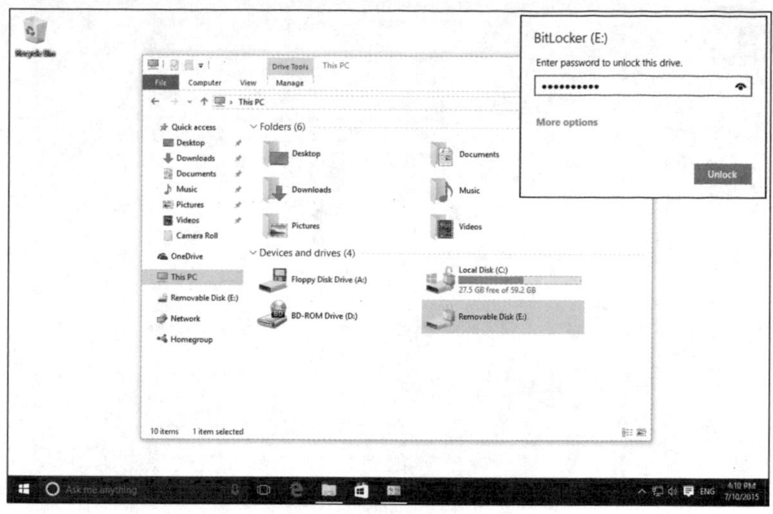

Figure 20-6: Unlocking a BitLocker encrypted drive.

6. **Double-click again on the removable drive in File Explorer to open it and see its contents.**
7. **Close File Explorer when you finish using the removable drive.**

Decrypt a BitLocker Encrypted Drive

The process for decrypting a BitLocker-protected drive is easy. First, unlock the drive by providing the appropriate encryption password, as previously shown in this chapter, and then follow these steps:

1. **In the search bar on the taskbar, type** bitlocker.

   A list of search results appears.
2. **Click Manage BitLocker.**

   The BitLocker Drive Encryption window appears.
3. **In the BitLocker Drive Encryption window that appears, find the drive that you want to decrypt and click the Turn Off BitLocker link (see Figure 20-7).**

   You receive a message saying that the drive will be decrypted.
4. **Click Turn Off BitLocker.**

   The decryption process starts immediately.
5. **Close the BitLocker Drive Encryption window.**

   You can resume using your computer.

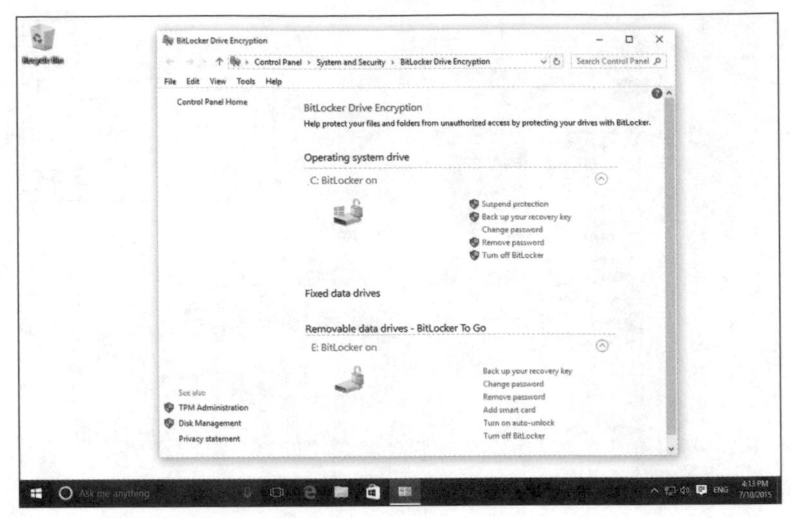

Figure 20-7: Decrypting a drive.

The decryption process is the same for operating system drives and removable drives. To completely turn off BitLocker, you need to decrypt all drives using the decryption procedure shown earlier.

Back Up your Files with File History

File History was first introduced in Windows 8 and continued in Windows 8.1 and now continues in Windows 10. With File History, you can back up the files in your Libraries (such as Documents, Pictures, and Music), Contacts folder, Favorites folder, and the Desktop. After this feature is turned on and the backup location is available, Windows handles the backups automatically. File History backs up only your libraries and the aforementioned folders. If you have some folders elsewhere and want to also back them up, you can include them in one of your user libraries.

File History also stores all the file versions you create, depending on how you set it to work. By default, File History keeps all versions of all files it backs up, forever. However, it can be set to keep files either until space is needed or for a limited time period (such as a month or three months). You can then use File History to revert to a previous version of a file, if you need to. This feature works best with external storage devices such as hard disks or large USB memory sticks that have sufficient space for the copied files. You can also make copies on network locations, such as folders from another computer or on a server. File copies can be restored at any time on the same computer or on other Windows devices and computers, which can be useful if your system crashes or encounters problems with corrupted data. By using File History, you can ensure that your important data is always backed up and available.

To turn on File History and use it to back up your files, plug an external hard disk into your Windows 10 computer or device or have a network drive available that can be used for this task; then follow these steps:

1. **In the search bar on the taskbar, type** file history.

   A list of search results appears.

2. **Click File History.**

   The File History window appears.

3. **Wait for File History to detect suitable drives for use; then click Turn On (see Figure 20-8).**

4. **If you're asked whether to recommend this drive to other members of your HomeGroup, make your choice.**

5. **Close File History.**

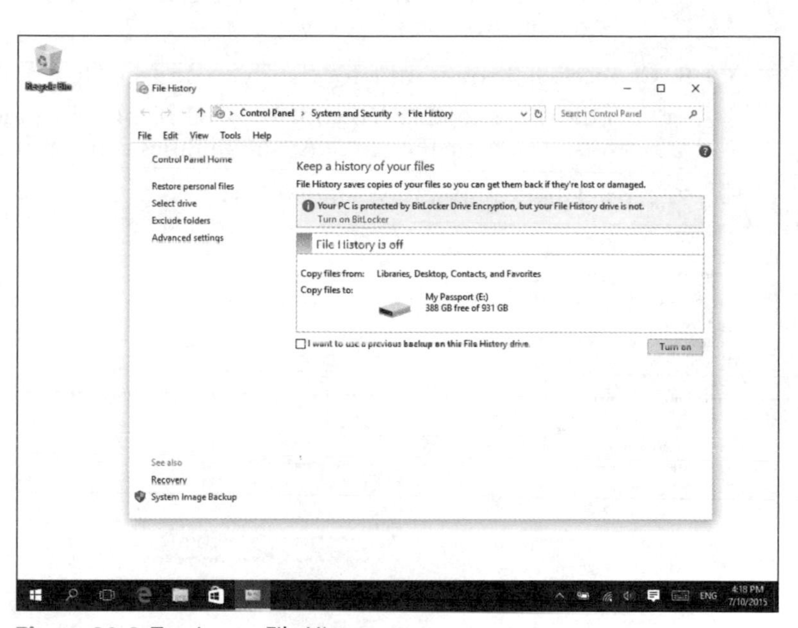

Figure 20-8: Turning on File History.

Restore Files with File History

With File History, you can restore complete folders and libraries, as well as individual files. If you want to restore a library, you select it and click Restore. If you want to restore only one file, browse to its location, select it and click Restore. To select more than one item, press and hold the Ctrl key on your keyboard while selecting each item with the mouse.

You can restore files to where they were initially copied on your computer or to a different location. Here's how the process works:

1. **In the search bar on the taskbar, type** file history.

   A list of search results appears.

2. **Click File History.**

   The File History window appears.

3. **Click Restore Personal Files, and the File History wizard opens.**

4. **Select the libraries and folders that you want to restore.**

5. **Click the Restore button (see Figure 20-9).**

   The Restore button is green; it has an arrow that suggests going back in time.

   You're asked to confirm that you want to replace the existing files with the ones from your backup. Figure 20-9 shows how to restore files with File History.

6. **Choose what you want File History to do (see Figure 20-9).**

   After the copying process completes, a File Explorer window opens showing the files, folders, and libraries you copied.

7. **Close File Explorer, then File History.**

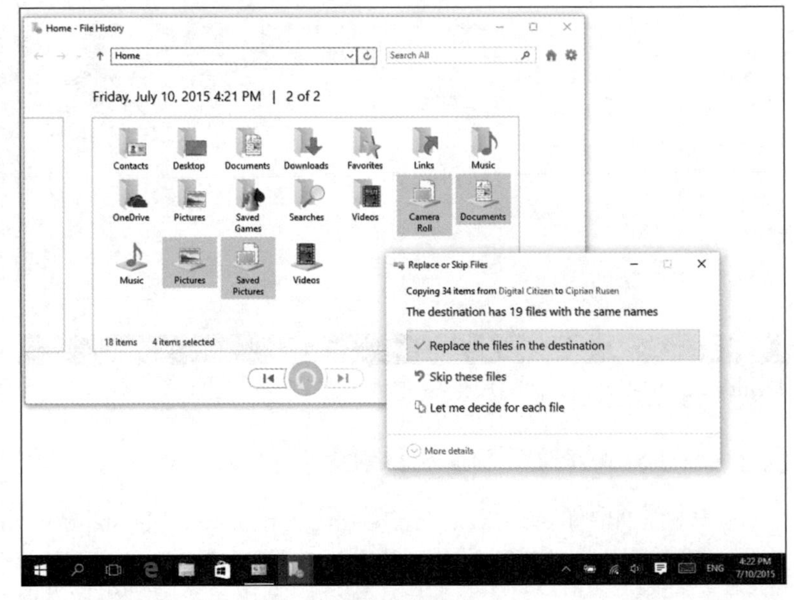

Figure 20-9: Restoring files with File History.

Configure File History

You can configure how File History works and adjust settings such as how often File History saves copies of your files and how long it keeps saved versions of your files. To set how it works, follow these steps:

1. **In the search bar on the taskbar, type** file history.

   A list of search results appears.

2. **Click File History.**

   The File History window appears.

3. **Click Advanced Settings.**

   The Advanced Settings window appears.

4. **Set how you want File History to work (see Figure 20-10) by setting how often it should save copies of files and for how long it should keep saved versions.**

5. **Click Save Changes.**

6. **Close File History.**

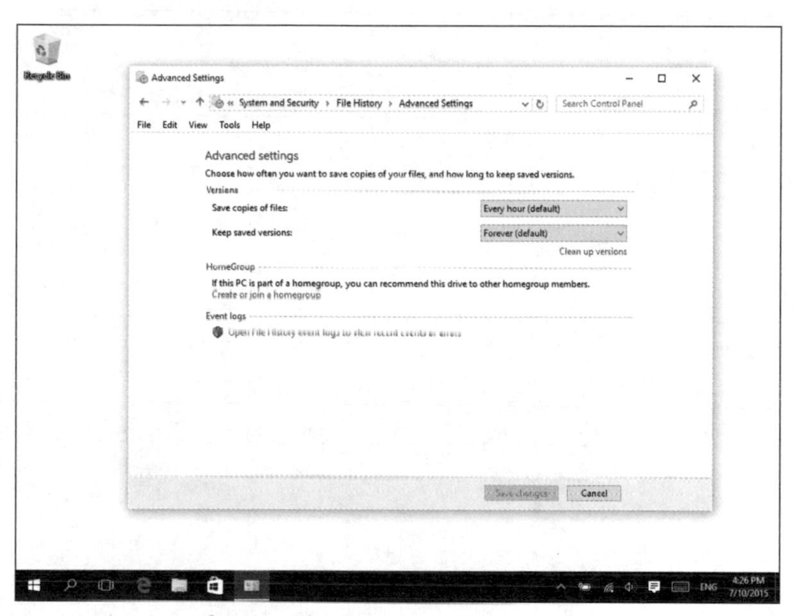

Figure 20-10: Configuring File History.

To exclude folders and libraries from backups, go to the File History window, click Exclude Folders, then click Add and select the folders that you want to exclude from the backup.

Turn Off File History

If you no longer want to use File History or you need to turn it off temporarily, here's what to do:

1. **In the search bar on the taskbar, type** file history.

   A list of search results appears.

2. **Click File History.**

   The File History window appears.

3. **Click Turn Off.**

4. **Close File History.**

CHAPTER TWENTY ONE

Personalizing User Accounts

User accounts make it possible for multiple people to share a computer, with each person having a private Documents folder, apps, email inbox, and Windows settings. When you have your own account, you can do all the customization you want to your Windows environment without affecting other user accounts. Other users will have their own visual customization, their own app settings, and so forth. Windows 10 provides several types of user accounts, each with its own characteristics. This chapter starts by detailing them and what's different from user account to user account.

This chapter also shows how to personalize your own user account and do things such as set up a PIN or a picture password for quick sign-ins, switch between sign-in options, and change your account picture. Finally, you see how to set the sign-in policy in Windows 10.

In This Chapter

- Understanding user accounts in Windows 10
- Understanding user account types and permissions
- Setting up a PIN
- Setting up a picture password
- Switching between sign-in options
- Changing the user account picture
- Setting the sign-in policy in Windows 10

Understanding the User Accounts That You Can Use

Just like in Windows 8, in Windows 10, several user accounts are available, each with its own characteristics.

In well-managed business environments, there is a network domain for the entire company or for a part of it. On this domain, each individual user has his or her own user account called a *domain user account.* When using a domain user account, your actions are limited by the access rights and privileges associated with the account. These rights and privileges are managed centrally by the IT department or by the network administrator and can't be changed by individual users.

With a domain user account, employees can log on to every computer in the company's network and quickly get access to their apps, files, and settings. A domain user account has two name formats that can be used to authenticate in Windows and in Windows apps:

- **Email address or User Principal Name (UPN)**: Specifies an Internet-style name, such as `UserName@Microsoft.com` and `ciprianrusen@wiley.com`.

  The parts of the UPN are

  - The user account name (before the @ character)
  - The separator (the @ character)
  - The domain name (after the @ character)

- **Down-level logon name:** Specifies a domain and a user account in that domain, such as DOMAIN\UserName and CONTOSO\John.Smith.

  The parts of a down-level logon name are

  - The domain name (before the \ character)
  - The separator (the \ character)
  - The user account name (after the \ character)

On your personal Windows devices as well as in smaller companies without a carefully managed IT environment, you don't use domain user accounts. Instead, you can use a Microsoft account or a local account.

A Microsoft account is an ID composed of an email address and password, which you can use to log on to most Microsoft websites, services, and properties such as Outlook.com, Xbox Live, and all Microsoft services (including OneDrive and Skype). You also use it in Windows 10 and Windows 8.1 for synchronizing your computer settings, for using the Windows Store to purchase apps, and for other activities.

If you're already using Outlook.com, OneDrive, or Xbox Live, you already have a Microsoft account. You can use the same email address and password in Windows 10.

If you don't have a Microsoft account, you can easily create one in Windows 10 or on the Microsoft websites. Using a Microsoft account in Windows 10 is very useful, particularly if you want to access all the features it has to offer without problems or limitations. In addition, a Microsoft account gives you access to almost all Microsoft products, services, properties, and websites. And you can use the same Microsoft account across many devices and have your settings, apps, and files synced automatically.

Local user accounts can be used only on your local computer. If you have multiple devices, you must create a separate local account for each device. A local account is the same as any account you've ever used to log in to a Windows 7 or Windows XP operating system. A local account grants you access to the system's resources in your own user space. You can install desktop apps, change settings, and work as usual. Although with local accounts you won't miss out on any familiar features in older versions of Windows, you can't access too many new features that Windows 10 has to offer, because local accounts can't use services like OneDrive or Skype, unless you manually enter a Microsoft account.

In Windows 10, you can sign in with domain user accounts, Microsoft accounts, and local user accounts. However, your work computer might not allow every type of user account. That's because the company may impose certain rules about which types of user accounts can be used on the company's computers. In a company with carefully managed networks, usually you can use only your domain user account; you can't create or use a local account or a Microsoft account.

Understanding User Account Types and Permissions

User accounts in Windows 10 can be administrator accounts or standard user accounts. Accounts with administrator permissions are specified by the word Administrator in the Accounts section of the Settings window (see Figure 21-1).

Administrators have full access to all user accounts. They can create and delete user accounts and change the name, password, and account types for other accounts. The administrator can also install software and hardware and configure every aspect of the operating system. As a rule, every computer must have at least one administrator.

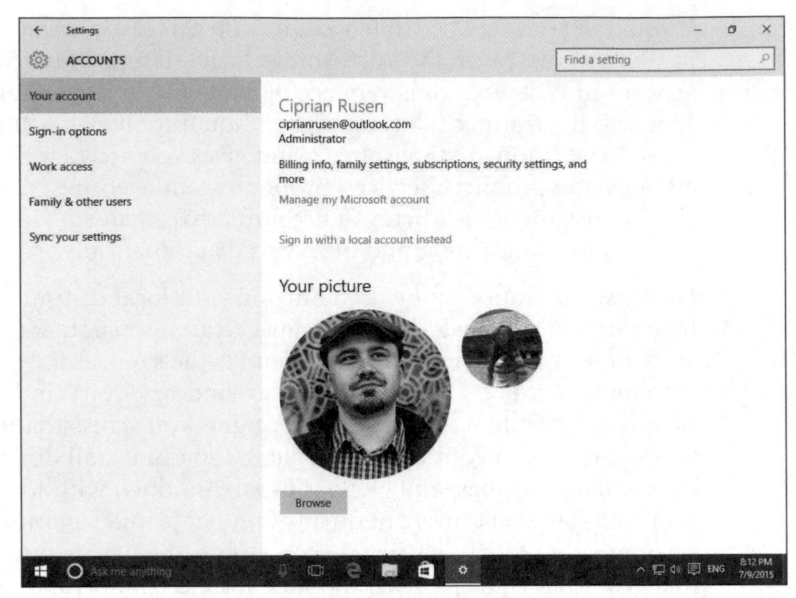

Figure 21-1: A user account that's set as an administrator.

A user account that isn't an administrator account is considered a standard user account and has limited permissions. Generally, a user with standard privileges has access to apps that have already been installed on the computer but can't install other software without the administrator password. Standard users can change their own passwords but can't change the account name or type without the administrator password.

In business environments, most users have standard user accounts with limited permissions that are set by the IT department or the network administrator. Individual users can't create and manage other user accounts. The rest of this chapter explains how to personalize your standard user account in Windows 10.

Set Up a PIN for Your User Account

To simplify how you log on to your computer, Windows 10 allows you to create a four-digit PIN associated with your user account. After you create a PIN, you can use it to log on quickly to your user account. Here's how to set up a pin for your account:

1. **Open Settings.**
2. **Click Accounts.**

   The settings for user accounts are shown.

3. **Click Sign-In Options.**

   Your sign-in settings are shown.

4. **Click the Add button in the PIN section.**

   You're asked to verify your account.

5. **Enter your user account password.**

6. **Click Sign In.**

   The Set Up a PIN window opens.

7. **Type the PIN that you want to set in the New PIN and Confirm PIN boxes (see Figure 21-2).**

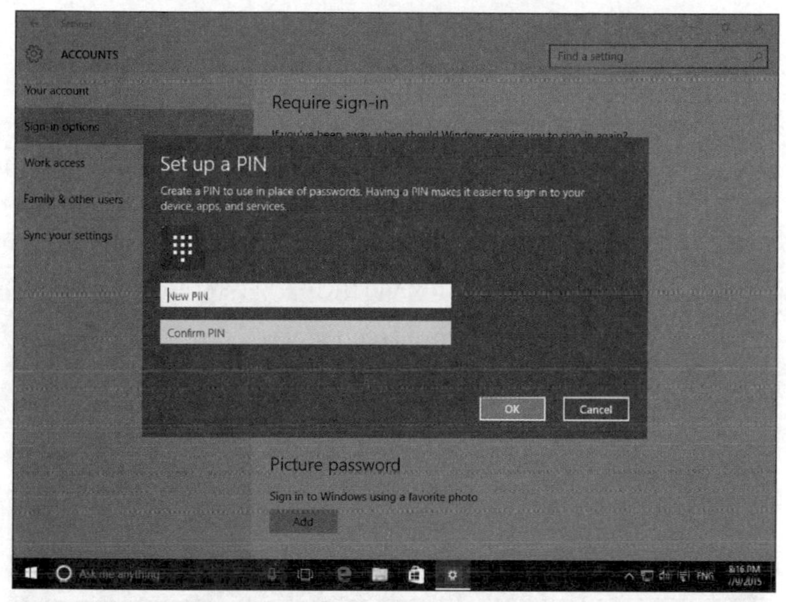

Figure 21-2: How to set up the PIN in Windows 10.

8. **Click OK.**

9. **Close Settings.**

If you forget your PIN, you have to reset it. To reset the PIN, follow the preceding steps and, at Step 4, click I Forgot My PIN; then follow the wizard's instructions for resetting the PIN.

Set Up a Picture Password for Your User Account

The concept of picture passwords was first introduced in Windows 8. A picture password has two complementary parts: a picture and gestures that you draw on it. These gestures can be taps, clicks, circles, or lines. If your user account has a complicated password, using a picture password can make it easier to log on to your Windows 10 devices. Even though this feature is particularly recommended for use on touch-enabled devices such as tablets, you can also employ it on a desktop computer by using a mouse.

To create a picture password for your user account, follow these steps:

1. **Open Settings.**
2. **Click Accounts.**

   The settings for user accounts are shown.
3. **Click Sign-In Options.**

   Your sign-in settings are shown.
4. **In the Picture Password section, click the Add button.**

   You're asked to first verify your account info and type your password.
5. **Type your password as requested; then click OK.**

   The wizard for setting the picture password appears.
6. **Click Choose Picture (see Figure 21-3).**

   A browsing window opens.

Figure 21-3: Welcome to picture password.

7. **Navigate to where you stored the picture you want to use for the password and select it.**
8. **Click Open.**

   The selected picture is now open.
9. **Drag the picture to the position that you want.**

   You can use your mouse (if you have one) or your finger (if you use touch).
10. **Click Use This Picture.**

    You're asked to set up three gestures as your picture password.
11. **Draw three gestures on your picture.**

    You can use any combination of circles, straight lines, and taps.
12. **Confirm the three gestures by drawing them again (see Figure 21-4).**

    You receive a message that you successfully created your picture password.
13. **Click Finish.**
14. **Close Settings.**

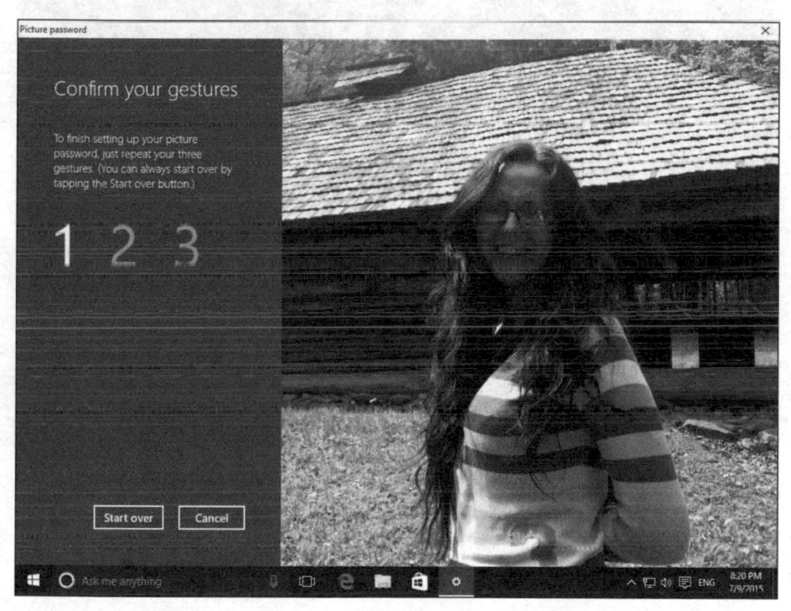

Figure 21-4: Confirming your gestures for the picture password.

Switch Between Sign-In Options

After you set up more than one way to sign in to Windows 10, you need to know how to switch between them when signing into Windows. When you're at the sign-in screen in Windows 10 and you want to use a way to sign in other than with your password, here's what to do:

1. **Select your user account from the list of available accounts.**

   Your user account picture appears.

2. **Click the Sign-In Options link.**

   A list of icons appears. Each icon represents a sign-in option. From left to right, they are picture password, password, and PIN.

3. **Click the icon for the sign-in option that you want to use (see Figure 21-5).**

4. **Sign in to Windows 10 using the option that you selected.**

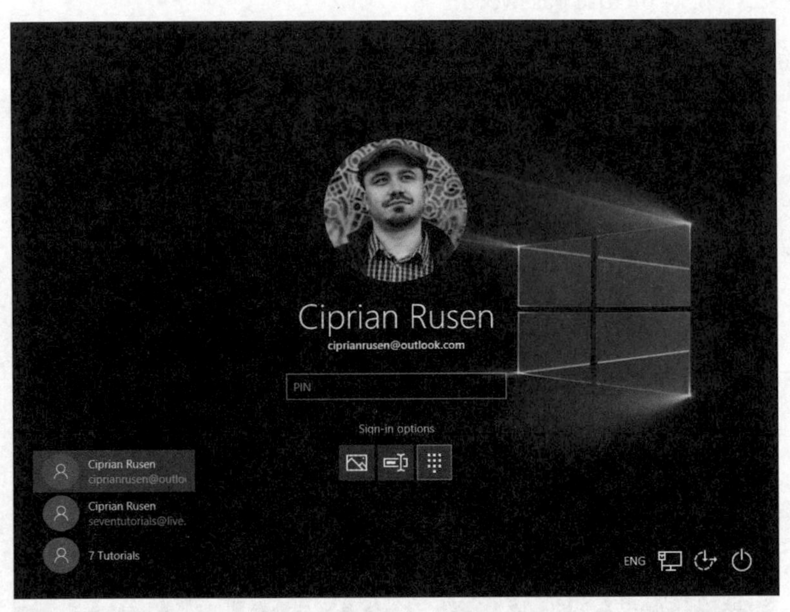

Figure 21-5: Selecting the sign-in option that you want to use.

Change Your User Account Picture

In Windows 10, you can set a picture for your user account, and you can change it at any time. The picture you use is shown when you sign in to Windows 10, on the Start Menu, in apps that use this picture, and so on.

To change the picture that you're using for your account, follow these steps:

1. **Open Settings.**
2. **Click Accounts.**

   The settings for user accounts are shown.
3. **In Your Account, click the Browse button (see Figure 21-6).**

   A browsing window opens.

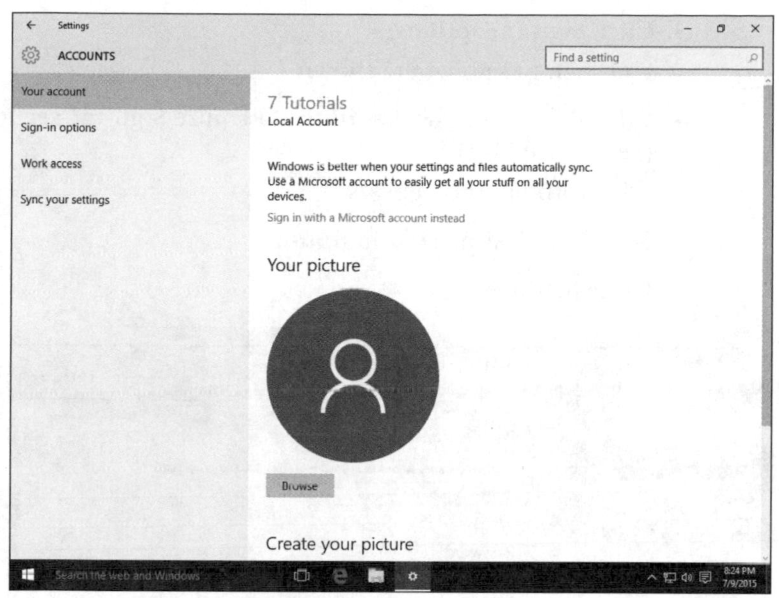

Figure 21-6: Changing your user account picture.

4. **Navigate to where you stored the picture that you want to use and select it.**
5. **Click Choose Picture.**

   The new picture is shown alongside the previous one, if one was set.
6. **Close Settings.**

Set the Sign-In Policy

You can set Windows 10 to require you to sign in again if you stop using it for a certain period of time. You can also set it to never ask you to sign in.

Setting Windows 10 to always require you to sign in after you're away from your computer is a very useful security precaution, especially in business environments where it's important that unauthorized people don't get access to your work.

Here's how to set the sign-in policy in Windows 10:

1. **Open Settings.**
2. **Click Accounts.**

   The settings for user accounts are shown.
3. **Click Sign-In Options.**

   Your sign-in settings are shown.
4. **Click the drop-down list in the "Require Sign-In" section (see Figure 21-7).**

   A list with options appears.
5. **Select the desired sign-in option.**
6. **Close Settings.**

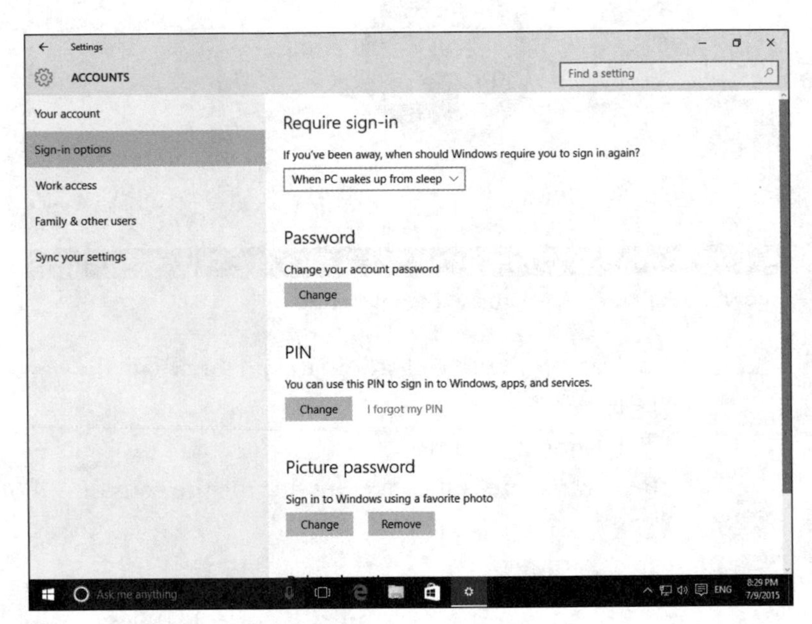

Figure 21-7: Setting the sign-in option.

CHAPTER TWENTY TWO

Sharing with Others on a Network

In This Chapter

- Adjusting network sharing settings
- Accessing what is shared on a network
- Sharing files on a network
- Using the HomeGroup feature for sharing with computers on your home network
- Ending sharing folders and libraries with others on a network
- Turning on the Sharing Wizard

You're probably connected to a network almost every time you use your work computer. One of the advantages of using a network connection is that it allows you to share resources with others and access shared resources from the network. This chapter shows you how to set up different network sharing settings in Windows 10 and how to share resources with others in your network.

If you take a work laptop home with you, you may need to share resources with others in your home network. To help you do that as easily and as securely as possible, Windows 10 offers the HomeGroup feature. This chapter shows how HomeGroup works and how to use it.

Enable Network Discovery

Network discovery allows Windows to find other computers and devices on a network. This feature is automatically turned on when you're connected to private networks like the one in your home or workplace. Network discovery is turned off when you're connected to public networks that shouldn't be trusted and you don't allow your PC to be discoverable on those networks.

If your Windows 10 computer or device can't view other computers on the network, two things are probably at fault: You either assigned the incorrect network profile (public instead or private) or network discovery is turned off for some reason. (Chapter 4 covers the basics of network profiles.)

Here's how to activate network discovery in Windows 10 for your active network profile:

1. **Open Settings.**

   The Settings window appears.

2. **Click Network & Internet.**

   Your network and Internet related settings are shown.

3. **In the panel on the left, click either Wi-Fi (if you're connected to a wireless network) or Ethernet (if you're connected to a network using a network cable).**

   A window with settings for your network appears.

4. **Find the Related setting section on the right, then click Change Advanced Sharing Settings.**

   The Advanced Sharing Settings window appears.

5. **Expand the network profile currently assigned to your network connection.**

   It is marked with the words "current profile" on the right side of its name.

6. **In the Network discover section, select "Turn on network discovery". Also, check the box that says "Turn on automatic setup of network connected devices" (see Figure 22-1).**

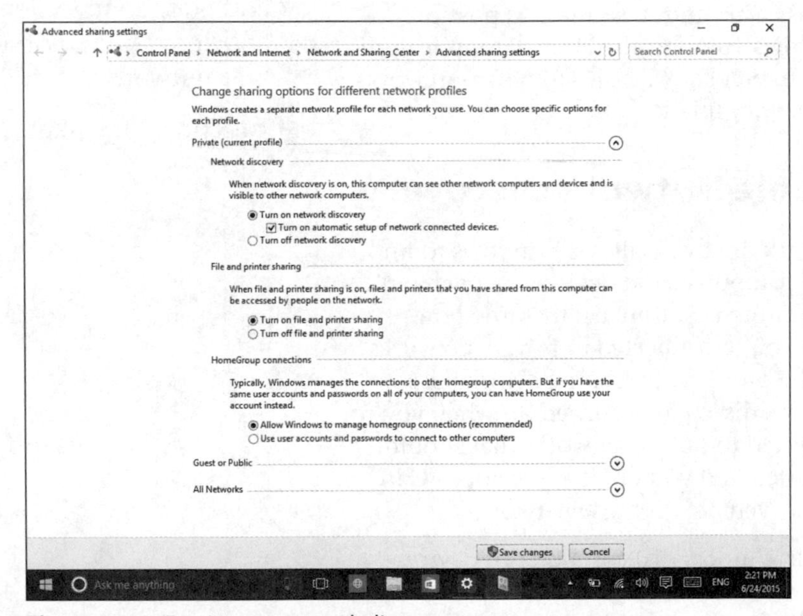

Figure 22-1: Turning on network discovery.

7. **Click Save changes.**
8. **Close the Settings window.**

You don't ever want to enable network discovery when you're connected to public networks. So, if you're connected to a public network like those in airports and cafes, be sure to set the profile to Public.

Enable File and Printer Sharing

When you're connected to private networks, Windows 10 automatically turns on the File and Printer Sharing setting. In this way, you can easily share folders, files, and printers with other computers and devices in your network. However, if your network administrator adjusts this setting, you may need to manually turn it on or off, depending on your needs.

Here's how to activate the File and Printer Sharing setting in Windows 10 for your active network connection:

1. **Open Settings.**

   The Settings window appears.
2. **Click Network & Internet.**

   Your network and Internet related settings are shown.
3. **In the panel on the left, click either Wi-Fi (if you're connected to a wireless network) or Ethernet (if you're connected to a network using a network cable).**

   A window with settings for your network appears.
4. **Find the Related setting section on the right, then click Change Advanced Sharing Settings (see Figure 22-2).**

   The Advanced Sharing Settings window appears.
5. **Expand the network profile currently assigned to your network connection.**

   It's identified as "current profile."
6. **In the File and Printer Sharing section, select Turn On File and Printer Sharing.**
7. **Click Save Changes.**
8. **Close the Settings window.**

If you assign the incorrect network profile to your network, turn back to Chapter 4 to find out how to change the profile. There's no need for you to turn on File and Printer Sharing in this situation. If you need to turn File and Printer Sharing off, follow the preceding steps and select Turn Off File and Printer Sharing in Step 5.

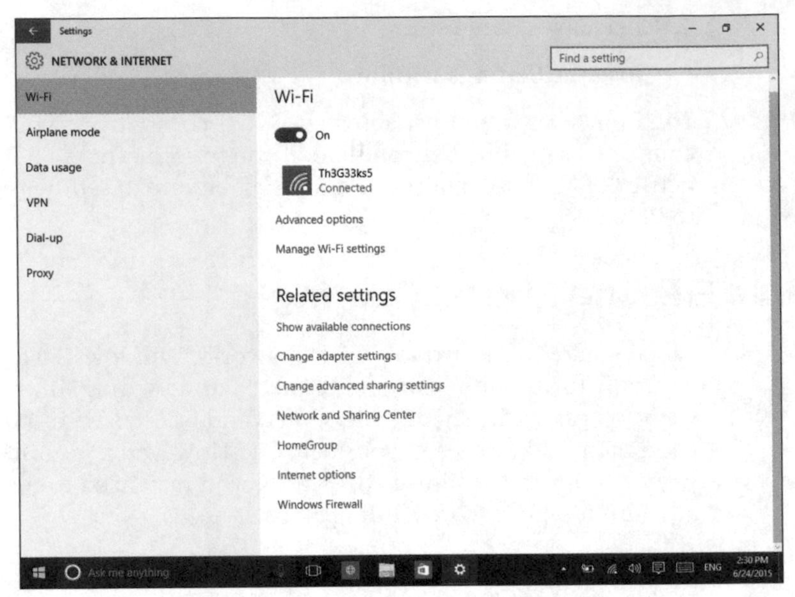

Figure 22-2: Accessing advanced sharing settings in Windows 10.

If you're connected to a public network like those in airports and cafes, be sure to assign Public as the profile for that connection. Also, don't enable the File and Printer Sharing setting when you're connected to public networks.

Enable Public Folder Sharing

The Public folder is located on your hard drive in C:\Users\Public. All user accounts registered in Windows have access to it. That's why it's named Public. Any file and folder found in C:\Users\Public is completely accessible to all users on the computer. Depending on your network sharing settings, this folder and its contents can also be accessed by all other computers and devices that are part of the same network.

To turn on Public Folder Sharing, follow these steps:

1. **Open Settings.**

   The Settings window appears.

2. **Click Network & Internet.**

   Your network and Internet related settings are shown.

3. **In the panel on the left, click either Wi-Fi (if you're connected to a wireless network) or Ethernet (if you're connected to a network using a network cable).**

   A window with settings for your network appears.

4. **Find the Related setting section on the right and click Change Advanced Sharing Settings.**

   The Advanced Sharing Settings window appears.

5. **Scroll down and expand the All Networks category of settings.**
6. **In the Public Folder Sharing section, select Turn On Sharing So Anyone with Network Access Can Read and Write Files in the Public Folders (see Figure 22-3).**

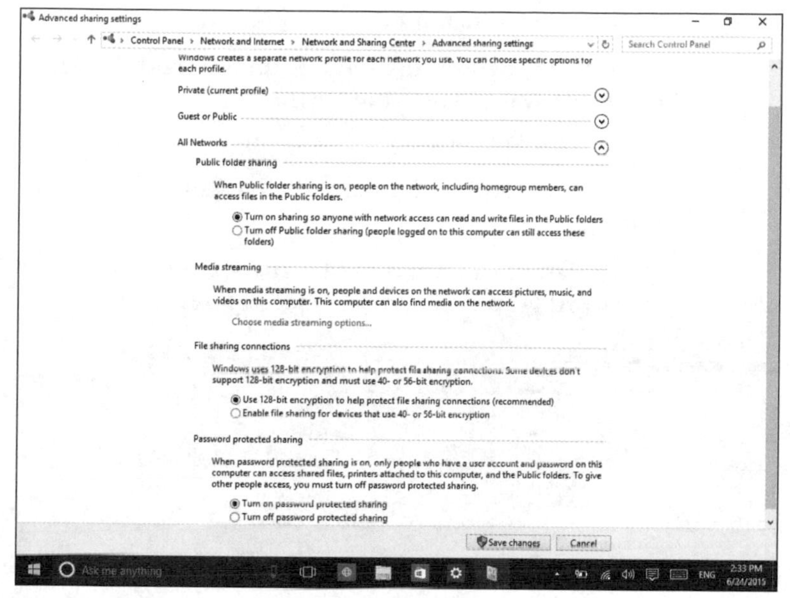

Figure 22-3: Turning on Public Folder Sharing.

7. **Click Save Changes.**
8. **Close the Settings window.**

If you need to turn Public Folder Sharing off, follow the preceding steps and select Turn Off Public Folder Sharing in Step 6.

Enable Password Protected Sharing

When Password Protected Sharing is turned on, only people who have a user account and password on your computer or network domain (in the case of business networks) can access shared files and printers attached to your Windows 10 computer or device, as well as your public folders. It's a good idea to avoid disabling Password Protected Sharing, but you may need to do that in some situations, such as when you want to give other people access.

To turn on Password Protected Sharing, follow these steps:

1. **Open Settings.**

   The Settings window appears.

2. **Click Network & Internet.**

   Your network and Internet related settings are shown.

3. **In the panel on the left, click either Wi-Fi (if you're connected to a wireless network) or Ethernet (if you're connected to a network using a network cable).**

   A window with settings for your network appears.

4. **Find the Related setting section on the right and click Change Advanced Sharing Settings.**

   The Advanced Sharing Settings window appears.

5. **Scroll down and expand the All Networks category of settings.**

6. **In the Password Protected Sharing section, select Turn On Password Protected Sharing (see Figure 22-4).**

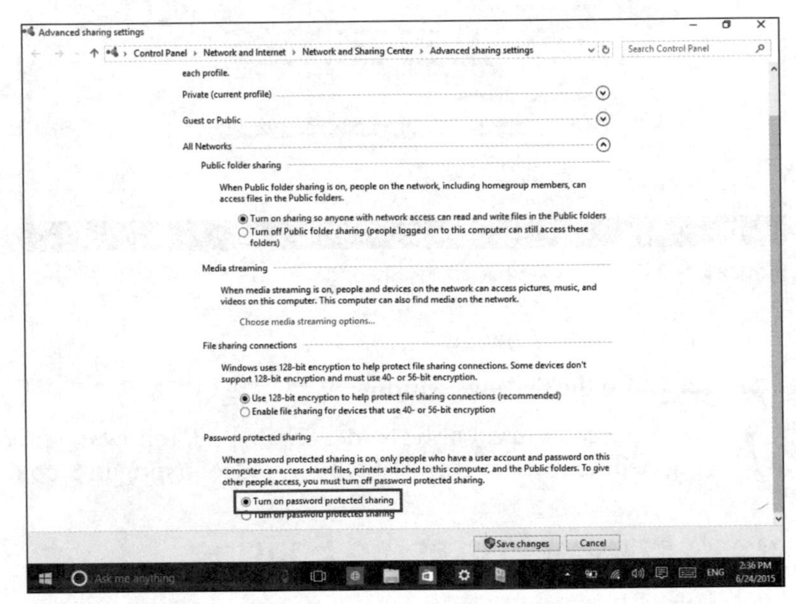

Figure 22-4: Turning On password protected sharing.

7. **Click Save Changes.**

8. **Close the Settings window.**

If you need to turn off Password Protected Sharing, follow the preceding steps and select Turn Off Password Protected Sharing in Step 5.

Access Shared Network Computers

You use File Explorer to access the folders and libraries that are shared by other computers in your network. If you're in a network domain, all you need is your domain username and password, and you can access anything you have permission to access. If you're on a local network without a network domain, you need an assigned user account and password on a computer in order to access its shared resources.

To access folders and libraries shared by others on the network, follow these steps:

1. **Click the File Explorer icon on the taskbar.**

   The File Explorer window appears.

2. **In the Navigation pane on the left, click Network.**

   A list of the computers and devices available on the network appears (see Figure 22-5 for an example).

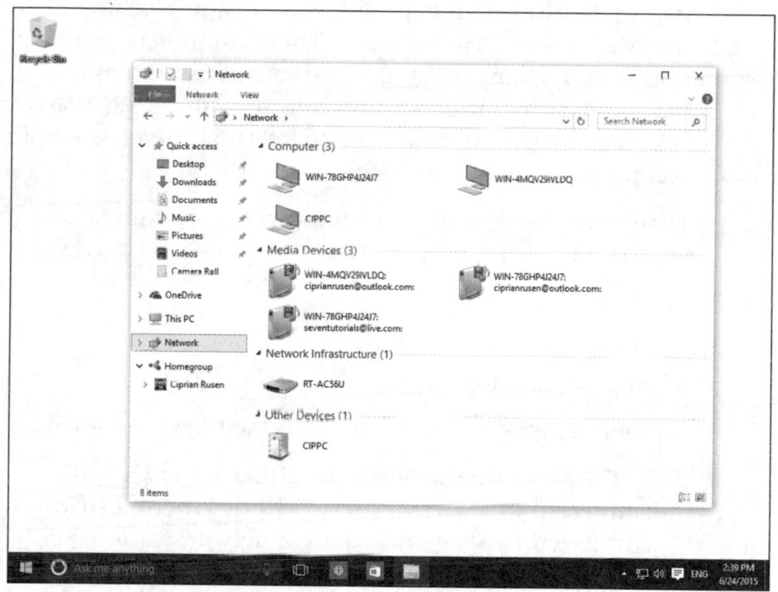

Figure 22-5: Accessing other computers in a network.

3. **Double-click the computer whose shared folders you want to access.**

4. **If asked, enter your network credentials for access to that computer's shared folders:**

   - If you're on a network domain, enter your username and password and click OK.

- If you're on a local network and not a network domain, first enter the name of the computer you want to access, then enter \ followed by a user account that exists on that PC. Next, type your password and click OK.

5. **Browse the folders that the computer shares with the network and access what you're interested in.**
6. **When you're done, close File Explorer.**

Join a HomeGroup

If you take your work computer home, connect it to your home network, and select a private network profile for it, you can use the HomeGroup feature.

A *HomeGroup* comprises a group of Windows computers and devices that can share content and devices with each other. The information and items shared with a HomeGroup aren't available to computers that are on the same network but aren't part of the HomeGroup. Windows 7, 8, and 10 computers and devices can join a HomeGroup. These computers, unlike older operating systems, aren't required to enter a username and password each time they connect to something that's shared with a HomeGroup. By design, there's no limit on the number of computers that can join a HomeGroup.

Here's how to connect your Windows 10 computer or device to an existing HomeGroup:

1. **Open Settings.**

   The Settings window appears.
2. **Click Network & Internet.**

   Your network and Internet related settings are shown.
3. **In the panel on the left, click either Wi-Fi (if you're connected to a wireless network) or Ethernet (if you're connected to a network using a network cable).**

   A window with settings for your network appears.
4. **Find the Related setting section on the right and click HomeGroup.**

   The HomeGroup window appears.
5. **Click Join Now (see Figure 22-6).**
6. **Click Next.**

   A list appears with the items that you can share with others on the HomeGroup.

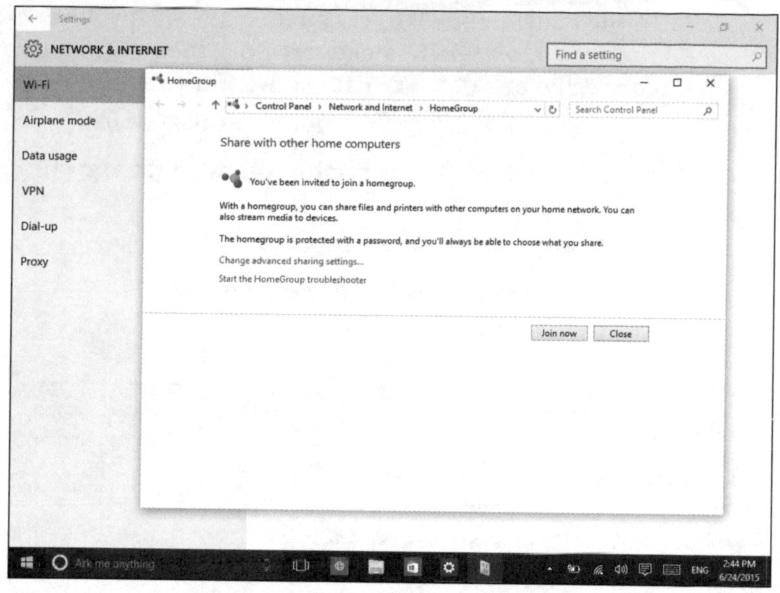

Figure 22-6: The wizard for joining a HomeGroup.

7. **Select which libraries and devices you want to share with the HomeGroup.**
8. **Click Next.**

   You're asked to enter the password for the HomeGroup.
9. **Type the password for the HomeGroup.**
10. **Click Next.**

    You're notified whether the computer has joined the HomeGroup.
11. **Click Finish.**

Create a HomeGroup

When you use your work computer at home, if you select a private network profile for your home network connection, you can create a HomeGroup and have other Windows computers and devices at your home join that HomeGroup.

In order to create a HomeGroup on your Windows 10 computer or device, follow these gates:

1. **Open Settings.**

   The Settings window appears.
2. **Click Network & Internet.**

   Your network and Internet related settings are shown.

3. **In the panel on the left, click either Wi-Fi (if you're connected to a wireless network) or Ethernet (if you're connected to a network using a network cable).**

   A window with settings for your network appears.

4. **Find the Related setting section on the right and click HomeGroup.**

   The HomeGroup window appears.

5. **Click Create a HomeGroup (see Figure 22-7).**

   The Create A HomeGroup wizard appears.

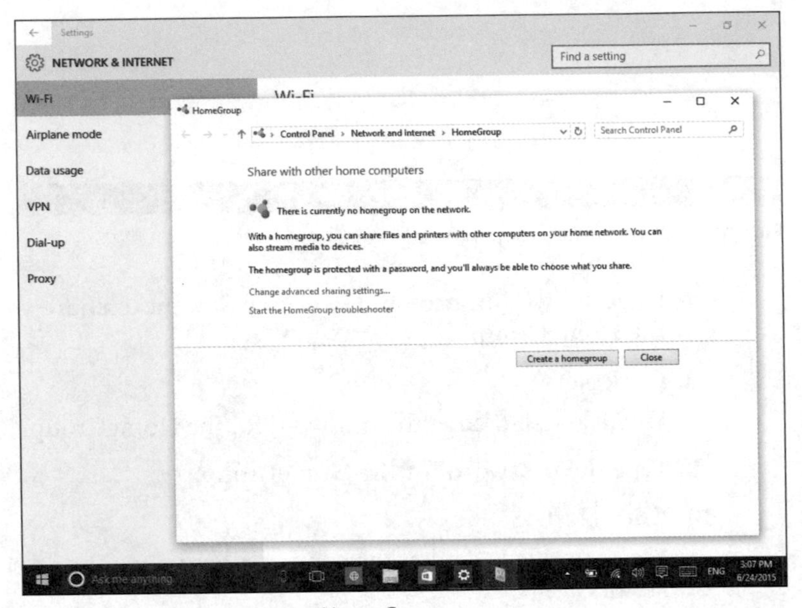

Figure 22-7: How to create a HomeGroup.

6. **Click Next.**

   A list appears with the items that you can share with others on the HomeGroup.

7. **Select which libraries and devices you want to share with the HomeGroup.**

8. **Click Next.**

   A secure password is automatically generated by Windows for your HomeGroup.

9. **Jot down the password so that you can share it with users who will use it to connect to the HomeGroup; then click Finish.**

10. **Close the HomeGroup window.**

Change a HomeGroup Password

If you can't remember the password that is automatically generated by Windows for your HomeGroup or if you want to change the password to something you can more easily remember, here's how to do so:

1. **Open Settings.**

   The Settings window appears.

2. **Click Network & Internet.**

   Your network and Internet related settings are shown.

3. **In the panel on the left, click either Wi-Fi (if you're connected to a wireless network) or Ethernet (if you're connected to a network using a network cable).**

   A window with settings for your network appears.

4. **Find the Related setting section on the right and click HomeGroup.**

   The HomeGroup window appears.

5. **Click Change The Password.**

   The Change Your HomeGroup Password wizard appears.

6. **Click Change the Password again (see Figure 22-8).**

   Windows automatically generates a new password for you.

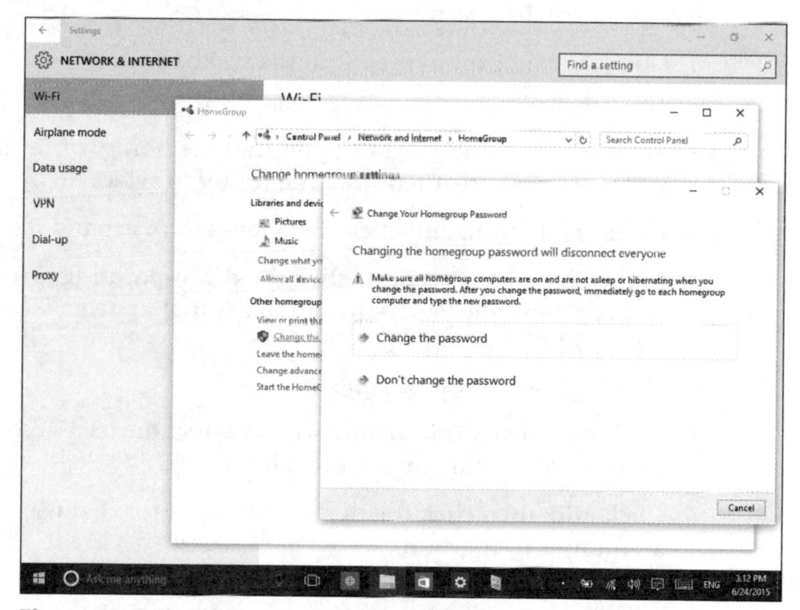

Figure 22-8: The Change Your HomeGroup Password wizard.

7. **Replace the password by typing the password that you want to use; then click Next.**

   You're informed that your HomeGroup password was successfully changed.

8. **Click Finish.**
9. **Close the Settings window.**

When your change the password of your HomeGroup, all the Windows computers and devices that have joined it using the old password are automatically disconnected from the HomeGroup. You must reconnect them to the HomeGroup, using the new password.

Share Folders and Libraries with Individual Users

You can share your folders and libraries with specific user accounts and with specific groups. For example, if you share a folder with the group Everyone, that folder is shared with everyone in your network. By default, all the user accounts with which you choose to share are granted Read permissions to the shared item. However, you can easily change the permissions to Read/Write permissions.

To share a folder or library with a specific user account or user group, follow these steps:

1. **Click the File Explorer icon on the taskbar.**

   The File Explorer window appears.

2. **Browse your computer until you find the library or folder you want to share; then click the folder to select it.**
3. **Go to the Ribbon and click the Share tab to expand it.**
4. **In the Share With section, click the down-pointing arrow and click Specific People from the list that appears (see Figure 22-9).**

   The File Sharing wizard appears.

5. **Click the down-pointing arrow and select the user account or user group that you want to share with.**
6. **Click Add; then click the permission level for that user account or user group.**

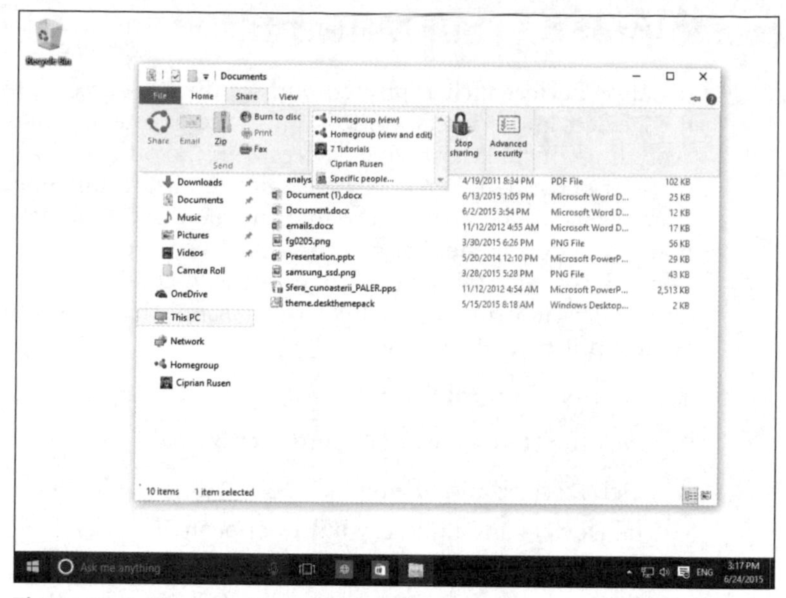

Figure 22-9: Sharing with specific people.

7. **Select the permission level that you want to assign to the selected user account (see Figure 22-10).**
8. **Click Share.**
9. **When you receive confirmation that the folder is shared, click Done.**

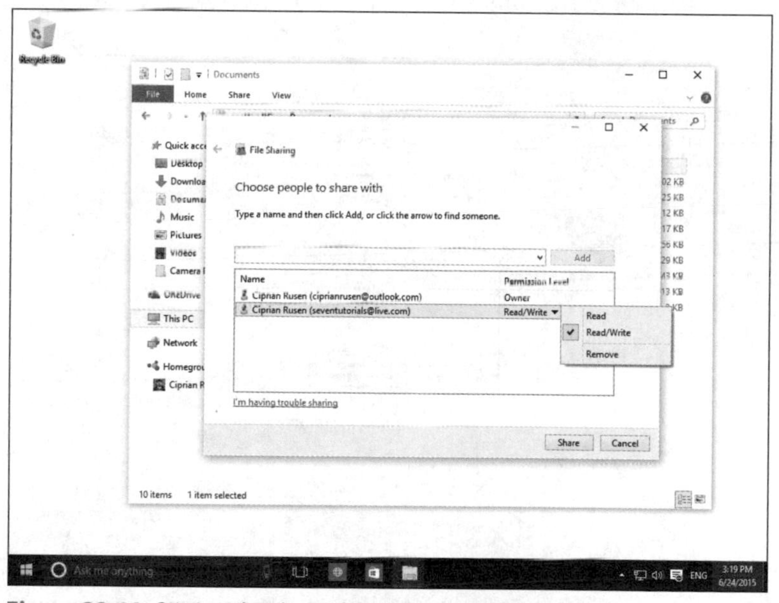

Figure 22-10: Setting the desired permission level.

Share a Printer on Your Network

Installed devices such as printers and scanners are accessible in the Devices and Printers window. From there, you can configure everything, including sharing devices with the other computers on your network. When you share a printer, its default Share Name is its model name. To change the name, you can type a new name during the sharing procedure. A shared printer on a network is shared with the entire network, including computers and devices that are outside the HomeGroup. Here's how to share a printer with your network:

1. **Open the Control Panel.**
2. **Click the Hardware and Sound section.**
3. **Click Devices and Printers.**

   The Devices and Printers window appears.
4. **Scroll down to the Printers section to view the printers installed on your computer.**
5. **Right-click the printer that you want to share.**

   The right-click menu appears.
6. **Click Printer Properties.**

   The Printer Properties dialog box appears.
7. **Click the Sharing tab.**
8. **Select the Share This Printer check box (see Figure 22-11).**

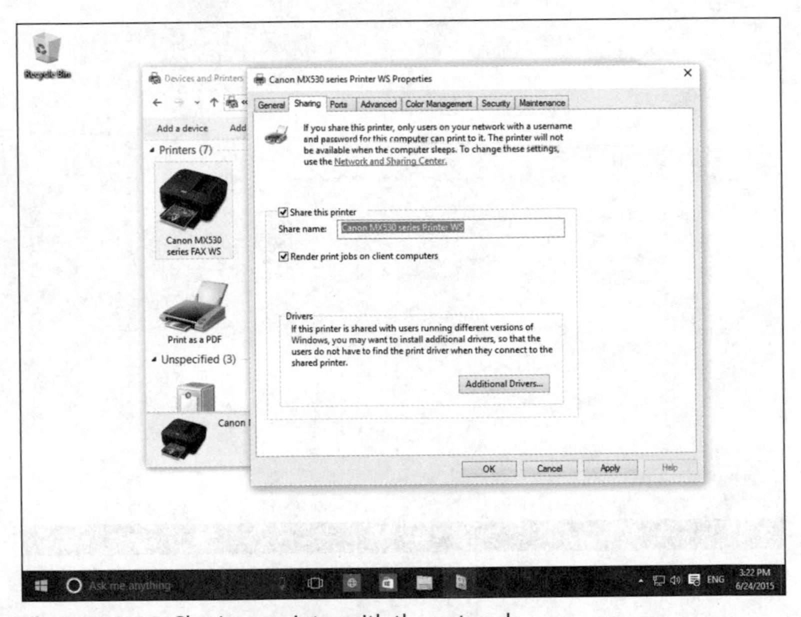

Figure 22-11: Sharing a printer with the network.

9. If you want, you can type a new name for your printer.
10. Click OK.
11. Close the Devices and Printers window.

Share Folders and Libraries with a HomeGroup

To share a folder or library with a HomeGroup, follow these steps:

1. Click the File Explorer icon on the taskbar.

   The File Explorer window appears.

2. Browse your computer until you find the library or folder that you want to share; then click the folder to select it.
3. Go to the Ribbon and click the Share tab to expand it (see Figure 22-12).

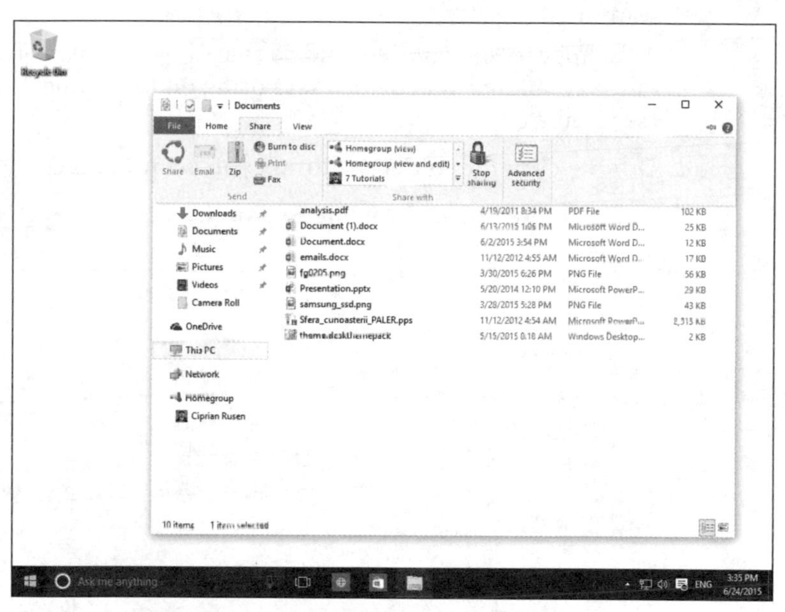

Figure 22-12: The Share tab on the File Explorer Ribbon.

4. In the Share With section, click either HomeGroup (view) or HomeGroup (view and edit) to assign the preferred level of permission.
5. Close File Explorer.

Access Shared Folders and Libraries on a HomeGroup

You use File Explorer to access the folders and libraries that are shared by computers on a given network. When you view what's shared by a HomeGroup, you don't see computer names as you do in the Network section. Instead, you see usernames. That's because a HomeGroup first shows the user accounts that are sharing with the HomeGroup and then lists what they're sharing.

To access folders and libraries shared on your HomeGroup, follow these steps:

1. **Click the File Explorer icon on the taskbar.**

   The File Explorer window appears.

2. **In the Navigation pane on the left, click HomeGroup.**

   A list appears showing all the user accounts that are sharing with the HomeGroup.

3. **Double-click the user account with the shared folders you want to access.**

   A list appears showing the folders shared by that user on each of the computers that he or she is using on the HomeGroup (see Figure 22-13).

4. **Double-click the folder or library you want to access.**
5. **When you're done, close File Explorer.**

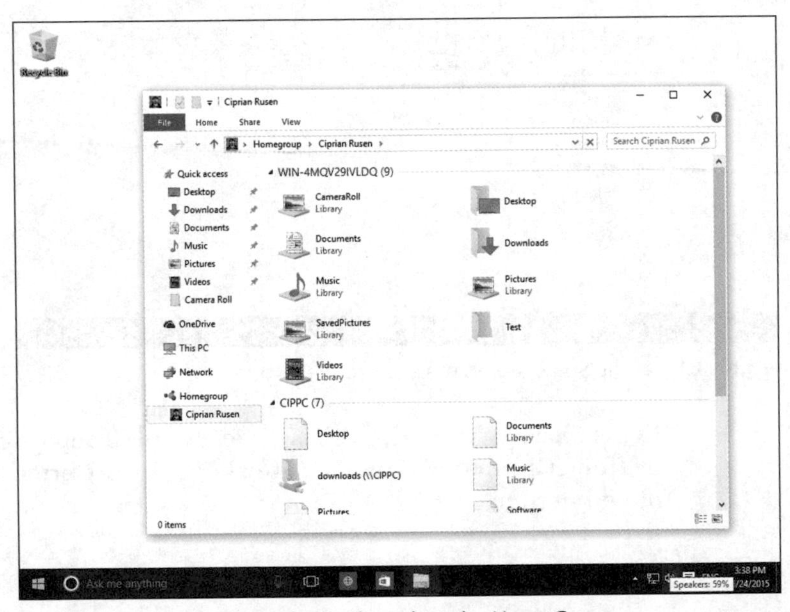

Figure 22-13: Accessing what is shared on the HomeGroup.

Stop Sharing Folders and Libraries

To stop sharing a folder or library, follow these steps:

1. **Click the File Explorer icon on the taskbar.**

   The File Explorer window appears.

2. **Browse your computer until you find the library or folder that you want to stop sharing. Click it to select it.**

3. **Go to the Ribbon and click the Share tab.**

4. **In the Share With section, click the Stop Sharing button (see Figure 22-14).**

5. **When you're done, close File Explorer.**

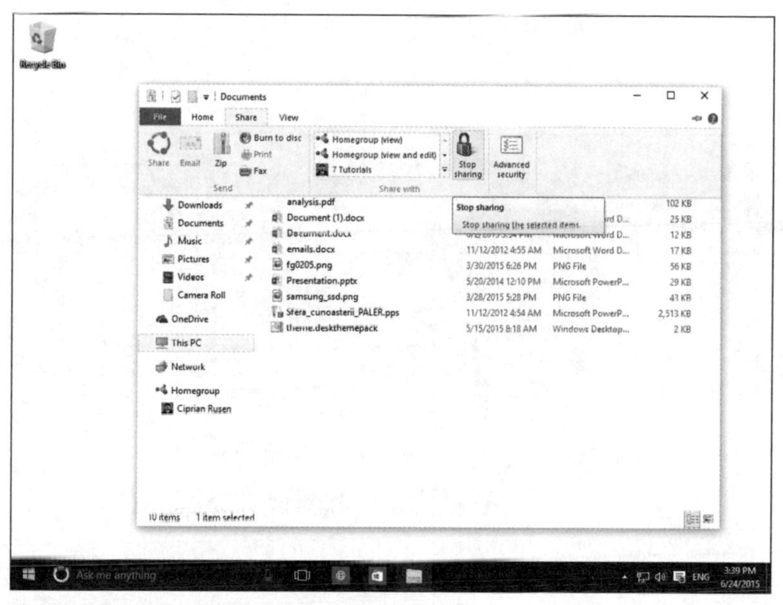

Figure 22-14: The Stop Sharing button.

Leave a HomeGroup

To leave the HomeGroup on your Windows 10 computer or device, follow these steps:

1. **Open Settings.**

   The Settings window appears.

2. **Click Network & Internet.**

   Your network and Internet related settings are shown.

3. **In the panel on the left, click either Wi-Fi (if you're connected to a wireless network) or Ethernet (if you're connected to a network using a network cable).**

   A window with settings for your network appears.

4. **Find the Related setting section on the right and click HomeGroup.**

   The HomeGroup window appears.

5. **Click Leave the HomeGroup.**

   The Leave The HomeGroup wizard appears.

6. **Click Leave the HomeGroup again (see Figure 22-15).**

   You're informed that you have successfully left the HomeGroup.

7. **Click Finish.**

8. **Close the Settings window.**

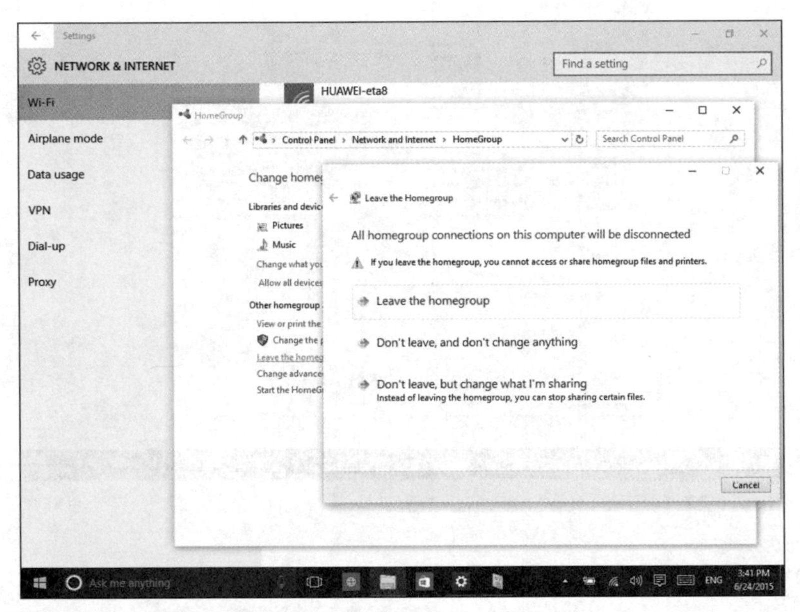

Figure 22-15: The Leave the HomeGroup wizard.

Enable the Sharing Wizard

The Sharing Wizard is designed so that you can easily share anything you want with the other computers and devices on your network. The wizard is turned on in Windows 10 by default. However, if it's turned off on your computer for some reason, the steps in this chapter on sharing over the network won't work, and when you try to share folders, you see a completely different set of sharing options and buttons. Here's how to turn on the Sharing Wizard so that you can perform the tasks in this chapter:

1. **Click the File Explorer icon on the taskbar.**

   The File Explorer window appears.

2. **Click the View tab to expand it.**

3. **Click the Options button located at the upper-right corner of the File Explorer window.**

   The Folder Options window appears.

4. **Click the View tab.**

5. **Scroll down the Advanced Settings list.**

6. **Select the Use Sharing Wizard (Recommended) check box (see Figure 22-16).**

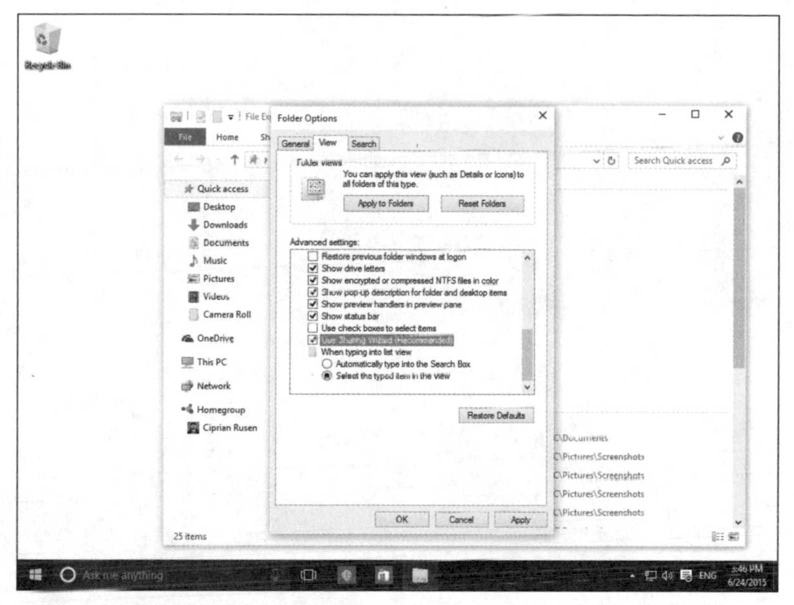

Figure 22-16: The Folder Options window.

7. **Click OK.**

   You return to the File Explorer window.

8. **Close File Explorer.**

If you want to turn the Sharing Wizard off, start the preceding steps; in Step 6, deselect Use Sharing Wizard.

CHAPTER TWENTY THREE

Improving Your Privacy and Security

In This Chapter

- Working with Windows Update
- Working with UAC
- Using Windows Defender
- Using Windows Firewall
- Improving your privacy
- Setting which apps can access your data
- Improving the security of your passwords

Security and privacy are especially important in business environments. Many employees work with confidential data that, if stolen, could be harmful to businesses. That's why most company networks have strict security rules and install several security tools. In this chapter, I present the key security features that Windows 10 offers. Your company may use some (or all) of them, so feel free to check out only the features pertinent to your needs, or check out all of them if you're just curious by nature.

Protecting your personal privacy is also important in today's computing world. By default, Windows 10 and your apps can access plenty of data about you; for example, your account name, picture, location, contacts, and calendar. This chapter shows you how to set all these privacy options so that Windows 10 and your apps can access only the data you allow.

Check Whether Windows Update Is Turned On

Depending on the size of the company you work for and your role in it, either you or an IT department is tasked with keeping Windows 10 up to date. If your company is a big one with a well-managed environment, the IT department probably manages updates. In this environment, you have no say about how your computer and devices are updated — and you don't have to worry about it, either. On the other hand, if you work for a small company, it may not have an IT department or even an IT person, so you may have to deal with Windows updates yourself. If that's the case, be glad that Windows Update is automatically turned on and Windows 10 updates itself automatically. I just recommend that you check whether Windows Update is turned on. Here's how to do so:

1. **Click Start.**

   The Start Menu appears.

2. **Click Settings.**

   The Settings window appears.

3. **Click Update & Security.**

4. **In the Update & security list of settings, click Windows Update (see Figure 23-1).**

   If Windows Update is already turned on, you see this message: Available Updates Will Be Downloaded and Installed Automatically.

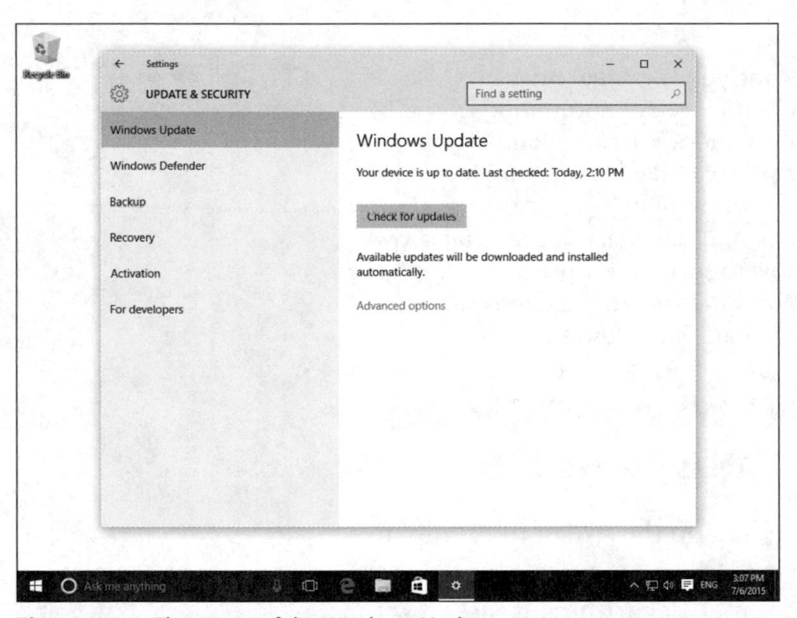

Figure 23-1: The status of the Windows Update service.

If Windows Update is turned off and you have the permission needed to change the setting, don't worry. I tell you how to turn on Windows Update in the following section.

Turn On Windows Update

Say that you start up your work computer and find that Windows Update is turned off. Assuming that your company doesn't have an official IT person and that you're allowed to change the Windows Update settings, here are the steps you can take to enable it:

1. **Open Settings.**
2. **Click Update & Security.**

   Your Windows update and Windows security settings are loaded.
3. **Click Windows Update to access this tool and its settings.**
4. **Click Advanced options.**
5. **In the Choose How Updates Are Installed drop-down list, select Automatic. (see Figure 23-2).**
6. **Close Settings.**

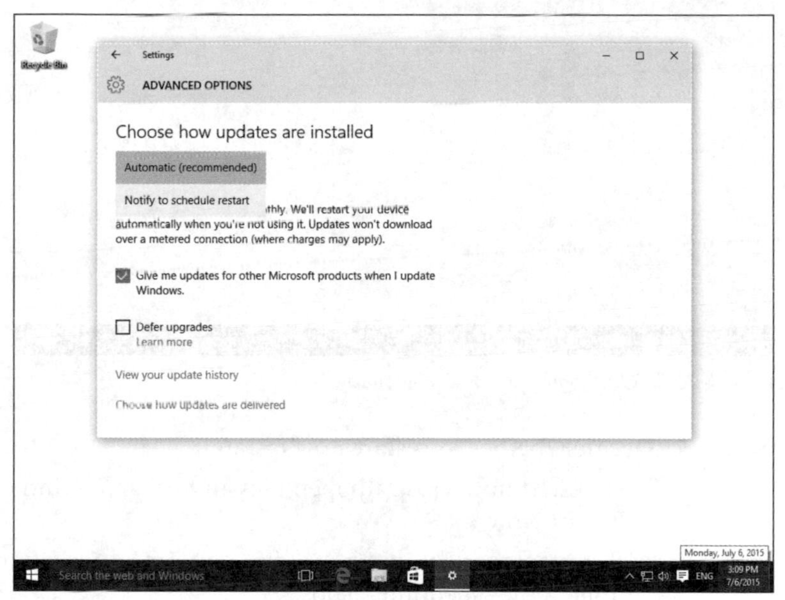

Figure 23-2: Turning on Windows Update.

Install Windows Updates

Once Windows Update is turned on, Windows 10 automatically checks for updates and installs them. However, unless prohibited by your IT department, you can manually check for updates and install them anytime you want. Here's how:

1. **Open Settings.**
2. **Click Update & Security, then click Windows Update.**

   Windows Update is now shown on the screen.
3. **Click Check for Updates.**

   If updates are available, they're automatically downloaded and installed (see Figure 23-3).

   For some updates, a restart may be required, and if so, Windows 10 automatically schedules it for you.

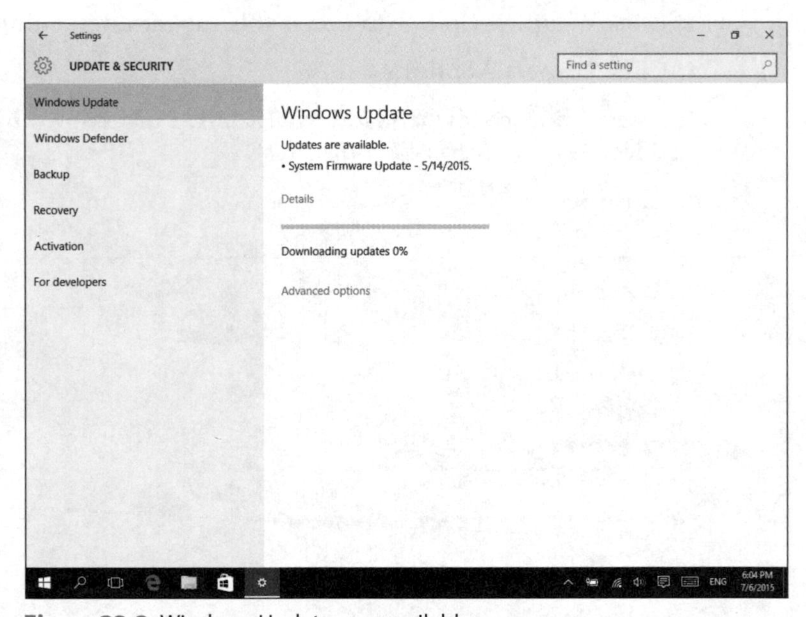

Figure 23-3: Windows Updates are available.

4. **Decide whether to restart now or later:**
   - To restart now, close all open files and programs and click Restart Now.
   - To restart your computer at a different time, specify the time in the scheduling fields.

Configure Windows Update

With Windows 10, you can now quickly download apps and updates from multiple sources. For example, you can download them from PCs on your local network as well as from PCs on the Internet. Here's how to configure this behavior:

1. **Open Settings.**
2. **Click Update & Security.**
3. **In the list of settings that appears, click Windows Update.**

   Windows Update is now shown on the screen.
4. **Click Advanced Options.**
5. **In the list with advanced options, click Choose How Updates Are Delivered.**
6. **Set the "Download Windows Updates and Apps from Other PCs in Addition to Microsoft" switch to On (see Figure 23-4).**

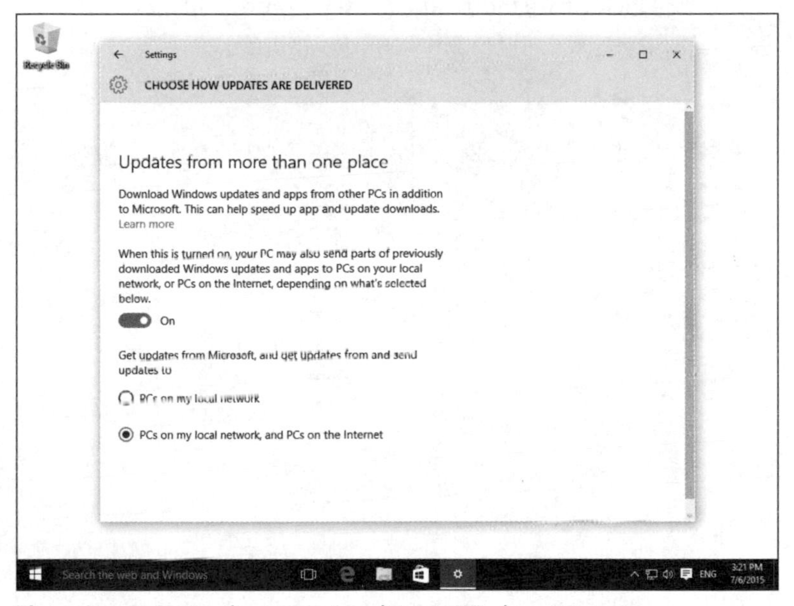

Figure 23-4: Setting how to get updates in Windows 10.

7. **Choose from the following sources for downloading apps and updates:**
   - PCs on My Local Network
   - PCs on My Local Network, and PCs on the Internet.
8. **Close Settings.**

Remove Unwanted Windows Updates

Generally, Windows updates are a good thing. They fix security problems and bugs, or they add new features and improvements to Windows. However, from time to time, Microsoft botches an update or a fix, causing all kinds of headaches for users like you and me.

If you've installed an update that causes problems on your Windows 10 computer or device, you can uninstall it at any time. Here's how:

1. **Open Settings.**
2. **Click Update & Security.**
3. **In the list of settings that appears, click Windows Update.**
4. **Click Advanced Options.**
5. **In the Advanced Options window, click View Your Update History.**

   The View Your Update History window appears.
6. **Click Uninstall Updates (see Figure 23-5).**

   The Installed Updates window appears.

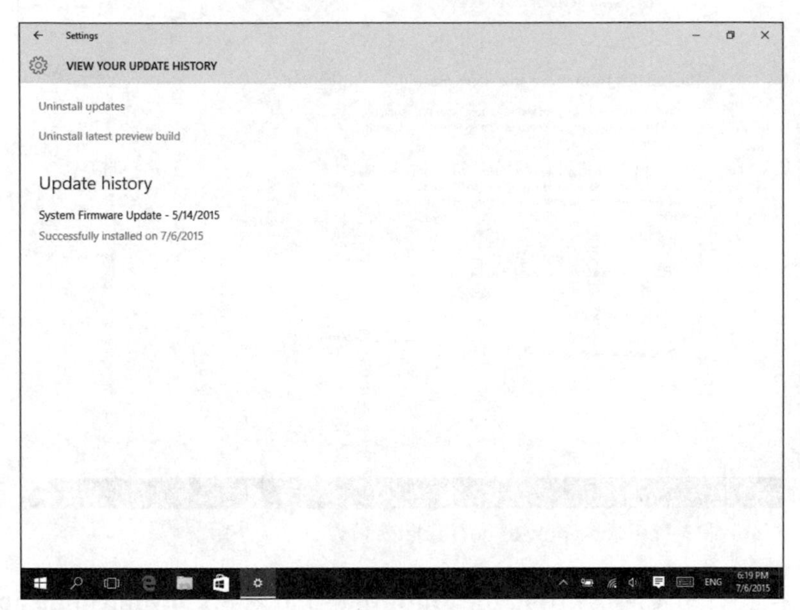

Figure 23-5: Viewing your update history.

7. **Select the update that you want to remove.**
8. **Click Uninstall.**
9. **When asked to confirm that you want to uninstall the selected updated, click Yes.**

10. **After the update is removed, close Installed Updates and Settings.**

Removing some Windows updates may require you to restart your computer. Before you restart the computer, don't forget to close all your opened files and apps, so you don't lose your work during the process.

Use UAC (User Account Control)

The User Account Control (UAC) is a security feature that helps prevent unauthorized changes to your Windows 10 computer or device. These unauthorized changes can be initiated by users, apps, viruses, or other types of malware. UAC ensures that these changes are made only with the administrator's approval. If these changes aren't approved by the administrator, they will never be executed, and the system will remain unchanged.

Desktop apps in Windows 10 don't run with administrator permissions and consequently can't make automatic changes to an operating system. When a desktop app wants to make system changes (such as modifications that affect other user accounts, modifications of system files and folders, or installation of new software), Windows 10 issues what's called a UAC confirmation dialog box, where users can confirm whether they want those changes to be made. If the user clicks No, the changes won't be made. If the user clicks Yes, the app receives administrator permissions and makes the system changes it's programmed to make (see Figure 23-6).

Figure 23-6: The User Account Control (UAC) prompt.

These permissions will be granted until the app stops running or the user closes it.

When using Windows Store apps, UAC is never triggered because, by design, these apps can't modify system settings or files.

If you're on a locked computer and your user account doesn't have administrator permissions, the UAC prompt asks you to enter the password for an administrator account, as shown in Figure 23-7. If you don't type the correct administrator password, then you can't run desktop apps that require administrator permissions.

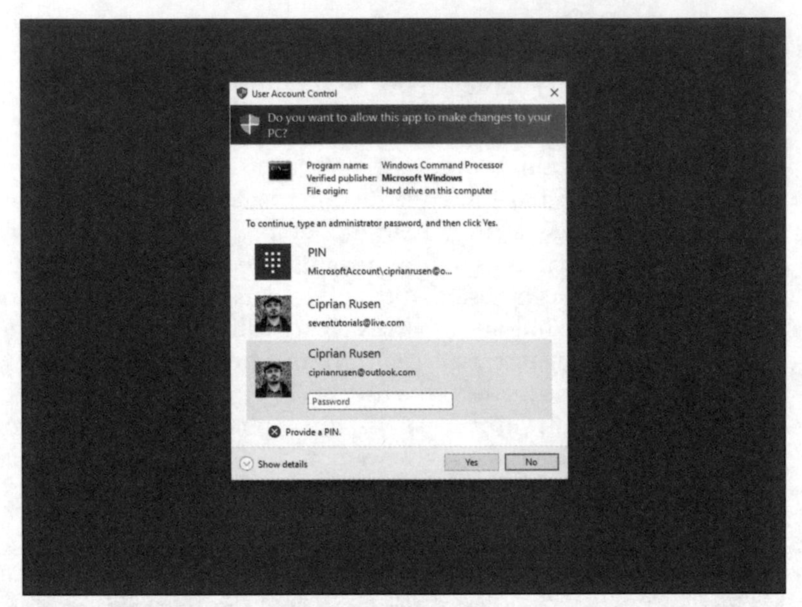

Figure 23-7: The UAC prompt on a locked down account.

When you encounter UAC prompts, it's important to pay attention to them. Look at the information displayed and determine which app wants administrator permissions. If it isn't an app that you started and want to run, click No.

Configure UAC

Depending on how your company's network is set up, you may or may not be able to change how UAC prompt works. If you're in a small company that doesn't have a network domain with rules and policies imposed by a network administrator or an IT department, you may be able to change how UAC prompts are shown. Follow these steps:

1. **Click in the search box on the taskbar.**
2. **Type uac.**

   A list of search results appears.
3. **Click "Change User Account Control settings".**

   The User Account Control Settings window appears.
4. **Set the UAC switch to the position you want.**

   You can choose one of the following options, shown in Figure 23-8:

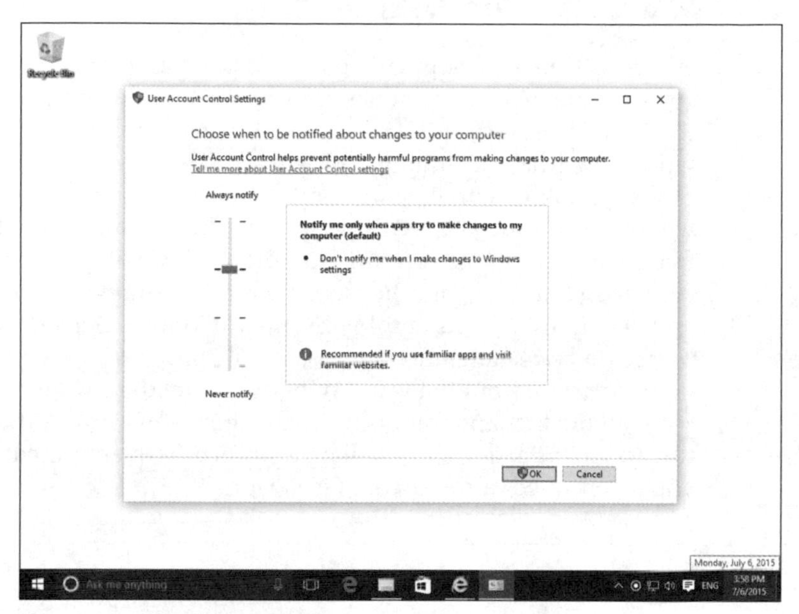

Figure 23-8: The UAC settings.

- *Always notify.*

  The UAC prompt is shown when apps try to install software or make changes to your computer and when you try to change Windows settings. The Desktop is dimmed when a UAC prompt is shown.
- *Notify me only when apps try to make changes to my computer.*

  This is the default setting for UAC. UAC prompts aren't shown when you try to make changes to Windows settings. The Desktop is dimmed when a UAC prompt is shown.
- *Notify me only when apps try to make changes to my computer (do not dim my desktop).*

  UAC prompts are not shown when you try to make changes to Windows settings, but the Desktop isn't dimmed when a UAC prompt is shown.

- *Never notify.*

  This is the equivalent of turning off UAC. I don't recommend that you use this setting.

5. **Click OK.**

   The User Account Control prompt is shown.

6. **Click Yes.**

   Your settings are applied.

Protect Yourself from Malware

Windows Defender originally provided protection only against spyware threats. With each new version of Windows, this product has been improved, and it now provides protection against more types of malware, including both viruses and spyware. Windows Defender doesn't compare in number of features and efficiency with most commercial security solutions, but it's one of the best free security solutions you can find for Windows. If your company hasn't installed another security product on the computers and devices used by its employees, then Windows Defender is turned on by default, and it automatically protects your computer or device from malware. Windows Defender automatically scans all the files and folders through which you browse. If a threat is identified, it's immediately cleaned or quarantined, and you're informed of this action (see Figure 23-9).

Figure 23-9: A Windows Defender prompt.

Depending on the threat, you may not need to do anything, or you may need to restart your computer or device in order for Windows Defender to disinfect your computer.

Pay attention to the prompts that Windows Defender displays. They're never false alarms, and these prompts should put you on guard that you're dealing with a possible malware infection.

Scan your device again after Windows Defender has dealt with threats. This scan gives Windows Defender the chance to make a complete scan and identify all infected files.

Scan for Viruses

As I mention earlier in this chapter, Windows Defender automatically monitors your computer for malware threats. However, if a malware sample (such as a virus) is detected, you should run a manual full-scan of your computer or of the drive where the threat was detected. Here's how to perform a manual scan with Windows Defender:

1. **Click inside the search box on the taskbar.**
2. **Type defender.**

   A list of search results appears.
3. **Click Windows Defender.**

   The Windows Defender window appears.
4. **In the Home tab, find the Scan Options section.**
5. **Select the type of scan that you want to perform (Quick, Full or Custom).**
6. **Click Scan now (see Figure 23-10).**
7. **Wait for the scan to finish.**
8. **If threats were detected, click Clean PC and follow the instructions for removing threats.**

   If no threats were detected, close Windows Defender.

At Step 5, if you've selected Custom, you're asked to select the location that you want to scan after Step 6. Browse your computer, select the folders or the drives that you want to scan and click OK.

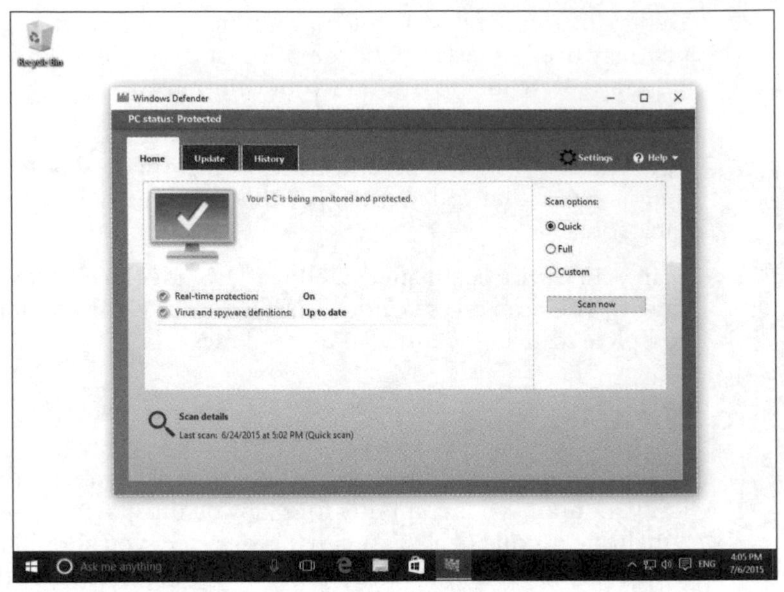

Figure 23-10: The Windows Defender desktop app.

Configure Windows Defender

If you're the administrator on your work computer and the company hasn't imposed any network-wide policies about how Windows Defender works, you may be able to configure some of its settings. For example, you can enable or disable its real-time protection engine, its cloud protection engine, and the automated sample submission for the malware samples it detects on your Windows 10 computer or device.

Here's how to access Windows Defender's settings and how to change them:

1. **Open Settings.**
2. **Click Update & Security.**
3. **In the list of settings that appears, click Windows Defender.**

   All Windows Defender related settings are shown.
4. **Set the Real-Time Protection switch to On or Off, depending on whether or not you want to enable this feature (see Figure 23-11).**
5. **Set the Cloud-Based Protection switch to On or Off, depending on whether or not you want to enable this feature.**

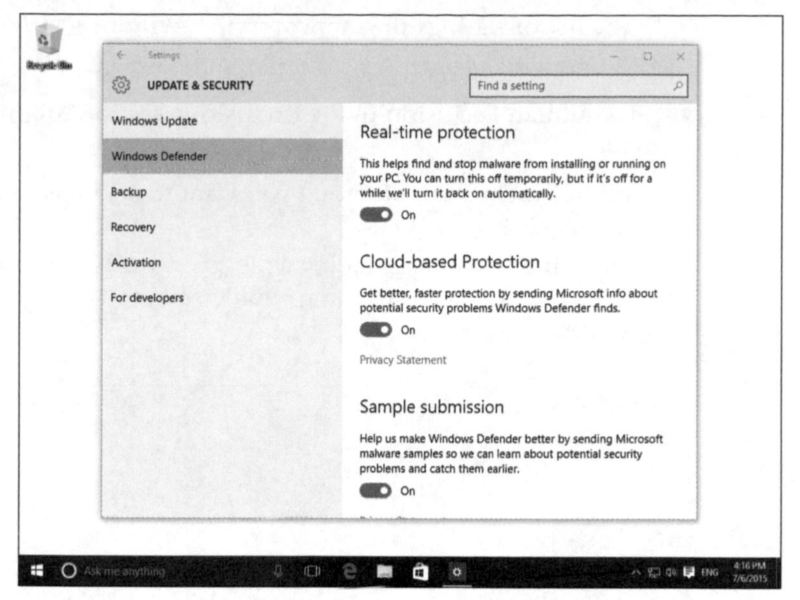

Figure 23-11: Windows Defender settings.

6. **Set the Sample Submission switch to On or Off, depending on whether or not you want to enable this feature.**
7. **Close Settings.**

If you don't have another antivirus installed, don't disable the real-time protection offered by Windows Defender. Doing so leaves your computer completely unprotected. Always have at least one antivirus product installed and active on your computer or device to keep you safe from viruses and other types of malware.

Set Exclusions for Windows Defender

In Windows 10, one of the new and useful features of Windows Defender is that it allows you to set advanced exclusions. These exclusions can be files, file locations, file extensions, and processes that you don't want Windows Defender to scan and block. In a typical business environment, these exclusions are defined by the network administrator or the IT department, but in smaller companies with environments that aren't tightly controlled, you may be able to define your own set of exclusions. Here's how:

1. **Open Settings.**
2. **Click Update & Security.**

3. **In the list of settings that appears, click Windows Defender.**

   All Windows Defender related settings are shown.

4. **Click Add an Exclusion in the Exclusions section on the right.**

5. **Find the type of exclusion that you want to set (see Figure 23-12).**

   If you're interested in excluding a file, go to the Files section. If you're interested in excluding a folder, go to the Folders section, and so on.

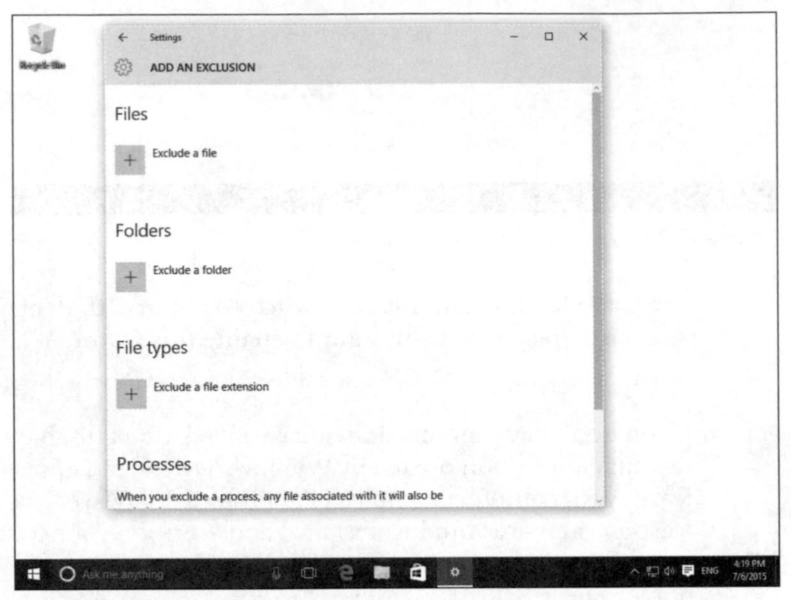

Figure 23-12: Adding an exclusion in Windows Defender.

6. **Click the appropriate Exclude button for the type of item that you want to exclude.**

7. **Select the item that you want to exclude and confirm your choice.**

   That item is now shown in the list of exclusions.

8. **Close Settings.**

Don't create a long list of exclusions. Doing so lowers the security of your system. Set exclusions only for the files, folders, or processes that you're completely certain are safe, or that Windows Defender has trouble scanning or dealing with.

Allow or Block Apps from Accessing Networks

Windows Firewall helps block unauthorized access to your computer while permitting authorized communications to and from your computer. In Windows 10, Windows Firewall filters both inbound and outbound network traffic, based on a set of applied rules and exceptions and on the type of network to which you're connected. If you aren't using a third-party security suite that includes a firewall, it's highly recommended that you use Windows Firewall because it provides a sufficient level of security.

By default, Windows Firewall has a predefined set of rules that are applied as soon as it's turned on. Windows Firewall allows you to perform tasks such as these: browse the Internet; use instant messaging apps; connect to a HomeGroup, if you're working from home; and share files, folders, and devices with other computers. The rules are applied differently depending on the network profile set for your active network connection.

Unless set otherwise by the network administrator, Windows Firewall allows all Windows Store apps to access the network. You see prompts for allowing or blocking access only for desktop apps.

If you're working in a large enterprise and the company network is administered by a network administrator or an entire IT department, the Windows Firewall rules are probably already set, and you can't change them. However, when you're running an app that's trying to access the network or the Internet and that app isn't in the list of rules set for the Windows Firewall, you'll probably receive a prompt from Windows Firewall, such as the one shown in Figure 23-13. In this prompt, you can allow or block the app that requires network or Internet access.

To allow an app to access the networks you connect to, select the network profile(s) you're interested in and then click Allow Access. If you want to block an app from accessing any network you're connected to, click Cancel.

Allow only apps that you know and trust. If you get a prompt from a dodgy app or one you're not familiar with, block its access to the network.

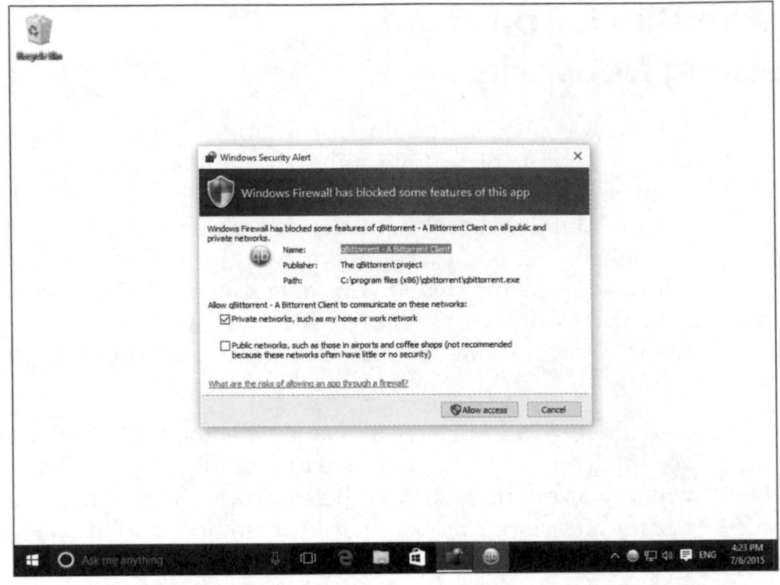

Figure 23-13: Allowing or blocking network access for an app with Windows Firewall.

Customize Apps That Are Allowed Through Windows Firewall

In managed business networks, the user generally can't customize which apps Windows Firewall allows to access the network and the Internet. However, in smaller companies, that kind of customization may be possible. If that's the case for you, here's how to customize the apps that are allowed to go through the Windows Firewall:

1. **In the search bar on the taskbar, type the word** firewall.
2. **Click the Allow an App Through Windows Firewall search result.**

   The list of Allowed Apps appears.
3. **Click Change Settings.**

   The list is now editable.
4. **Select the app that you want to customize by clicking it (see Figure 23-14).**

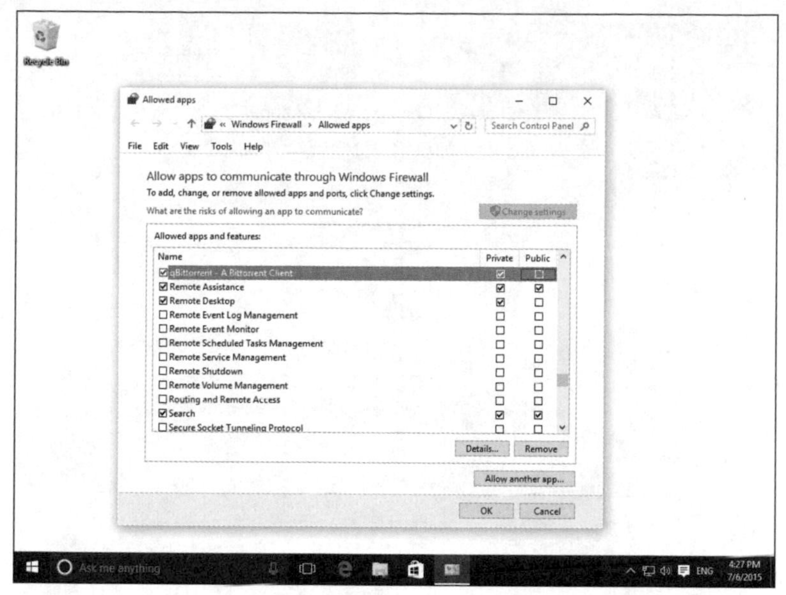

Figure 23-14: The list of allowed apps that can communicate through Windows Firewall.

5. **Check the network profile(s) where you want to allow access and uncheck the network profile(s) where you want to block access.**
6. **Click OK.**

Customize Your Privacy

Windows 10 and your apps can get access to lots of personal data and use that information to show personalized information and notifications. For example, apps can access your name, picture, advertising ID, location, contacts, calendar, and more. Luckily, Windows 10 gives you the tools you need to control which personal information is accessed and by which apps. Here's how to customize several general privacy related settings:

1. **Open Settings.**
2. **Click Privacy.**

   The list of privacy-related settings appears.
3. **Click General (see Figure 23-15).**
4. **Set the privacy settings that you want to enable to On.**

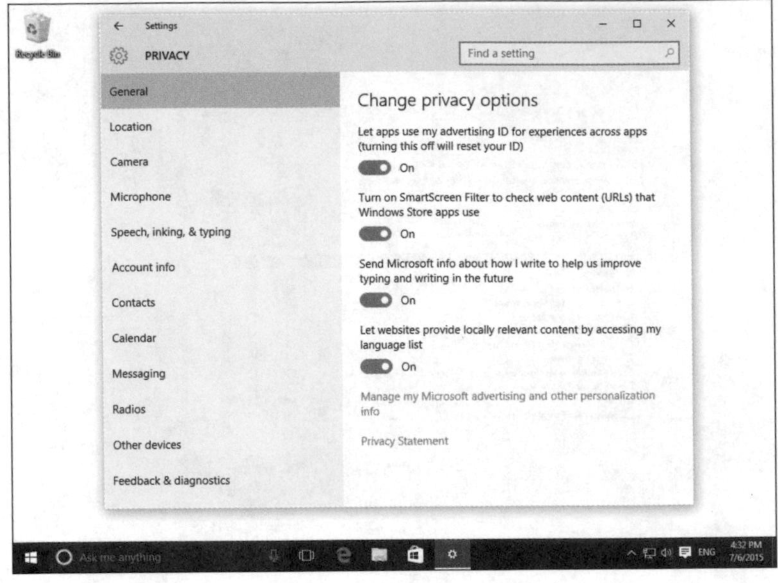

Figure 23-15: General privacy related settings in Windows 10.

5. **Set the privacy settings that you want to disable to Off.**
6. **Close Settings.**

Clear Your Location Data and Disable Location Services

By default, Windows 10 apps as well as the operating system can request your location and location history. If you don't want them to access your location, follow these steps to disable location services:

1. **Open Settings.**
2. **Click Privacy.**

   The list of privacy-related settings appears.
3. **Click Location.**
4. **Click the Change button under "Location for this device is on."**
5. **Set the Location For This Device switch to Off (see Figure 23-16).**
6. **Close Settings.**

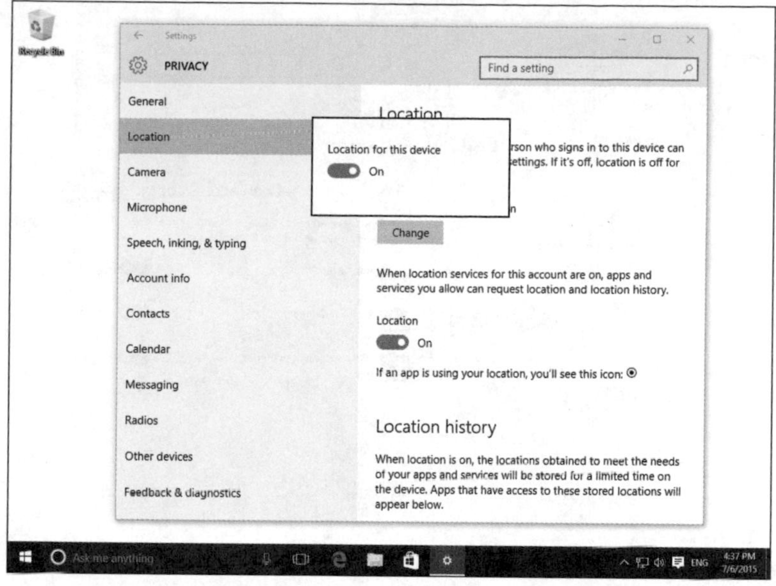

Figure 23-16: Enabling or disabling the location in Windows 10.

If you want your location history cleared, in the Location window, click the Clear button (it's below Clear history of this device).

Control Apps That Access Your Contacts

By default, Windows 10 apps can access your contacts when they need to. You can block some apps from accessing your contacts as well as all the apps you install. Here's how:

1. **Open Settings.**
2. **Click Privacy.**

   The list of privacy-related settings appears.
3. **Click Contacts and a list of apps that need access to your contacts is shown (see Figure 23-17).**
4. **If you want to disable access to your contacts for all apps, set the available switch to Off for all apps in the list.**

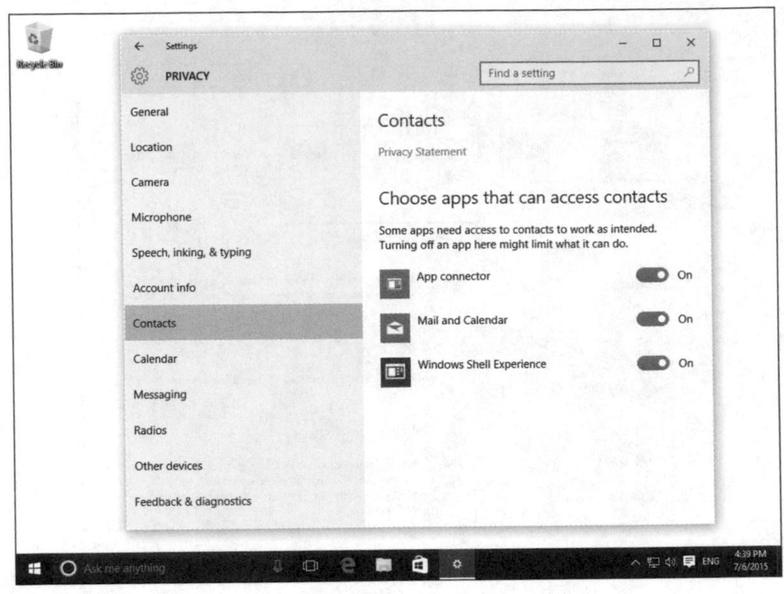

Figure 23-17: The apps that need access to your contacts.

5. **If you want to block only one app from accessing your contacts, set its switch to Off.**
6. **Close Settings.**

Control Which Apps Can Access Your Calendar

By default, Windows 10 apps can access your calendar when they need to. You can block some apps from accessing your calendar as well as all the apps you install. Here's how:

1. **Open Settings.**
2. **Click Privacy.**

   The list of privacy-related settings appears.
3. **Click Calendar and a list of apps that need access to your calendar is shown (see Figure 23-18).**
4. **If you want to disable access to your calendar for all apps, set the Calendar switch to Off.**
5. **If you want to block only one app from accessing your calendar, set its switch to Off.**
6. **Close Settings.**

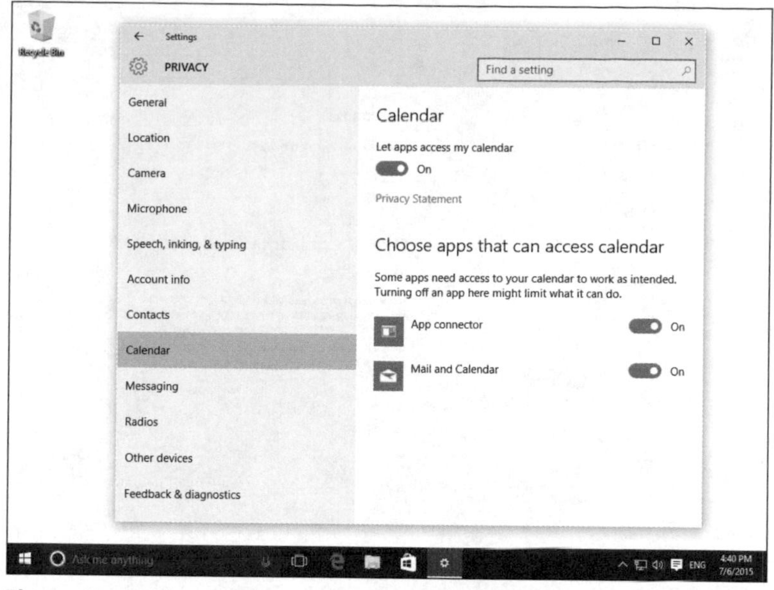

Figure 23-18: The apps that need access to your calendar.

Control Apps That Read or Send Messages

If you have a tablet with a SIM card installed or a laptop that's connected to a 3G USB modem, you can use the SIM card or the modem to send and receive SMS or MMS messages. If that's the case for your device, by default, Windows 10 apps can read or send messages. You can block some or all the apps you install from accessing your messages or from sending messages. Here's how:

1. **Open Settings.**
2. **Click Privacy.**

   The list of privacy-related settings appears.
3. **Click Messaging and a list of apps that need to read or send messages is shown (see Figure 23-19).**
4. **If you want to disable access to your messages for all apps, set the Messaging switch to Off.**
5. **If you want to block only one app from accessing your messages, set its switch to Off.**
6. **Close Settings.**

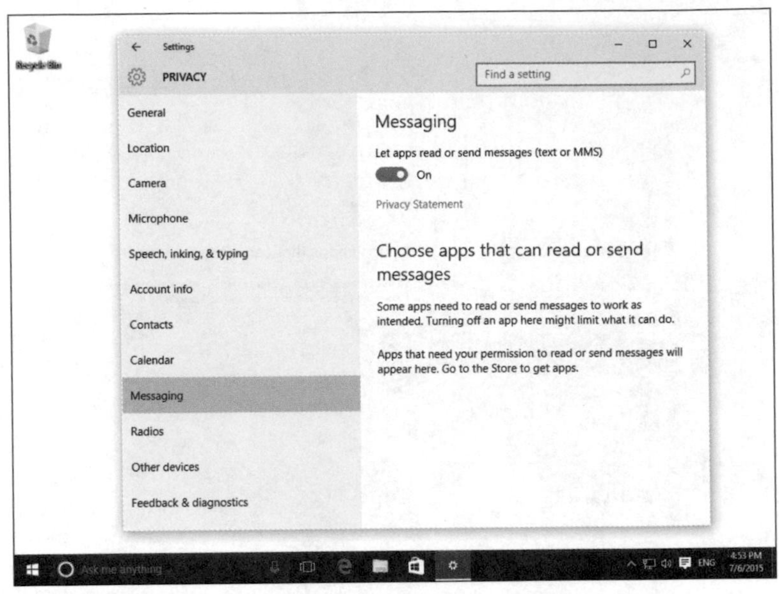

Figure 23-19: The apps that need to read or send messages.

Increase the Security of Your Passwords

Regardless of how good your company's security products are, your computer or devices are still vulnerable to security problems if you don't use good judgment about password security. If you use the same password everywhere, a malicious user might break into a forum or social website you're using and steal your password. That user can then use your password and the email address you used when you registered with the forum or social website to access more personal data and information from your Inbox, your accounts on social networks, and so on.

In corporate environments, you may be forced to change your password every month, but that doesn't mean that you aren't using guessable passwords. Large companies tend to be regular targets for hackers. Industrial espionage is also a common problem in large companies, and good password habits are critical for keeping your data safe.

To expose yourself as little as possible, follow these guidelines:

- Don't use passwords with fewer than six characters. They're especially easy to break.

  Your passwords should be at least eight characters long and shouldn't be recognizable words.

- Include letters, numbers, and special characters such as +, #, and $ in your password.
- Don't reuse the same password.
- Use password-management solutions such as LastPass, KeePass, or RoboForm that help you securely store and use your passwords.

  These solutions help you identify your duplicate passwords, change them to new random passwords, generate secure passwords automatically, and store them safely so that you can use them whenever needed, and never lose them again.

CHAPTER TWENTY FOUR

Preventing Problems with Windows 10

Prevention is one of the best ways to ensure that you'll have a long, pleasant, and safe computing experience. Windows 10 helps you do so by including prevention tools such as System Restore, Optimize Drives, Storage Sense, System Maintenance, and the System Health Report. This chapter shows when and how to use them.

Also, you find some practices that can help you stay out of trouble when using any Windows computer or device.

In This Chapter

- Creating a system restore point
- Enabling System Restore
- Defragmenting and optimizing partitions
- Setting where new apps, games, and files are stored
- Performing recommended system maintenance
- Preventing problems through best practices

Manually Create a System Restore Point

System Restore is a system recovery tool that allows you to reverse the changes made to the Windows operating system. It's like an Undo button but for changes made to system files and settings such as drivers, registry keys, and installed programs. System Restore is turned on by default. Each time you make a significant change to Windows, such as the installation of drivers and apps, System Restore makes periodic snapshots (which are known as *restore points*) of your system's hard drive. You can also create manual restore points, and doing so is recommended, especially after setting up a new Windows 10 computer or device.

Later, if you encounter issues with Windows 10, you can easily revert back to any of the existing restore points and continue to use Windows as if the recent system changes never happened.

System Restore is very useful when you encounter faulty drivers that destabilize your system or after you install apps that cause problems.

Here's how to use System Restore to manually create a system restore point:

1. **In the search bar on the taskbar, type** system restore.

   A list with search results appears.

2. **Click the Create a Restore Point search result.**

   The System Properties window opens.

3. **Click the Create button at the bottom right side of the System Properties window.**

   You're asked to type a description to help you identify the restore point.

   If the Create button is grayed out, this feature is currently disabled. See the next section to find out how to turn on System Restore, assuming, of course, that your user account has administrator permissions on your computer.

4. **In the available text box, type a description for the restore point (see Figure 24-1).**

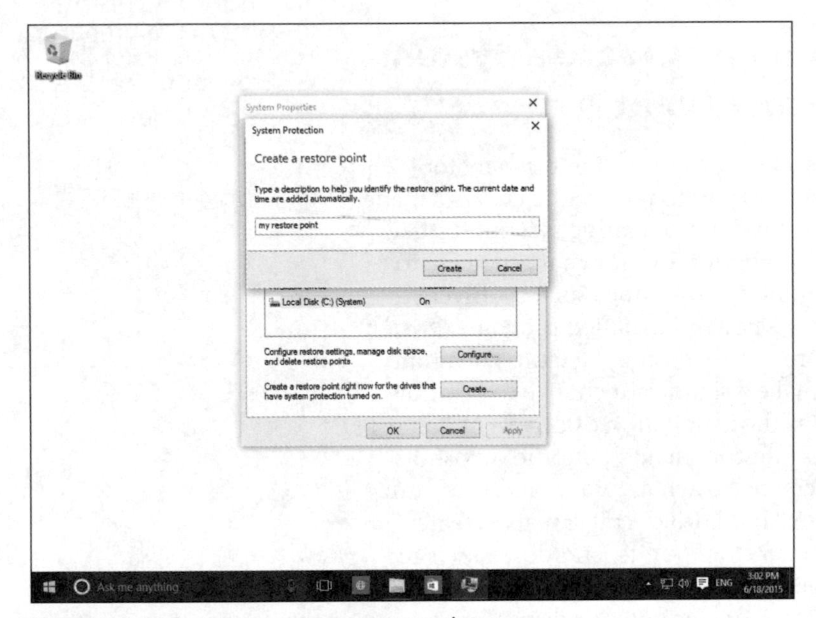

Figure 24-1: Creating a system restore point.

5. **Click Create.**
6. **After Windows lets you know that the restore point is created, click Close.**
7. **Click OK in the System Properties window.**

Chapter 25 shows how to use System Restore when you encounter problems.

Turn On System Restore

If your user account has administrator permissions on your computer, follow these steps to quickly activate System Restore:

1. **In the search bar on the taskbar, type** system restore.

   A list with search results appears.

2. **Click the Create a Restore Point search result.**

   The System Properties window appears.

3. **Select local disk drive (C:) from the list of available drives.**
4. **Click Configure.**

   The System Protection window for your local list drive (C:) opens.

5. **Click Turn On System Protection (see Figure 24-2).**
6. **Click OK twice.**

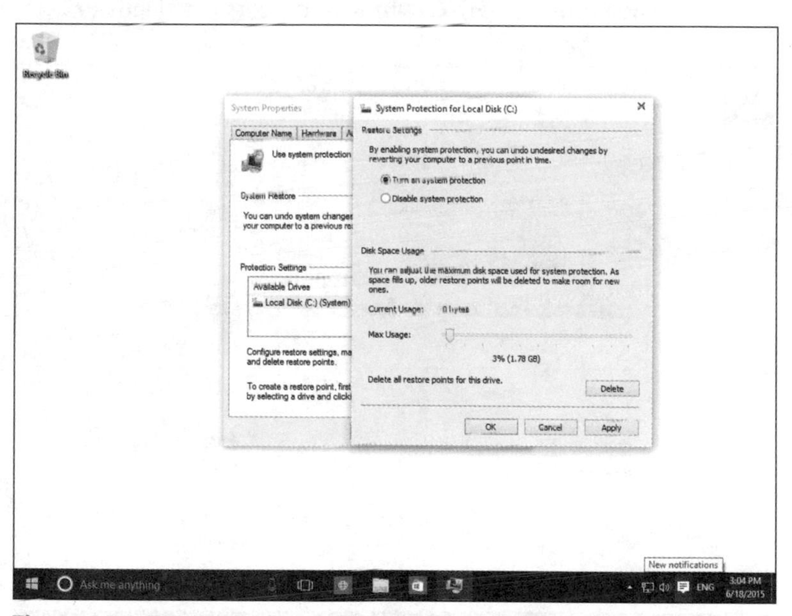

Figure 24-2: Turning On System Restore.

In very locked-down business network environments, your user account may not have the permissions needed to turn on and work with System Restore. If that's the case, both the Configure and Create buttons are disabled in the System Properties window.

Defragment and Optimize Partitions

When you defragment a partition, the files stored on it are rearranged to occupy continuous storage locations. This process minimizes the time it takes the hard drive to find all the fragments of your files, thereby decreasing the time it takes you to access them. The startup time for Windows is also improved.

USB drives and SSDs have a limited number of read/write cycles, so don't use up your cycles by defragmenting. Doing so isn't necessary, which is why the Optimize Desktop app doesn't show you those types of drives. You can use the Optimize Drives tool only to optimize partitions on classic hard disks.

Although Windows automatically defragments your drives in the background once a week, you can also choose to defragment manually. Here's how:

1. **In the search bar on the taskbar, type** defragment.

   A list with search results appears.

2. **Click the Defragment and Optimize Your Drives search result.**

   The Optimize Drives window appears (see Figure 24-3).

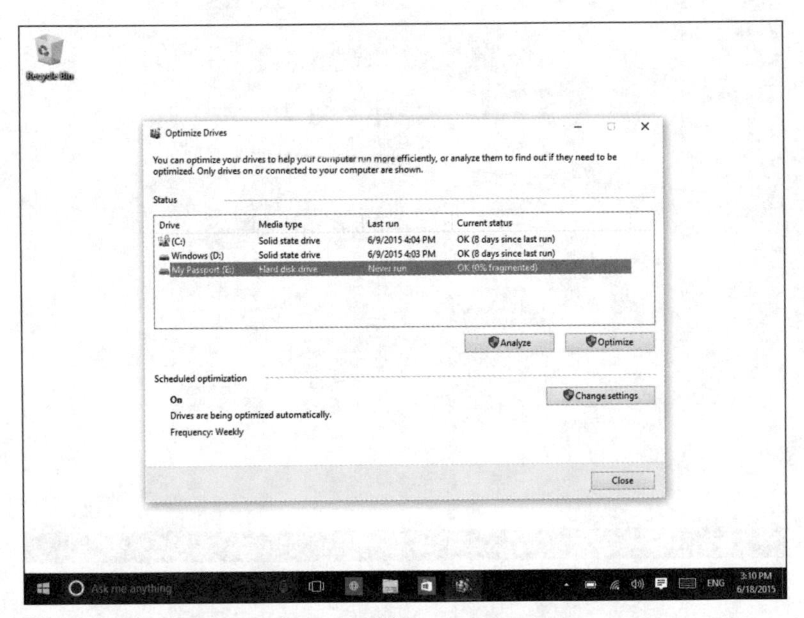

Figure 24-3: Defragmenting a partition.

3. **Select the partition that you want to defragment.**
4. **Click Optimize.**

   The process may take a couple of minutes to finish because it includes several optimization passes.
5. **When the process finishes, click Close.**

Control Where Standard Files Are Stored by Default

If you have a tablet, a hybrid device, or a laptop that has internal storage available on a hard disk or SSD and an external microSD card, you may want to set where your files are saved by default. Doing so places them where you want them and helps you keep track of them. Using the new Storage Sense feature, you can easily set where your new apps, documents, pictures, music, and videos are stored.

Here's how to set up the Storage Sense feature in Windows 10:

1. **Open Settings.**
2. **Click System.**

   A list with system settings appears.
3. **Click Storage.**

   A list with storage related settings appears.
4. **In the Save Locations section, select where you want to save your new apps, documents, music, pictures, videos, and so on (see Figure 24-4).**
5. **Close Settings.**

If your Windows 10 device has little storage space, you may want to save your new apps and games to the microSD card that you're using, instead of the internal storage provided by your device. Because music and video files can take up a lot of space, you may want to store those on the microSD card as well.

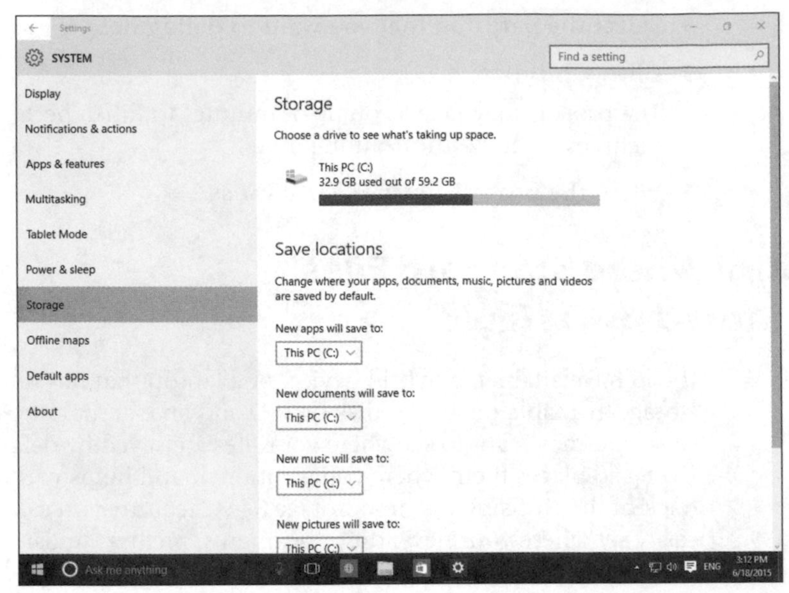

Figure 24-4: Setting the storage locations in Windows 10.

Perform Recommended System Maintenance

Windows 10 includes the System Maintenance tool, which is a hidden tool that you can run on demand to find out if there are issues with your system. This tool checks for unused files and shortcuts, performs maintenance tasks, checks whether the system time is set correctly, and so on. If problems are found, the System Maintenance tool fixes them automatically.

To manually run the System Maintenance tool, follow these steps:

1. **In the search bar on the taskbar, type** maintenance.

   A list with search results appears.

2. **Click the Perform Recommended Maintenance Tasks Automatically search result.**

   The System Maintenance wizard starts.

3. **Click Next (see Figure 24-5).**

   The wizard begins the process of detecting possible issues.

4. **If the wizard recommends that you do the troubleshooting as an administrator, click Try Troubleshooting as an Administrator.**

   When the wizard finishes, it shows a summary of its findings. If it finds issues, it also shows you actions that you can take.

5. **Click Close.**

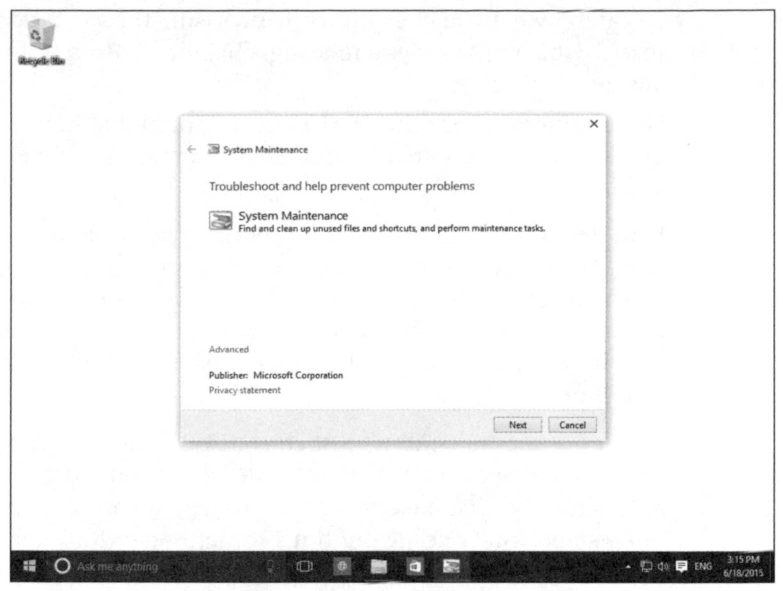

Figure 24-5: Starting the System Maintenance wizard.

Prevent Problems with Your Windows Computer or Device

Just as in medicine, when you're dealing with computers, prevention is a much better tool than medication. That's why, if you want to face as few issues as possible, the best approach is to consider these simple, effective rules:

- Don't download apps and programs from untrusted sources. Stick to websites that have a good reputation and with well known software.

  If you need to download and install an app that you know nothing about, before you even consider downloading it, search on Google or Bing for information about it.

- When you install apps, never use the quick install option; always use the custom install.

  Many free desktop apps bundle all kinds of junk and third-party apps that you don't need. If you always choose to install them quickly and don't go for a slower custom install where you configure in detail what gets installed, you're just asking for trouble. You may install toolbars that hijack your computer, useless desktop apps that take up space and system resources, apps that display ads you don't want, and so on.

- Be careful what you click on while browsing the web. It doesn't matter which browser you're using, clicking random links and ads invites trouble.

  Use browser add-ons like WoT (Web of Trust) that help you quickly evaluate the trustworthiness of the websites that you're visiting.

- Shut down your Windows computer or device from time to time. Usually, you want your devices to start as fast as possible, so you might use Sleep and other low-power modes. However, a simple shut down once a week helps Windows update files, shut down processes, and start from scratch the next time you turn it on.

- Read error messages; don't just click through them. When you encounter an error message in Windows 10, don't just click OK automatically. First, take some time to read it completely and understand what's going on. If it's something serious, take a screenshot of that message, so that you can share it with your company's IT support department or someone else who can help you solve the problem.

- Use a security product on your Windows device. At the very least, use the built-in Windows Defender and Windows Firewall to protect your computer or device from malware and network attacks. The best idea is to purchase a commercial security product from a well-known security company such as Kaspersky, Bitdefender, Norton, or ESET.

- Keep Windows 10 and your security software up to date at all times. Yes, updates are annoying, but they're also very useful. Keeping your software up to date means that your system is less likely to get infected by malware and is less vulnerable to all kinds of threats, and you get new features and bug fixes that are rolled out on a regular basis.

- Perform regular maintenance using the tools covered in this chapter to keep your system in good shape.

CHAPTER TWENTY FIVE

Fixing Common Problems with Windows 10

Windows 10 is the most reliable version of Windows yet, but that doesn't mean you'll never encounter problems with it on your computers or devices. For example, maybe an app doesn't respond to your commands or the storage runs too low on your Windows 10 tablet. Or perhaps a driver causes Windows to crash, which you can fix only by booting into Safe Mode. Or perhaps, down the road, you find that you've used Windows 10 for such a long time that performance isn't that great anymore and a refresh or reset of your PC would be a welcome change.

This chapter explores the most common problems that you might encounter when you use Windows 10 and then shows you how to fix those problems. Also, you find advice on how to approach the people in your company's IT department so that they can understand the problems that you're encountering and how to fix them as soon as possible.

In This Chapter

- Using Task Manager to fix all kinds of problems
- Freeing up storage space with Disk Cleanup
- Finding out which apps and games use the most storage space
- Troubleshooting problems using the built-in troubleshooting wizards
- Solving problems with the Microsoft Fix It Solution Center
- Booting into Safe Mode
- Resetting Windows 10

Start Task Manager

Task Manager is one of the most useful tools that you can use to troubleshoot performance problems with your Windows

10 computers and devices. With it, you can view which apps are running, which aren't responding, which apps consume too many system resources, which make your system's startup time longer, and so on.

The fastest way to start Task Manager is to press Ctrl+Shift+Esc on your keyboard. You can also use a mouse or touch gestures. Here are the steps for starting Task Manager:

1. **Right-click the Start button.**

   A pop-up menu appears showing several options.

   You can also access the pop-up menu by pressing Windows+X on your keyboard. You can also use search by typing **task manager** in the search bar on the taskbar and clicking the appropriate search result.

2. **Click Task Manager to start it (see Figure 25-1).**

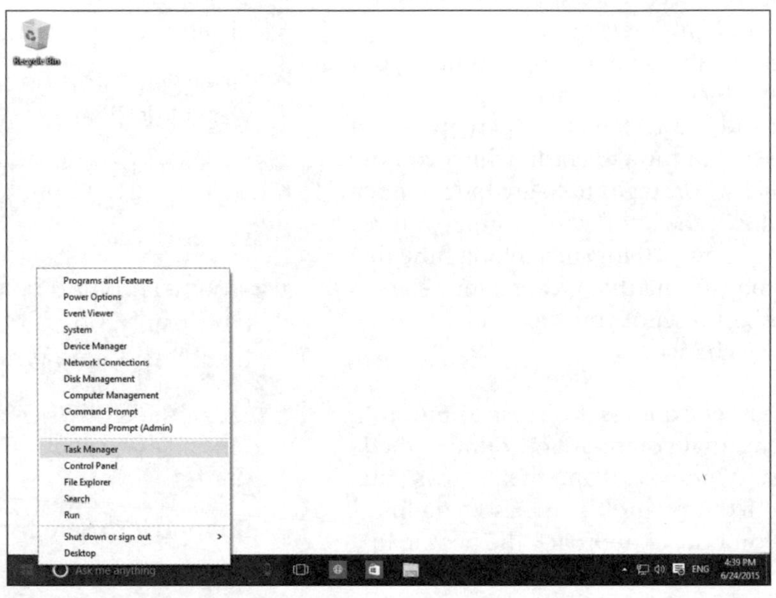

Figure 25-1: Starting Task Manager.

View All Running Apps and Processes

When you start Task Manager, you see a list of only the apps that you're running (see Figure 25-2). The only data shown for each app is its name. In this list, you see both apps from the Windows Store and desktop apps.

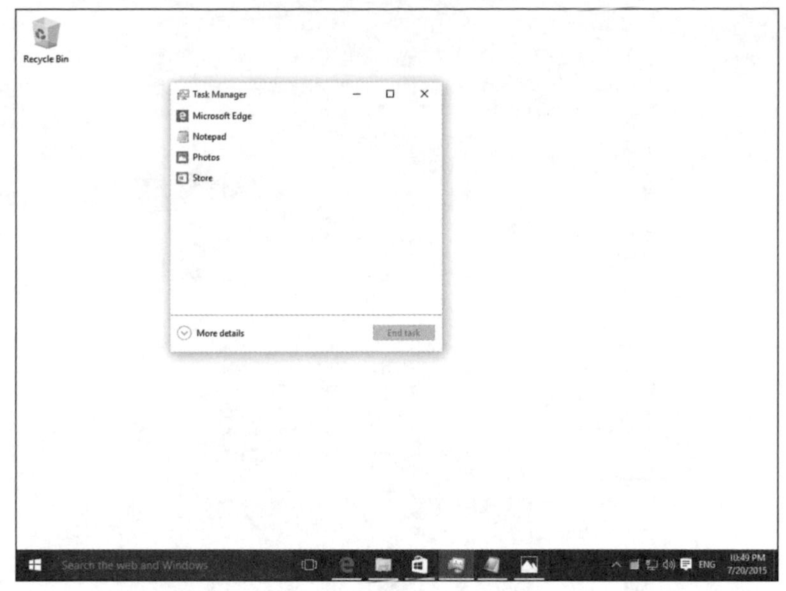

Figure 25-2: Task Manager in Windows 10.

To view a more complete list with all the apps that you're running and the processes started by Windows 10, click More Details at the bottom-left corner of Task Manager. A new Task Manager window appears with many tabs that contain lots of detailed information. By default, the Processes tab is loaded, and there you see a long list of running apps and processes, split into the following categories:

- **Apps**: The apps that you're running
- **Background processes:** Processes that are started either by Windows 10 or by the apps that you install
- **Windows processes:** Processes that are automatically started by Windows 10 and that are required in order for the operating system to function correctly

All these tabs are shown in Figure 25-3. For each entry, you see the percentage of the CPU (processor) it's using, how much RAM memory it's using, how much data it writes on the disk, and how much of your network connection it's using.

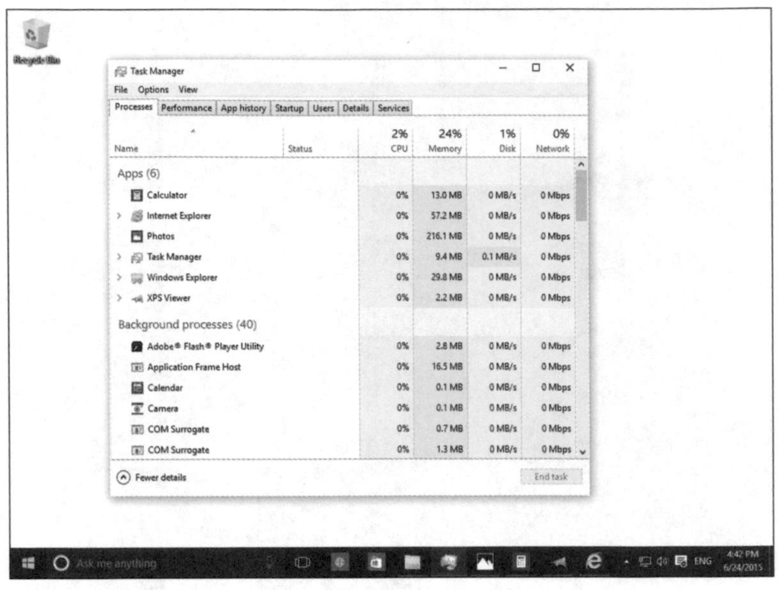

Figure 25-3: The Processes tab in Task Manager.

End Apps That Aren't Responding

At times, some apps may stop responding to your commands, making it impossible to use them. When that happens, it's best to force them to close using Task Manager and then start them again. To close an app, follow this procedure:

1. **Start Task Manager.**
2. **In the list of running apps, select the app that you want to close by clicking it.**
3. **Click the End Task button in the bottom-right corner of the Task Manager window.**

Check Which Apps Use the Most System Resources

Task Manager offers you the tools you need to find out which apps are using most of your computer's resources. This information is especially useful when apps start running too slowly or when your computer doesn't seem to understand what you want it to do. If you find an app that's using too many resources, you can use the End Task option to close it and free up system resources so that your computer and apps will run faster.

Here's how to find the apps that use the most resources:

1. **Start Task Manager.**
2. **If the Processes tab isn't shown, click More Details.**
3. **In the Processes tab, click the CPU column to sort apps and processes by processor usage.**
4. **Identify the apps that use more of your system's processor than you want (see Figure 25-4).**

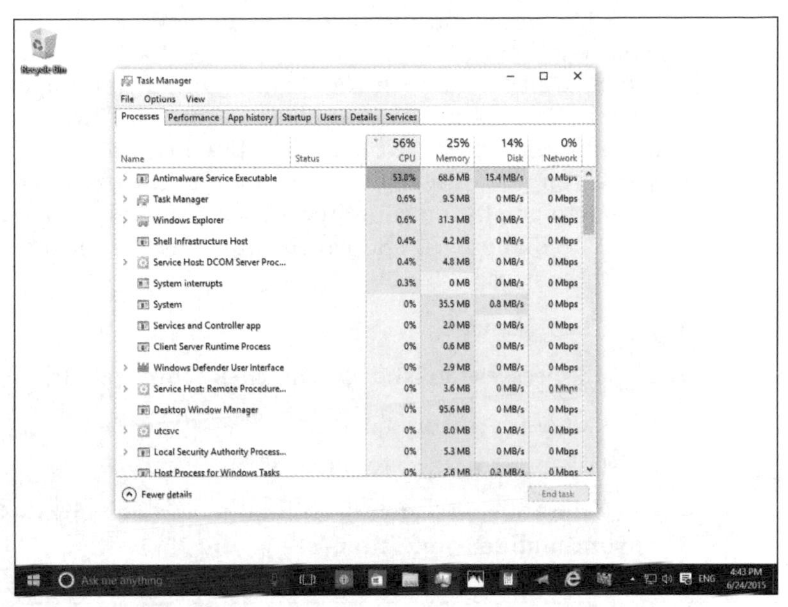

Figure 25-4: The apps that use the most CPU power.

5. **Click the Memory column to sort apps and processes by memory usage.**
6. **Identify the apps that use more of your system's RAM memory than you want.**
7. **Click the Disk column to sort apps and processes by hard disk usage.**
8. **Identify the apps that write the most data on your system's hard disk.**
9. **Click the Network column to sort apps and processes by network usage.**
10. **Identify the apps that use more of your system's network connection than you want.**

11. **Click the Name column to view apps and processes using the default view offered by Task Manager, which is sorted by name and type.**
12. **Close Task Manager.**

Find Apps That Use the Most Data

When you're on the go, chances are that you use a 3G or 4G mobile connection to connect to the Internet and to your company's VPN (virtual private network) service. When you work on your Windows 10 device, your apps most likely consume the data plan available through your connection. If you're approaching the traffic limit of your data plan, you may want to know which apps used most of your mobile Internet connection. This way, you can stop using those apps or limit their use and expend the remaining traffic on your monthly data subscription to apps that you need to use. To find which apps consume the most data, follow these steps:

1. **Start Task Manager.**
2. **If the Processes tab isn't shown, click More Details.**
3. **Click the App History tab.**

   A list of apps and their resource use appears.
4. **Click the Metered Network column to sort apps by their use of your mobile connection (see Figure 25-5).**

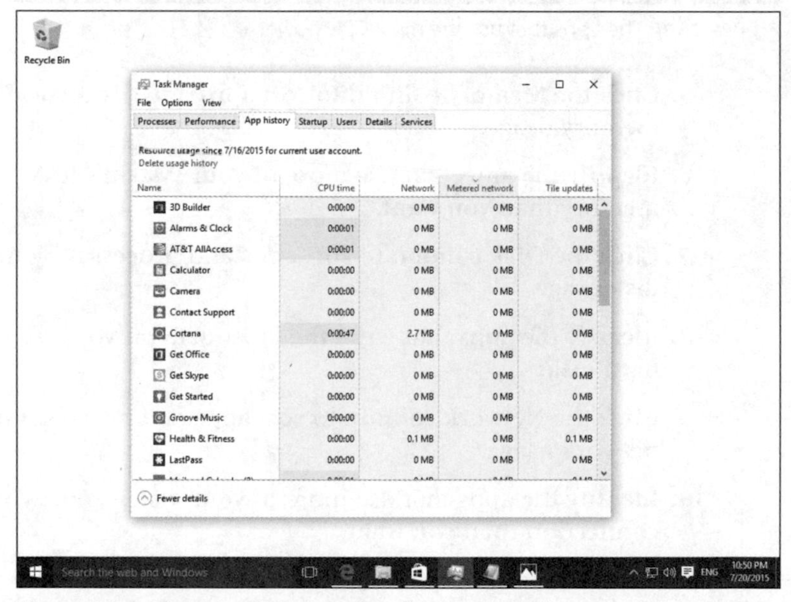

Figure 25-5: The apps that use most of your metered connection.

5. **Identify which apps are using most of your data plan.**

6. **Close Task Manager.**

As shown in this exercise, the App History tab offers several other columns of data. The CPU Time column tells you the amount of time each app used on the processor, the Network column tells you how much network traffic each app generated when connected to wireless networks or cable, and the Tile Updates column tells you how much data was used to update the tiles of each app.

Identify Apps That Make Windows Start Slowly

Another useful way to use Task Manager is to find which apps start when Windows 10 is loaded and which of them make Windows start more slowly. To locate this information, follow these steps:

1. **Start Task Manager.**

2. **If the Processes tab isn't shown, click More Details.**

3. **Click the Startup tab.**

   The list of startup apps appears.

4. **Click the Startup Impact column to see the apps sorted by their impact on your system's startup time.**

5. **Identify the apps that have a high impact on your system's startup (see Figure 25-6).**

6. **Close Task Manager.**

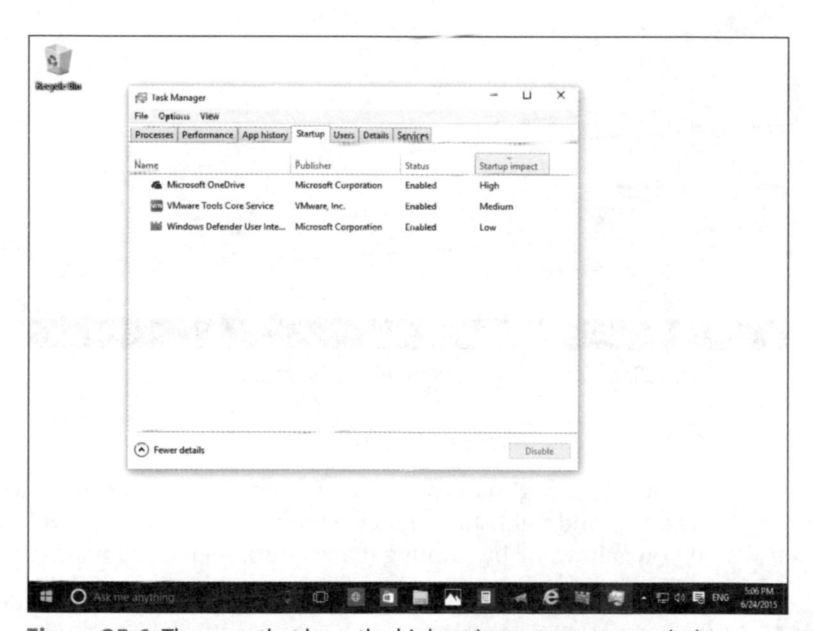

Figure 25-6: The apps that have the highest impact on startup timings.

Stop Apps from Running at the Windows Startup

If Windows 10 takes a long time to start, you may want to disable some of the apps that run at startup, or at least those that have a high impact on the startup procedure. To do so, follow these steps:

1. **Start Task Manager.**
2. **If the Processes tab isn't already shown, click More Details.**
3. **Click the Startup tab.**

   The list of startup apps appears.
4. **For each app that you want to disable from running at startup, follow these steps (see Figure 25-7):**

   a. *Click an app that you want to disable.*

   b. *Click the Disable button on the bottom-right corner of the Task Manager window.*

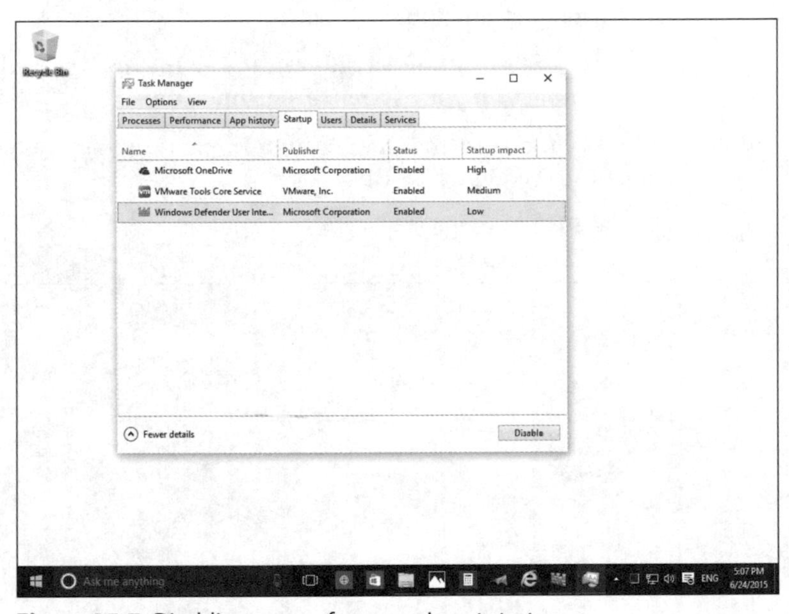

Figure 25-7: Disabling an app from running at startup.

5. **Close Task Manager.**

Before choosing to disable an app from running at startup, check its name and publisher, and take the time to find out what it does. If you gain value by running it at startup, then don't disable it.

WARNING!

Never disable an app from running at startup if it was installed by a driver. Your system won't perform at its best if you do.

Increase Disk Space Using Disk Cleanup

If you're running out of disk space on your Windows 10 computer or device, you can use the Disk Cleanup tool. This tool scans your system for files that can be removed and then helps you remove them. These unnecessary files can be of several types, such as temporary Internet files, log files made by the apps that you installed, thumbnails, and temporary files.

To free up some space on your computer or device, follow these steps:

1. **Click in the search bar on the taskbar.**
2. **Type the words** disk cleanup.

   A list of search results appears.
3. **Click Free Up Disk Space by Deleting Unnecessary Files.**
4. **If you have more than one partition on your Windows 10 computer or device, you're asked to select which one you want to scan. Select the partition you're interested in.**

   Disk Cleanup automatically starts and scans your computer for files that can be safely removed. When it finishes, you see a list of the types of files that can be removed.
5. **Select the types of files that you want to remove (see Figure 25-8).**

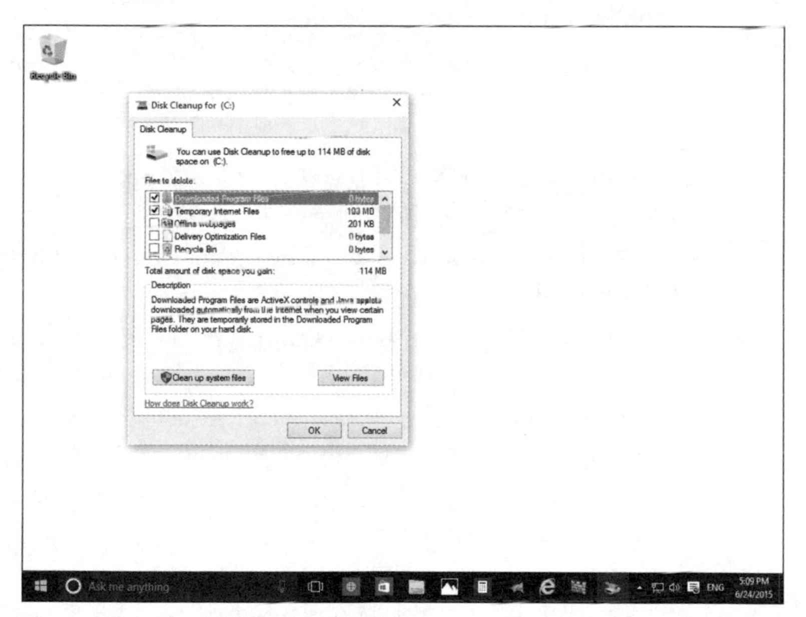

Figure 25-8: The Disk Cleanup tool.

6. **Click OK.**

   You're asked to confirm that you want to permanently delete the files.

7. **Click Delete Files and wait for Disk Cleanup to do its job.**

After Step 4, if you click Clean Up System Files instead of moving forward with Step 5, Disk Cleanup restarts and rescans your computer. This time, it looks also for system files that can be cleaned up like previous Windows installation files, temporary Windows installation files and so on. Select the types of files that you want to remove and continue with steps 6 and 7.

Check How Your Storage Space Is Used

Windows 10 includes a new feature called Storage. You can use it to find how storage space is used on your computer or device. This information is useful because you know how the storage space is used and understand what you can delete to save some space.

When displaying how your storage space is used, Storage splits things into the following categories:

- **System and Reserved:** This space is for files that Windows requires in order to run. Never delete system files even if you're running out of space.
- **Apps and Games:** These are the apps and games that are installed on your computer or device.
- **Pictures, Music, and Videos:** This is the space occupied by the files in your Pictures, Music, and Videos user folders and libraries.
- **Mail:** This is the space occupied by the Mail app for storing your email messages.
- **Maps:** This is the space occupied by the maps that you have downloaded.
- **Documents:** This is the space occupied by the files in your Documents user folder and library.
- **OneDrive:** This is the space occupied by the OneDrive folder and the files that you're synchronizing to the cloud.
- **Other Users:** This is the space used by other user accounts on your computer or device.
- **Temporary Files:** Includes temporary files that are generated by Windows or the apps that you're using.
- **Other:** These are unrecognized files and folders that can't be classified by Windows 10.

Their order isn't the same as the order of the preceding list; Windows 10 automatically sorts all these categories by the amount of storage space they take. Therefore, these categories are in a different order on your computer or device.

When you open any of the preceding items, Windows 10 offers you different options for creating storage space in the item's category. To find how the storage space is used on your computer or device, follow these steps:

1. **Open Settings.**
2. **Click System.**

   Your system settings are shown.
3. **Click Storage.**

   Now you can see the total storage space that's used on your computer or device.
4. **Click This PC.**

   Windows 10 takes a few seconds to analyze how your storage space is used.
5. **Check each category and find how much storage space it uses (see Figure 25-9).**
6. **When done, close Settings.**

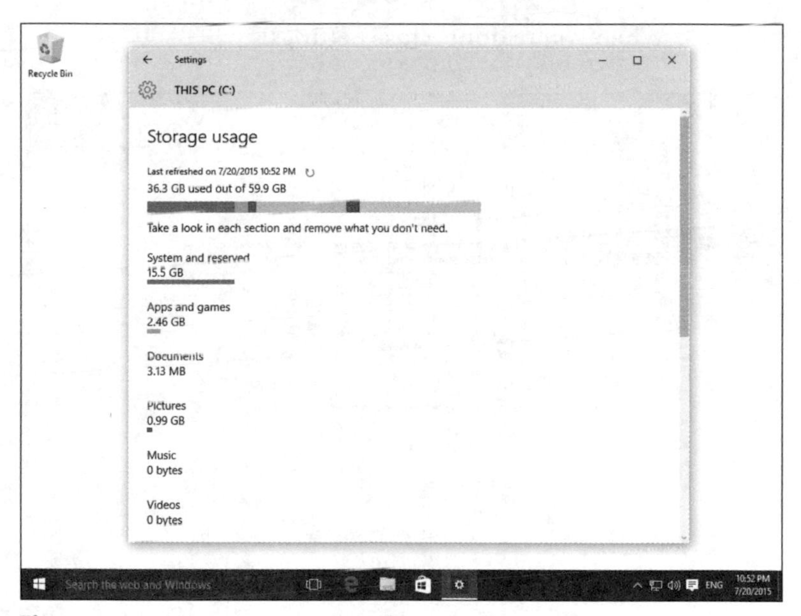

Figure 25-9: Using your storage space.

If you have a microSD card plugged into your Windows 10 tablet or laptop, you can use Storage to view how storage space is used on it, too.

Find Which Apps and Games Use the Most Storage Space

If you're close to running out of storage space on your Windows 10 computer or device, one thing you can do is find out which apps and games from the Windows Store use the most space. If you don't use some of those apps and games, you can uninstall them and free up storage space.

If you want to find how much storage space each installed app and game uses, follow these steps:

1. **Open Settings.**
2. **Click System.**

   Your system settings are shown.
3. **Click Apps & Features.**

   Windows 10 analyzes all installed apps.
4. **Look at the list of apps and games and identify those that require the most storage space (see Figure 25-10).**
5. **When you're done, close Settings.**

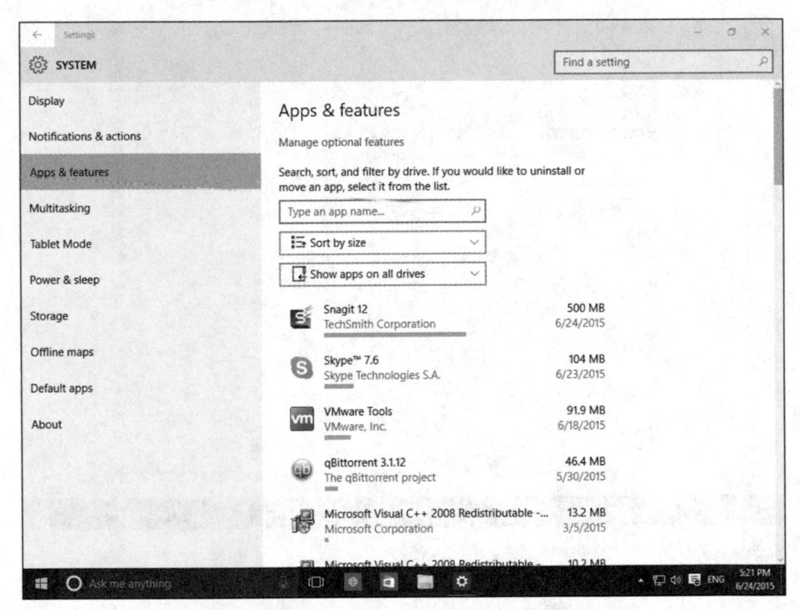

Figure 25-10: Installed apps and games and their size on disk.

You can remove the apps and games you no longer need to use straight from the App Sizes section. Simply click the app that you want to remove and then click Uninstall twice to remove it.

Troubleshoot Problems Using the Windows Troubleshooting Wizards

Windows 10 includes many troubleshooting wizards that can help you solve lots of problems. For example, you can fix issues with programs that aren't compatible with Windows 10 and with problems related to Internet Explorer and to the hardware for different components, such as the network card, the sound card, printers, and Internet connections. You can find these wizards in the Troubleshooting panel, and they're easy to use (see Figure 25-11).

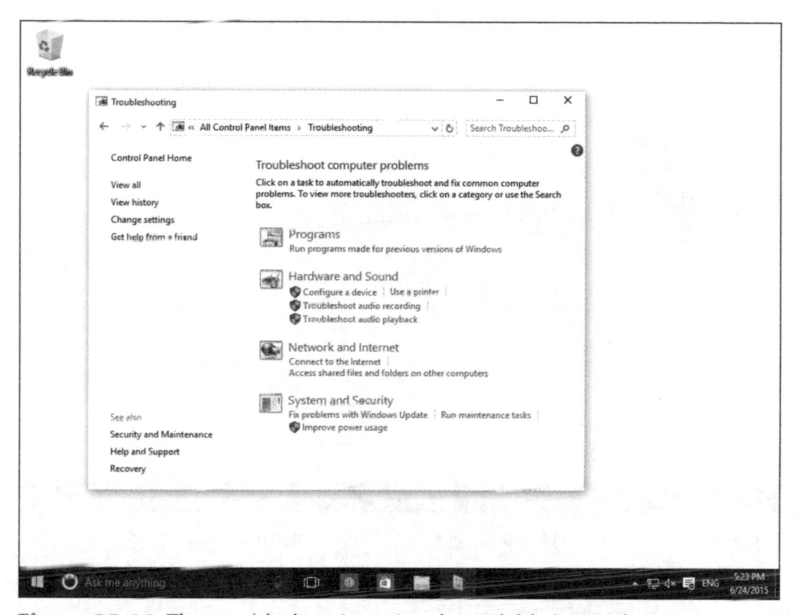

Figure 25-11: The troubleshooting wizards available in Windows 10.

With the help of these wizards, you can identify both what's causing the problems you're having and the solutions to fix them. In some scenarios, the troubleshooting wizards automatically fix the problem.

Here's an example of how these troubleshooting wizards work. For this example, mute the sound on your device. The Playing Audio troubleshooter can find and fix the problem.

1. **Click in the search bar on the taskbar.**
2. **Type** troubleshooting.

   A list of search results appears.

3. **Click the Troubleshooting search result.**

   The Troubleshooting window appears.

4. **Click Hardware and Sound.**

   The Hardware and Sound window appears.

5. **Click Playing Audio to start this troubleshooting wizard.**

6. **Click Next (see Figure 25-12).**

   Wait for the troubleshooter to identify the problems that you're having. When it finishes, you receive a message telling you that the troubleshooting is completed and that the problems were found and fixed automatically.

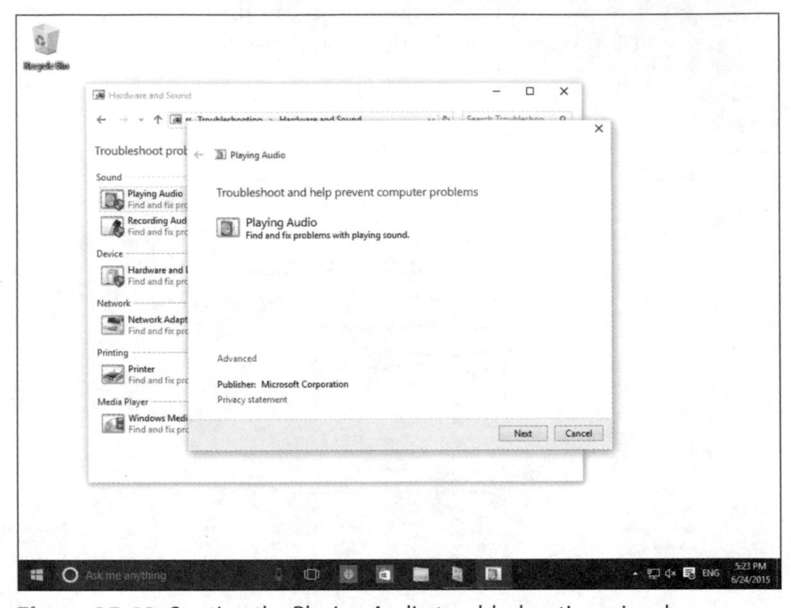

Figure 25-12: Starting the Playing Audio troubleshooting wizard.

7. **Click Close.**

The sound is no longer muted on your Windows 10 computer or device.

Solve Problems Using the Microsoft Fix It Solution Center

Microsoft has created a portal named Microsoft Fix it Solution Center that helps you fix many problems with Microsoft products and services. It covers products like Windows, Internet

Explorer, Windows Media Player, Xbox, Office, and many others. The address of this portal is `http://support2.microsoft.com/fixit`.

When you use this portal, you select the product you're having problems with; then you select what you're trying to do. You're given a list of problems and solutions. Many solutions are offered in the form of an executable file that you download and run on your computer. In that case, that executable file automatically fixes the problem for you. Other solutions are given in the form of text instructions with detailed steps to follow.

Here's an example of using the Microsoft Fix it Solution Center to solve a problem with Internet Explorer:

1. **Start Internet Explorer or your favorite web browser.**
2. **Browse to** `http://support2.microsoft.com/fixit`.
3. **In the Select a Problem Area section, click the Windows icon (see Figure 25-13).**

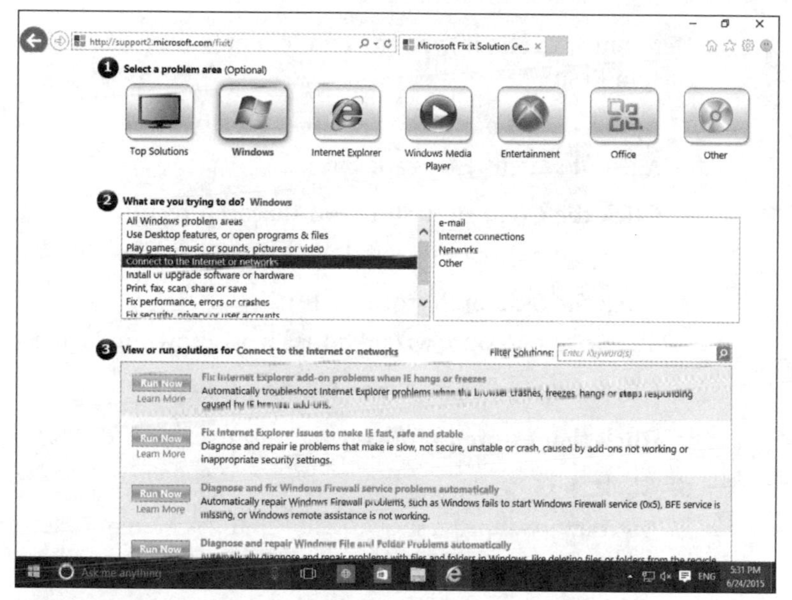

Figure 25-13: Using the Microsoft Fix it Solution Center.

4. **In the What Are You Trying to Do box, click to select Connect to the Internet or Networks.**
5. **In the View or Run Solutions section, select Fix Internet Explorer Add-On Problems When IE Hangs or Freezes.**
6. **Click the Run Now button for that problem.**
7. **Save the file to your computer.**

8. **When the download is complete, click Run.**
9. **When an UAC prompt appears, click Yes.**

   The downloaded file does the necessary fixing.
10. **When the Microsoft Fix It file is done, close it.**

Restore Windows to a Previous State with System Restore

System Restore is a system recovery tool that allows you to reverse the changes that were made to the Windows operating system. It's like an Undo button but for changes that were made to system files and settings. (Chapter 24 introduces the functions of System Restore).

If System Restore is enabled (as shown in Chapter 24), when you encounter issues with Windows 10, you can easily revert back to any of the existing restore points and continue to use Windows as if recent system changes never happened.

Here's how to restore your system to a previous state, using System Restore:

1. **In the search bar on the taskbar, type** system restore.

   A list of search results appears.
2. **Click the Create a Restore Point search result.**

   The System Properties window opens.
3. **Click the System Restore button.**

   The System Restore wizard appears, as shown in Figure 25-14.
4. **Click the Next button (see Figure 25-14).**
5. **Click the restore point you want to use.**
6. **Click Next.**

   A summary appears showing the changes System Restore will make.
7. **Click Finish to confirm that you want the changes to be made.**

   You're warned that once it starts, System Restore can't be interrupted, as shown in Figure 25-15.
8. **Click Yes to confirm that you want to continue (see Figure 25-15).**

   Windows 10 prepares to restore your system to the selected state and then restarts. The process generally takes a couple of minutes and may involve a restart.

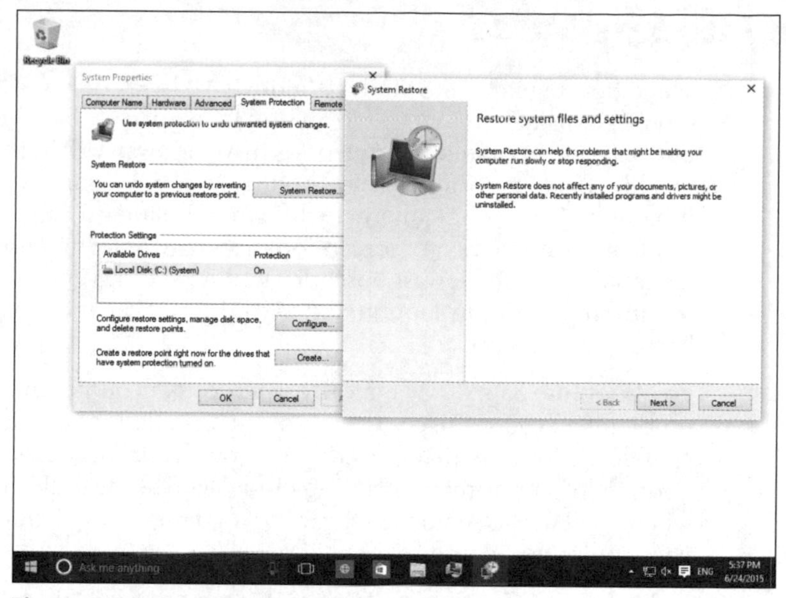

Figure 25-14: Starting the System Restore wizard.

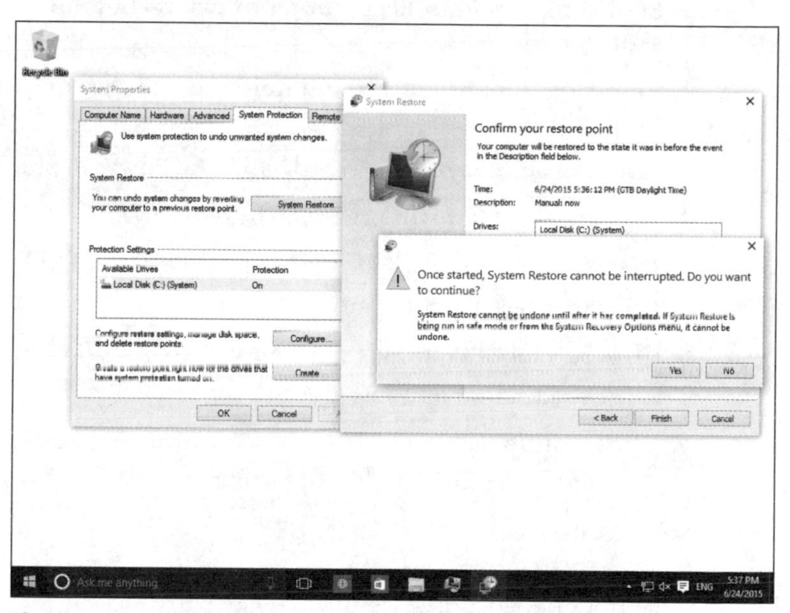

Figure 25-15: The System Restore wizard asking you to confirm that you want to continue.

9. **Log in to Windows 10.**

   You're informed that the restoration is successful.

10. **Click Close.**

Boot into Safe Mode

When booting into Safe Mode, Windows 10 loads only the bare essentials needed to function. You don't have access to anything but the core programs and functions of Windows, which don't include the drivers for your networking devices, meaning you usually can't access the Internet while in the standard Safe Mode. While in Safe Mode, your screen looks pretty wonky because it's set to run at the lowest possible graphics settings and at the minimum resolution supported by Windows. Also, the desktop background is black.

You boot into Safe Mode typically when you encounter major problems, such as disk corruption or the installation of poorly configured software that prevents Windows 10 from successfully booting into its normal operating mode. Safe Mode is also useful when you have to remove malware or rogue software that harms your computer.

To boot into Safe Mode, follow these steps:

1. **Start your Windows 10 computer or device, but don't sign in.**
2. **At the log in screen, press and hold the Shift key on your keyboard.**
3. **With the Shift key still pressed, click the Power menu.**
4. **With the Shift key still pressed, click Restart.**

   Windows restarts, and you're asked to choose an option.
5. **Click to select Troubleshoot.**
6. **Click Advanced Options (see Figure 25-16).**

   A list of advanced options appears.
7. **Click Startup Settings.**

   The Startup Settings window appears.
8. **Click Restart.**

   Your Windows 10 computer or device restarts. A list of startup settings is loaded (see Figure 25-17).
9. **To choose from the Safe Mode startup options, press one of the keys from 4 to 6 (see Figure 25-17).**

   Windows 10 now loads into Safe Mode.
10. **Log in to your account.**

If Windows 10 still doesn't start, you need to boot using a System Recovery disc or USB stick.

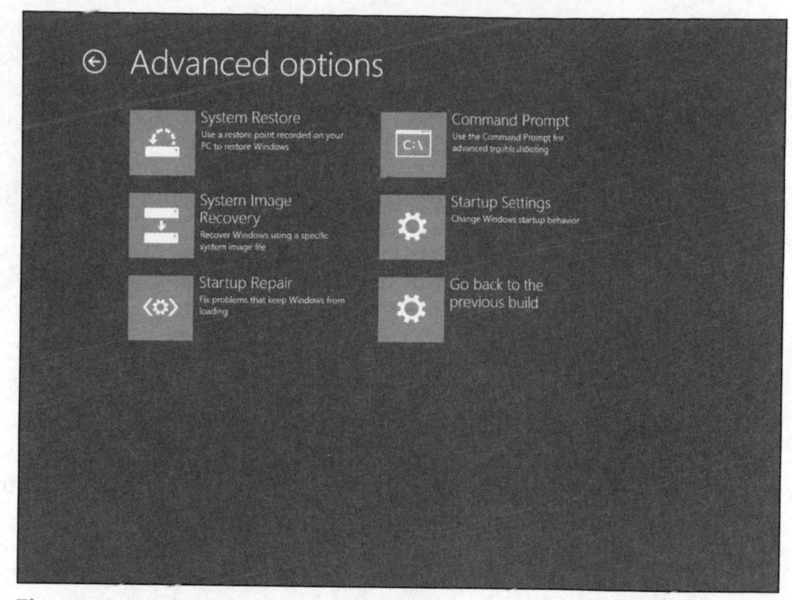

Figure 25-16: The Advanced Options screen.

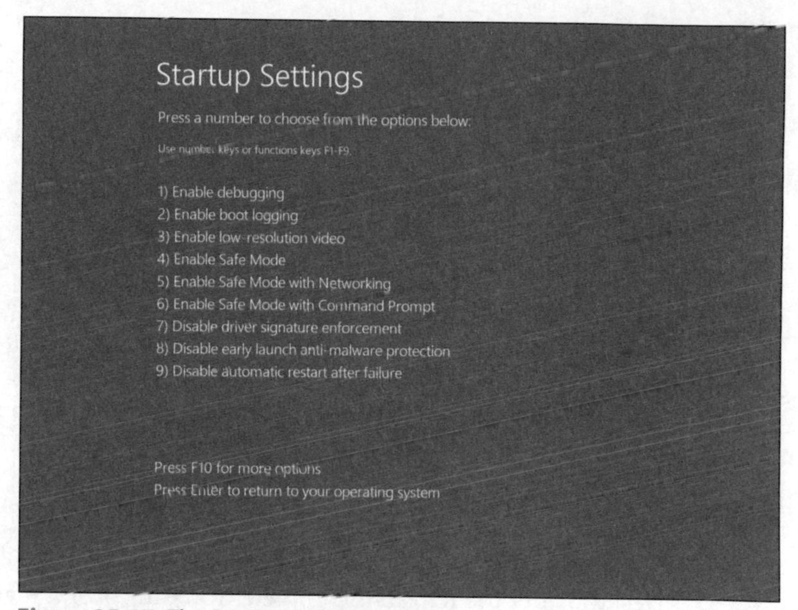

Figure 25-17: The Startup Settings screen.

Refresh Your Installation

If you have problems with your Windows 10 computer or device and you can't fix them, it may help to refresh your Windows 10 installation. This process is similar to reinstalling Windows but with some differences:

- You won't lose your photos, music, videos, documents, and other personal files. At least not if they're stored on the Desktop or in the standard user folders and libraries that come with Windows: Documents, Downloads, Music, Pictures, and Videos.
- Your user account settings are kept as you set them, and your Windows Store apps remain installed.
- All system settings are restored to their factory defaults, and all desktop apps and drivers are uninstalled. However, a list of these apps is saved on the Desktop in a file named Removed Apps.html.
- The previous Windows 10 installation is stored on your C: drive in a folder named Windows.old. If the refresh process goes as expected and you solve your problems, remove this folder manually or by using Disk Cleanup.

To refresh your Windows 10 installation, follow these steps:

1. **Open Settings.**
2. **Click Update & Security.**

   Your settings related to Windows Update and your system's security are loaded.
3. **Click Recovery.**
4. **In the Reset this PC section on the right, click Get Started.**

   You're asked to choose an option.
5. **Click Keep my files (see Figure 25-18).**

   You may receive a message that says "Some files are missing. Your Windows installation or recovery media will provide these files." If that happens, insert a Windows 10 installation disc or a recovery disc so that you can continue with the refresh process.
6. **When you're ready to go ahead, click Next.**

   A list appears showing all the apps that you need to reinstall. This list also is stored on a Removed Apps.html on your Desktop after the refresh is complete. You can consult it at that time, then manually download and install the apps that have been removed.
7. **Click Next.**

   You're informed about what happens when you Reset Windows 10 using the settings that you have made so far.
8. **Click Reset (see Figure 25-19).**

   Windows 10 restarts and begins the refresh process, which takes a couple of minutes and requires several restarts.

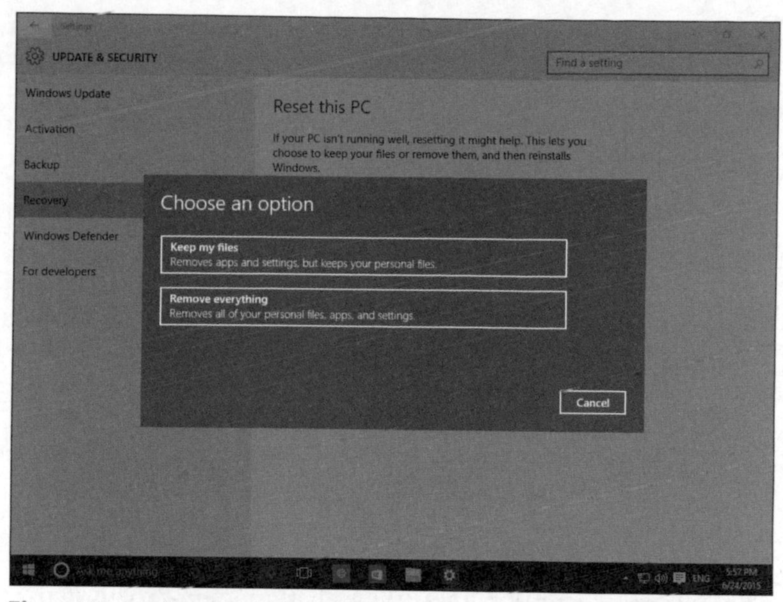

Figure 25-18: Starting the refresh process on your Windows 10 installation.

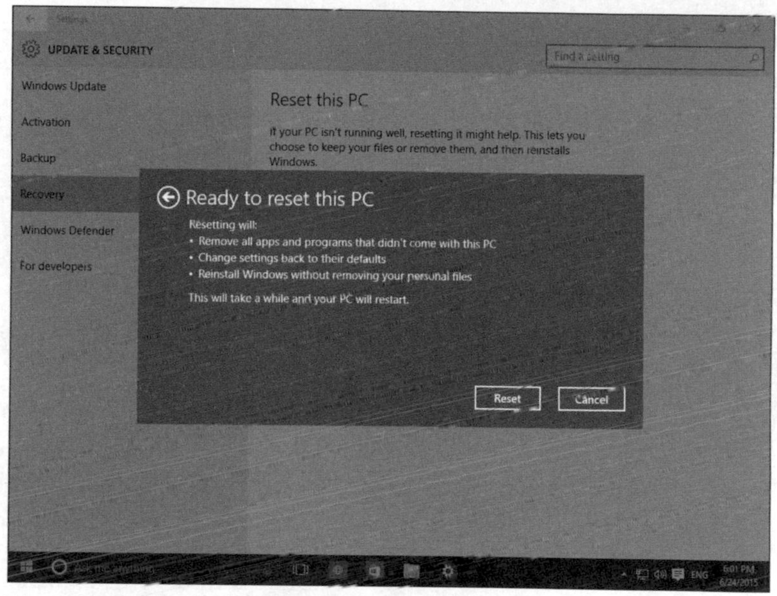

Figure 25-19: Confirming that you want to refresh your PC.

9. When the refresh is finished, log in to Windows 10 using your user account.

10. Once Windows 10 sets up its apps and settings for you, reinstall the desktop apps and the drivers that you need to use.

The Removed Apps.html file on your Desktop shows which desktop apps you need to manually reinstall to return your Windows 10 computer or device to its previous condition.

Reset Your Installation

Another way to fix your computing problems is to use the Reset feature. Doing so is equivalent to reinstalling Windows 10, which means that all your apps and files are removed and that Windows 10 is reinstalled from scratch. However, before starting this process, you can opt to have Windows 10 remove your files and back up your old Windows 10 installation and place it in a Windows.old folder on your C: drive; or you can opt to have Windows fully clean and format the system drive and then reinstall Windows 10 without keeping the old installation. As you can imagine, this process takes much longer than a refresh process, so you need to arm yourself with some patience.

To reset your Windows 10 installation, follow these steps:

1. **Open Settings.**
2. **Click Update & Security.**

   Your settings related to Windows Update and your system's security are loaded.
3. **Click Recovery.**
4. **In the Reset this PC section on the right, click Get Started.**

   You're asked to choose an option.
5. **Click Remove Everything.**

   You're asked whether you want to clean the drives too, as shown in Figure 25-20.
6. **Click the option you prefer (either removing your files or removing your files and cleaning the drive).**

   You may receive a message that says "Some files are missing. Your Windows installation or recovery media will provide these files." If that happens, insert a Windows 10 installation disc or a recovery disc so you can continue with the reset process. If everything is okay, you're shown a summary of what happens when you reset your computer.
7. **Click Reset.**

   Windows 10 now restarts and begins the reset process, which takes a couple of minutes and several restarts. Once the reset process is done, you're asked to configure Windows 10, as though you just installed it from scratch.

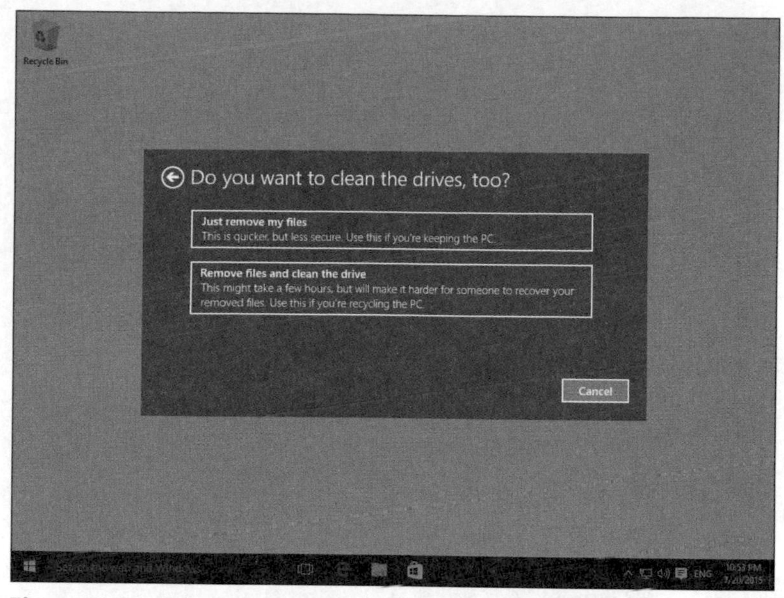

Figure 25-20: Selecting whether you want to clean the drives.

8. **Click the language that you want to use, then set the Country, App Language, Keyboard Layout, and Time Zone that you want (see Figure 25-21).**

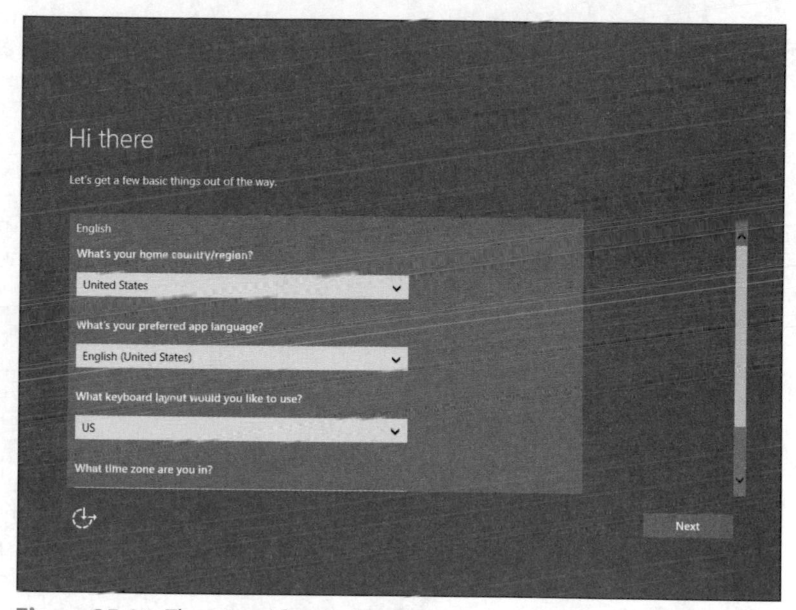

Figure 25-21: The wizard for configuring Windows 10.

9. **Click Next.**

   The license agreement appears.

10. **Read the license agreement; then click Accept.**

    You're asked to set up the settings for Windows 10.

11. **To accept the default settings, click Use Express Settings.**

    You can customize the settings later, after logging in to Windows 10.

    You're asked to choose how you will connect to Windows 10.

12. **Select the option you prefer, click Next.**

13. **Enter your username and password in the fields where this information is requested.**

14. **Click Next.**

    Windows 10 now sets up your account and apps.

15. **Begin to configure Windows 10 as you want it and install the apps and drivers that you need.**

Get Help from Your Company's IT Department

When you use Windows 10 at work, you may encounter issues that you can't fix on your own, even after reading this chapter. When that happens, contact the IT support team at your company and talk with them about your issues. Be sure to follow these guidelines:

- **Describe your issues clearly and completely.** It's very important that the IT staff understand what's wrong with your Windows 10 computer or device so that they can help you more effectively.
- **Describe accurately what you were doing when the problem occurred.** Use your own words, You don't have to be very technical. However, be as detailed and as accurate as possible in your description of the problem.
- **Ask for clarification if you don't understand something.** If technical terms or questions seem foreign to you, don't hesitate to ask the IT support team to use simpler, more accessible language. Doing so increases the effectiveness of your dialogue and also the chances of getting your problem solved faster.

- **Keep calm and be level-headed.** Don't take your computing issues personally and express your frustration in a non-constructive manner. Explain your problems calmly and be patient. The IT support team is there to help you as fast as possible.
- **Set some time aside for solving your problem.** If you haven't figured things out on your own, your problem probably isn't that easy to understand and fix. Don't expect it to be solved in five minutes. Allow the IT support team time to understand what's going on and what the best fix is.
- **Learn from your mistakes.** If you repeat the same mistakes, you repeat the same problems. When a problem is solved, ask the IT support team to explain what was wrong and what you can do to make sure that the problem doesn't reoccur in the future.

Index

• A •

• B •

• C •

• D •

• E •

• F •

• G •

• H •

• I •

• K •

• L •

• M •

• N •

• O •

• P •

• Q •

• R •

• S •

• T •

• U •

• V •

• W •

• Z •

About the Author

Ciprian Adrian Rusen is a recognized Windows Consumer Expert and a Microsoft Most Valuable Professional (MVP). He has published several books about Windows and Microsoft Office, and he's a very active tech blogger at `www.7tutorials.com`.

On this website, you can find many tutorials about Windows, Android, Windows Phone, and Xbox One. If you want to keep up to date on the latest Microsoft consumer products, be sure to subscribe to his blog, too.

Dedication

To Ana-Maria, for making the spring of 2015 a truly memorable one. Also to my sister, who has always been my best friend and supporter. I love you both!

Authors' Acknowledgments

A big thank-you goes to Steve Hayes for giving me the chance to work on my first *For Dummies* project and for making things easy and flexible, while keeping track of the deadlines that we needed to meet.

I also want to thank Marte Brengle, my teammate at 7 Tutorials, for patiently double-checking all my writing and pointing out mistakes I failed to notice.

Publisher's Acknowledgments

Project Editor: Pat O'Brien

Technical Editor: Brian Underdahl

Editorial Assistant: Claire Brock

Sr. Editorial Assistant: Cherie Case

Production Editor: Kinson Raja